Sustainable Consumption and Production, Volume II

Ranjula Bali Swain · Susanne Sweet
Editors

Sustainable Consumption and Production, Volume II

Circular Economy and Beyond

palgrave
macmillan

Editors
Ranjula Bali Swain
Center for Sustainability
Research and Misum
Stockholm School of Economics
Stockholm, Sweden

Department of Economics
Södertörn University
Stockholm, Sweden

Susanne Sweet
Center for Sustainability Research and
Department of Marketing and
Strategy
Stockholm School of Economics
Stockholm, Sweden

ISBN 978-3-030-55287-9   ISBN 978-3-030-55285-5 (eBook)
https://doi.org/10.1007/978-3-030-55285-5

This Palgrave Macmillan imprint is published by the registered company Springer Nature Switzerland AG
The registered company address is: Gewerbestrasse 11, 6330 Cham, Switzerland

Preface

The ongoing COVID-19 pandemic has been created and propagated by the over-arching socio-economic environment and activities that are pushing the physical boundaries of Earth and its biodiversity. Return to normal cannot be a return to the same re-enforcing systems that have created such risks in the first place. Urgency is evident and the proportion of action has to be greater than the risks that our 'business as usual' scenario imposes—not what is convenient and easy to implement. Circular economy is one such transformative change to reduce material and resource use; prolong life of products by reuse, repairing, re-furbishing or re-manufacturing and; at the end of a product's life, recycling the material and put it into productive use again. This volume addresses the knowledge gaps and potential and necessary developments to reach a circular economy.

This volume is part of a two volume work on Sustainable Consumption and Production. The initial process of work on these volumes began when Bali Swain was Visiting Professor to University of California, Berkeley and Sweet was the Research Manager of a eight years long cross-disciplinary research programme, Mistra Future Fashion, with the aim of a systemic transformation towards sustainability in the fashion industry. We would like to thank two anonymous reviewers and our publishing team at Palgrave Macmillan led by Wyndham Hacket Pain and Rachel Sangster, supported by Lavanya Devgun, Anette Lindqvist, Arun Kumar Anbalagan, Ashwini Elango. We thank Mimi Choudhury for excellent copyediting support and Suneethi Raja for subject indexing. We gratefully acknowledge the contributing authors, for their participation in the digital two-days International Sustainable Consumption and Production book workshop at Stockholm School of Economics during October 2019. We express our gratitude to Swedish Research Council for Sustainability (Formas), the Swedish Energy Agency, and Mistra for research funding to the editors of this volume. We acknowledge Mistra Center for Sustainable Markets, Misum, for the financial and administrational support for copyediting of this work.

Stockholm, Sweden
June 2020

Ranjula Bali Swain
Susanne Sweet

Contents

Notes on Contributors

Saman Amir is a Ph.D. candidate in Business Administration and a researcher at Center for Sustainability Research at Stockholm School of Economics (Handelshögskolan). Her research area is circular systems analysis and implementation using simulation models to understand and measure the economic and environmental trade-offs of circular supply chains and circular business models.

Farazee M. A. Asif holds a Ph.D. degree and works in the Department of Production Engineering as senior researcher. His research falls in the area of Circular Economy with manufacturing focus. His research mainly deals with modelling and simulation of complex systems relevant to circular manufacturing systems.

Ulrich Atz, Dipl-Volks is a Research Associate at the NYU Stern Center for Sustainable Business with over a decade in experience in using data science for research, government and business. Prior to joining New York University, he worked at the Open Data Institute in London, where he managed the Startup Programme evaluating hundreds of startups on their triple bottom line. He holds a Diploma in Economics from the University of Mannheim and a M.Sc. in Social Research Methods (Statistics) from the London School of Economics.

Frank Boons is an economic sociologist who has contributed to the field of environmental sciences on the topics of contested technological change, responsible innovation and the governance of material and energy flows. He has specialised in systemic and processual approaches to analysis and policy advice. In addition to his publications on these topics, he has held editorial roles at the *Journal of Cleaner Production* and the *Journal of Industrial Ecology*. His current research interest is in how economies transition to become more sustainable, with increased circulation as one possible pathway.

Catherine Casson is a Lecturer in Enterprise at Alliance Manchester Business School. Her research is interdisciplinary across history and management, drawing on her training as a medieval historian at the University of York, UK. Her publications include articles in Economic History Review, Business History Review and Urban History and the co-authored book The Entrepreneur in History: From Medieval Merchant to Modern Business Leader (Palgrave Macmillan: Basingstoke, 2013).

Elyse Douglas is a Senior Scholar at the NYU Stern Center for Sustainable Business focusing on the ROSI methodology. She was previously Executive Vice President and Chief Financial Officer of Hertz Global Holdings, Inc. Her prior experience includes finance roles at Coty Inc., Nabisco, JPMorgan (previously Chase Manhattan Bank), and she served as a board member of Assurant, Inc. where she was a member of the Audit Committee and chaired the Finance and Risk Committee until May 2019. She is a Certified Public Accountant and chartered financial analyst.

Dr. Enrico Fontana is a Lecturer at Sasin School of Management (Thailand) and an affiliated researcher at Mistra Centre for Sustainable Markets at Stockholm School of Economics (Sweden). He obtained his Ph.D. degree in Business Administration from Stockholm School of Economics. His Ph.D. and current work are focused on corporate social responsibility and sustainable value chains in South and East Asia. Enrico has published his work in multiple academic outlets, including *Journal of Business Ethics*, *Journal of Cleaner Production*, *European Business Review*, *Culture and Organization and Corporate Social Responsibility* and *Environmental Management*. Before embarking on his Ph.D. studies, Enrico worked for six years as market manager in the apparel industry in Asia and Europe.

Jenny Yi-Chen Han is a Research Associate for the Gender, Environment and Development research theme at Stockholm Environment Institute, SEI Asia, Bangkok. She holds a Masters degree (distinction) in Sociology and Global Change from the University of Edinburgh.

Her thesis was conducted in conjunction with Mistra Future Fashion at Center for Sustainability Research at SSE, where she looked at valuation mechanisms and symbolic associations that drive consumption practices within sustainable fashion markets. Previously, Jenny worked as an Academic Program Assistant for the Gender and Sexuality Programme at a non-profit foundation in Copenhagen, Denmark.

Cary Y. Hendrickson is a social scientist trained in economic geography (Ph.D., University of Rome La Sapienza, 2017), environmental science and technology (Ph.D., Autonomous University of Barcelona, 2017), sustainability science (Lund University, 2009) and environmental economics (Michigan State University, 2004). Her research is situated at the intersection of political economy, environmental geography and development studies. She is currently a postdoctoral researcher at the University of Rome La Sapienza, studying the extent to which the sharing economy transforms traditional markets through the introduction of decentralised market mechanisms and various forms of non-monetary, mutual, transitive or generalised reciprocity. Past research examined how market-based environmental policies impact livelihoods, linking rural communities to global environmental value chains and transforming institutions for natural resource management.

Maryna Henrysson is a researcher at the Energy Systems Division, Department of Energy Technology at the Royal Institute of Technology, Sweden. Maryna holds a Ph.D. in low-carbon development governance from Technical University of Denmark with focus on the politics of energy systems' transformation and climate change mitigation and a MSc degree in environmental studies and sustainability science from Lund University. Maryna's research has been focused on the politics of international knowledge regimes and the roles of institutions in development of national climate change mitigation policies and the role of non-state actors in climate governance, in particular. Maryna currently investigates the collaborative governance of innovation in industrial strategy of circular economy in agri-food and energy systems. She is also working with developing a framework for assessment of urban circularity.

Helen Holmes is a Lecturer in Sociology. Her work explores materiality, consumption and diverse forms of economy, especially the circular economy. In particular, Helen focuses upon social perspectives of objects and materials, to illuminate the lived everyday relationships we have with things. She has extensive expertise in using ethnographic methods to study micro level practices. Helen has published widely in high quality journals including *Sociology*, *The Sociological Review*, *Work, Employment and Society* and *Geoforum*.

Tracy Van Holt is the Director of Academic Research at the NYU Stern Center for Sustainable Business, where she draws upon more than 15 years' research experience focused on food systems, landscapes and commodity chains. At the start of her career, she spent many years in the field learning how people at the beginning of many commodity chains live and work, and adapt to environmental and market changes. Now her research is taking her to examine more deeply how companies are working to solve sustainability and wellbeing challenges in their supply chains, and how investors make sense of environmental, social and governance issues in companies.

Julia Kasmire researches and teaches on how to use new forms of data for social scientists with the UK Data Service and the Cathie Marsh Institute at the University of Manchester. She approaches this task as an interesting combination of thinking like a computer (essential for data sciences) and thinking like a human (essential for social sciences) in the context of complex adaptive systems. She is deeply committed to equality, diversity and inclusivity and is currently dabbling with stand-up comedy as a form of science communication.

Clara My Lernborg defended her doctoral thesis in Business Administration at Stockholm School of Economics in 2019. Her research interests include CSR, sustainable fashion and private governance. She is currently working in the development sector with climate change issues.

Lin Lerpold is an Associate Professor at the Stockholm School of Economics in the Department of Marketing and Strategy and Director of Center for Sustainability Research. She is also a member of the board of the Stockholm School of Economics Institute for Research, Vice Chair in the board of directors of AP2, and a senior advisor for Global Utmaning. Lin was the founding director of SSE's sustainability centre, Mistra Center for Sustainable Markets. Before that, she served as the Associate Dean for SSE MBA programmes and has been a Visiting Fellow at the LSE, Center for the Studies of Human Rights and Visiting Professor at INSEAD, Strategy Department.

Johanna Mair is Professor of Organization, Strategy and Leadership at the Hertie School. Her research focuses on how novel organisational and institutional arrangements generate economic and social development. Mair is also the Distinguished Fellow at the Stanford Center on

Philanthropy and Civil Society, Academic Editor of the Stanford Social Innovation Review and Co-Director of the Global Innovation for Impact Lab. She is a Senior Research Fellow at Harvard Kennedy School and has held visiting positions at Harvard Business School and INSEAD. She serves on the board of foundations and organisations and advises companies, governments and social impact investors on social innovation. In 2008, the Aspen Institute recognised her as a 'Faculty Pioneer' in Social Entrepreneurship Education.

Jennie Perzon is a Ph.D. candidate in Business Administration and a researcher at Center for Sustainability Research at Stockholm School of Economics (Handelshögskolan). She holds a Master of Business Law and a Master of Business Administration from Bond University and an MSc from University of Southern California. Her 15 years as a management consultant at Accenture includes both global and local projects within the area of corporate citizenship and sustainability. Inspired by the work with both NGOs and multinational corporations she developed an interest in multi stakeholder collaboration and collective impact. With a particular focus on capabilities her research focuses on ecosystem models for sustainable change.

Malvina Roci is a Ph.D. candidate in Production Engineering at KTH Royal Institute of Technology. Her research is focused on developing analysis methods and tool to support manufacturing industry in its transition from linear to circular manufacturing systems that are economically viable and environmentally sustainable.

Malte B. Rödl is Research Associate at the Sustainable Consumption Institute at The University of Manchester. Their research looks at meaning-making processes and how established understandings of 'normality' influence new technologies and associated debates.

Funda Sezgi is Chief Operating Officer at Norrsken HQ, Stockholm, Sweden. She has a doctoral degree in Strategic Management from the IESE Business School, University of Navarra and has been a doctoral scholar at the Scandinavian Consortium for Organizational Research, Stanford University.

Örjan Sjöberg is Professor of Economic Geography and Research Director at Center for Sustainability Research, Stockholm School of Economics (SSE), a position held since 2001. Upon receiving his Ph.D. in human geography (Uppsala University 1991), he joined SSE where over the years he has taught courses on economic geography, international economics, globalisation, institutions and economic development, Asian and transition economies, urban studies as well as business and climate change. In addition to being the author of a monograph on rural change under central planning and the editor of several collections of articles, his research has appeared in e.g. *Annals of the Association of American Geographers*, *Economic Geography*, *Environment and Planning A*, *Geoforum*, *International Journal of Urban and Regional Research*, *Urban Studies* and in several area studies journals.

Dr. Ingrid Stigzelius is a researcher and lecturer at Stockholm School of Economics within the Department of Marketing and Strategy and Center for Sustainability Research. Her primary research interest lies at the intersection of markets and consumption and how various socio-material practices work to produce green, political consumers as well as a more sustainable business and society.

Ranjula Bali Swain is a Research Director and Visiting Professor at Center for Sustainability Research & Misum, Stockholm School of Economics and Professor of Economics, Södertörn University. She is affiliated to the Center for European Research in Microfinance (CERMi), at the Solvay Brussels School of Economics and Management, has worked as an Expert at the International Labour Organisation, Geneva; and has been visiting professor at University of California, Berkeley, Stanford University, Tufts University, University of Pretoria, South Africa and UN Sustainable Development Solutions Network, New York, USA. Her research interests include Microfinance, Sustainable Development and Circular Economy.

Susanne Sweet is Research Director, Center for Sustainability Research and Associate Professor at Stockholm School of Economics in the Department of Marketing and Strategy. She was a founding senior researcher of SSE's sustainability centre, Mistra Center for Sustainable Markets and a research manager for a large international cross-disciplinary research programme Mistra Future Fashion, (www.mistrafuturefashion.com), between 2011 and 2019 aiming to a systemic change of the Swedish fashion industry leading to sustainable development of the industry and wider society. Her research covers a broad range of topics on corporate sustainability and responsibility and in 2007 she received the Globe Award for 'For an outstanding and tangible research in the field of CSR'.

Daniel Welch is a Lecturer in Sociology and a researcher at the Sustainable Consumption Institute. His research interests include the sociology of consumption, cultural sociology and social theory. He has published in journals including *The Journal of Consumer Culture*, *Environment and Planning A* and the *Journal for the Theory of Social Behaviour*.

Professor Tensie Whelan leads the Center for Sustainable Business at NYU Stern School of Business, which she launched in 2016. Previously, amongst other roles, she served as President of the Rainforest Alliance, Vice President at National Audubon Society, Managing Editor of Ambio (published by the Royal Swedish Academy of Sciences) and sits on the board of Aston Martin and the advisory boards of Arabesque and Inherent Group.

Harald Wieser is a Research Fellow at the Sustainable Consumption Institute, University of Manchester. In his doctoral research, he examined market dynamics with respect to the frequency at which consumer durables are exchanged through an historical case study of the British mobile phone market. Previously, he has published on the roles of households in reducing resource use, looking at how food and durable goods are consumed and the work that goes into preventing waste. His research interests lie in the possibilities of slower material flows and their implications for the environment and social justice.

List of Figures

List of Tables

CHAPTER 1

Sustainable Consumption and Production: Introduction to Circular Economy and Beyond

Ranjula Bali Swain and Susanne Sweet

Introduction

With the current path of global population growth and expansion of consumption and production, the resource availability and resilience of the Earth Systems are under threat. Transformative changes require transformative ideas and innovative thinking. Given the overwhelming evidence provided by Intergovernmental Panel on Climate Change

R. Bali Swain (✉)
Center for Sustainability Research and Misum, Stockholm School of Economics, Stockholm, Sweden
e-mail: ranjula.bali@hhs.se

Department of Economics, Södertörn University, Stockholm, Sweden

S. Sweet
Center for Sustainability Research and Department of Marketing and Strategy, Stockholm School of Economics, Stockholm, Sweden
e-mail: susanne.sweet@hhs.se

R. Bali Swain and S. Sweet (eds.), *Sustainable Consumption and Production, Volume II*,
https://doi.org/10.1007/978-3-030-55285-5_1

(IPCC, 2014), the international impetus of Sustainable Development Goals (Agenda 2030) and the Paris Agreement, public, private and third sector parties need to transform and adapt to sustainable development goals (SDGs). In recent studies, Bali Swain and Ranganathan (2020), Bali Swain (2018), Ranganathan and Bali Swain (2018), Spaiser, Ranganathan, Bali Swain, and Sumpter (2016), and UNSD (2020) provide empirical evidence that SDGs are conflicting, interlinked with trade-offs and synergies, and sometimes contradictory. These interlinkages imply that a number of technological, social and economic interrelationships on the individual and system levels have to be addressed to achieve SDGs. Goals on sustainable consumption and production (SDG12) are related to circular economy (CE) approaches, such as 12.2, achieving the sustainable management and efficient use of natural resources; 12.3 and 12.5 substantially reduce waste generation through prevention, reduction, recycling and reuse.

In this chapter, we present an introduction to sustainable consumption and production through circular economy. Circular economy is an approach to reduce material and resource use; prolong life of products by reuse, repairing, refurbishing or remanufacturing and; at the end of a product's life, recycle the material and put it into productive use again.

CE and sustainable development are also closely related concepts (Pauliuk, 2018). Some researchers argue that CE succeeds sustainable development as sustainable development is based on linear thinking strategies (Sauve, Bernard, & Sloan, 2016). Others argue that sustainability is a broader concept as CE is an instrument to operationalize sustainable development principles (Kirchherr, Reike, & Hekkert, 2017; Kopnina & Blewitt, 2014). Still others suggest that CE is not a comprehensive model of sustainable development and addresses only a subset of SDGs (Schröder, Anggraeni, & Weber, 2018). Sustainability aims to integrate the environmental, economic and social dimensions, whereas, CE concentrates on environmental issues and is set within the industrial context (D'Amato et al., 2017; Sauve et al., 2016). Geissdoerfer, Savaget, Bocken, and Hultink (2017) is one of the few studies that focus on the social issues and the environmental, economic and social dimensions of sustainable development.

Circular Economy

CE is not a new concept. People in different historical periods recycled and reused, and it was driven by technological, societal, cultural, political, economic and religious circumstances. During medieval times, production was labour intensive, and the waste was used to produce other items. To be responsible and take care of belongings and materials was promoted as positive behaviour with religious significance. The Industrial Revolution period between 1750 and 1850 deterred recycling and reuse through the boom in mass production (Stobart, Hann, & Morgan, 2007; Stobart & Van Damme, 2010). The shift from small scale to mass production, with improvements in transportation resulted in greater volumes and lower prices for consumers. The World Wars, however, resulted in resource scarcity, and thus promoted reuse and recycling. Disruptions in supply chains led to schemes to recycle metal, paper and textiles. In addition to manufacturing limits on the volume of new clothing and household items, new 'utility' designs were introduced to conserve the raw materials. Necessity, and indeed legislation, therefore encouraged recycling and reuse.

Pearce and Turner (1990) were the first to use the term CE, but it was Boulding (1966), who discussed the closed system to emphasize the limited natural resources available for human activities. CE is an umbrella concept with its origin in industrial ecology, environmental science and ecological economic, and does not have well-defined boundaries with concepts such as Green Economy and Bioeconomy (Blomsma & Brennan, 2017; D'Amato et al., 2017; Korhonen, Honkasalo, & Seppälä, 2018; Lazarevic & Valve, 2016; Merli, Preziosi, & Compora, 2018). It also has strong roots in ideas related to cradle-to-cradle design (Braungart & McDonough, 2002) and natural capitalism (Hawken, Lovins, & Lovins, 1999). Bioeconomy also plays the critical role of biological engine of CE, concentrating on the renewability of material end energy in closed loops (European Commission, 2015).

The European Commission's circular economy action plan adopted by the EU in 2015, defines circular economy as:

> ...an economy [that] aims to maintain the value of products, materials and resources for as long as possible by returning them into the product cycle at the end of their use, while minimising the generation of waste.

This process starts at the very beginning of a product's lifecycle: smart product design and production processes can help save resources, avoid inefficient waste management, and create new business opportunities (European Commission, 2015, 2019).

CE is thus an evolving concept and there is no consensus or commonly accepted definition of CE (Kirchherr et al., 2017; Rizos, Tuokko, & Behrens, 2017; Yuan, Bi, & Moriguichi, 2006). One currently prominent approach to address the sustainable challenges connected to consumption and production is to close material loops using CE approaches. CE principles are driving to overcome the challenges of today's linear take-make-dispose production and consumption patterns through keeping the value of products, materials and resources circulating in the economy as long as possible (Ellen MacArthur Foundation, 2012, 2015; Geissdoerfer et al., 2017; Haas, Krausmann, Wiedenhofer, & Heinz, 2015; Kirchherr et al., 2017; Merli et al., 2018).

Consequently, a transition towards CE will impact whole systems of provision of products and services (Checkland, 2000). For example, by working with CE principles, (a) manufacturers need to implement Circular Manufacturing Systems (CMS), including designing products which should last significantly longer and be designed for easy repair, refurbishing and remanufacturing; (b) consumers and households need to adapt to different consumption patterns and business models, such as sharing, renting or service models; and (c) at a societal level, policies and infrastructure for waste management, supporting pricing, taxation and fee models, education and communication etc., need to be implemented. Thus, CE is an approach that is characterized by planned organization and governance for regenerative and restorative systems of consumption and production to propagate inclusive and equitable societal prosperity by maintaining the value of resources, materials and products, and avoiding wastage.

With its origin in the field of industrial ecology, CE developed into an independent concept connected to environmental sustainability, mostly employing tools and methods for modelling processes and supporting decision-making for CE implementation—for example, using Life Cycle Assessment and Material Flow Analysis. In a systematic analysis of CE literature, Merli et al. (2018) broadly identify three approaches at the macro, micro and meso level. The first set of literature focuses on the changes in social and economic dynamics at the macro and administrative level. The second set of literature focuses on the implementation of circular processes at the firm or micro level. The remaining literature addresses industrial symbiosis experiences at the meso level.

The CE literature on the macro level is focused on the change in social and economic dynamics in China and the European Union. China implements a national top-down policy for CE with focus on cities and provinces (Geng & Doberstein, 2008; Yuan et al., 2006). The European Union, on the other hand, identifies patterns for a circular-oriented society following a bottom-up approach, and is thus focused on circular cities, country-level waste management and the interrelations of waste flows among member states (Pomponi & Moncaster, 2017).

The second set of literature is micro level, and concentrates on firms and consumers. The bottom-up approach of the European Action Plan for CE aims to reach sustainability practices and culture to all stakeholders in society through innovative forms of consumption and production, in which actions are implemented at all value chain stages (Ghisellini, Cialani, & Ulgiati, 2016; Manninen, Koskela, Antikainen, & Dahlbo, 2017; Saavedra, Iritani, Pavan & Ometto, 2017).

The meso-level literature with respect to China examines the planning and evaluation of eco-industrial parks pilot projects and networks focusing on environmental improvements (Geng, Fu, Sarkis, & Xue, 2012). The European meso-level literature consists of the industrial symbiosis experiences based on the industrial ecology paradigm and is a widely used model to implement CE principles. This may support the transition towards CE through the identification of alternative use of materials and waste flows (Saavedra et al., 2017).

One of the main objectives of CE is to minimize waste production and maximize its reuse as material and energy sources (D'Amato et al., 2017; Song, 2013). The European Union Action Plan for CE binds the legislative proposals to reduction of waste generation and management objectives (European Commission, 2015). However, critics suggest that EU targets on improving recycling rates are deficient in developing societal changes that are essential for a global transition towards CE (Haupt & Zschokke, 2017).

Cleaner production is an essential strategy that has been dominating CE literature (Bilitewski, 2012; Ellen MacArthur Foundation, 2015; Ghisellini et al., 2016). Business model strategies for CE is another important area. Researchers have mainly focussed on studying the closing material loops strategy; slowing the loops, on the other hand, requires a change of consumption and production patterns, which is only marginally studied. Another under-researched area in CE is the role of consumers and consumption (Geels, McMeekin, Mylan, & Southerton, 2015; Pogutz & Micale, 2011). In recent years, a growing body of research on the link between sustainable development and consumption practices has focused on the role of consumption in CE; for example, sharing economy, collaborative consumption, reuse, second-hand, product-service system, repairs, etc. (Camacho-Otero, Boks, & Pettersen, 2018).

In spite of the different models for take-back systems that have been around for a long time, CE has not become a major part of industry and market practices. Instead we have witnessed increased consumption of natural resources and growing waste issues with impacts on land and the seas. The complexity involved in implementing CE thinking and practices through the whole value chain has hampered the move towards sustainable development and a CE. The challenge is to adapt social and institutional changes which are able to transform the upstream process of production and consumption (Bocken, Ritala, & Huotari, 2017). It requires changes to redesign the goods and services, sharing and performance economy, and dematerialization practices to fulfill everyday needs (European Commission, 2015; Hobson, 2015; Merli et al., 2018). As Hobson (2015) argues, CE has to develop beyond cleaner production practices, and greater efforts need to be invested in the 'profound transformative change' that is required to go beyond the take-make-dispose linear model. The CE model requires a transformation of current societies, and their consumption and production practices that are related to a wide range of human needs.

Circular Economy and Beyond

Work has begun recently to address the complexity of the transition towards a circular economy (Bocken, Boons, & Baldassarre, 2019; Boons & Bocken, 2018). The process of changing from linear to circular modes of provision is a sociotechnical transition (Boons & Bocken, 2018). Studies of such transitions have pointed to the tensions and dynamics in relation to mature markets to retain economic growth. In particular, the material flows, the strategies and activities of the actors, and potential pathways of such transformations for particular sectors and contexts are of importance. In this volume, researchers from various disciplines push the frontiers of this transformation towards a circular economy.

Recent research investigates how firms may capture CE principles into their business model s and practices. Boons (Chapter 2), addresses the existing knowledge gap on creating sustainable business models for a CE, discussing the practices of consumption and production that are a key part of the currently unsustainable societies that we live in. These practices generate flows of materials and energy that have three basic impacts on natural ecologies: they (1) require the extraction of natural resources beyond sustainable rates of replenishment, (2) disturb ecological cycles (such as the hydrological cycle and climate dynamics) and (3) use natural ecosystems as sinks through the dispersion of discarded human-made materials. The embeddedness of socio-material systems within natural ecologies has been acknowledged for a long time, although there is a rich history of ideas on the analytical and normative framings that have been in use throughout the centuries. A currently popular way of framing this embeddedness is in terms of (un)sustainable business models. Boon begins by outlining this framing, including the more general work on business models, which includes an assessment of its added value when compared to previous framings. The chapter further provides a critical analysis of the sustainable business model framing, describing a way forward to retain the added value while addressing the criticisms.

Casson and Welch (Chapter 3) investigate the idea of the circular economy by looking at practices of reuse and recycling in medieval and later periods. They employ historical data on the United Kingdom's reuse and recycling to think about contemporary practices. They further examine how the CE functions in an imagined future in contemporary practice. They conclude that circularities of material flows in economies are always embedded in institutional contexts that are conditioned by contentious social actors mobilizing their own cultural repertoires and norms and values around consumption.

In recent years, the growing political interest has led to the penetration of CE into sustainable production and consumption, expanding from its industrial roots into best practice approaches for different types and scales of businesses, and consumer activities. Most sustainability transition research relates to shifts in the provision of societal needs such as energy, mobility and food, etc. (Köhler et al., 2019). However, CE requires reconfiguration of the *temporalities* of material flows. CE makes us think beyond conventional boundaries of closed loop systems to consider other spaces and scales in which circular practices occur. In Chapter 4, Holmes, Weiser and Kasmir discuss critical approaches to circular economy research: time, space and evolution. They focus on the micro practices of circularity and lived experiences of being circular, with an emphasis on the material. Approaching the CE from a temporal perspective, they address inherent tensions among different CE strategies, and identify the necessity of coordinating activities across production, distribution and consumption. Instead of presenting CE as a coherent and uniform solution to the elimination of waste, Holmes, Weiser and Kasmir suggest that it is better to adopt CE as an umbrella concept. In terms of multiple spaces and scales, CE practices can be identified in a range of spaces and scales and involving activities which are traditionally identified as consumption. They argue for a deeper understanding of the 'doing' of circularity and recognition of the labour (which blurs the boundaries of production and consumption), and skills involved. Finally, they argue that no matter how circular it is, the material, energy and information flowing through an economy causes inevitable and irreversible evolutionary responses. Understanding these changes across temporal and spatial scales is necessary to ensure a systemic change that is sustainable, equitable and just.

Innovative practices and decentralized systems for local and urban food production are rapidly emerging in diverse forms across Europe. In Chapter 5, Henrysson and Hendrickson investigate the coupling of food waste from agri-food value chains and energy systems to critically analyse how circularity strategies are developed in practice. They examine the pressures in potential urban food and energy system transitions within the context of diverse societal-level discourses on food systems, urban sustainability, and the promotion of the circular. Employing a qualitative comparative case study, Henrysson and Hendrickson examine the local stakeholders' practices and perceptions of urban transitions. Their empirical data is collected from Sweden, Italy, Spain, Germany, the United Kingdom, Romania and Finland. They use multiple and shared visions of circularity and societal transition towards sustainability of actors engaged in local agri-food value chains to identify tensions, synergies and potential for alignment with energy policies and programmes aimed at developing a more circular urban economy.

Another challenge is the industrial production and excessive consumption of animal meat, which is increasingly related to environmental, ethical and health issues. Meat alternatives such as those made from plant-based proteins, or growing animal tissue in laboratories, is becoming popular, with increased interest in meat-free and meat-reduced diets. In Chapter 6,

Rödl reviews the growing markets and trends as well as the sustainability potential of meat alternatives. The chapter also investigates how these trends may constitute opportunities and threats to the meat industry. Assuming that all 'meats' are mutually substitutable, it is argued that 'non-animal meats' can be considered a further step in the industrialization of agriculture; thus, the social, symbolic and financial capital of the global meat industries enables them to continue 'producing meat' and to use these trends for further growth.

Related to the study of the potential of a circular transformation of the system are the perceptions and practices of users in those systems (Sweet, Aflaki, & Stalder, 2019; Sweet & Wu, 2019). A common stream of sustainability consumer studies shows a gap between intentions of sustainable consumption and actual behaviour. One prominent explanation of why this occurs points to consumer lock-ins that relate to conflicts between everyday practices and how institutions, markets and objects are organized in ways that can influence the possibilities of engaging in sustainable consumption (Stigzelius, 2017). The theoretical literature investigates some of these social practices of consumption to provide insights into how users engage with a physical product and understand how those practices facilitate or hinder the establishment of routes of circulation (Han & Sweet, Chapter 9; Holmes, 2018, 2019; Warde, 2005).

Stigzelius (Chapter 7) delves deeper into sustainable food consumption to better understand how the consumer becomes a sustainable actor across different moments of consumption, and thereby improve the understanding of the connections between production, markets and consumption in this process. The chapter takes a practice perspective on the study of sustainable (food) consumption where consumers' capacity to act sustainable is not merely dependent on individual motives and merits, but is seen as a collective result involving both social and material actors. The chapter theorizes how a practice perspective can provide a constructive middle path between individual agency and structure, to rather focus on the building of capacities through various practices. Through empirical examples from practices in production, exchange and consumption of food, the chapter illustrates how sustainable consumption is a collective achievement wherein sustainable consumers are both being produced and are part of producing sustainable consumption.

The hospitality industry is one of the fastest growing sectors worldwide. With increasing levels of affluence, the demand for eating out, leisure activities and travel is rising. While this is reflective of the switch in consumption from material things to experiences, this switch imposes large demands on the physical resources at humanity's disposal. It produces travel-related emissions, puts high pressure on sensitive environments, and increases shopping. Lerpold and Sjöberg assess the social sustainability component in Chapter 8. Both positive (regional development, employment, incomes, integration) and less attractive (precarious work, displacement of indigenous or low-income residents) features are discussed.

In Chapter 9, Han and Sweet explore the valuation mechanisms and symbolic associations that drive consumption practices within second-hand fashion markets. Their chapter argues that while participants claim that they engage within second-hand markets primarily due to environmental motivation, the practice is largely driven by gaining symbolic and cultural capital. These symbolic associations demonstrate that second-hand shopping is not only responsible consumerism but also about engendering concepts that transcend sustainability. Han and Sweet argue that the increasing acceptance of alternative business models within fashion requires a stronger cultural narrative than simply a diluted notion of 'green consumption'. In this way, it is speculated that one aspect of prolonging the life of a garment is to continuously create and recreate its symbolic value for consumers.

Circular Fashion is presented as the solution to multiple sustainable production and consumption issues in the fashion and textile market. Lernborg (Chapter 10) investigates how the idea of 'circular fashion' is translated in the fashion market. Using coding circularity definitions and messages in sustainability reports and consumer-directed messages in social media, Lernborg argues that there is partial translation of circular fashion. New market actors translate circular fashion to sustainable consumption (reuse), whereas traditional fashion actors translate it to production aspects (recycle).

In a globalized world aiming towards sustainable development, organizations need to meet new criteria for success, demanding new forms of operation and collaboration. New forms of collaborations are emerging with multiple partners. To understand what capabilities are needed to succeed and how capabilities manifest themselves in a collaborative process, Perzon (Chapter 11) makes an in-depth qualitative study of a collaboration within the fashion industry. Employing dynamic capabilities as a theoretical model to understand the multistakeholder collaboration and relying on the antecedents of dynamic capabilities, Perzon argues for the importance of a collaborative culture grounded in personal conviction and a generous mindset.

In Chapter 12, Amir, Malvina and Farazee present an overview of the modelling and simulation of circular manufacturing systems. Emphasizing the circular aspects of manufacturing systems leads to another level of complexity that needs to be understood in terms of the performance of the system from economic, environmental and social perspectives. This demands a better understanding through analysis of the interdependencies among business models, product design, supply chains and consumption patterns interactions by modelling the effects of these interactions to provide a scientific method of decision-making. The authors discuss the role of modelling simulation for prediction and improved decision-making in complex situations. They also present case studies where simulation is used as a tool to enhance decision-making to advance the transition towards circular systems implementation.

In Chapter 13, Fontana problematizes the inherent notion of buyers' change agency in Global Value Change (GVC) literature. He argues for a deeper understanding of the contribution of the developing countries' manufacturers to multistakeholder initiatives (MSIs) and their ability to advance the SDGs. Employing the case of socially proactive manufacturers operating in the Bangladeshi apparel supply chain, the DBL Group (DBL), Fontana conceptualizes a three-step governance process based on: (1) learning (2) integrating and (3) scaling. This process highlights how developing countries' manufacturers can participate with MSIs to lead and diffuse social sustainability programmes in the chain. The chapter concludes with a discussion on the implications of the buyers' change agency assumed in GVC literature.

For businesses to undertake transformative sustainable practices, it is critical to determine if sustainable practices may lead to a positive financial return for the business. To answer this critical question, practitioners and researchers need to value the return on sustainability investment (ROSI). Atz, Van Holt, Douglas, and Whelan (Chapter 14) apply a five-step methodology that systematically monetizes sustainability by monetizing potential and realized financial benefits via mediating factors (i.e. financial drivers) across two types of industries. Investigating the Brazilian beef supply chains that committed to deforestation-free beef and the automotive industry, they find substantial value from implementing sustainability strategies. Their results show that the beef supply chain yields a potential net present value (NPV) between 0.01 and 12% of annual revenue, depending on the supply chain segment. Whereas, for an automotive company, the five-year NPV based on realized benefits is 12% of annual revenue. They thus argue that monetizing sustainability can lead to competitive advantage and shared value for multiple stakeholders.

The concluding Chapter 15 by Sezgi and Mair addresses the issue of scaling social innovation efforts. The authors adopt an organizational perspective on scaling in order to focus on the role of control in organizational achievements. Although the level of control exerted differs from one organizational setting to another, control is essential in any type of organization to coordinate organizational members towards coherent goals. A better understanding of how organizations scale, the mechanisms they put into use for achieving differing degrees of control under different organizational modes, can help both organizations and entrepreneurs align their strategies with appropriate design features. In order to shed light on the mechanisms at play, the authors investigate Aravind Eye Care System, a nonprofit organization based in India providing eye care services to poor people. Aravind serves as a unique setting for zooming into organizational modes since it is a rare example of an organization that applies three organizational modes simultaneously.

References

Bali Swain, R. (2018). A critical analysis of the sustainable development goals. In W. Leal, et al. (Eds.), *Handbook of sustainability science and research* (pp. 341–355). Cham, Switzerland: Springer.

Bali Swain, R., & Ranganathan, S. (2020). *Modelling interlinkages between sustainable development goals using network analysis, draft, Misum*. Sweden: Stockholm School of Economics.

Bilitewski, B. (2012). The circular economy and its risks. *Waste Management, 32,* 1–2.

Blomsma, F., & Brennan, G. (2017). The emergence of circular economy: A new framing around prolonging resource productivity. *Journal of Industrial Ecology, 21,* 603–614.

Bocken, N., Boons, F., & Baldassarre, B. (2019). Sustainable business model experimentation by understanding ecologies of business models. *Journal of Cleaner Production, 208,* 1498–1512.

Bocken, N. M. P., Ritala, P., & Huotari, P. (2017). The circular economy: Exploring the introduction of the concept among S&P 500 firms. *Journal of Industrial Ecology, 21,* 487–490.

Boons, F., & Bocken, N. (2018). Towards a sharing economy—Innovating ecologies of business models. *Technological Forecasting and Social Change, 137,* 40–52.

Boulding, K. E. (1966). The economics of the coming spaceship earth. *Journal of Environmental Quality, 1,* 1–8.

Braungart, M., & McDonough, W. (2002). *Cradle to cradle: Remaking the way we make things*. London: Vintage Books.

Camacho-Otero, J., Boks, C., & Pettersen, I. N. (2018). Consumption in the circular economy: A literature review. *Sustainability, 10*(8), 2758.

Checkland, P. (2000). Systems thinking, systems practice: Includes a 30-year retrospective. *Journal-Operational Research Society, 51*(5), 647.

D'Amato, D., Droste, N., Allen, B., Kettunen, M., Lähtinen, K., Korhonen, J., ... Toppinen, A. (2017). Green, circular, bio economy: A comparative analysis of sustainability avenues. *Journal of Cleaner Production, 168,* 716–734.

Ellen MacArthur Foundation. (2012). *Towards the circular economy Vol. 1: An economic and business rationale for an accelerated transition.* Cowes, UK: Ellen MacArthur Foundation.

Ellen MacArthur Foundation. (2015). *Delivering the circular economy: A toolkit for policy makers.* Cowes, UK: Ellen MacArthur Foundation.

European Commission. (2015). *An EU action plan for the circular economy.* European Commission. Retrieved from https://doi.org/10.1017/CBO9781107415324.004.

European Commission. (2019). *Report on the implementation of the Circular Economy Action Plan.* European Commission. Retrieved from https://doi.org/10.1259/arr.1905.0091.

Geels, F. W., McMeekin, A., Mylan, J., & Southerton, D. (2015). A critical appraisal of sustainable consumption and production research: The reformist, revolutionary and reconfiguration positions. *Global Environmental Change, 34,* 1–12.

Geissdoerfer, M., Savaget, P., Bocken, N. M. P., & Hultink, E. J. (2017). The circular economy—A new sustainability paradigm? *Journal of Cleaner Production, 143,* 757–768. https://doi.org/10.1016/J.JCLEPRO.2016.12.048.

Geng, Y., & Doberstein, B. (2008). Developing the circular economy in China: Challenges and opportunities for achieving 'leapfrog development'. *International Journal of Sustainable Development and World Ecology, 15,* 231–239.

Geng, Y., Fu, J., Sarkis, J., & Xue, B. (2012). Towards a national circular economy indicator system in China: An evaluation and critical analysis. *Journal of Cleaner Production, 23,* 216–224.

Ghisellini, P., Cialani, C., & Ulgiati, S. (2016). A review on circular economy: The expected transition to a balanced interplay of environmental and economic systems. *Journal of Cleaner Production, 114,* 11–32.

Haas, W., Krausmann, F., Wiedenhofer, D., & Heinz, M. (2015). How circular is the global economy? An assessment of material flows, waste production, and recycling in the European union and the world in 2005. *Journal of Industrial Ecology, 19,* 765–777. https://doi.org/10.1111/jiec.12244.

Han, J., & Sweet, S. (Forthcoming). Consumers practicing slow consumption: Exploring how value is constructed in the second-hand fashion market? In R. Bali Swain & S. Sweet (Eds.), *Sustainable consumption and production.* London: Palgrave Macmillan.

Haupt, M., & Zschokke, M. (2017). How can LCA support the circular economy? 63rd discussion forum on life cycle assessment, Zurich, Switzerland, November 30, 2016. *International Journal of Life Cycle Assessment, 22*(5), 832–837.

Hawken, P., Lovins, A., & Lovins, H. (1999). *Natural capitalism: Creating the next industrial revolution.* New York: Little, Brown and Company.

Hobson, K. (2015). Closing the loop or squaring the circle? Locating generative spaces for the circular economy. *Progress in Human Geography, 40*(1), 88–104.

Holmes, H. (2018). New spaces, ordinary practices: Circulating and sharing within diverse economies of provisioning. *Geoforum, 88,* 138–147.

IPCC. (2014). *Climate change 2014: Synthesis report.* Contribution of working groups I, II and III to the Fifth Assessment Report of the Intergovernmental Panel on Climate Change. IPCC, Geneva, Switzerland, 151 pp.

Kirchherr, J., Reike, D., & Hekkert, M. (2017). Conceptualizing the circular economy: An analysis of 114 definitions. *Resources, Conservation and Recycling.* https://doi.org/10.1016/j.resconrec.2017.09.005.

Köhler, J., Geels, F. W., Kern, F., Markard, J., Onsongo, E., Wieczorek, A., … Fünfschilling, L. (2019). An agenda for sustainability transitions research: State of the art and future directions. *Environmental Innovation and Societal Transitions, 31,* 1–32.

Kopnina, H., & Blewitt, J. (2014). *Sustainable business: Key issues.* New York: Routledge Earthscan.

Korhonen, J., Honkasalo, A., & Seppälä, J. (2018). Circular economy: The concept and its limitations. *Ecological Economics, 143,* 37–46.

Lazarevic, D., & Valve, H. (2016). Narrating expectations for the circular economy: Towards a common and contested European transition. *Energy Research and Social Science, 31,* 60–69.

Manninen, K., Koskela, S., Antikainen, R., & Dahlbo, H. (2017). Do business models capture the circular economy value propositions? *Journal of Cleaner Production, 129,* 81–92.

Merli, R., Preziosi, M., & Compora, A. (2018). How do scholars approach the circular economy? A systematic literature review. *Journal of Cleaner Production, 178,* 703–722.

Pauliuk, S. (2018). Critical appraisal of the circular economy standard BS 8001: 2017 and a dashboard of quantitative system indicators for its implementation in organizations. *Resources, Conservation and Recycling, 129,* 81–92.

Pearce, D. W., & Turner, R. K. (1990). *Economics of natural resources and the environment*. Baltimore: Johns Hopkins University Press.

Pogutz, S., & Micale, V. (2011). Sustainable consumption and production: An effort to reconcile the determinants of environmental impact. *Society and Economy, 33*(1), 29–50.

Pomponi, F., & Moncaster, A. (2017). Circular economy for the built environment: A research framework. *Journal of Cleaner Production, 143,* 710–718.

Ranganathan, S., & Bali Swain, R. (2018). Sustainable development and global targets: A dynamical systems approach to aid evidence-based policy making. *Sustainable Development, 26*(6), 812–821.

Rizos, V., Tuokko, K., & Behrens, A. (2017, April). *The circular economy: A review of definitions, processes and impacts* (CEPS Research Report No 2017/8).

Saavedra, Y. M. B., Iritani, D. R., Pavan, A. L. R., & Ometto, A. R. (2017). Theoretical contribution of industrial ecology to circular economy. *Journal of Cleaner Production, 170,* 1514–1522.

Sauve, S., Bernard, S., & Sloan, P. (2016). Environmental sciences, sustainable development and circular economy: Alternative concepts for trans-disciplinary research. *Environmental Development, 17,* 48–56.

Schröder, P., Anggraeni, K., & Weber, U. (2018). The relevance of circular economy practices to the sustainable development goals. *Journal of Industrial Ecology, 23*(1), 77–95.

Song, X. Y. (2013). Analysis on green hotel marketing management under the background of circular economy. *Applied Mechanics and Materials, 291–294,* 1478–1481.

Spaiser, V., Ranganathan, S., Bali Swain, R., & Sumpter, D. (2016). The sustainable development oxymoron: Quantifying and modelling the incompatibility of sustainable development goals. *International Journal of Sustainable Development and World Ecology, 24*(6), 457–470.

Stigzelius, I. (2017). *Producing consumers: Agencing and concerning consumers to do green in everyday food practices* (Published PhD dissertation). Stockholm School of Economics, Sweden.

Stobart, J., Hann, A., & Morgan, V. (2007). *Spaces of consumption leisure and shopping in the English town, c. 1680–1830*. London: Routledge.

Stobart, J., & Van Damme, I. (2010). Introduction. In J. Stobart & I. Van Damme (Eds.), *Modernity and the second-hand trade: European consumption cultures and practices, 1700–1900* (pp. 1–15). Basingstoke: Palgrave Macmillian.

Sweet, S., Aflaki, R., & Stalder, M. (2019). *The Swedish market for pre-owned apparel and its role in moving the fashion industry towards more sustainable practices* (A Mistra Future Fashion Report 2019:13).

Sweet, S. & Wu, A. (2019). *Second-hand and leasing of clothing to facilitate textile reuse—Identifying sources of value generation from the perspective of businesses and user* (A Mistra Future Fashion Report 2019:13).

UNSD. (2020). *Second report of sustainable development goals interlinkages*. UN IAEG Interlinkages Working Group. Retrieved from https://unstats.un.org/unsd/statcom/51st-session/documents/2020-2-SDG-IAEG-Rev-EE.pdf.

Warde, A. (2005). Consumption and theories of practice. *Journal of Consumer Culture, 5*(2), 131–153.

Yuan, Z., Bi, J., & Moriguichi, Y. (2006). The circular economy: A new development strategy in China. *Journal of Industrial Ecology, 10,* 4–8.

CHAPTER 2

From Business Models to Modes of Provision: Framing Sustainable Consumption and Production

Frank Boons

Introduction

Practices of consumption and production are a key part of the currently unsustainable societies that we live in. While human beings engage in these practices to provide for their needs, these practices inevitably generate flows of materials and energy as they involve the transformation and geographical displacement of matter. Even if we consider the delivery and use of services such as hospitality, it is evident that this is impossible without the use of artefacts and physical infrastructure (Jones, Hillier, & Comfort, 2016).

Consequently, practices of consumption and production have three basic impacts on natural ecologies (Commoner, 1972): (1) they require the extraction of natural resources, which can extend beyond sustainable

F. Boons (✉)
Sustainable Consumption Institute, University of Manchester, Manchester, UK
e-mail: frank.boons@manchester.ac.uk

R. Bali Swain and S. Sweet (eds.), *Sustainable Consumption and Production, Volume II*,
https://doi.org/10.1007/978-3-030-55285-5_2

rates of replenishment, (2) disturb ecological cycles (such as the hydrological cycle and climate dynamics) and (3) use natural ecosystems as sinks through the dispersion of discarded human-made materials. In addition, these practices potentially have consequences for the well-being of those performing them, as well as others. There is thus also a social impact of consumption and production practices.

This chapter takes a critical look at a currently dominant way of framing these practices, and their social and ecological impact: sustainable business models. The next section, "Antecedents of Framing the Impact of Production and Consumption" starts with a concise historical overview of the way in which business, seen as being primarily responsible for production, has been linked to social and environmental impact, and how this was eventually complemented to include consumption practices. This provides the context, in the section "The Business Model Label as a New Way of Framing Sustainable Consumption and Production", for understanding how the business model, a currently popular way of framing production and consumption among academics, and increasingly also among business managers and policymakers, constitutes a clear departure from earlier framings. The advantages of this new framing are discussed in the section "Advantages of the Business Model Framing", while a closer look at drawbacks takes centre stage in the section "Limitations of the Business Model Construct for Sustainable Consumption and Production". This leads us to, in the section "Towards a Comparative Understanding of Modes of Provision", a plea for using the notion of modes of provision as a term to understand and facilitate sustainable practices of delivery and use for human needs.

Antecedents of Framing the Impact of Production and Consumption

The idea of socio-material systems being embedded within natural ecologies has an intellectual history that goes back centuries (Glacken, 1967), with a variety of analytical and normative framings that have been in use throughout these centuries. Since the 1960s, the notion of society, and business in particular, impacting on the natural environment, initially constructed to consist of the 'sectors' air, water and land, gained traction. Within the then industrialized world, more specifically the United States and Europe, governments adopted a regulatory approach to contain the impacts of production activities on these environmental sectors.

This reflected an adversarial relationship between government and business, which was ideologically supported by a division of responsibility where 'business' was assumed to take responsibility for maximizing profit, while the state served to set limits to the means for achieving profit (Friedman, 1970, 2007). This relates specifically to Western countries with an economy functioning along capitalist lines; for a view on the state-led economy of the USSR (see Ziegler, 1986). The notion of social responsibility was also used more specifically to refer to the social impact of firms (Carroll, 2008).

With the publication of the United Nations' Brundtland Report, *Our Common Future*, the term sustainable development, and its nominalization 'sustainability', became a dominant framing (Brundtland, Khalid, Agnelli, Al-Athel, & Chidzero, 1987). This new term, and the way in which it was constructed, redefined the scope considerably in two fundamental ways. First, the focus on environmental impact of human societies ignored that, as humans engage in these practices, they potentially create an impact on the well-being of themselves and others, in the present as well as on future generations. This constitutes the 'social' dimension of sustainability, which was now seen in an explicit relation to environmental impact. The second broadening of scope related to the governance of the social and environmental impact associated with human societies, and economic activities in particular. While previously the antagonistic dichotomy between business and government was at the heart of a legalistic approach to minimize impact, in the 1990s the term sustainability became associated with collaborative approaches between members of societal sectors, infusing emerging notions such as Corporate Social Responsibility (Carroll, 2008; for a critical perspective see Banerjee, 2008).

In that period the relative lack of attention for consumption as a driver for negative ecological and social impact became more apparent. Political and academic initiatives led to definitions of sustainable consumption, and perspectives that integrate sustainable consumption and production have since emerged (Geels, McMeekin, Mylan, & Southerton, 2015; Pogutz & Micale, 2011). In the past two decades, for instance, research on the link between sustainable development and consumption practices has blossomed, looking at the role of consumption in the circular economy (Camacho-Otero, Boks, & Pettersen, 2018).

The Business Model Label as a New Way of Framing Sustainable Consumption and Production

The concise historical exposé above uses the terms consumption and production without defining them. The initial formulation of sustainable consumption under the guidance of the Norwegian Ministry of the Environment (1994) defines consumption as 'the use of goods and services that respond to basic needs and bring a better quality of life'. Production is usually defined in terms of activities performed by business firms, more specifically activities associated with organizing and executing the transformation of matter to produce goods and services. Defined in this way, 'goods' and 'services', exchanged across markets, are the linking pin between separate practices of consumption and production.

The new framing of business models emerged at a time when this compartmentalized view proved to be ill-suited to newly emerging activities (see Ghaziani & Ventresca, 2005; Nielsen & Lund, 2014; Schweizer, 2005; Zott, Amit, & Massa, 2011). While the term had been used before, it gained traction in relation to new trends in Western economies. Two trends are of particular relevance. First, the extensive outsourcing of 'non-core' activities that business firms engaged in during the 1980s and 1990s created 'core' firms surrounded by a network of supplying and supporting firms. This made it less straightforward to locate the precise source of value creation. Second, technological change, in particular the development of computers linked through wireless networks, enabled firms to develop completely new types of services. As the Internet took shape, it provided a vehicle for economic activity where the traditional notion of a market, and separate producers and consumers became less useful; as users created content, they played a dual role. Also, given the free accessibility of the Internet, the way in which firms could appropriate value became less straightforward. As a result, whereas previously the strategies and organizational characteristics of firms had been framed in terms of a fixed legal entity which embodies the R&D, production, marketing and sales activities related to product/market combinations, there was an increased need to have a language that enabled the analysis of new forms. David Teece was among the first to articulate this, using a language of value creation and value appropriation as the central concepts; the firm was one particular form in which value could be created and appropriated, and one which by then had a rich embedding of supporting legal and cultural rules (Teece, 2010 is a consolidation of his contribution to the concept since the 1990s).

As the overview provided by Massa, Tucci, and Afuah (2017) reveals, there is considerable difference in the scope of business model definitions. An influential one is provided by Zott & Amit: 'A business model [is a] set of activities, as well as the resources and capabilities to perform them—either within the firm or beyond it through cooperation with partners, suppliers or customers' (2010: 217). '[It depicts] the content, structure, and governance of transactions designed so as to create value through the exploitation of business opportunities' (p. 219). While this definition, as others, focuses on the 'business' side of things, it includes the customer/user as an active participant. Thus, the business model concept brings in users, and the way they participate in value creation, as an explicit element. This is also clear from the popular business model canvas, a design-oriented tool where user-elements comprise three out of nine elements that together constitute a business model (Osterwalder & Pigneur, 2010).

Advantages of the Business Model Framing

The framing of sustainable consumption and production in terms of business models has a number of distinct advantages, which stem from the concept being sensitive to (evolving) characteristics of the wider economic system, as well as its explicit focus on articulating a value proposition as a starting point for understanding and designing practices of production and consumption. Five advantages are discussed in more detail below.

More Inclusive Definitions of Value Created

Perhaps most crucially, the language of value creation, which was originally designed to allow for innovative ways of designing profitable business activities in a rapidly changing economy with digital technology at its core, allowed for a wider range of 'definitions of value' (Boons, 2009). It thus became a convenient way for combining the social and environmental values associated with sustainable development with economic value as traditionally defined from an economic, marketing or business perspectives. As one of the first articulations of the 'sustainability business model' Stubbs and Cocklin (2008), presented case studies of firms where environmental and social priorities were seen as 'shaping' the business model.

Slight differences in labels can be seen to denote fundamentally different approaches: several publications (Lüdeke-Freund, Schaltegger, & Dembek, 2019; Schaltegger, Hansen, & Lüdeke-Freund, 2016: 6) put forward the notion of the 'business model for sustainability' which they define as a construct that 'helps describing, analysing, managing, and communicating (1) a company's sustainable value proposition to its customers, and all other stakeholders, (2) how it creates and delivers this value, (3) and how it captures economic value while maintaining or regenerating natural, social, and economic capital beyond its organizational boundaries'. This definition acknowledges the vital role of stakeholders beyond the firm in achieving sustainable value. A definition that focuses on the process needed to achieve this involvement is provided by Boons and Lüdeke-Freund (2013: 13; for a practice-based definition, see Boons & Laasch, 2019):

1. The value proposition provides measurable ecological and/or social value in concert with economic value, reflecting a business-society dialogue concerning the balance of economic, ecological and social needs as such values are temporally and spatially determined.
2. The firm actively involves its suppliers, who take responsibility towards their own as well as the focal company's stakeholders, avoiding shifting its own socio-ecological burdens to its suppliers.
3. The customer interface motivates customers to take responsibility for their consumption as well as for the focal company's stakeholders. The focal company does not shift its own socio-ecological burdens to its customers.
4. The financial model reflects an appropriate distribution of economic costs and benefits among actors involved in the business model and accounts for the company's ecological and social impacts.

Bocken, Short, Rana, and Evans (2014) provide an insight into the diversity of business models that relate to sustainability in one form or another. Drawing on a literature review they derive so-called 'archetypes' of sustainable business models which seek to create and deliver value in three broad categories: technical (which comprises value propositions relating to eco-efficiency and closed loop systems), social (including product stewardship and advancing sufficiency) and organizational (including business models based in bottom of the pyramid thinking and open innovation).

An Orientation to (Re-)design and Innovation

As articulated by Doganova and Eyquem-Renault (2009), the business model construct performs functions beyond providing an analytical lens; it plays an active role in processes of strategizing, innovation and organizational change. This makes sense given the history of the concept, emerging in a period of flux and transformation of the economy in general. It thus facilitates the discussion of (re-)designing practices of production and consumption. This makes it an attractive construct to handle questions which link it to the normative agenda of imagining sustainable ways of creating and delivering value.

Two notions are relevant here. The first is business model innovation (Geissdoerfer, Vladimirova, & Evans, 2018; Massa & Tucci, 2013; Schneider & Spieth, 2013), which consists of the design of business models 'from scratch', as well as the reconfiguration of existing business models. Both are relevant from the perspective of sustainability, which involves the activities from new market entrants as well as from incumbent firms (see also section on societal transitions below). Also, the distinction has been linked to the market maturity (Massa & Tucci, 2013): business model innovation is a possible strategy to retain market share once product and process innovations have been exhausted, for instance through adopting a service-oriented business model.

A second notion is that of business model experimentation. As a counterweight to the sometimes simplistic view on how business model innovations actually come about, attention has been given to the actual process through which this takes place. In the context of delivering sustainable value, Roome and Louche (2016) provide a detailed account of two cases which show that it involves a complex of (inter)actions where incremental change emerges over a longer period (Boons & Laasch, 2019; Whiteman & Kennedy, 2016 for a more generic process-orientation). This has been further developed into approaches to facilitate sustainable business model experimentation (Bocken, Boons, & Baldassarre, 2019).

Bridging to Incorporate Work on Product-Service Systems

A further advantage of the business model construct is that it provides a conceptual bridge to empirical research on product-service systems (PSS). Such systems have been the focus of environmental scientists interested in sustainable consumption and production for a longer time. Moving to a PSS involves a shift from users owning products to them being provided with the service delivered by that product. This shift can potentially result in superior resource efficiency in the provision of human needs. Empirical research provides mixed evidence for PSS delivering improved resource efficiency and sustainability in general (Tukker, 2015; Tukker & Tischner, 2006). Nevertheless, the core idea of moving from product sales to service delivery is exactly what is meant with the concept of business model reconfiguration. Thus, it is possible to connect a substantial body of empirical evidence relating to sustainable consumption and production to the study of sustainable business models.

Addressing the Micro–Macro Challenge: Business Model Innovation and Societal Transitions

Socio-economic imaginaries such as the 'circular economy' and 'sustainable cities' require a transformation of current societies, which comprise consumption and production practices related to a wide range of human needs. Provision for these needs is highly interrelated, which suggests that something like a 'circular economy' is more than the accumulation of individual circular business models.

Transition theory (see Köhler et al., 2019 for an overview) seeks to understand and help facilitate the transformation of larger socio-economic systems. A significant part of this work is directed at the so-called sustainability transitions (Markard, Raven, & Truffer, 2012). As suggested recently (Bidmon & Knab, 2018), the construct of a business model fits well with this highly developed and empirically grounded research lineage. Transitions are seen to start with the emergence of 'strategic niches', in which firms, users and other stakeholders experiment with new technologies, and the practices they suggest, to provide for human needs. When such experimentation is successful, it can grow to compete with, and eventually replace, an existing sociotechnical system. The business model construct is helpful in detailing what is needed to be successful and the understanding of business model experimentation enriches insights from transition theory on strategic niche management (Schot & Geels, 2008).

The link between transition theory and business models has been conceptually developed for the sharing economy by Boons and Bocken (2018). Using the metaphor of an ecosystem, they detail the mechanisms through which sharing business models can replace non-sharing business models. An empirical example of interacting business models in the evolution of the market for electric vehicles is provided by Bohnsack, Pinkse, and Kolk (2014). They detail how incumbents and new entrants experiment with business models and thus shape the evolving socio-economic system of private mobility.

An Explicit Look at the Shifting Boundary Between Production and Consumption

As mentioned above, the business model construct emerged in a period when taken-for-granted practices of production and consumption were challenged. Previously ingrained practices of production revolving around mass production of stock products constituted a major part of the economy, with users purchasing the ownership of those products without having the influence to shape those products in any fundamental way (this is true even when acknowledging that user practices can greatly affect the performance of products, and even the function they perform). With e-commerce and other applications of digital technology as a major trigger, alternative practices of production and consumption could now be conceptualized.

Crucially, such alternative practices involve a shift in the boundary between consumption and production. This boundary is less rigid than is assumed in traditional marketing and economics perspectives. In fact, users have to engage in consumption work to be actually able to use the product they have obtained. Also, implementing recycling and reuse requires them to do additional consumption work (Glucksmann, 2016; Wheeler & Glucksmann, 2013). Thus, the user is involved in the value creation process, rather than a passive recipient of a value created by a distant producer. This shifting boundary has consequences for social and environmental impact: for instance, the shift of meal preparation from consumer to producer that is implied in portioned ingredients available at retailers, results in increased use of packaging material, which has a negative environmental impact that is complemented by a potential reduction in the food waste resulting from a meal.

A more fundamental boundary shift is implied by the concepts of 'prosumer' (Ritzer, 2015, 2019) and 'collaborative consumption' (Perren & Grauerholz, 2015). Here users take on the role of actual producers, for instance through installing renewable energy technologies like solar panels and wind turbines which then feed-into the main grid. Apart from the environmental impact consequences (Leismann, Schmitt, Rohn & Baedeker, 2013), this often relates to complex changes in social relations, with users organizing themselves in some form to participate effectively in the wider system of provision.

Limitations of the Business Model Construct for Sustainable Consumption and Production

Inevitably, a construct highlights features of the world we inhabit at the cost of downplaying or ignoring others. The advantages presented above have thus to be seen as connected to a few fundamental limitations that come with conceptualizing sustainable consumption and production in terms of business models. Two key limitations are discussed in detail below, together with kernels of existing ways of addressing them.

Business (Model) as Usual

A key limitation of the construct, at least in the way it is routinely employed, lies in the wider economic system it invites us to assume. The language of 'business' and 'value appropriation' in particular leads users of the construct towards ways of providing for human needs that presuppose a profit-oriented economic system (see Boons & Bocken, 2018 for further development of this point). This frames the search for more sustainable practices of production as one in which a 'business case' must exist: profitability is taken as a condition for viability. This limits not only the range of production practices considered; it also has consequences for the consumption practices that come into view, as well as the possible boundaries between the two. Important trends such as commoning, providing for human needs in a way that does not require ownership relations (Bollier & Helfrich, 2015; Turner, 2017), as well as community-based networks of reuse, are thus left out of scope. These are crucial not just for their potential to reduce environmental impact; as community-based forms they may also contribute substantially to social sustainability. For some, such new forms of sustainable production and consumption constitute an antidote to the neoliberal market economy that has invaded global societies and which is one of the drivers of continued exploitation of natural resources and social relationships (note that in some accounts labels like 'sustainable development' and 'green economy' are seen as devices for keeping that system in place (Neusteurer, 2017; Wanner, 2015).

In this framing, it becomes relevant to empirically assess the relative merits of a variety of consumption and production practices using an inclusive language. For some, this work can be done using the notion of 'not-for-profit business models'. An alternative that avoids the word 'business' can be found in the language of 'modes of provision' (McMeekin & Southerton, 2007). This term refers to instituted ways in which the provision for human needs is performed within a society. This language is silent about the specific social practices and materialities that constitute a mode of provision, which can range from state-led provision to profit-oriented to communal forms. A comparison of modes of provision in terms of sustainability then comes into view, as is for instance provided by Lennon, Dunphy, and Sanvicente (2019) and Hess (2011) when comparing communal and for-profit provision in the energy market. Similarly, in seeking to address the negative social and ecological impacts of the current fast fashion trend, looking at modes of provision would juxtapose business models, and viable and existing non-profit networks for sharing and reuse (see Holmes, 2018 on such networks) as viable alternatives. This perspective brings into view the complicated nature of the fast fashion phenomenon: as Joy, Sherry, Venkatesh, Wang, and Chan (2012) report, there is a discrepancy of consumers' awareness of the unsustainability of fast fashion, and their continuation of engagement with it. At the same time, local networks of reuse do exist. Zamani, Sandin, and Peters (2017) show the environmental impact of fast fashion and discuss how extending the lifetime of clothing items through collaborative consumption is an alternative. They indicate that the environmental benefit of this switch depends on how this is organized logistics.

The inclusive language of modes of provision is also helpful when engaging with the macro process of sustainability transitions. Taking an inclusive view allows the assessment of how emerging sustainable (for-profit) business models are replacing non-profit/informal modes of provision, as for instance when car sharing business models compete with communal forms of carpooling, of business-led routes of clothing recycling substituting informal networks of reuse (Boons & Bocken, 2018).

Assessing the Sustainability of Modes of Provision

Much of the work on business models, even when specifically dealing with sustainability, lacks an explicit analysis and assessment of the environmental and/or social impacts it presumably brings. Often a positive impact is implicitly assumed (see Boons, 2013 for an assessment of literature on business and the environment in this respect).

As the work of Zamani et al. (2017) shows, assessing the environmental and social impact of a mode of provision is complicated. When envisioning, enacting and understanding sustainable production and consumption, a comparative assessment of such community-based, non-profit forms with profit-oriented business models is nevertheless required. While the assessment of products has become standardized in the analytical technique of life cycle assessment, a similarly agreed upon approach to assessing and comparing specific modes of provision is currently lacking. Boons and Bocken (2018) provide a conceptual proposal for assessing the contribution of a mode of provision to ecological sustainability relative to the practices of production and consumption it replaces. Some empirical work has been done in this area: Manninen et al. (2018) provide an assessment method for delivery on environmental value proposition of circular business models. Suckling and Lee (2015) provide a life cycle assessment of mobile phones under different business models (ownership versus a cloud-based product-service system). Kjaer, Pigosso, Niero, Bech, and McAloone (2019) show how a set of conditions must be met before PSS/circular business models actually lead to increased resource efficiency/decoupling.

Towards a Comparative Understanding of Modes of Provision

The construct of a business model enables a distinct perspective on sustainable consumption and production. It starts to bring into focus the alternative ways of defining, creating and delivering sustainable value, and it enables an understanding of sustainable transitions to increase sustainable value at the macro level. At the same time, in its current usage it is limiting in foregrounding profit-based practices of production and consumption. For this reason, the language of modes of provision is proposed, as it can capture the benefits delivered by the business model construct, while drawing in a more inclusive range of practices of production and consumption. This allows a more complete comparative analysis of such practices that will help facilitate processes of sustainable development. In order for this to work, a major gap to fill is to connect such analysis with standardized forms for assessing the social and environmental impacts of modes of provision in a meaningful way.

References

Banerjee, S. B. (2008). Corporate social responsibility: The good, the bad and the ugly. *Critical Sociology, 34*(1), 51–79.

Bidmon, C. M., & Knab, S. F. (2018). The three roles of business models in societal transitions: New linkages between business model and transition research. *Journal of Cleaner Production, 178,* 903–916.

Bocken, N. M., Boons, F., & Baldassarre, B. (2019). Sustainable business model experimentation by understanding ecologies of business models. *Journal of Cleaner Production, 208,* 1498–1512.

Bocken, N. M., Short, S. W., Rana, P., & Evans, S. (2014). A literature and practice review to develop sustainable business model archetypes. *Journal of Cleaner Production, 65,* 42–56.

Bohnsack, R., Pinkse, J., & Kolk, A. (2014). Business models for sustainable technologies: Exploring business model evolution in the case of electric vehicles. *Research Policy, 43*(2), 284–300.

Bollier, D., & Helfrich, S. (Eds.). (2015). *Patterns of commoning*. The Commons Strategy Group and Off the Common Press.

Boons, F. (2009). *Creating ecological value: An evolutionary approach to business strategies and the natural environment*. Cheltenham: Edward Elgar Publishing.

Boons, F. (2013). Organizing within dynamic ecosystems: Conceptualizing socio-ecological mechanisms. *Organization & Environment, 26*(3), 281–297.

Boons, F., & Bocken, N. (2018). Towards a sharing economy—Innovating ecologies of business models. *Technological Forecasting and Social Change, 137*(C), 40–52.

Boons, F., & Laasch, O. (2019). Business models for sustainable development: A process perspective. *Journal of Business Models, 7*(1), 9–12.

Boons, F., & Lüdeke-Freund, F. (2013). Business models for sustainable innovation: State-of-the-art and steps towards a research agenda. *Journal of Cleaner Production, 45,* 9–19.
Brundtland, G. H., Khalid, M., Agnelli, S., Al-Athel, S., & Chidzero, B. (1987). *Our common future*. New York.
Camacho-Otero, J., Boks, C., & Pettersen, I. N. (2018). Consumption in the circular economy: A literature review. *Sustainability, 10*(8), 2758.
Carroll, A. B. (2008). A history of corporate social responsibility: Concepts and practices. In *The Oxford handbook of corporate social responsibility*. Oxford: Oxford University Press.
Commoner, B. (1972). *The closing circle: Confronting the environmental crisis*. New York: Random House.
Doganova, L., & Eyquem-Renault, M. (2009). What do business models do? Innovation devices in technology entrepreneurship. *Research Policy, 38*(10), 1559–1570.
Friedman, M. (1970, September 13). The social responsibility of business is to increase its profits. *The New York Times Magazine*, pp. 122–124.
Friedman, M. (2007). The social responsibility of business is to increase its profits. In W. C. Zimmerli, K. Richter, & M. Holzinger (Eds.), *Corporate ethics and corporate governance* (pp. 173–178). Berlin and Heidelberg: Springer.
Geels, F. W., McMeekin, A., Mylan, J., & Southerton, D. (2015). A critical appraisal of sustainable consumption and production research: The reformist, revolutionary and reconfiguration positions. *Global Environmental Change, 34,* 1–12.
Geissdoerfer, M., Vladimirova, D., & Evans, S. (2018). Sustainable business model innovation: A review. *Journal of Cleaner Production, 198,* 401–416.
Ghaziani, A., & Ventresca, M. J. (2005). Keywords and cultural change: Frame analysis of business model public talk, 1975–2000. *Sociological Forum, 20*(4), 523–559.
Glacken, C. J. (1967). *Traces on the Rhodian shore: Nature and culture in Western thought from ancient times to the end of the eighteenth century* (Vol. 170). Los Angeles: University of California Press.
Glucksmann, M. (2016). Completing and complementing: The work of consumers in the division of labour. *Sociology, 50*(5), 878–895.
Hess, D. J. (2011). Electricity transformed: Neoliberalism and local energy in the United States. *Antipode, 43*(4), 1056–1077.
Holmes, H. (2018). New spaces, ordinary practices: Circulating and sharing within diverse economies of provisioning. *Geoforum, 88,* 138–147.
Jones, P., Hillier, D., & Comfort, D. (2016). Sustainability in the hospitality industry. *International Journal of Contemporary Hospitality Management, 28*(1), 36–67.

Joy, A., Sherry, J. F., Jr., Venkatesh, A., Wang, J., & Chan, R. (2012). Fast fashion, sustainability, and the ethical appeal of luxury brands. *Fashion Theory, 16*(3), 273–295.

Kjaer, L. L., Pigosso, D. C., Niero, M., Bech, N. M., & McAloone, T. C. (2019). Product/service-systems for a circular economy: The route to decoupling economic growth from resource consumption? *Journal of Industrial Ecology, 23*(1), 22–35.

Köhler, J., Geels, F. W., Kern, F., Markard, J., Onsongo, E., Wieczorek, A., & Fünfschilling, L. (2019). An agenda for sustainability transitions research: State of the art and future directions. *Environmental Innovation and Societal Transitions, 31*, 1–32.

Leismann, K., Schmitt, M., Rohn, H., & Baedeker, C. (2013). Collaborative consumption: Towards a resource-saving consumption culture. *Resources, 2*(3), 184–203.

Lennon, B., Dunphy, N. P., & Sanvicente, E. (2019). Community acceptability and the energy transition: A citizens' perspective. *Energy, Sustainability and Society, 9*(1), 35.

Lüdeke-Freund, F., Schaltegger, S., & Dembek, K. (2019). Strategies and drivers of sustainable business model innovation. In F. Boons & A. McMeekin (Eds.), *Handbook of sustainable innovation* (pp. 101–123). Cheltenham: Edward Elgar Publishing.

Manninen, K., Koskela, S., Antikainen, R., Bocken, N., Dahlbo, H., & Aminoff, A. (2018). Do circular economy business models capture intended environmental value propositions? *Journal of Cleaner Production, 171*, 413–422.

Markard, J., Raven, R., & Truffer, B. (2012). Sustainability transitions: An emerging field of research and its prospects. *Research Policy, 41*(6), 955–967.

Massa, L., & Tucci, C. L. (2013). Business model innovation. In M. Dodgson, D. M. Gann, & N. Phillips (Eds.), *The Oxford handbook of innovation management* (pp. 420–441). Oxford: Oxford University Press.

Massa, L., Tucci, C. L., & Afuah, A. (2017). A critical assessment of business model research. *Academy of Management Annals, 11*(1), 73–104.

McMeekin, A., & Southerton, D. (2007). *Innovation and final consumption: Social practices, instituted modes of provision and intermediation*. Manchester: Center for Research on Innovation and Competition.

Neusteurer, D. (2017). The concept of green economy and its role in hegemonic neoliberal capitalism. *Socijalna Ekologija, 25*(2016)(3), 311–323.

Nielsen, C., & Lund, M. (2014). A brief history of the business model concept. In C. Nielsen & M. Lund (Eds.), *The basics of business models*. Aarhus: Ventus.

Norwegian Ministry of the Environment. (1994). *Sustainable consumption symposium report*. Oslo: Symposium on Sustainable Consumption, 19–20 January 2004.

Osterwalder, A., & Pigneur, Y. (2010). *Business model generation: A handbook for visionaries, game changers, and challengers*. Hoboken: Wiley.

Perren, R., & Grauerholz, L. (2015). Collaborative consumption. *International Encyclopedia of the Social & Behavioral Sciences, 4*, 139–144.

Pogutz, S., & Micale, V. (2011). Sustainable consumption and production: An effort to reconcile the determinants of environmental impact. *Society and Economy, 33*(1), 29–50.

Ritzer, G. (2015). Prosumer capitalism. *The Sociological Quarterly, 56*(3), 413–445.

Ritzer, G. (2019). Contemporary capitalism and the 'new' prosumer. In F. F. Wherry & I. Woodward (Eds.), *The Oxford handbook of consumption* (pp. 75–94). Oxford: Oxford University Press.

Roome, N., & Louche, C. (2016). Journeying toward business models for sustainability: A conceptual model found inside the black box of organisational transformation. *Organization & Environment, 29*(1), 11–35.

Schaltegger, S., Hansen, E. G., & Lüdeke-Freund, F. (2016). Business models for sustainability: Origins, present research, and future avenues. *Organization & Environment, 29*(1), 3–10.

Schneider, S., & Spieth, P. (2013). Business model innovation: Towards an integrated future research agenda. *International Journal of Innovation Management, 17*(01), 1–34.

Schot, J., & Geels, F. W. (2008). Strategic niche management and sustainable innovation journeys: Theory, findings, research agenda, and policy. *Technology Analysis & Strategic Management, 20*(5), 537–554.

Schweizer, L. (2005). Concept and evolution of business models. *Journal of General Management, 31*(2), 37–56.

Stubbs, W., & Cocklin, C. (2008). Conceptualizing a 'sustainability business model'. *Organization & Environment, 21*(2), 103–127.

Suckling, J., & Lee, J. (2015). Redefining scope: The true environmental impact of smartphones? *The International Journal of Life Cycle Assessment, 20*(8), 1181–1196.

Teece, D. J. (2010). Business models, business strategy and innovation. *Long Range Planning, 43*(2–3), 172–194.

Tukker, A. (2015). Product services for a resource-efficient and circular economy—A review. *Journal of Cleaner Production, 97*, 76–91.

Tukker, A., & Tischner, U. (2006). Product-services as a research field: Past, present and future. Reflections from a decade of research. *Journal of Cleaner Production, 14*(17), 1552–1556.

Turner, M. D. (2017). Political ecology III: The commons and commoning. *Progress in Human Geography, 41*(6), 795–802.

Wanner, T. (2015). The new 'passive revolution' of the green economy and growth discourse: Maintaining the 'sustainable development' of neoliberal capitalism. *New Political Economy, 20*(1), 21–41.

Wheeler, K., & Glucksmann, M. (2013). Economies of recycling, 'consumption work' and divisions of labour in Sweden and England. *Sociological Research Online, 18*(1), 114–127.

Whiteman, G., & Kennedy, S. (2016). Sustainability as process. In A. Langley & H. Tsoukas (Eds.), *The SAGE handbook of process organization studies* (pp. 417–431). London: Sage.

Zamani, B., Sandin, G., & Peters, G. M. (2017). Life cycle assessment of clothing libraries: Can collaborative consumption reduce the environmental impact of fast fashion? *Journal of Cleaner Production, 162*, 1368–1375.

Ziegler, C. E. (1986). *Environmental protection in the Soviet Union*. IIUG.

Zott, C., & Amit. R. (2010). Business model design: An activity system perspective. *Long range planning, 43*(2-3), 216–226.

Zott, C., Amit, R., & Massa, L. (2011). The business model: Recent developments and future research. *Journal of Management, 37*(4), 1019–1042.

CHAPTER 3

Histories and Futures of Circular Economy

Catherine Casson and Daniel Welch

Introduction

In this chapter we aim to put the idea of 'Circular Economy' into a wider perspective by viewing it through both a historical lens and a lens turned to the future. Observing a phenomenon through a historical perspective is perhaps a more commonplace exercise than through a futures perspective, but while each necessarily draws on different methods and resources, both perspectives share commonalities. As the historian of technology Johan Schot puts it, 'history is never only about recovering the past; it is a looking glass which makes us understand the present and the future' (2016: 445). To consider reuse and recycling from a long historical perspective helps draw attention to the extent to which such practices are always within a social and cultural context. As the following section

C. Casson (✉)
Alliance Manchester Business School, Circular Economy Group, The Sustainable Consumption Institute, University of Manchester, Manchester, UK
e-mail: catherine.casson@manchester.ac.uk

D. Welch
Department of Sociology, Circular Economy Group, The Sustainable Consumption Institute, University of Manchester, Manchester, UK
e-mail: Daniel.Welch@manchester.ac.uk

R. Bali Swain and S. Sweet (eds.), *Sustainable Consumption and Production, Volume II*,
https://doi.org/10.1007/978-3-030-55285-5_3

makes clear, it would be entirely wrong to see the reuse of goods and the recycling of materials in the past as being simply driven by necessity and scarcity. Rather, the practices of reuse and recycling have always been framed and conditioned by institutional arrangements and by cultural expectations and norms. Where and when price incentives have a role to play are in themselves functions of social regulation.

While to transpose the idea of 'Circular Economy' too literally into the historical past would obviously be anachronistic, turning to the future perspective allows us to ask where exactly 'The Circular Economy' is located temporally. What is 'The Circular Economy'? Certainly, we can understand it as a set of ideas in the here and now, and existing practices that draw on those ideas. But those ideas are orientated to the future—the future realization of the Circular Economy. According to the most prominent nongovernmental proponent of the idea, the very concept of waste would be eliminated in the future Circular Economy (EMF, n.d.). 'The Circular Economy' is an ambition, composed of targets, policy instruments, 'action plans' and 'pathways', expectations and aspirations. It is an *imagined future*. The second part of this chapter explores how we might understand 'Circular Economy'—or '*The* Circular Economy', because the definite article makes a difference—in terms of an imagined future. It draws upon a small but burgeoning field of social future studies that take seriously the future's critical role in the present (Adam & Groves, 2007; Beckert, 2016; Jasanoff & Kim, 2015; Mische, 2009; Urry, 2016).

Applying a Historical Lens to Circular Economy

Creating incentives for reuse and recycling can be challenging, and requires an awareness of barriers as well as opportunities. Historical evidence has a benefit that contemporary data often lacks, namely, that it is possible to examine both the context to attempts at recycling and reuse, and to assess their outcome. This facilitates both the identification of incentives and deterrents, and the causes of successes and failures (Boons, 2009; Fountaine, 2008).

The industrial revolution of c.1750–c.1850 has been identified as a pivotal historical moment which deterred recycling and reuse (Stobart, Hann, & Morgan, 2007; Stobart & Van Damme, 2010). The shift from small scale to mass production resulted in greater volumes and lower prices. Improvements in transport through investment in canals and railways enhanced distribution networks. Consumers were therefore provided with a greater variety of products, while competition between producers intensified. As a result, there were deterrents to the reuse of goods. Producers, however, were aware of the opportunities for recycling through transferring waste from one process to the raw materials for another. During the nineteenth century, for example, abattoirs and meat-packing firms in France and America began to engage in lard, tallow and glue production in order to reduce the volume of waste. In some cases, the initiative was taken by the firm, while in others it was imposed by local authorities anxious to make environmental improvements (Rosen, 2007).

In contrast, the period 1939–1945 is associated with intensive and successful recycling and reuse. World War II disrupted supply chains and required the reallocation of resources for armament production. In Britain, government-led schemes recycled metal, paper and textiles. Limitations were placed on the volumes of new clothing and household items that could be manufactured and 'utility' designs were introduced to conserve the raw materials that were used. Necessity, and indeed legislation, therefore encouraged recycling and reuse.

Recycling and reuse became less popular in the following decade. New goods were once more easily available. Women entering the workplace were looking for labour-saving opportunities in the home and no longer had the time to invest in collecting and sorting items for recycling, or for repairing objects for reuse. The creation and use of man-made fibres such as lycra, also became more widespread from the 1950s onwards. While these were frequently durable, which had the potential to promote reuse, they did not biodegrade easily and were difficult to process for recycling.

Focusing on the period c. 1760 onwards suggests that lower prices and greater choice in new goods deterred the reuse of goods. Change in the composition of items from organic to synthetic, meanwhile, limited the opportunities for recycling (O'Connor, 2011). Necessity appears to have been the prime motivator for recycling and reuse, particularly limited availability and the high cost of new alternatives. When this was removed, there appear to have been little incentive for consumers to reuse or recycle. On some occasions reuse and recycling were actively promoted by local and national governments, either to prevent unpleasant waste (the meat industry) or to address resource scarcity (WWII) (Rosen, 2007; Summers, 2015; Thorsheim, 2015). However, such interventions were sometimes restricted in scope, focusing on particular industries, locations or time periods.

Concerns about the environmental and welfare effects of mass production and intensive industrialization, however, led some to investigate alternative methods. English entrepreneur William Morris advocated a return to the production processes of the middle ages, which he associated with environmentally sustainable production, centred on small workshops or the household and using organic materials. He established his home furnishing production in the nineteenth century using those principles. Morris also believed that consumption was more responsible in previous centuries, as people only possessed items for their essential requirements and, with fewer possessions, valued each one more (Harvey & Press, 1991).

To what extent was Morris correct in his perception of the middle ages as a period of successful recycling and reuse? It is possible to investigate the reality through surviving evidence. Documents produced by trade organizations and local and central government give a perspective on the production and distribution of manufactured items. Consumer perspectives are revealed through wills (which detailed possessions) and via household inventories and domestic manuals.

Compared to subsequent periods, medieval production was relatively labour intensive. It is estimated that to produce a piece of cloth in the 1540s took a total of 978 hours (50 for wool sorting, 572 for yarn preparation, 130 for weaving, 90 for cleansing, thickening and stretching, 120 for finishing, eight for dyeing and eight for packing and transport) (Lee, 2018: 72–73). Most processes were reliant on organic materials (such as wool, metals, clay and wood) which were time-consuming to collect and whose availability could fluctuate. Under such circumstances there might be strong incentives to reuse items or to re-enter them into production through recycling. Yet, the period c.1200–c.1500 also witnessed an industrial revolution, characterized by the growth of towns and an expansion in the scale and scope of manufacturing. Prices of some goods were lowered through the introduction of labour-saving technology, such as mechanical mills for thickening cloth. Married women were expected to focus on household management. However, single and widowed women could be wage earners and, along with skilled male workers, could command competitive wages with some spare money for fashion items. The range of goods on offer, especially in towns, was high. London, for example, had 52 goldsmiths' shops on the Strand (Alsford, 2019). Incentives to buy new goods rather than reusing old ones therefore existed.

Responsible care of items was promoted as a positive behaviour in the middle ages in the domestic sphere. A manual written by an elderly husband to his new (young) wife in the late 1300s records instructions for preventing damp and insects damaging household linens and clothes, and recipes for stain removers (Greco & Rose, 2009: 220–221). The couple seems to have been well-off financially, suggesting that financial constraints were not the only motivation for such advice. Instead, scholars have suggested, conservation of household items was part of a wider set of behaviour through which a wife demonstrated her and her family's 'good order, simplicity and respectability' (Greco & Rose, 2009: 57–58). She was to care for her existing expensive clothes, such as feathers and furs, rather than following the 'new fashions' and to set herself apart from 'foolish or ignorant women who do not care about their own estate or that of their husband' and go around in 'disarray' (Greco & Rose, 2009: 57).

Social connections also incentivized the reuse of items, as recorded in testator bequests. Here, the motivation seems to have depended on the status of the recipient. Bequests made to servants usually had a practical dimension. John Baret II, for example, was a citizen of Bury St Edmunds who had business interests in the cloth trade. He died in 1467. He bequeathed his servant John Aleyn a horse and sets of Baret's clothes and bedding. If Aleyn were to take up an apprenticeship in a craft, then the executors were instructed to 'helpe hym therto with my goodes' (Merry, 2000: 254). However, commemoration after death was a significant motivation, especially for bequests to family members and friends. Medieval religious beliefs emphasized the need to pray for the soul of the dead person, to ease their passage through purgatory and ensure their arrival in heaven. Bequests of items could ensure that the deceased was remembered and prayed for by the recipient. Baret II records the household items bequeathed to his niece Jenete in unusual detail, including:

> my grene hanggyd bedde steynyd with my armys ther in that hanggith in the chambyr ovir kechene with the curtynez the grene keveryng longgyng therto another coverlyte ij blanketts ij peyre of good shetes…the fethirbeed is hire owne at her maistresse gaf hire at London and a basyn and an euer of laten cownterfet therto and more stuff I have not ocupyed of hirs. (Merry, 2000: 268)

Baret II had no children and that may have intensified his wish to ensure remembrance through the reuse of his possessions. The detailed descriptions may also stem from his business interests in the cloth trade, and experience of keeping inventories of stock.

Distribution of reused items outside of the domestic environment was a more contentious issue in the middle ages. Consumer protection appears to have been one reason. The trade organizations which managed many crafts had rules relating to quality control, and specialized in the sale of new goods (Casson, 2020). When consumers purchased from a member of a trade organization, such as the tailors or the skinners, they were doing so under the assumption that the goods would be of a certain quality and new. Manufacturers who broke the rules damaged consumer confidence. Particularly serious were attempts to alter old clothes so that they appeared to be new, by dyeing, re-shearing leather or raising the nap of cloth. In London in 1303–1304, for example, skinner Simon de Canterbury was censured for selling customer Geoffrey le Lacer 60 lambskins 'of which eleven were false and counterfeited out of old skins, being newly sheared again' (Davis, 2010: 273). Likewise, the repair of items using old material was prohibited.

There are indications, however, that there was a willingness among consumers to buy second-hand items. In 1321 in London, for example, at least 41 traders were present at a night-time market of second-hand goods (Davis, 2010: 275). Manufacturers of new goods, however, were reluctant to permit second-hand trade. Alongside concerns about quality control, it is also likely that the second-hand trade was seen as competing with new products. The local and central government had additional concerns. London's civic authorities frequently expressed the fear that second-hand markets provided an outlet for stolen goods (Davis, 2010: 275). Central government, meanwhile, feared that access to second-hand clothing distorted the social hierarchy. Those of lower incomes might be able to buy second-hand clothes previously owned by people of higher status, and thus practice deception in their social status. Attempts were made to curtail this perceived threat through legislation, notably the Statute of Diet and Apparel of 1363 which detailed appropriate apparel according to income level (Anon, 1810–1828: 278–283). Craftsmen, for example, were not to 'wear cloth worth more than 40 shillings for a whole cloth…nor wear bejewelled cloth', while knights with an income of 200 marks per year were permitted to wear cloth of a much higher value of six marks for the whole cloth (Anon, 1810–1828: 278–283).

Recycling waste material into other parts of the production process was an option for medieval manufacturers. The most detailed surviving evidence relates to textile production. Flocks (coarse tufts and refuse of wool, removed before spinning and shearings cut from the cloth) and thrums (unwoven ends of the warp threads left on the loom, and other pieces of waste thread or yarn after weaving) were waste products from cloth production. There is evidence that they were used as stuffing and quilting for bedding—which appears to have been an acceptable purpose (Lee, 2018: 132, 165–167). However, the reintroduction of this by-product into the manufacturing of lengths of cloths or the felting of hats was more controversial and was banned by a number of urban trade organizations, because use of a 'waste' by-product was considered to damage the quality of items.

In conclusion, the evidence from the period c.1250–c.1500 lends some support to Morris's belief that medieval people cherished their possessions. However, rather than being solely motivated to reuse out of necessity, they seem to have been incentivised by the personal associations communicated through reuse. Conserving of resources was praised in the domestic environment, but largely deterred outside of it. Trade organizations and local and central government frequently introduced legal constraints on the circulation of reused items, and on the recycling of waste products into related areas of production. Sometimes these concerns were for wider social benefit, notably consumer protection and the maintenance of law and order. However, attempts to limit consumers from actively purchasing second-hand clothing were more self-serving, and motivated by a desire to limit competition for the producers of new goods and to maintain the social hierarchy.

This brief historical excursion helps underscore how practices of the reuse of goods and recycling of materials have always been embedded in social and cultural, as well as economic, contexts. Indeed, it underscores how the 'the economy' is itself a historical artefact (Mitchell, 2008). The medieval legal restraints on the economic circulation of reused items such as clothing may seem bizarre to us today, but they are no more or less historically contingent than our contemporary regulations about what can be reused, repaired and recycled, and by whom. As the following section demonstrates, when we consider what a future Circular Economy might look like we are forced to consider exactly these questions.

Imagined Futures of the Circular Economy

We now turn from a historical perspective to the challenge of seeing things from the perspective of the future. The conventional social scientific viewpoint sees present conditions as outcomes emerging from the past. There is growing scholarly interest, however, in thinking through what it means to take seriously the critical role that representations and expectations of the future play in the present. Imagined futures can come to serve as visions guiding public or corporate policy, channelling funding, influencing technological design, orienting social movements or providing political legitimation. Projects and visions of collective futures embody expectations of future states, pragmatic beliefs about the way the world works and beliefs about the nature of 'the common good' (Adam & Groves, 2007; Beckert, 2016; Brown, Rappert, & Webster, 2000; Jasanoff & Kim, 2015; Mische, 2009, Urry, 2016). In other words, the way we frame our understandings of the future *today* helps shape the future tomorrow. 'The Circular Economy' can be understood as an *imagined future* in this sense.

Imagined futures—and the understandings, expectations and beliefs they carry with them—may come to invest, inform and motivate different areas of the social world, such as professional practices, political projects and everyday consumption. Sustainable consumption is an example of such a future-oriented project. Since the Rio Earth Summit in 1992, 'sustainable consumption' has come to encompass explicit visions of the future, developed in reports, scenarios, vision documents and even fiction. Sustainable consumption has also become a field for specialized professional practices, including for example, academic scholarship (of which this Handbook is an example), sustainability communications within corporations and marketing agencies, and technical practices such as Life Cycle Analysis. In turn these visions, ideas and professional practices, and their associated aspirations and expectations, have come to inform the everyday consumption practices of ordinary people.

The discourse of 'Circular Economy' has grown to prominence in recent years, in many instances superseding the discourse of 'sustainable consumption and production'. The European Union (EU), for example, has reframed policy commitments to 'sustainable production and consumption' in terms of Circular Economy. In 2008, the EU launched a 'Sustainable Consumption and Production Action Plan'. Since then, the European Commission reframed its commitments to waste reduction and recycling in terms of the Circular Economy and in 2015 launched a 'Circular Economy Action Plan' (EC, 2015).[1] This is not simply a case of swapping old buzzwords for new ones. Circular Economy is a specific constellation of ideas, drawing on inheritance in the field of 'industrial ecology', 'cradle-to-cradle' design (Braungart & McDonough, 2002) and 'natural capitalism' (Hawken, Lovins, & Lovins, 1999). It can be argued that in this transition much of the social scientific insight into consumption developed in dialogue with the field of sustainable consumption has been lost in the mainstream discourse of circular economy (Mylan, Holmes, & Paddock, 2016). This has real consequences. Imagined futures of Circular Economy carry usually implicit models of consumption, and of what interventions in everyday consumption might look like (Welch, Keller, & Mandich, 2016).

Such implicit models frame what is considered plausible and possible and thus have very real effects on policy and interventions for behavioural and social change. The 2015 EU Circular Economy Action Plan (EC, 2015), for example, opens the section on 'Consumption' by noting that:

> the choices made by millions of consumers can support or hamper the circular economy. These choices are shaped by the information to which consumers have access, the range and prices of existing products, and the regulatory framework. (EC, 2015)

Here consumption is framed as the aggregate of consumer choices resulting from rational economic behaviour. This is an individualistic, voluntaristic and economistic understanding of consumption that has been widely challenged by social scientific approaches to sustainable consumption. The Action Plan therefore presents a vision of consumption in a future Circular Economy that is reduced to purchasing and recycling. The full potential of policy interventions into consumption and of business models that could be envisioned under the aegis of 'the Circular Economy' are likely to thus remain unrealized in policies framed by the understanding of consumption in this document (Welch & Southerton, 2019).

[1] At the time of writing (2020) the second EU Circular Economy Action Plan was being finalized.

Analysing Social Futures

We turn now briefly to some of the analytical and theoretical resources through which we might approach the Circular Economy as an imagined future. The significance of expectations and guiding visions has been a growing field of social scientific analysis for over 20 years (see Borup, Brown, Konrad, & Van Lente, 2006; Brown et al., 2000). Central to this 'sociology of expectations' has been the study of how expectations shape scientific and technological change and the field of social studies of science, technology and society (STS) has been the dominant orientation, although the expectations literature also draws on sociology, economics and philosophy of science. As Brown et al. put it, this work seeks to shift the analytical gaze 'towards the phenomenon of future orientation itself'; a shift from '*looking into* the future to *looking at* how the future…is constructed and managed, by whom and under what conditions' (Brown et al., 2000: 4). Here 'the future' is understood as 'a contested object of social and material action' (2000: 3). It is contested between social actors seeking to secure specific kinds of futures—for example social movements on the one hand and corporations on the other—that engage in a range of rhetorical, representational, organizational and material activities through which they hope to shape understandings and expectations of the possibility and plausibility of their desired futures. These expectations of imagined futures can come to play a critical role in the realization of the futures desired by different actors—motivating action, mobilizing resources and legitimating specific courses of action. Expectations can be understood, according to Borup et al. (2006: 286), as 'wishful enactments of a desired future' and 'promissory commitments that become part of a shared agenda and thus require action' (ibid., 289).

Arguably the mainstream discourse of Circular Economy is more strongly a promissory discourse than that of 'sustainable consumption and production'. The latter was of course future-oriented and often framed in terms of the promise of science and technology, particularly through understandings of ecological modernization. However, 'the Circular Economy' is arguably more strongly oriented by, as Gregson, Crang, Fuller, and Holmes (2015: 221) put it, 'idealized visions' of technological progress. While the prosaic reality is, thus far, largely one of enhanced, post-consumer waste management, the vision is of a new, producer-led, industrial revolution of 'industrial symbiosis' with products designed for end-of-life recyclability as new material inputs to 'circular' production processes (ibid.). This vision is strongly framed through the model, or metaphor, of a nutrient cycle, with 'the economy' conceived as a system of 'closed loop' cycles of materials and resources playing the role of nutrients (see, e.g. EMF, n.d.). As Gregson et al. (2015) note, such a guiding vision raises important questions concerning the spatial boundedness of such a system, as well as, we might add, questions on the presumed relationships between the circulation of resources and the circulation of capital.

Visions of the Circular Economy can also be understood as what Jasanoff and Kim (2009) have named 'sociotechnical imaginaries'. Sociotechnical imaginaries are 'collectively held and performed visions of desirable futures…animated by shared understandings of forms of social life and social order attainable through…advances in science and technology'. (Jasanoff, 2015: 19). 'Sociotechnical imaginaries' articulate the relationship of science and technology to political power and policy; they are 'visions of what is good, desirable, and worth attaining for a political community' (Jasanoff & Kim, 2009: 122). They are both 'descriptive of attainable futures and prescriptive of the futures that ought to be attained' (ibid. 120). Sociotechnical futures mobilize groups of actors around specific visions and 'master narratives' (Jasanoff, 2015). Work in this area stresses that guiding visions, such as that of the Circular Economy, are co-constituted with policy frameworks and strategies for achieving those visions, such as the EU Circular Economy Action Plans, which act as the driver towards the imagined future (Birch, 2016). Jasanoff and Kim's (2009) work stressed the national identity of sociotechnical imaginaries, the co-production of sociotechnical imaginaries and national science policy, and the relationships between national sociotechnical imaginaries. More recent work has examined how, before sociotechnical imaginaries stabilize and become dominant within a political community, such as the EU, there are usually a range of potential or emergent visions or imagined futures competing for influence (Birch, 2016). This raises questions about the processes of contention between actors championing competing imagined futures and the policies, technologies and practices involved in such power struggles, and which kinds of social actors—for example, NGOs, social movement organizations or corporations—are able to engage with, or are excluded from, the development of future visions of society (Birch, 2016).

Another set of issues raised by the idea of competing imagined futures concerns how those imaginaries mobilize wider cultural repertoires of understandings, beliefs and values (Welch & Ehgartner 2019; Welch et al., 2016). Such cultural repertoires include beliefs about the nature of the common good or the conventional forms of worth used to justify imagined futures. Welch et al. (2016), for example, note how the EU Circular Economy Action Plan (2015) is framed primarily through market-based understandings of profit-maximization and competition and industrial-based understandings of efficiency, productivity and instrumentality, while ecological understandings are largely absent. Another aspect of the cultural repertoires that imagined futures draw upon are the understandings through which we orient ourselves to future possibilities. Such understandings include beliefs about individual and collective agency, about the nature of society, pragmatic beliefs about the way the world works, as well as cosmological beliefs such as believing in fate. The cultural sociologist Ann Mische (2009) uses the term 'dimensions of projectivity' to describe the different dimensions of orientation to the future that are made up of those understandings. Mische (2009) identifies nine distinct dimensions. These include, for example, 'contingency', the degree to which projections are imagined as predetermined or uncertain; 'extension' in time, such as utopian movements' vision of long-term transformation, or the short term of business and electoral cycles; and 'volition', the sense of whether the future is moving towards us, is beyond our control, or whether we make the future ourselves.

Contested Imagined Futures of Circular Economy

Having introduced some of the analytical, social scientific resources through which we might explore the Circular Economy as an imagined future, we turn to a concrete example. Recent controversies around the EU's Ecodesign Directive can be understood in terms of contestation between competing imagined futures of the Circular Economy. In October 2019, the European Commission ratified new regulations to be included in the Ecodesign Directive, which enshrines environmental regulations relating to product design, in this case for a range of goods including televisions, 'white goods' and lighting products.

The new regulations represented a partial settlement between two rival groups of actors promoting different imagined futures of Circular Economy. On the one hand were the consumer goods corporations and their political advocates within the EU policymaking apparatus and on the other, a coalition of citizens' organizations (themselves EU-wide representatives of smaller, usually nationally based organizations), such as the European Environmental Bureau (the largest network of environmental citizens' organizations in Europe), BEUC (representing 45 consumer organizations) and Repair.eu, a coalition of 'Right to Repair' campaign groups.

The corporate camp mobilized an imagined future of Circular Economy drawing on the tropes of technological progress and renewed economic growth through the 'fourth industrial revolution'; the 'idealized vision' noted by Gregson et al. (2015: 221) of a new, producer-led industrial revolution of 'industrial symbiosis'. This vision, drawing on the market and industrial understandings and values noted above, segued closely with the official EU Circular Economy policy as represented by the 2015 Action Plan. The corporations lobbied for legislation that would frame 'eco-design' in terms of energy efficiency and products designed for end-of-life, producer-controlled recyclability and the circular flows of material envisaged—the 'nutrients' of the Circular Economy—firmly under corporate control.

Contesting this vision of a top-down, producer-controlled Circular Economy was the growing 'Right to Repair' movement. While consumer and environmental interests, and the organizational actors representing them, had an important part to play, it was the 'Right to Repair' movement that galvanized support, and, critically, offered an alternative vision of Circular Economy. The movement consists of increasingly widespread grassroots initiatives, and some well-organized 'hub' organizations, such as the Repair Café Foundation and the UK's Restart Project. Repair Cafés are often temporary spaces where volunteers open the doors to the public to bring everyday items for repair. The first Repair Café opened in Amsterdam in 2009—10 years later there are over 1500 worldwide. The improbable cause of the repairability of refrigerators and washing machines became a contested political issue due to the success of the movement.

The Right to Repair seeks to push back against the growing monopoly on repair exercised by manufacturers of products that are co-constituted by the increasing prevalence of software in everything from domestic white goods to cars and farm machinery, and a regime of guarantee terms, regulations or intellectual property laws that militates and legislates against amateur repair. In the USA, farmers legally restrained from repairing their own tractors, and even the US military unable to maintain its own equipment in the field due to restrictions imposed by manufacturers. 'Right to Repair' bills in 20 US states have been stalled or defeated by a concerted corporate campaign, in which Apple has paid a critical role, on grounds of safety, security and intellectual property risks (Ehgartner & Hirth, 2019).

With slogans such as 'Move slow and fix things' and 'In a disposable society to repair is to rebel' the Repair movement has articulated a vision of a sustainable future that was not dominated by ideas of corporate-led innovation (*The Economist*, 2018). Rather, it offers grassroots engagement in material culture rooted in popular appeal to notions of the value of thrift and distaste at the 'throwaway society'. Nearly 200,000 citizens across Europe signed petitions calling for the 'Right to Repair' to be enshrined in the Ecodesign Directive, and the issue gained mainstream media coverage including, for example, a feature on 'Fixing the throwaway economy' on the popular BBC Breakfast show (2018).

A poster available from the Restart Project (2017), which specializes in organizing repair cafes to fix electronic goods, is headed 'This is the world we are working towards, and it's nearer than you think' above an illustration featuring aspects of an imagined future, including 'Electronics become heirlooms with extended software support' and 'Move beyond recycling and resource efficiency'. The organization's website introduces the rationale for the poster thus:

> We know what world (or off-world) we do *not* want to see — WALL-E painted that sad picture. But we felt we needed to envision the world we would like to see. Taking the design of a circuit board for inspiration—the operative heart of our gadgets—our "Restarted Future" poster illustrates the life-force of the circular economy. There are so many possibilities for the move towards a more sustainable relationship with our gadgets: from repair in schools, to 3D printing new spare parts, to the more efficient use of resources in manufacturing. (Restart Project, 2017: n.p.)

The core demands of the Right to Repair movement are an end to legislation restricting repair on intellectual property grounds, guaranteed access to spare parts and repair information for all, and 'design for disassembly' with widely available tools. The Ecodesign Directive therefore became the site of struggle of rival imagined futures of the Circular Economy. A critical axis of dispute on the framing of the Directive was whether the emphasis should lie on energy efficiency or efficiency in materials. With few exceptions, the focus of the Ecodesign Directive, supported by corporate actors, was on the energy efficiency of household appliances in use, arguing that energy consumption remains a core issue for climate change, which their technical innovation could increasingly mitigate. From this same position, industry representatives argued against the inclusion in the Ecodesign Directive of non-energy using products such as furniture and clothing. For the Right to Repair movement, a key issue was to prove the importance of increasing the efficiency of resource use for mitigating climate change, and the Ecodesign Directive was seen as a critical site to set precedents around wider sustainability issues relating to the design. A second core axis of dispute was between design for disassembly, advocated by Right to Repair activists, against design for recyclability advocated by the corporations. While this could be framed in terms of a clash between consumer rights and intellectual property rights, it was also a contest between fundamental elements of the rival imagined futures. On the one hand, a Circular Economy based on technical innovation in which material flows would be controlled and managed by producers and retailers; and, on the other, a Circular Economy that reconfigured consumers' relations to products in a far more fundamental way.

Between an early draft of the Directive in August 2018 to the draft of October 2018, following corporate lobbying, the framing shifted fundamentally from one vision to another, as repair advocates were quick to point out. The Table 3.1, taken from a document prepared by the European Environmental Bureau (EEB) and allies, demonstrates this shift in relation to the proposed regulations on washing machines.

The EEB (2018: n.p.) went on to note its disappointment that:

> Rather than facilitating the provision of information on repair, the regulation now justifies the significant restriction of information on repair, which conflicts directly with circular economy principles.

By the final version of the Ecodesign Directive, campaigners succeeded in pushing back the framing to one in which flows of materials in the future Circular Economy were not understood solely in terms of 'recovery and recycling', but it was a partial victory. Repair campaigners won concessions with producers having to provide access to key spare parts for professional repairers for up to 10 years after selling the last unit of a model, and a 'design for disassembly'. This created a major precedent, with the repairability of products legally built into legal design standards.

Table 3.1 From EEB (2018: n.p.)

Early draft of regulation (August 2018)	*Latest draft of regulation (October 2018)*
Requirements for disassembly for the purpose of repair and for material recovery and recycling while avoiding pollution	**Requirements for dismantling for material recovery and recycling while avoiding pollution**
Household washing machines and household washer-dryers shall be designed so that the access to and the removal of the following components (when present) is possible without the use of any tool which is not readily available for purchase: [...]	Manufacturers shall ensure that household washing machines and household washer-dryers are designed in such a way that the materials and components referred to in Annex VII to Directive 2012/19/EU can be removed without the use of any tool which is not readily available for purchase
Manufacturers shall document the sequence of dismantling operations needed to access the components listed above, including for each of these operations, the type and the number of fastening techniques(s) to be unlocked, and tool(s) required. This information should be accessible under the same conditions as the repair and maintenance information under (3)	Manufacturers shall provide information free of charge about preparation for reuse and treatment of household washing machines and household washer-dryers to preparation for reuse facilities and to treatment and recycling facilities, as provided in Point 1 or Article 15 of Directive 2012/19/EU

However, a major loss to campaigners was the restricting of access of spare parts and repair information to professional repairers licensed by producing corporations, excluding non-licensed and amateur repairers.

Recent developments suggest, however that the Right to Repair movement's vision for the Circular Economy is gaining traction in EU policymaking, with the publication in December 2019 of a European Commission 'Green Deal' document, which looks forward to the updated 2020 Circular Economy Action Plan. If implemented in the proposed form, Repair.eu notes reducing and reusing materials will be prioritized before recycling them and:

> The [2020] Circular Economy Action Plan will include measures to encourage businesses to offer, and to allow consumers to choose, reusable, durable and repairable products. It will analyse the need for a 'right to repair', and curb the built-in obsolescence of devices, in particular for electronics. (Repair.eu, 2019: 8)

Conclusion

The longue durée takes us from the medieval guild restriction on the sale of second-hand clothing to our contemporary intellectual property regime where American farmers are banned from repairing their own tractors, and in the EU only professional repairers accredited by manufacturers have the right to access product spare parts and repair manuals. The circularities of material flows in economies are thus always embedded in institutional contexts. They are always also conditioned by contentious social actors mobilising their own cultural repertoires. And critical to those repertoires are norms and values around consumption, whether the valorisation of the medieval wife's prudent household management or distaste at 'the throwaway society', and cultural understandings of the future, whether William Morris's utopian socialism or the Right to Repair movement's vision of a Circular Economy of empowered citizen-consumers.

Funding Information

Daniel Welch's contribution to this chapter has been supported by funding from the UK Economic and Social Research Council grant ES/R007942/1 "Imagined Futures of Consumption".

References

Adam, B., & Groves, C. (2007). *Future matters: Action, knowledge, ethics*. Leiden and Boston, MA: Brill.

Alsford, S. (Ed.). (2019). *A perspective on English towns in the fifteenth century*. http://users.trytel.com/~tristan/towns/florilegium/introduction/intro03.html. Accessed 24 January 2020.

Anon. (1810–1828). *Statutes of the realm*. London: George Eyre and Andrew Strahan.

BBC Breakfast. (2018, November 5). *BBC One*.

Beckert, J. (2016). *Imagined futures: Fictional expectations and capitalist dynamics*. Cambridge, MA: Harvard University Press.

Birch, K. (2016). Emergent imaginaries and fragmented policy frameworks in the Canadian bio-economy. *Sustainability, 8*, 1007. https://doi.org/10.3390/su8101007.

Boons, F. (2009). *Creating ecological value: An evolutionary approach to business strategies and the natural environment*. Cheltenham: Edward Elgar.

Borup, M., Brown, N., Konrad, K., & Van Lente, H. (2006). The sociology of expectations in science and technology. *Technology Analysis & Strategic Management, 18*(3–4), 285–298.

Braungart, M., & McDonough, W. (2002). *Cradle to cradle: Remaking the way we make things*. London: Vintage Books.

Brown, N., Rappert, B., & Webster, A. (2000). Introducing contested futures: From looking into the future to looking at the future. In N. Brown, B. Rappert, & A. Webster (Eds.), *Contested futures: As sociology of prospective techno-science*. Aldershot: Ashgate.

Casson, C. (2020). Guilds. In T. da Silva Lopes, C. Lubinski & H. J. S. Tworek (Eds.), *The Routledge companion to the makers of global business* (pp. 159–170). Abingdon: Routledge.

Davis, J. (2010). Marketing secondhand goods in late medieval England. *Journal of Historical Research in Marketing, 2*, 270–286.

European Commission (EC). (2015). *Closing the loop—An EU action plan for the circular economy*. European Commission (COM614). http://ec.europa.eu/environment/circular-economy/index_en.htm. Accessed 27 August 2020.

The Economist. (2018, October 20). Repair is as important as innovation.

European Environment Bureau (EEB). (2018). *Briefing on resource efficiency provisions in Ecodesign 2018*. https://eeb.org/eu-to-deny-citizens-longer-lasting-and-repairable-popular-consumer-products-media-brief/. Accessed 20 January 2020.

Ehgartner, U., & Hirth, S. (2019). *The right to repair and endangered practices*. Discover Society Issue 75. https://discoversociety.org/2019/12/04/the-right-to-repair-and-endangered-practices/.

EMF (Ellen MacArthur Foundation). (n.d.). *What is the circular economy?* www.ellenmacarthurfoundation.org/circular-economy/what-is-the-circular-economy.

Fountaine, L. (Ed.). (2008). *Alternative exchanges: Secondhand circulations from the sixteenth century to the present*. New York and Oxford: Berghahn Books.

Greco, G. L., & Rose, C. M. (Trans. & Ed.). (2009). *The good wife's guide (Le Ménagier de Paris): A medieval household book*. Ithaca and London: Cornell University Press.

Gregson, N., Crang, M., Fuller, S., & Holmes, H. (2015). Interrogating the circular economy: The moral economy of resource recovery in the EU. *Economy and Society, 44*(2), 218–243.

Harvey, C., & Press, J. (1991). *William Morris: Design and enterprise in Victorian Britain*. Manchester and New York: Manchester University Press.

Hawken, P., Lovins, A., & Lovins, H. (1999). *Natural capitalism: Creating the next industrial revolution*. New York: Little, Brown.

Jasanoff, S. (2015). Future imperfect: Science, technology and the imaginations of modernity. In S. Jasanoff & S. H. Kim (Eds.), *Dreamscapes of modernity: Sociotechnical imaginaries and the fabrication of power*. Chicago: Chicago University Press.

Jasanoff, S., & Kim, S. H. (2009). Containing the atom: Sociotechnical imaginaries and nuclear power in the United States and South-Korea. *Minerva, 47,* 119–146.

Jasanoff, S., & Kim, S.-H. (2015). *Dreamscapes of modernity: Sociotechnical imaginaries and the fabrication of power*. Chicago and London: The University of Chicago Press.

Lee, J. S. (2018). *The Medieval Clothier*. Woodbridge: The Boydell Press.

Merry, M. L. (2000). *The construction and representation of urban identities: Public and private lives in late medieval Bury St Edmunds* (PhD Dissertation). University of Kent.

Mische, A. (2009). Projects and possibilities: Researching futures in action. *Sociological Forum, 24*(3), 694–704.

Mitchell, T. (2008). Rethinking economy. *Geoforum, 39,* 1116–1121.

Mylan, J., Holmes, H., & Paddock, J. (2016). Re-introducing consumption to the 'Circular Economy': A sociotechnical analysis of domestic food provisioning. *Sustainability, 8,* 794.

O'Connor, K. (2011). *Lycra: How a fiber shaped America*. New York and London: Routledge.

Repair.eu. (2019). *European Green Deal's implications for right to repair*. https://repair.eu/news/european-green-deal-promises-reusable-durable-and-repairable-products/. Accessed 20 January 2019.

Restart Project. (2017). *Restarted future: A tour of our new poster*. https://therestartproject.org/news/restarted-future-poster/. Accessed 20 January 2019.

Rosen, C. M. (2007). The role of pollution regulation and litigation in the development of the U.S. meatpacking industry, 1865–1880. *Enterprise & Society, 8*(2), 297–347.

Schot, J. (2016). Confronting the second deep transition through the historical imagination. *Technology and Culture, 57*(2), 445–456.

Stobart, J., Hann, A., & Morgan, V. (2007). *Spaces of consumption leisure and shopping in the English town, c. 1680–1830*. London: Routledge.

Stobart, J., & Van Damme, I. (2010). Introduction. In J. Stobart & I. Van Damme (Eds.), *Modernity and the second-hand trade: European consumption cultures and practices, 1700–1900* (pp. 1–15). Basingstoke: Palgrave Macmillian.

Summers, J. (2015). *Fashion on the ration: Style in the second world war*. London: Profile Books.

Thorsheim, P. (2015). *Waste into weapons: Recycling in Britain during the second world war*. Cambridge: Cambridge University Press.

Urry, J. (2016). *What is the future?* Chichester: Wiley.
Welch, D., Keller, M., & Mandich, G. (2016). Imagined futures of the circular economy. In N. Spurling & L. Kuijer (Eds.), *Everyday futures*. Lancaster: Institute for Social Futures. http://wp.lancs.ac.uk/everydayfutures/essay-collection/.
Welch, D., & Ehgartner, U. (2019). Imagined futures of consumption: Lay expectations and speculations. *Discover Society, 73*. https://discoversociety.org/2019/10/02/imagined-futures-of-consumption-lay-expectations-and-speculations/. Accessed 2 October 2019.
Welch, D., & Southerton, D. (2019). After Paris: Transitions for sustainable consumption. *Sustainability: Science, Practice and Policy, 15*(1), 31–44.

CHAPTER 4

Critical Approaches to Circular Economy Research: Time, Space and Evolution

Helen Holmes, Harald Wieser, and Julia Kasmire

Introduction

Traditional approaches to circular economy (CE) focus on large-scale manufacturing and industrial processes, and their adoption of closed loop, cradle-to-cradle processes for maximum resource efficiency. In brief, closed loop processes capture excess energy and waste resources which are then reused within the manufacturing loop. Such systems are positioned in opposition to take-make-dispose models of production which follow a linear trajectory from resource extraction to production processes to

H. Holmes (✉) · H. Wieser · J. Kasmire
Circular Economy Group, Sustainable Consumption Institute, University of Manchester, Manchester, UK
e-mail: Helen.Holmes@manchester.ac.uk

H. Wieser
e-mail: Harald.wieser@manchester.ac.uk

J. Kasmire
e-mail: Julia.kasmire@manchester.ac.uk

R. Bali Swain and S. Sweet (eds.), *Sustainable Consumption and Production, Volume II*,
https://doi.org/10.1007/978-3-030-55285-5_4

disposal. The latter system is deemed to have both a negative environmental and economic impact through the loss of valuable resources and energy, whilst the former is seen to conserve resources and have less of an environmental footprint.

In recent years, the concept of CE has become a global hallmark of sustainable production and consumption. Propelled by political interest, the scope of CE as a model for sustainable resource use has expanded dramatically from its industrial roots into best practice approaches for all types and scales of businesses, and even consumer activities. The Ellen MacArthur Foundation is now solely focused on promoting circularity, 'designing out waste and pollution, keeping products and materials in use, and regenerating natural systems' (Ellen MacArthur Foundation, 2019). The European Commission has spent three years implementing its Circular Economy Action Plan (European Commission, 2019), which includes common EU targets for waste reduction, the development of a Circular Plastics Alliance to tackle the growing plastics challenge and a focus on engaging consumers in circular practices. In the UK, the main waste management government advisory and not-for-profit organisation, WRAP (Waste and Resources Action Programme) has similarly adopted CE as their overarching objective moving forward. Each of its action plans, consumer campaigns and voluntary agreements with business have CE principles at their core (WRAP, 2019).

Whilst the CE does not represent a comprehensive model of sustainable development, addressing only a sub-set of Sustainable Development Goals (Schröder, Anggraeni, & Weber, 2018), a transition to CE practices would potentially have far-reaching implications and produce both environmental and societal benefits. In particular, the CE touches upon important issues that receive little attention in alternative models of sustainable consumption and production. Whereas most sustainability transition research concerns the *directionality* of change (Köhler et al., 2019; Røpke, 2012) relating to shifts in the provision of societal needs such as energy, mobility and food among others, the CE is fundamentally an intervention that calls for a reconfiguration of the *temporalities* of material flows. Furthermore, CE affords us the opportunity to think beyond conventional boundaries of closed loop systems to consider other spaces and scales in which circular practices occur.

In research and beyond, the CE discourse has revitalised long-standing debates concerning temporalities, from the longevity of products, repair, reuse to servitisation (Cooper, 2010; Crocker & Chiveralls, 2018). Yet, remarkably little explicit attention is devoted to the temporalities or spatialities inscribed in such strategies, how they interrelate and what they imply for the organisation and management of individual household practices of everyday life in the social metabolism of society at large. In this chapter, we open up the CE concept to examine the relations among different CE strategies and how these are in turn linked to practices and material flows beyond what is generally regarded as the scope of CE interventions. In so doing, we want to direct attention to the challenges of examining CE through the lens of both temporality and spatiality, and to the problems of anticipating adaptive change within CE over multiple time-scales and spatial frames.

The chapter begins with the varying roles of products in the CE and examines divergent claims in the CE discourse relating to the temporal reconfiguration of material flows. The discussion of alternative CE strategies reveals a fundamental tension that sets strict limits on their mobilisation as complementary solutions to environmental pressures. Following this, we continue our focus on material flows to question the spaces and scales in which CE traditionally occurs, considering the everyday embeddedness of CE and practices of circularity which are often hidden or invisible. The final section turns attention to how material flows drive change within complex adaptive systems, specifically focusing on how such systems can respond to changes in material flow in unexpected and undermining ways over different temporal or spatial scales.

The Temporalities of Material Flows: The Environmental Rationales for a CE

Put forward as an alternative to the linear economy in which material flows go through a predetermined temporal sequence of resource extraction, manufacturing, distribution, consumption and waste, the CE is an inherently temporal concept. Yet, aside from broad commitments to circularity and slower flows, the CE discourse is conspicuously silent on how the temporalities of material flows are to be reconfigured in practice. Adopting a 'temporal gaze' (Adam, 2000) on the CE, our first point is to direct attention to the struggles and complexities involved in shifting the temporalities of material flows. At the most fundamental level, a focus on time reveals that the CE does not so much represent an overarching temporal order as a collection of configurations with partly mutually incompatible temporalities.

The multiplicity of CE configurations that can be found in practice runs counter to recent efforts at establishing a common definition (Kirchherr, Reike, & Hekkert, 2017) and quantitative indicators for measuring progress towards a CE (Moraga et al., 2019). Arguably a key affordance of the CE is that it operates as an 'umbrella concept', creating a discursive space within which previously disparate approaches to the management of material resources can be discussed (Blomsma & Brennan, 2017). Reviews of the concept trace its origins in a wide range of such approaches, including biomimicry, cradle-to-cradle, industrial ecology, the blue economy and the performance economy, many of which continue to inform thinking on CE practices (Blomsma & Brennan, 2017; Ghisellini, Cialani, & Ulgiati, 2016; Reike, Vermeulen, & Witjes, 2018).

The central instrument through which the different ideas from these approaches are brought together are the various 'R frameworks' that underpin many definitions of the CE (Kirchherr et al., 2017; Reike et al., 2018). In their most basic form, they consist of three R's—Reduce, Reuse, Recycle, which represent the key principles according to which material flows should be organised. More significant than the number of principles and the shared first letter, however, is that R principles are typically hierarchically ordered, with recycling or recovery being positioned as the least preferable from an environmental point of view. What is notable about this step of hierarchisation, which itself can be traced back to 'Lansink's Ladder' and the concept of the 'waste hierarchy' (Kemp & van Lente, 2011), is that it establishes equivalency among a series of waste management strategies that allows them to be ranked on a single scale. From a temporal perspective, however, there are significant incompatibilities between CE strategies that resist any straightforward rankings on a one-dimensional scale. This is to say that it is insufficient to discuss interventions merely in terms of their radicalness—from a recycling-centred economy to a more fully circular economy that integrates also strategies higher up on the waste hierarchy (Allwood, 2014; Reike et al., 2018; Stahel, 2010; van Buren, Demmers, van der Heijden, & Witlox, 2016). Rather than a clear priority list, there are inherent tensions between strategies.

A tension that has permeated the CE discourse since its early days, exists between strategies focused on the *tempo* versus those prioritising the *duration* of material flows. The basic difference between these two types of strategies has been discussed in the literature in terms of *closing* and *slowing* loops (Bakker, Balkenende, & Poppelaars, 2019; Bocken, de Pauw, Bakker, & van der Grinten, 2016; Stahel, 2010), a terminology that we take up here. But rather than positioning them as complementary strategies, as has become the norm in today's CE discourse, attention to their temporal implications reveals that the closing and slowing of loops are partly contradictory aims. They originate in different concerns relating to 'clashes of temporalities' (Bensaude-Vincent, 2018).

The concern relating to the tempo or speed at which materials flow through the economy can be rooted in debates over the acceleration of technological change and the recognition of a clash of temporalities between technological innovation and biological cycles. Following this argument, technological change has outpaced nature's capacity for regeneration:

> contemporary society uses up natural resources like gas and oil at rates much higher than necessary for their reproduction, and produces and dumps large amounts of toxic waste at faster speeds than the ecosystem is able to dispose of them. (Rosa, 2009: 12)

Similar concerns had already been articulated by Boulding (1966), for whom a growing 'cowboy economy' was untenable on a planet with finite resources. He suggested that under such conditions the material throughput needed to be minimised, with priority being given to the maintenance of existing stocks through more long-lasting products. More recently and in the narrower discourse surrounding the CE, the centrality of speed has been most forcefully put forward by Walter Stahel. To Stahel (2010), a central guideline is the 'inertia principle', which foregrounds the importance of retaining the integrity of products. By preserving the state of a high-value product for as long as possible, less energy needs to be invested than if the product had to be disassembled and transformed into a new one.

The focus on the slowing down of material flows does not always constitute an optimal solution, however—it can potentially produce even adverse environmental effects. To critics such as Michael Braungart, co-founder of the cradle-to-cradle approach, '[product] longevity is a catastrophe for the environment and innovation'.[1] The cradle-to-cradle

[1] http://www.klimaretter.info/forschung/hintergrund/20693-kritiker-murks-studie-ist-selber-murks (retrieved on 12 December 2019).

approach strongly challenges the attention paid to speed, suggesting that a CE model predicated on slower flows fails to overcome the take-make-dispose sequence characteristic of the linear economy, instead postponing the production of waste only (Braungart, McDonough, & Bollinger, 2007). Besides taking issue with the continued production of waste, the cradle-to-cradle approach further insists that the pursuit of longevity itself can produce detrimental outcomes for the environment. A case in point is the use of non-biodegradable materials such as plastics, which can prolong the life of products, but ultimately resist a re-entry into biological cycles. Similarly, the use of potentially more durable, heavy metals and complicated designs may increase the energy and resource intensiveness in production and recycling processes (Murray, Skene, & Haynes, 2017). Furthermore, the strategy based on product longevity involves inevitable risks in so far as the potential environmental hazards and toxicity of materials may be unknown at the time of production (Korhonen, Honkasalo, & Seppälä, 2018). This includes potential gains in efficiency, which may reduce environmental damage resulting from a product's use and justify earlier replacements (van Nes & Cramer, 2006). Such issues arise when the longevity of products is not synchronised with the pace of change in science and technology.

In contrast to the emphasis on speed, the cradle-to-cradle approach derives from concerns relating to the duration of material flows. Here, the linear economy is rejected for accepting that resources turn into waste, and its strict separation of biological and technical cycles that makes it difficult for used materials to re-enter biological cycles. Instead of releasing nutrients or food for successive processes of valorisation, it is argued that the linear economy gradually 'downcycles'—reduces the quality of—materials (Braungart et al., 2007). This second 'clash of temporalities' thus concerns the limited duration of technical flows compared to the infinite flows in nature (Bensaude-Vincent, 2018). Crucially, cradle-to-cradle does not imply a mere reliance on recycling. The key is to design products so as to avoid toxic materials and ensure that their components can be disassembled. However, rather than constituting a complementary strategy to product longevity, this approach is in many ways antithetical to the idea of creating an integrated and 'inert' product. Approaching design from a particle rather than a product perspective (Blomsma, 2016), the ideal product is modular, flexible, biodegradable and easy to disassemble.

In light of this, it is not surprising that this approach centred on the duration of material flows has received considerable criticism, too. In environmental terms, the main problems relate to its relative neglect of the energy input required to allow materials to circulate, and how the law of entropy creates biophysical limitations to the speeding up of such flows (Allwood, 2014). Frequent dis- and re-assembly of the same product tends to be relatively inefficient and comes at a high energy cost due to the lack of economies of scale. Moreover, it has been argued that recycling and reuse tend to legitimise more frequent acquisitions of new products (Gregson, Crang, Laws, Fleetwood, & Holmes, 2013; Valenzuela & Böhm, 2017; Wieser, 2016). The idea of 'decoupling' resource use from economic growth may thus face comparable structural problems as it did previously in other domains (Korhonen et al., 2018).

Table 4.1 summarises the tension in temporalities discussed so far by setting the strategies of closing and slowing loops in relation to one another. The arrow indicates that the two strategies work in opposing directions, but cannot be strictly separated in practice. As Blomsma (2016) suggests, the two are partly mediated by approaches to modular designs. Even intermediate solutions, however, cannot overcome what are fundamentally different approaches to the temporalities of material flows. One such intermediate solution is repair. In contrast to the general positioning of repair as a practice that complements other practices for product longevity, a temporal lens directs attention to important tensions between the two. The Fairphone, for example, is based on a modular design that makes it possible for owners to replace single components. In the context of expectations of ever thinner phones and the preference for 'premium' materials like metal and glass, however, the bulky and plasticky feel of the Fairphone that allows for its modularity in the first place, may render it more quickly obsolete than intended by the manufacturer. Moreover, modular designs carry the risk of consumers using this to customise mobile phones and replace their components at a more frequent rate than an integrated design would have allowed (see Proske & Jaeger-Erben, 2019).

As this example further indicates, any solution will need to be coordinated across social agents if the temporalities of material flows are to be changed in a sustainable manner. A perspective on the temporal dynamics of material flows highlights the need to design CE configurations that spread across production, distribution and consumption: without such an integration, the continuity of flows cannot be secured. Equally, a high

Table 4.1 The continuum between closing and slowing loops strategies

	Closing loops ←——→	*Slowing loops*
Temporal dimension	Duration	Tempo
Material perspective	Particles/molecules	Products
Matters of environmental concern	Scarcity of material resources; toxic materials	Energy use; greenhouse gas emissions in production
CE strategies	Biodegradable, modular products	Long-lasting products
CE approaches	Cradle-to-cradle, biomimicry	Performance economy, material efficiency
Relation between technical and biological cycles	Dissolved	Synchronised

Source Author's creation

degree of synchronisation is necessary to ensure that the existing stock is used at its highest capacity and additional extractions of resources can be avoided. A precondition for this is to consider the varying spaces and scales at which materials circulate.

The Spatiality of Material Flows: Revealing the Hidden Places of CE

In keeping with the above questioning of divergent claims within the CE discourse, in what follows we add a further layer to the temporal lens to explore the spatiality of CE. Continuing the focus on material flows, we consider the multiple and often invisible spaces of CE and circular practices. As noted, whilst traditionally the realm of manufacturing and industry, in recent years a push towards CE and circularity in other spheres and sectors has become part of the political rhetoric of CE policy. The Ellen MacArthur Foundation (2019) for example, discusses the need for circular practices within urban planning and farming, whilst the EU Commission has conducted a study into how to engage consumers in CE practices (2018). Thus, there is a sea change occurring in CE discourse away from traditional notions of manufacturing and heavy industry into the previously unchartered territory of consumers, households, third sector and government departments.

Two elements mark this shift most starkly and form the basis for the following discussion. First, is a clear signalling of a move away from production into the realms of consumption and consumer practice (yet, as we discuss, this dichotomy must also be challenged). Second, is a significant shift in scale from the macro power houses of manufacturing and industry to the meso-level activities of SMEs, and micro-scale activities of the consumer and household. Yet, whilst encouraging circular activities across a spectrum of production and consumption activities, and also across multiple spaces and scales seems like an excellent idea for ensuring future sustainable global resource use, little instruction is given in CE discourse as to how this should occur. Whilst the actors, scales and sometimes sectors are identified, the practicalities and potential circular activities are not. In our work, we seek to answer some of these questions, using in depth qualitative and empirical research to explore the micro practices of circularity and experiences of circular behaviour within a range of spaces. Such research is time consuming and labour intensive, yet it yields an alternative version of CE; one that encompasses the novel CE spaces of consumers, households and third sector organisations, but which also recognises that many circular activities are not essentially new or original. Indeed, as we have argued elsewhere (Holmes, 2018), circular practices of reciprocity, sharing and communal resource networks have been a feature of neighbourhoods, communities and societies for centuries (Pahl, 1984).

The household is a case in point. In other work developed by our research institute (Mylan, Holmes, & Paddock, 2016) we have illustrated how the domestic is a crucial site of circular activities. Focusing on material flows of food in and out of the home, our research illustrates how often mundane and invisible acts such as shopping, cooking and eating involve circular practices. From reusing leftover food, such as making a new meal from the previous night's dinner, to various 'ridding' strategies such as giving surplus food to a neighbour or putting it outside for wildlife, small acts of circularity and careful use of resources are everyday occurrences within households. Such activities are not remarkable, nor are they necessarily anything new, but they flag how circular practices do occur in the domestic and consumer sphere and, importantly, at the micro scale. Identifying such practices provides the much-needed evidence to support grand political narratives that consumers should be adopting circular approaches.

Third sector organisations offer another ideal example of how circularity at the micro scale is put into practice. Our work has focused on a spectrum of communal and grassroots enterprises to illuminate the circular activities and experiences embedded within them (Holmes, 2018, 2019; Pesch, Spekkink, & Quist, 2019). From repair cafes to clothes swaps to communal food groups, we have identified circular material flows in a wide range of third sector activities. Linking to the above discussion on temporality, repair initiatives are of particular interest. The Repair Café network now spans the globe with over 1500 cafés established. People can take in their broken items, primarily electrical appliances, and learn the skills to mend them from expert volunteers. It is estimated that repair cafés worldwide prevented 350,000 kilos of waste in 2018 (Repair Café Network, 2019). Given the growing issue of electrical waste, currently estimated at 500 million metric tonnes (UN University, 2019), repair cafés offer an important and vital space for diverting electronic waste from landfills. They also highlight that models of repair are crucial to circular systems; of course, repair only really slows down the loop, rather than closing it.

Clothes swaps offer another micro model of circularity through consumption practices. Whilst no formal or global clothes swap model has been established, they are becoming a regular feature of urban space. In Manchester, UK where our institute is based, there are several clothes swapping events advertised on social media every month. As our research has illustrated (Holmes, 2018), clothes swaps offer consumers the chance to access items of clothing which are 'new' to them, fulfilling desires perpetuated by the fashion industry around having 'a new look', whilst offering a trusted space to dispose of their unwanted items to what they deem as good homes where their items will be looked after (see also Henninger, Burklin, & Niinamaki, 2019). Like repair cafés, clothes swaps are perceived to slow down the loops of consumption and production.

Thus, our work offers practical evidence that CE policy needs to encourage and implement circular strategies at the micro level, but it also raises a number of important questions. As we have discussed, are micro practices of circulation really anything new? Are the clothes swaps of the contemporary era simply a more organised, digitally mediated version of jumble sales (McRobbie, 1989) or reciprocal circulations of baby clothes (Clarke, 2001)? Are repair cafés a more concentrated version of asking a knowledgeable neighbour or relative to fix a broken item? Societies have always had some mechanisms of trying to conserve resources and retain the value in materials. The current culture of disposal in the Global North has changed this, but as our research shows, these activities still exist. Moreover, they exist for many reasons other than simply preventing waste. They are a crucial part of the fabric of a functioning society, enabling the maintenance and development of social relationships, caring for those around us, overcoming social inequalities, displaying moral standing and so forth (Holmes, 2019; Mock et al., 2019). These components of micro circular practices are just as vital as the (temporary) diversion of waste from landfills.

Similarly, our work is important because of its focus on what is primarily determined as the sphere of consumption. As discussed, a key feature of the contemporary CE discourse is this shift from the realm of production to consumption. Yet whilst our research focuses on consumer activities, we would argue that such practices do not easily fall into the category of consumption. Indeed, as we have argued through our work on domestic circular practices (Mylan et al., 2016: 794), rather than recognising consumers as 'users' of materials and products, we understand them as 'doers' of activities. Thus, in keeping with the ethos of circularity and the previous focus on temporality, neither materials nor those they come into contact with, are static. Rather, what we identify is the labour and work which goes into these circular activities; labour which at times is both consumptive and productive. Take for example the repair café—our broken electrical appliance requires our labour to be fixed. Our reusing of leftover food at home to make another meal demands our skills and time to produce something new. These 'prosumption' activities, as Ritzer (2014) terms it, blend the dichotomous spheres of production and consumption in ways that CE discourse so far overlooks. Hence, a further and developing area of our research is focused on how the CE is enacted through practices of 'consumption work' (Welch, Hobson, Holmes, Wheeler, & Wieser, 2019; Wheeler & Glucksmann, 2015), that is, the work and labour the consumer undertakes to consume. So, activities such as repairing broken items or upcycling our favourite item of clothing are forms of 'consumption work' which are configured by circular practices.

Therefore, CE discourse needs to recognise not only how material flows script the temporality of their consumption, but also how they are embedded within particular spatial, social and relational contexts. Many micro scale circular practices are not necessarily new; they are often established means of 'getting by', organised in new and novel forms (Holmes, 2018). Yet, a focus on the micro scale of CE activities opens up CE narratives to different spheres of opportunity (Schroder, Anantharaman, Anggraeni, & Foxon, 2019 on CE in the Global South); spheres which recognise and challenge the dichotomous nature of 'consumption' versus 'production' and provide potential blueprints for CE good practice models. Nonetheless, perhaps the contemporary global emphasis on CE is not required at all, due to the circuitous nature of ecosystems and economies, as our final section on how an evolutionary perspective also opens up CE debates.

Material Flows Drive Evolutionary Adaptation

It is important to note that all economies (regardless of their circularity) are complex systems because they have component parts that interact in non-trivial ways by exchanging matter, energy and information. Natural ecosystems, economies and other complex systems with living components evolve when matter, energy or information flows change, with each evolutionary adaptation triggering further changes (van Dam,

Nikolic, & Lukszo, 2012). Adaptations ripple back and forth, as opportunities and competitive advantage are seized or undermined, creating new opportunities in the process. Despite the ubiquity of evolutionary change, traditional economic theories have assumed equilibrium to be an economy's natural, general or default state (Arthur, 2013), although the possibility of non-equilibrium economic states has begun to be explored more recently. Circular economies then, would have a circular equilibrium.

Evolution is voracious; eventually something will adapt to use every resource. Thus, both ecosystems and economies can be understood as constantly striving towards circularity. For example, early life was nearly eliminated by a catastrophic build-up of the toxic waste product, oxygen (O_2), but O_2-breathers evolved and created a complete O_2–CO_2 cycle (Lane, 2003). Evolution is also irreversible; no adaptive change can ever be undone. Removing O2-breathers would not return the earth to its early state, but disrupting the O_2–CO_2 cycle would cause new problems. The voracity and irreversibility of evolution apply to all temporal and spatial scales. If this means that economies will, if left alone, evolve towards circularity, then what is the role for CE studies or management? Three key features of that role are explored with an illustrative example: plastic.

First, plastic-eaters will evolve, for good or ill. Evolution seeks complete cycles (e.g. water, O_2–CO_2, food chains, etc.) by driving adaptions to occupy or consume every resource. Indeed, preventing materials, energy or information from moving through a cycle is difficult and has motivated considerable effort to, for example, protect jumpers from moths, preserve food or keep wasps out of attics. Eventually, something will evolve to consume plastic because it contains potentially valuable energy and chemical content. Plastic-eating bacteria may already exist as research shows the existence of some plastic-dissolving enzymes (Yang, Yang, Wu, Zhao, & Jiang, 2014), although plastic-eaters may evolve from fungi, plants, invertebrates or anything else. Such a development may seem very positive as, being non-biodegradable, (micro-)plastic waste accumulates at problematic rates. However, in the absence of plastic-eaters, the non-biodegrability of plastic is actually a valuable property. The biological inertness of plastic makes it uniquely useful for maintaining sterile tools and surfaces in clinical settings (Hammon et al., 2014), for effective food packaging (Marsh & Bugusu, 2007), and for creating safely sealed health and beauty products (Johnston, 2003). The development of a plastic-eater would trigger adaptive changes in these areas as well as many more on which economies have come to depend. This may be seen as comparable to the growing problems of antibiotic resistance; an extremely useful innovation is undermined by inappropriate or excessive use that drives evolutionary adaptation.

Second, evolution is always co-evolution. Modern economies entail unprecedented changes in material flows, including both resource use and waste creation, that prompt adaptive changes throughout complex evolutionary webs. Plastic, for instance, has been found in deep oceans (Woodall et al., 2014), inside animals, and even in bottled water. The prevalence of plastic pollution reveals a strange dichotomy in human attitudes. Plastic is valued because it is (currently) non-biodegradable but is also discarded into the environment or otherwise poorly managed as if it were biodegradable. This creates some fairly obvious problems of plastic waste accumulation as long as it remains non-biodegradable. At the same time, (micro-)plastics are creating new problems as they are increasingly ingested. Just because a material resource can be eaten does not mean it should be eaten, as is clear from the dubious feeding practices blamed for mad cow disease.

Third, plastic is neither the first nor last circularity challenge. Turning limited petrochemicals into plastics with no plan for their circularity is a current problem, but evolutionary pressure has driven materials, resources or processes to be abandoned or adapted before. For example, new fuels were found when old ones became scarce or were not sufficient for the demands of new industries and technologies, with knock-on effects on health, landscapes and more. Similarly, agricultural development makes some species numerous and others (near) extinct, also with consequences for health, society, international trade and much more. The future will surely have its own problems in relation to nanomaterials, rare earth metals or biotechnology.

Together, these three points suggest that any complex adaptive system with humans will benefit from the study and management of material, energy and information flows. As a complex adaptive system, evolutionary pressures will drive innovations, which will trigger inevitable and irreversible changes in the economy. Many of those changes can be understood as moves towards circularity at multiple, overlapping and potentially conflicting time-frames and spatial scales, but those changes will not all be positive for the people within the economy. Some changes may undermine the value of previous changes, provoke scarcity, generate waste problems or produce other unexpected consequences. Thus, human attention and effort is needed to ensure that any negative outcomes of the inevitable and irreversible evolutionary path can be ameliorated through careful consideration, critical reflection, thoughtful study and dedicated management. For example, innovations seeking a patent could be required to provide impact plans that demonstrate consideration for how innovations might be (mis-)used, how evolution towards circularity might interact with that (mis-)use and how identified problems could be addressed. Similarly, those who produce, distribute or use material flows could take responsibility for its further flow throughout the economy, perhaps by agreeing to appropriate use or end-of-use disposal plans, or by paying into a fund that manages economic circularity.

Conclusion

As this chapter has illustrated, taking a critical approach to contemporary CE discourse illuminates practices and material flows beyond the scope of what is generally regarded as CE interventions. Through a focus on temporality and space, we have questioned current claims about CE and offered different research framings and possibilities. Approaching the CE from a temporal perspective, we have addressed inherent tensions between different CE strategies and pointed to the necessity of coordinating activities across production, distribution and consumption. Instead of positioning the CE as a coherent and uniform solution to the elimination of waste, we suggest that it is more fruitful to embrace it as an umbrella concept for articulating specific CE configurations that work best in a given situation: configurations that create synergies between different strategies and are adapted to the temporalities of everyday life and nature. Thinking about the multiple spaces and scales of CE similarly opens up CE to new areas of research. As we have illustrated, CE practices can be identified in a range of spaces and scales and involving activities which are traditionally identified as consumption. In particular, our work has illuminated the importance of micro activities of circularity, and the need to recognise everyday embedded household, domestic and communal activities if CE rhetoric around consumer engagement is to be successful. Similarly, we have critiqued the shift in CE discourse from the sphere of production to consumption, arguing for a deeper understanding of the 'doing' of circularity and recognition of the labour and skills involved—labour which often blurs the boundaries of production and consumption. Finally, through a focus on adaptive change, we have shown that no matter how circular it is, the material, energy and information flowing through an economy triggers inevitable and irreversible evolutionary responses. A careful study of the temporal and spatial scales of these changes and an increased understanding of the conflicting pressures of co-evolution is necessary to ensure that in the entire system changes are as sustainable, equitable and just as possible.

References

Adam, B. (2000). The temporal gaze: The challenge for social theory in the context of GM food. *British Journal of Sociology, 51*(1), 125–142.

Allwood, J. M. (2014). Squaring the circular economy: The role of recycling within a hierarchy of material management strategies. In E. Worrell & M. A. Reuter (Eds.), *Handbook of recycling: State-of-the-art for practitioners, analysts, and scientists* (pp. 445–477). Waltham, MA: Elsevier.

Arthur, W. B. (2013). *Complexity and the economy*. Oxford: Oxford University Press.

Bakker, C., Balkenende, R., & Poppelaars, F. (2019). Design for product integrity in a circular economy. In M. Charter (Ed.), *Designing for the circular economy*. Abingdon and New York: Routledge.

Bensaude-Vincent, B. (2018). Of times and things: Technology and durability. In S. Loeve, X. Guchet, & B. Bensaude-Vincent (Eds.), *French philosophy of technology: Classical readings and contemporary approaches* (pp. 279–298). Cham: Springer International.

Blomsma, F. (2016). *Making sense of circular economy: How practitioners interpret and use the idea of resource life-extension* (PhD Dissertation). Imperial College London.

Blomsma, F., & Brennan, G. (2017). The emergence of circular economy: A new framing around prolonging resource productivity. *Journal of Industrial Ecology, 21*(3), 603–614.

Bocken, N. M. P., de Pauw, I., Bakker, C., & van der Grinten, B. (2016). Product design and business model strategies for a circular economy. *Journal of Industrial and Production Engineering, 33*(5), 308–320.

Boulding, K. E. (1966). The economics of coming spaceship earth. In H. Jarrett (Ed.), *Environmental quality in a growing economy* (pp. 3–14). Baltimore, MD: Resources for the Future/Johns Hopkins University Press.

Braungart, M., McDonough, W., & Bollinger, A. (2007). Crade-to-cradle design: Creating healthy emissions—A strategy for eco-effective product and system design. *Journal of Cleaner Production, 15*(13–14), 1337–1348.

Clarke, A. (2001). *The practice of the normative: The making of mothers, children and homes in north London*. Retrieved from: http://discovery.ucl.ac.uk/1317584/1/252292.pdf. Accessed 26 June 2019.

Cooper, T. (2010). The significance of product longevity. In T. Cooper (Ed.), *Longer lasting products: Alternatives to the throwaway Society* (pp. 3–37). Surrey, UK: Gower Publishing.

Crocker, R., & Chiveralls, K. (Eds.). (2018). *Subverting consumerism: Reuse in an accelerated world*. London and New York: Routledge.

EU Commission. (2018). *Consumers engagement in the circular economy*. Retrieved from: https://ec.europa.eu/info/live-work-travel-eu/consumers/sustainable-consumption_en. Accessed 12 December 2019.

European Commission. (2019). *Circular Economy Action Plan*. Retrieved from: https://ec.europa.eu/environment/circulareconomy/first_circular_economy_action_plan.html. Accessed 10 November 2019.

Ellen MacArthur Foundation. (2019). *The circular economy in detail*. Retrieved from: https://www.ellenmacarthurfoundation.org/explore/the-circular-economy-in-detail. Accessed 12 December 2019.

Ghisellini, P., Cialani, C., & Ulgiati, S. (2016). A review on circular economy: the expected transition to a balanced interplay of environmental and economic systems. *Journal of Cleaner Production, 114*, 11–32.

Gregson, N., Crang, M., Laws, J., Fleetwood, T., & Holmes, H. (2013). Moving up the waste hierarchy: Car boot sales, reuse exchange and the challenges of consumer culture to waste prevention. *Resources, Conservation and Recycling, 77*, 97–107.

Hammon, M., Kunz, B., Dinzl, V., Kammerer, F. J., Schwab, S. A., Bogdan, C., …, Schlechtweg, P. M. (2014). Practicability of hygienic wrapping of touchscreen operated mobile devices in a clinical setting. *PloS One, 9*(9): e106445.

Henninger, C., Burklin, N., & Niinamaki, K. (2019). The clothes swapping phenomenon: When consumers become suppliers. *Journal of Fashion Marketing and Management, 23*(3), 327–344.

Hobson, K., & Lynch, N. (2016). Diversifying and de-growing the circular economy: Radical social transformation in a resource-scarce world. *Futures, 82*, 15–25.

Holmes, H. (2018). New spaces, ordinary practices: Circulating and sharing in diverse economies of provisioning. *Geoforum, 88*, 138–147.

Holmes, H. (2019). Unpicking contemporary thrift: Getting on and getting by in everyday life. *The Sociological Review, 67*(1), 126–142.

Johnston, R. G. (2003). *Tamper-indicating seals: Practices, problems, and standards* (Technical Report). Los Alamos National Laboratory.

Kemp, R., & van Lente, H. (2011). The dual challenge of sustainability transitions. *Environmental Innovations & Societal Transitions, 1*(1), 121–124.

Kirchherr, J., Reike, D., & Hekkert, M. (2017). Conceptualizing the circular economy: An analysis of 114 definitions. *Resources, Conservation and Recycling, 127,* 221–232.

Köhler, J., Geels, F. W., Kern, F., Markard, J., Onsongo, E., Wieczorek, A., …, Wells, P. (2019). An agenda for sustainability transitions research: State of the art and future directions. *Environmental Innovation and Societal Transitions, 31,* 1–32.

Korhonen, J., Honkasalo, A., & Seppälä, J. (2018). Circular economy: The concept and its limitations. *Ecological Economics, 143,* 37–46.

Lane, N. (2003). *Oxygen: The molecule that made the world*. New York: Oxford University Press.

Marsh, K., & Bugusu, B. (2007). Food packaging—Roles, materials, and environmental issues. *Journal of Food Science, 72*(3), R39–R55.

McRobbie, A. (1989). *Zoot suits and second-hand dresses: An anthology of fashion and music*. Boston: HarperCollins.

Mock, M., Omann, I., Polzin, C., Spekkink, W., Schuler, J., Pandur, V., …, Panno, A. (2019). "Something inside me has been set in motion": Exploring the psychological wellbeing of people engaged in sustainability initiatives. *Ecological Economics, 160,* 1–111.

Moraga, G., Huysveld, S., Mathieux, F., Blengini, G. A., Alaerts, L., Van Acker, K., …, Dewulf, J. (2019). Circular economy indicators: What do they measure? *Resources, Conservation & Recycling, 146,* 452–461.

Murray, A., Skene, K., & Haynes, K. (2017). The circular economy: An interdisciplinary exploration of the concept and application in a global context. *Journal of Business Ethics, 140,* 369–380.

Mylan, J., Holmes, H., & Paddock, J. (2016). Re-introducing consumption to the 'circular economy': A sociotechnical analysis of domestic food provisioning [Special issue]. *Sustainability, 8*(8), 794.

Pahl, R. E. E. (1984). *Divisions of labour*. Oxford: Blackwell.

Pesch, U., Spekkink, W., & Quist, J. (2019). Local sustainability initiatives: Innovation and civic engagement in societal experiments. *European Planning Studies, 27*(2), 300–317.

Proske, M., & Jaeger-Erben, M. (2019). Decreasing obsolescence with modular smartphones?—An interdisciplinary perspective on lifecycles. *Journal of Cleaner Production, 223,* 57–66.

Reike, D., Vermeulen, W. J. V., & Witjes, S. (2018). The circular economy: New or Refurbished as CE 3.0?—Exploring controversies in the conceptualization of the circular economy through a focus on history and resource value retention options. *Resources, Conservation and Recycling, 135,* 246–264.

Repair Café Network. (2019). *Repair cafes prevent 350,000 kgs of waste*. Retrieved from: https://repaircafe.org/en/. Accessed 8 December 2019.

Ritzer, G. (2014). Prosumption: Evolution, revolution or eternal return of the same? *Journal of Consumer Culture, 14*(1), 3–24.

Røpke, I. (2012). The unsustainable directionality of innovation—The example of the broadband transition. *Research Policy, 41*, 1631–1642.

Rosa, H. (2009). *Social acceleration: A new theory of modernity*. University Park, PA: Pennsylvania State University Press.

Schröder, P., Anantharaman, M., Anggraeni, K., & Foxon, T. J. (Eds.). (2019). *The circular economy and the Global South: Sustainable lifestyles and green industrial development*. London: Routledge.

Schröder, P., Anggraeni, K., & Weber, U. (2018). The relevance of circular economy practices to the sustainable development goals. *Journal of Industrial Ecology, 23*(1), 77–95.

Stahel, W. R. (2010). *The performance economy* (2nd ed.). Basingstoke, UK and New York: Palgrave Macmillan.

UN University. (2019). *Future E-waste scenarios*. Retrieved from: https://collections.unu.edu/eserv/UNU:7440/FUTURE_EWASTE_SCENARIOS_UNU_190829_low_screen.pdf. Accessed 14 December 2019.

Valenzuela, F., & Böhm, S. (2017). Against wasted politics: A critique of the circular economy. *Ephemera: Theory and Politics in Organization, 17*(1), 23–60.

Van Buren, N., Demmers, M., van der Heijden, R., & Witlox, F. (2016). Towards a circular economy: The role of Dutch logistics industries and governments. *Sustainability, 8*, 647.

van Dam, K. H., Nikolic, I., & Lukszo, Z. (Eds.). (2012). *Agent-based modelling of socio-technical systems* (Vol. 9). Dordrecht: Springer Science + Business Media.

Van Nes, N., & Cramer, J. (2006). Product lifetime optimization: A challenging strategy towards more sustainable consumption patterns. *Journal of Cleaner Production, 14*(15–16), 1307–1318.

Welch, D., Hobson, K., Holmes, H., Wheeler, K., & Wieser, H. (2019, December). Consumption work in the circular economy: A research agenda. *Discover Society*.

Wheeler, K., & Glucksmann, M. (2015). *Household recycling and consumption work: Social and moral economies*. Basingstoke, UK: Palgrave Macmillan.

Wieser, H. (2016). Beyond planned obsolescence? Product lifespans and the challenges to a circular economy. *GAIA, 25*(3), 156–160.

Woodall, L. C., Sanchez-Vidal, A., Canals, M., Paterson, G. L. J., Coppock, R., Sleight, V., …, Thompson, R. C. (2014). The deep sea is a major sink for microplastic debris. *Royal Society Open Science, 1*(4), 140317.

WRAP. (2019). *Circular Economy and Resource Efficiency Experts*. Retrieved from: https://www.wrap.org.uk. Accessed 12 December 2019.

Yang, J., Yang, Y., Wu, W. M., Zhao, J., & Jiang, L. (2014). Evidence of polyethylene biodegradation by bacterial strains from the guts of plastic-eating waxworms. *Environmental Science and Technology, 48*(23), 13776–13784.

CHAPTER 5

Scope for Circular Economy Model in Urban Agri-Food Value Chains

Maryna Henrysson and Cary Y. Hendrickson

New Urban Agenda: A Call for Transformation

There is a growing recognition that unprecedented societal transformations, including in production and consumption modes, will be required to achieve the ambitious objectives of the 2030 Agenda for Sustainable Development. Much of this transformation will have to take place in urban areas, which currently account for more than half the world's population, a proportion that is expected to increase by 68% by 2050 (UN DESA, 2019). In addition to the well-recognized contribution of 75% of global greenhouse gas emissions, the material footprint of urban areas also needs to be acknowledged (Swilling et al., 2018). Cities consume 75% of global material resources and 80% of the world's global energy supply

M. Henrysson (✉)
Department of Energy Technology, School of Industrial Engineering and Management, KTH Royal Institute of Technology, Stockholm, Sweden
e-mail: maryna.henrysson@energy.kth.se

C. Y. Hendrickson
Department of Methods and Models for Economics, Territory and Finance, Università Di Roma "La Sapienza", Rome, Italy

R. Bali Swain and S. Sweet (eds.), *Sustainable Consumption and Production, Volume II*,
https://doi.org/10.1007/978-3-030-55285-5_5

(UNEP-DTIE Sustainable Consumption and Production Branch, 2015), and urban areas are the epicentres of socio-economic activity, where 80% of the global GDP is generated (UN-HABITAT, 2016). If urgent action is not taken to address the status quo, total demand for resource stocks (such as fossil fuels or biomass) is expected to reach 130 billion tonnes by 2050, and even under optimistic scenarios, it is unlikely the economy can fill the gap of approximately 40 billion tonnes expected by then (UNEP, 2011). Such shortages will expose cities, countries, and businesses to significant risks.

Over the past decade, significant efforts have been made to define sustainable urban areas as both an aspirational normative ideal and as a creative, experimental, and innovative practice (Caprotti et al., 2017), setting goals and indicators to measure desirable progress in the advancement of complexity of urban systems (SDG 11) (United Nations, 2015; Pact of Amsterdam, 2016). The SDGs also recognize that cities play a central role in the development and implementation of sustainable food systems, with the responsibility of ensuring access to healthy food, and helping address environmental issues (SDG 2, SDG 12.3). As urban diets shift towards more animal-based protein and processed foods, the demand on land and water resources to supply food for consumption in cities will continue to increase. Urban food policy issues are increasingly linked to wider social and environmental justice, and equity debates, also because of the crucial role the agri-food sector plays in terms of meeting socio-economic objectives. Urban food issues and policies are often seen as part of wider socio-economic issues that cities face, such as environmental protection and the protection of public space (Mares & Peña, 2010). To address these multiple challenges, a large number of cities have committed to creating a "better" food system (Candel, 2019), yet at the same time, the debate over how to achieve the necessary changes to meet the transformational demands at different scales is still open.

In response to a growing number of practitioners and scholars advocating circular economy as a model that holds great promise for transforming current (wasteful) economic models of organizing production and consumption, we look at the structural and agency-related factors related to the principles of circularity within an urban setting. The advent and proliferation of bottom-up approaches and diversified communities of practice are at the same time gaining increasing importance, especially in terms of the potential to lead the societal transition towards more sustainable societies. Cities have experienced a growing number of collective actions advancing societal transformation through a variety of practices, and grassroots or community-led initiatives have emerged as part of a response to collective dissatisfaction with the speed and "profoundness" of top-down political approaches. The diversity of scale, strategies, types of production systems and value chain these organizations target, and the networks they create, might help shed light on the relevance of small-wins societal innovations that have the potential to generate wider societal spillover effects. By changing perceptions within public authorities or investors and demonstrating the alternatives as plausible scenarios of development, they are capable of shifting the perceptions of what is possible and laying claim to democratizing the knowledge and expertise necessary for the integration of material and social "capital" in socio-technical and socio-ecological systems.

In this chapter, we zoom in on both the emergence of two types of grassroots or community-led initiatives (that is, in the energy and agri-food sectors) and their potential contribution for experimentation with applying circular economy principles in practice. This potential for cross-sectoral coupling and synergies, based on existing social capital and resource flow circularity between alternative urban agri-food networks and community-led energy initiatives, is discussed. We draw parallels between developments of alternative and community-based energy and food communities and suggest that different framings, such as in narrow technological-focused innovations, can slow down recognition and benefit from interdependencies of food and energy infrastructures, networks, and institutions.

Our specific objectives are to highlight sources of tensions in strategical alignments that can either facilitate or hinder the uptake and integration of circular economy principles in urban systems. There is a need to understand the potential of combining alternative urban agri-food networks with community-led energy initiatives to lead a sustainable transformation. We argue that better understanding also requires a recognition of how the uptake of visions or strategies of circularity is affected by the availability and strength of social networks (or capital), driving forces behind their emergence and persistence, and technological solutions within and for these grassroots initiatives.

We recognize three fundamental conditions to building resilient sustainable urban food networks: assessment of urban flows based on a coupled systems-perspective, the diversification of knowledge, and overcoming structural and cultural resistance to change. With these three challenges in mind, we discuss why community-led initiatives and alternative economies in food waste and loss and urban energy debate deserve to be looked at more seriously when considering support to circular economy approaches, modelling, and adaptation in the urban context. Finally, we offer some concluding remarks on the challenges to establishing cross-sectoral linkages and the need to create an enabling policy environment.

Although the purpose of the chapter is to highlight structural and agency-related factors considerations that need to be addressed, we do not cover all forms of grassroots organizations and their potential contributions to enhancing circularity. Overall, this chapter calls attention to the need to address interventions in complex socio-ecological systems, and systems of production and consumptions from a systems thinking perspective that not only includes material and energy flows, technological advancements, and investment needs, but also the interdependencies of all actors in the urban context and the benefits of the diversity of visions and motivation and knowledge clusters. Understanding the visions of urban circular economy and the underlying "motivations and needs to pursue circular economy model" of the communities of practice is crucial to developing scientific evidence and reduce policymaking uncertainty in addressing pressing urban transformational challenges. Solving urban sustainability dilemmas, which is the core challenge for the global economy and well-being, therefore, requires new and visionary concepts for sustainable pathways, one of which is the circular economy model.

Cities and the Rise of Circular Economy

Circular economy is often celebrated for its potential as a mobilization mechanism to engage a broad variety of actors and a model that presents feasible and comprehensive solutions for sustainable development (Fratini, Georg, & Jørgensen, 2019; Geissdoerfer, Savaget, Bocken, & Hultink, 2017; Sauvé, Bernard, & Sloan, 2016). While originating in academic literature more than half a century ago, the circular economy concept has most actively been promoted by the private sector. Lately, concept and policies for circular economy gained high-level political traction, and they are rapidly being adopted by agenda-setting actors. The concept has been broadly taken up and inspired new governmental, along with individual, action plans and practices for industries and community-led organizations. In the European Union context, for instance, where support to circular economy has been given the highest priority, the European Commission emphasizes that the realization of a circular economy should benefit cities, regions, and people (European Commission, 2020). The European Commission, under the Circular Economy Package (European Commission, 2015, 2019), introduced targets for priority sectors including key areas of action for food value chains, among others. In concert, European Commission promotes a zero-waste food programme for Europe (European Commission, 2014). In this, the circular economy is envisioned as a model of development with the goal of creating and sustaining "a carbon neutral, resource-efficient, and competitive economy" (European Commission, 2015: 2), and it is also one of the main facets that integrates Europe's new agenda for sustainable development, the Green Deal (European Commission, 2019) and the European Union Urban Agenda (Pact of Amsterdam, 2016). Together, these strategies seek to advance political and technological interventions that fit wider global targets, such as the SDGs related to energy (SDG 7), sustainable cities and communities (SDG 11), and reducing food loss and waste (SDG 12.3) (United Nations, 2015). In this way, food systems and reducing food waste and loss,[1] are increasingly seen for their potential to contribute to sustainable cities, energy, and production and consumption.

Recent and ongoing efforts to introduce circular economy principles in urban systems have taken various forms and have been initiated by a range of actors. Growing numbers of cities have been experimenting with varied visions and strategies of what a circular economy would look like (Bocken, Schuit, & Kraaijenhagen, 2018; Bolger & Doyon, 2019; Christis, Athanassiadis, & Vercalsteren, 2019; Fratini et al., 2019; Petit-Boix, & Leipold, 2018; Ziskind & Guna, 2018), even though barriers in implementation persist with market, cultural, and regulatory barriers

[1]The FAO's definitional framework, food waste is delimited by three dimensions: "**food loss, food waste, and food wastage**. **Food loss** refers to a decrease in mass (dry matter) or nutritional value (quality) of food that was originally intended for human consumption. These losses are mainly caused by inefficiencies in the food supply chains, such as poor infrastructure and logistics, lack of technology, insufficient skills, knowledge and management capacity of supply chain actors, and lack of access to markets. In addition, natural disasters play a role. **Food waste** refers to food appropriate for human consumption being discarded, whether or not after it is kept beyond its expiry date or left to spoil. Often this is because food has spoiled but it can be for other reasons such as oversupply due to markets, or individual consumer shopping/eating habits. **Food wastage** refers to any food lost by deterioration or waste. Thus, the term "wastage" encompasses both food loss and food waste" (FAO, 2014).

prevailing over technological deficiencies (de Jesus & Mendonça, 2018; Kirchherr et al., 2018).

The circular economy model of organization of production and consumption aims to challenge wasteful linear economic model and offers a vision of a wider transformation of socio-technical system, where inputs are reduced, regenerative processes are embedded in loops created to reuse and cascade energy and material flows (Geissdoerfer et al., 2017).There is no lack of definitions of circular economy and contestation over the concept, and they have been criticized on several grounds (Kirchherr, Reike, & Hekkert, 2017; Korhonen, Nuur, Feldmann, & Birkie, 2018). Definitions encompassing social, cultural, behavioural aspects are often overlooked or confused in definitions and concepts about the circular economy (cf. Murray, Skene, & Hynes, 2017), and little attention has been given beyond considerations of the circular economy in terms of physical and material resources (Kirchherr et al., 2017). Moreover, current discourses revolving around eco-efficiency and resource optimization explicitly support the claim of neoclassical economists that any limiting production factor can be substituted by technological innovation (Giampietro, 2019). Broader definitions of circular economy have also been aligned and consistent with such techno-centric narratives of green growth. Despite attempts to define or establish a common interpretation of the circular economy that refer to a *desired* or *intended* outcome, the operationalization of a circular economy model for the transformation of the current economic model towards a more sustainable one remains to be seen (Giampietro, 2019).

Given the dense spatial concentration of resources, knowledge, and economic activity in urban agglomerations, cities are strategically placed as key sites for experimentation with circular model-driven transformations. Meanwhile, scholars of urban sustainability have for long questioned the prevalence of techno-managerial views favoured at the expense of other dimensions of sustainability (cf. Bulkeley & Betsill, 2005). While the concept of circular economy withstands validity and legitimacy trials that are crucial for a successful and broad adoption (Blomsma & Brennan, 2017), it is important to be clear about what one means by the circular economy model in a particular context. Our understanding follows Prendeville, Cherim, and Bocken (2018: 176), who define a circular city as "a city that practices CE principles to close resource loops, in partnership with the city's stakeholders (citizens, community, business and knowledge stakeholders), to realize its vision of a future-proof city". Similarly, we treat urban agri-food network based on principles of circularity as *an economic system and model for provision of agri-food goods and services characterized by deliberate organization and governance for regenerative and restorative systems of production and consumption to perpetuate inclusive and equitable societal prosperity by maintaining the value of resources, materials, and products and avoiding wastage.*

The performance of circular economy targeting food systems can be measured by relying on, and making the most, of a diversity of material and energy flows, socio-technical and knowledge networks, social capital, and cross-sectorial cooperation. If a circular economy model can be seen as an alternative economic model with the objective of creating resilient and sustainable production and consumption systems, its related aspirational goals and operationalized strategies should stimulate growth in varied and concurrent actors, strategies, scales of intervention, and be coherent with wider efforts towards the achievement of the SDGs. With such an understanding, the diversity of visions and interest, and the means and mechanisms of implementation that can bring tangible change and create an impact, need to be taken into account.

Alternative and community-led initiatives provide such an example for further investigation, as they exist (in many cases) relatively independently from institutional and political attention and therefore also the constraints therein (Seyfang & Haxeltine, 2012; Smith, Voß, & Grin, 2010). We direct our attention to specific communities that offer a fertile testing ground in terms of innovative, flexible models of development. Alternative and community-led initiatives operating in the agri-food and energy domains provide such an example, as they exist (in many cases) relatively independently from institutional and political attention and therefore also the constraints therein (Seyfang & Haxeltine, 2012; Smith et al., 2010).

Community Economies and Grassroots-Led Transformation

In practice, there is a great variety of state-led, technology-led, market-led, and community-led urban experimentations and innovative practices modelled around circular economy principles in both the food and energy domains. Grassroots- or community-led initiatives have the potential to provide the transformative elements that are unachievable by top-down policies targeting individual behaviour or through technological innovation could ever achieve (Moloney, Horne, & Fien, 2010; Wolfram,

2018). Such experimentations are often promoted and at the same time hindered by a range of policies and measures that do not abide by sectoral domains or distinctions. National and municipal policies are not the only institutional and structural factors that enable and frame transformations towards circular economy model.

Grassroots initiatives have been described as a community that shares new rules and practices, which provide new and diverse market options, while at the same time aim to transform the entire market system (Geels & Raven, 2006; Hargreaves, Hielscher, & Seyfang, 2013; Smith, Hargreaves, Hielscher, Martiskainen, & Seyfang, 2016). They differ from other innovations as they originate in civil society and are mostly inspired by ideological communal values, and are context-specific. However, there is concern as to whether circular economy initiatives, in a similar vein as earlier, more broadly framed as sustainable development initiatives, are more effective when driven from bottom-up, by citizens and the private sector, instead of implemented through top-down policies.

Two main types of factors associated with the persistence and growth of grassroots organizations are those related to the individuals involved in the activities and the external, wider contextual factors (e.g., administrative environment, legal and regulatory framework, financial systems). A socio-technical transitions-perspective to studying advancements of grassroots organizations and their influence on wider unsustainable systems conceptualize community-based collective actions as initiators of alternative pathways of innovation that may provide the necessary radical and integrated socio-technical changes to solve environmental and social problems (Van Oers, Boon, & Moors, 2018). In such an interpretation, grassroots communities offer "visions of radical transition pathways and mobilize marginalized values, organizational forms, and institutional logics" (Martin & Upham, 2016; Martin, Upham, & Budd, 2015: 6). However, some authors have also argued that these initiatives are incapable of achieving this alone, and thus require scalar and re-interpretive shifts (Schot & Geels, 2008; Seyfang & Haxeltine, 2012). While they attract scholarly interest (often due to their outsider nature with respect to traditional economies), it is not unusual for non-profits to grow into "business-like" entities with commercialization strategy (Martin et al., 2015).

The Potential in Coupling Community Energy Initiatives and Alternative Food Networks as More Circular Economies

Here we introduce two widely diffused community-led and alternative systems: alternative food networks and grassroots-led energy initiatives. Alternative and community-based food networks are increasingly playing a bigger role in commodity production and food security, emerging as potential sources of locally retained added value and therefore catalysts for economic development and income generation (Marsden & Smith, 2005; Stefani, Romano, & Cei, 2017). We define alternative agri-food systems by their difference from conventional, industrial systems of food production, distribution, and consumption (Paül & McKenzie, 2013). They include, but are not limited to, systems that shorten the distance within value chains (i.e., between consumers and producers), facilitate direct marketing of goods, and provisioning methods. Small self-subsistence-oriented collectives of food producers, community-supported agriculture or consumer cooperatives, urban communal gardens, farmers markets, and urban food sharing platforms are examples of such developments taking this route (Bos & Owen, 2016; Rosol, 2020).

Community-supported agriculture offers a different business model in terms of organizing their value chains but often, similar to energy communities, they struggle to survive for a number of reasons (Hargreaves et al., 2013). If their role in the legitimization of alternative transformational pathways is recognized, societal innovators are believed to open the access to knowledge and investments available through public policy and venture capital.

Innovative community-based and alternative agri-food systems are important for the benefits they offer in terms of the environment or local economy, and they are also increasingly linked to emerging concepts of the circular economy and issues like reducing food waste and loss. Alternative economic, as well as more conventional, models across the entire agri-food sector are embracing strategies for circularity as a pathway to addressing the sustainability of urban food networks and problems with food waste and loss encompassing the entire value chain from producers, to manufacturers, to retailers, and big kitchens. However, the role locally based, alternative agri-food systems play in achieving objectives for urban circularity remains relatively under-researched.

Alternative energy communities are also typically locally based, non-commercial, decentralized and small-scale, or characterized by distributed peer-to-peer market design. Such grassroots energy systems can be broadly defined as "formal or informal citizen-led initiatives which propose collaborative solutions on a local basis to facilitate the development of sustainable energy technologies" (Bauwens, Gotchev, & Holstenkamp, 2016), that are involved in the provision or production of energy.

There are a diverse body of projects and networks that support individual households in becoming prosumers or introducing more stringent energy efficiency measures. Citizens act as prosumers in local energy communities that with varying degrees of self-coordination optimize the energy exchange between units of production and local demand. Historically, in places like Denmark and Finland, initiatives like district heating cooperatives or wind energy cooperatives have predominately relied on the early proactive engagement of actors with limited access to resources and expertise in development of renewable energy projects. However, they possessed uniquely localized knowledge of not only biophysical conditions and industrial and infrastructural conditions, but also knowledge and resources in terms of local social capital.

In addition to well-known Danish wind cooperatives framed as a form of alternative democratized decentralized energy system, Denmark also provides insight for democratic transitions to ownership of electricity production and new forms of cooperative market organization. Peer-to-peer food and farm cooperatives have existed for decades on a larger scale in both Sweden and Denmark, where dairy and grain farmers are organized in what has now emerged as large-scale industrial agricultural organizations, including organic farmers as well, who control and own "the entire farm-to-fork" chain. Productive and distributive knowledge and expertise are centralized in one place, and this type of ownership has facilitated capitalization of opportunities to capture what was once lost value (in waste), and redirection to create new productive value in its reuse. In Denmark, farmers with the support of a variety of societal groups, including research and development communities, were the first to mobilize the opportunities of decentralized biogas development in response to energy supply shortages (Raven & Geels, 2010). Grassroots and farm cooperatives are experimenting with different strategies aimed at capturing "lost" or "wasted" value and finding alternative markets and uses for food and waste loss streams. For instance, grain harvest residues are used to produce agro-ethanol, alternative grain protein bio-based polymers are used in plastics, bio-methane is fed into the distributed gas grid, a side stream from cheese production is used to extract protein for new protein value chains. The unique form of ownership, types of networks, and knowledge accumulation, as well as expectations in these cases facilitates a high level of collaboration that takes place at every step of the value chain. Advanced technology, research, and knowledge are extensive, available, and have developed across sectors in a form of circular production systems.

Community energy and alternative agri-food systems have the potential for interdependency, involving shared as well as conflictual terminology and conceptualizations, and as exemplified by the issue of food waste and loss. While the benefits of integrating food and energy systems are increasingly recognized, a range of obstacles to its deployment in the urban context remain, including commonly recognized issues such as a lack of policy coherence, consumer acceptance, and/or infrastructure. Food and energy security issues are also complex and intertwined with pressing issues like climate change, social justice, and poverty, among others. In terms of governance, energy and food policies must also account for cross-jurisdictional city region systems, and integrate broader movements from civil society, the private sector, financial institutions, and non-state actors such as research and academic institutions.

Current vertically organized energy and agri-food systems, in terms of technical and commercial market design, as well as supportive institutional frameworks, are still organized according to the traditional value chain of energy production, transport, storage, and distribution. However, an emerging market for distributed and smaller-scale energy production that enables the transition from supply-driven to demand-side EU energy policy is evolving. Agri-food systems are also dynamic, shifting, and influenced by varied interactions among scales of production, actors, sectors, and policies. Food systems are essential in linking consumers and producers, as well as governance issues that connect to health, employment, land use planning, etc., and may be underappreciated for their potential role in leading the transition to a circular economy (Borrello, 2016; European Commission, 2018; Principato, Ruini, Guidi, & Secondi, 2019). At the same time, food waste and loss is unique in its complexity being connected to various economic, societal, and environmental issues and sectors and scales (Buzby & Hyman, 2012; Gustavsson, Cederberg, Sonesson, Van Otterdijk, & Meybeck, 2011). While substantial environmental impacts from food occur in the production phase (agriculture, food processing), households influence these impacts through their dietary choices and habits (Richards & Hamilton, 2018). From a market perspective, consumer behaviour can play an important role in driving changes in agricultural practices, as demand for agri-food products that meet social and environmental objectives or low-carbon or renewable energy supplies increase (ibid). This has consequences for the environment-related, food-related energy consumption and waste generation, where the food sector is widely recognized as accounting for a large portion of global greenhouse gas emissions, as well as total energy consumption (Buzby & Hyman, 2012).

Recent research on local stakeholders' practices and perceptions of urban transitions has also shown the extent to which wider discourses on food waste and loss, and sustainable energy systems are coupled and complementary. In a study based on empirical data from grassroots organizations in Finland, Italy, Germany, Romania, Spain, and the United Kingdom, the aims and ambitions of community-led organizations in the food, energy, and transport sectors were examined and a range of shared outcome-related aims and aspirations, as well as guiding rationalities, were found to be motivating factors for the rise of these initiatives (Fischer, Holstead, Hendrickson, Virkkula, & Prampolini, 2017). Despite the different sectors of focus, this research showed that the shared values and interrelated aims and aspirations for achieving sustainable, resilient, and equitable development underlie the motivations to participate, and the emergence of this form of self-organization.

Obstacles in Creating Cross-Sectorial Synergies

The circular economy model appeals to a variety of stakeholders in addressing complexity and co-dependence of urban food and energy systems. The performance of circular economy initiative relies on various sources of material and energy flows, networks of actors, and integrated and coordinated cooperation, yet, commonly known actions have focused on either the micro or household level, meso level of product systems, or macro-level institutional and governance issues, overlooking community-based or grassroots efforts in alternative energy and agri-food systems.

The two types of grassroots or alternative communities for energy and food discussed above are examples where these factors manifested their historical development. Learning from these developments, we identify three considerations that need to be addressed in order to more effectively adapt circular economy models in building resilient sustainable urban food networks. These fundamental challenges are to be overcome in the realization of circular economy within the urban landscape: path-dependency in production and infrastructure patterns, knowledge claims (whose vision of the circular economy is more sustainable, desirable, and based on which values), and cross-value chain inequalities in bearing the costs of implementation and change (both upstream and downstream investments that will be needed). We see these as interlinked and related to the potential and role for grassroots organizations within circular food waste and loss management and agri-food systems, as described below.

First, as one of the clear advantages in operationalization, circular economy models are based on closed-loop systems and cascading principles (Ellen MacArthur Foundation, 2013; Velenturf, Archer, Gomes, Christgen, Lag-Brotons, & Purnell, 2019). The optimization of food management, technology, and diet—and the maximization of synergies systems requires comprehensive understanding of cross-interdependence of urban systems: energy and material flows, information and knowledge flows. To be able to build self-reliant networks the capacity and quality of material and energy flows should be accounted for. This needs both quantification and qualitative assessments of networks and systems performance, and includes peri-urban areas, incorporating water and land resources, ecosystem services, production and manufacturing practices, infrastructure access, transportation, consumption patterns, and financial feasibility. In the policy documents underlying the New Urban Agenda in the EU, development towards urban sustainability is often narrowly interpreted as increased material or resource efficiency, for example, regarding waste. Urban resource consumption is structural, therefore, accounting and optimization of waste infrastructure and energy demand, in urban agri-food systems, in particular, is not enough (Bahers, Tanguy, & Pincetl, 2020).

Second, the challenge related to identification and evaluation of urban flows links to the issue of knowledge claims, the role of experts, and indicators and metrics (as from above) as instruments in the governance of resources. Understanding which urban systems (as well as defining these boundaries) are included in the approaches or not, and thus what types of circular economy practices take place and which indicators are applied to measure progress, makes socio-technical imaginaries that govern the operationalization of urban circularity explicit (Kovacic, Strand, & Völker, 2019). As emphasized in works on sustainability transitions, the establishment of legitimacy is of special importance for technologies that are challenging the incumbent practices (Markard, Wirth, & Truffer, 2016). Therefore, acknowledgement that subjectivity, values, and power dynamics are fundamental factors determining the framing, contestation, and design of options to enhance resilience, efficiency, and sustainability performance of urban spaces is important for validating circular economy concept and legitimization of its operational principles. Collective action of community-based grassroots initiatives are important sources of pragmatic, moral, and cognitive legitimacy and associated legitimation strategies, but the practices and perceptions of urban transitions from the view of different actors, especially community-based initiatives vary greatly, and within an urban development context, knowledge becomes a crucial commodity. Largely engineering-based expertise lies with powerful private sector actors that are big enough to carry out the task of assessing the city flows (as seen in challenge we identify above), and are exemplified as in the case of Amsterdam city, strongly led by circular assessment and monitoring practice (Metabolic, 2018). However, there are tensions in these knowledge claims, as for instance, in the energy domain, it is becoming more broadly accepted among researchers that smaller-scale, cheaper, and mass employed technologies can enable faster transition (Wilson, Grubler, Bento, Healey, De Stercke, & Zimm, 2020). Advances in the circular economy are both steered direct towards interventions and also framed as opportunities for innovation and citizen-led transitions. As there have been a multitude of transformational sustainability pathways differing in goals and the means to achieve them advocated worldwide, decision-makers are facing a challenge to make explicit what transformation is to be achieved (Caprotti et al., 2017; Linnér & Wibeck, 2020).

Last, and of no less importance, are explanations of the resistance to change and path creation. While there is a need for a profound transformation in our ways of understanding and managing urban agri-food networks, the material infrastructure and governance regimes are characterized by a high degree of path-dependency and resistance to change.

Grassroots or community-led organizations in the energy and agri-food sectors demonstrate the diversity of agendas and interests in transformative practice and vision, both internally and externally, and unpacking these will require a basic framework for the different ways in which various actors interpret the concepts of transformation. The major tensions found in a study of European grassroots food, transport, and energy initiatives included issues related to resistance to change and claims over knowledge, such as the politicization of their work, the prioritization of financial goals and management of the organizations, which mirror tensions in larger, societal-level discourses on the plurality of aims and ambitions of different actors within the circular economy and similar sustainability initiatives (Fischer et al., 2017). For instance, narratives of integration in production, consumption, and land use may be diffused and prevalent in the Transition Towns movement. In this, shared values, as well as the agency of actors as both independent agents and members belonging to wider communities, are often identified as key elements in explaining the emergence of community-led organizations (Farla, Markard, Raven, & Coenen, 2012). Yet, these values and roles change, for instance, in terms of the expectations and visions at play in many grassroots or community-led initiatives, such as alternative energy or agri-food systems (Neal, 2013). Thus, we see a diversity of aims and resulting conflicts at a practical level as potential hindrances that should also be acknowledged in attempts to establish or support hybrid policy environments.

The governance structure of two complementary systems in energy and food domains, tied by visions of economic circularity, are also seemingly at odds. We interpret tensions among the potential for urban food and energy system transitions with the scalar limits of localized production–consumption–distribution networks as reflective of larger, diverse societal-level discourses on food systems, urban sustainability, and promotion of the circular economy as part of the sustainable socio-technical transition (Fischer et al., 2017). We echo similar findings and argue that these tensions need to be more widely explored—both in research around urban circular economy transformations, as well as at the practical level.

Beyond looking at technological changes in organizational structures, we wish to emphasize the implications for actors' motivations and transaction costs, and the consequences for the speed and efficiency of adopting circular economy models. Innovations derived from community economies and grassroots organizations face challenges to establish and maintain viability (Seyfang & Haxeltine, 2012). Some scholars also see spillover effects and maturation, expansion, and marketization of grassroots technology adaptation and practice and wider acceptance of sustainable transformation practices as requiring public authorities to create more opportunities for communities through increased support (for instance, public procurement and investment) (Bunt & Harris, 2010). Overall, we echo other scholars' calls for greater attention to critical perspectives on the discourses, aspirations, and conditions that are influencing the practices and the related impacts of community-led organizations (Fischer et al., 2017; Tornaghi, 2014).

The Importance of Community-Led Cities and More Circular Economies: Seeking Ways to Create an Enabling Environment

Issues such as the three addressed in this chapter are quite problematic; thus, if we do not put them front and centre, the investments, both financial and institution-building, cities and private actors are now making might be in vain. At the same time, there is a great deal to learn from the motivations behind and visions of community-led development to achieve resilient, sustainable, and/or equitable cities, and how they emerge to provide services or goods not provided by the government or unavailable in the market. Despite the potential to create cross-sectoral synergies and increasing circularity for community-led energy and alternative food systems, there are complex issues that cut across socio-economic systems and spatial scales and require the balancing of competing and parallel objectives. Envisioning and implementing the transformations required for any model of the circular economy will require special attention to cross-sectoral integration, as well as consideration of the way trade-offs are accounted for and tensions resolved across various socio-technical and socio-ecological domains.

The growing demand for agri-food commodities and goods in cities is a prime driver of climate change, biodiversity loss, depletion of water resources, land degradation, and increasing demand for energy and material resources (Springmann et al., 2018). When responding to these challenges, cities should encourage and stimulate food sustainability proposals and rethink their approach and role as policymakers, consumers, and agenda-setters towards sustainable food systems. This will require political debate and commitment at the city level, that in turn requires proactive engagement of a wide range of actors, including those associated with the agri-food value chains that extend beyond city and national borders, public institutions, the private sector, and civil societies. Both are crucial in order to establish better food governance models and lead the development of tangible transformations of production and distribution systems, as well as consumption behaviour in cities. Currently, tensions and trade-offs between various goals of sustainable transformation can be seen in the shared and also contested visions of circularity, as well as the diverse societal transitional pathways of actors engaged in local agri-food value chains. Simultaneously, this diversity points towards tenable synergies and potential for alignment with other energy and transportation policies and programmes that are aimed at developing a more circular urban economy through more grounded and bottom-up evolution of societal practices and behaviour.

There is little doubt that cities have a leading role to play in driving sustainable, resilient, and equitable development and changes in the way current systems of production are organized. Cities must face this challenge and accept their responsibility to create an enabling environment for social and business innovation to empower its citizens, build capacity and encourage the necessary shifts towards responsible consumption behaviour, all seen as key to improving their overall sustainability performance. We hope that the challenges and issues outlined above will add to the wider debate around how diverse actors both in the Global South and in the North will further shape implementation of the New Urban Agenda.

References

Bahers, J. B., Tanguy, A., & Pincetl, S. (2020). Metabolic relationships between cities and hinterland: A political-industrial ecology of energy metabolism of Saint-Nazaire metropolitan and port area (France). *Ecologcal Economics, 167*, 106447. https://doi.org/10.1016/j.ecolecon.2019.106447.

Bauwens, T., Gotchev, B., & Holstenkamp, L. (2016). What drives the development of community energy in Europe? The case of wind power cooperatives. *Energy Research & Social Science, 13*, 136–147. https://doi.org/10.1016/j.erss.2015.12.016.

Blomsma, F., & Brennan, G. (2017). The emergence of circular economy: A new framing around prolonging resource productivity. *Journal of Industrial Ecology, 21*(3), 603–614. https://doi.org/10.1111/jiec.12603.

Bocken, N. M. P., Schuit, C. S. C., & Kraaijenhagen, C. (2018). Experimenting with a circular business model: Lessons from eight cases. *Environmental Innovation and Societal Transitions, 28,* 79–95. https://doi.org/10.1016/J.EIST.2018.02.001.

Bolger, K., & Doyon, A. (2019). Circular cities: Exploring local government strategies to facilitate a circular economy. *European Planning Studies, 27*(11), 2184–2205. https://doi.org/10.1080/09654313.2019.1642854.

Borrello, M. (2016). *Circular economy in the agri-food sector: Going beyond sustainability-challenges and consumers' participation* (PhD Thesis). University of Naples Federico II, Naples. http://www.fedoa.unina.it/id/eprint/10839.

Bos, E., & Owen, L. (2016). Virtual reconnection: The online spaces of alternative food networks in England. *Journal of Rural Studies, 45,* 1–14. https://doi.org/10.1016/j.jrurstud.2016.02.016.

Bulkeley, H., & Betsill, M. M. (2005). Rethinking sustainable cities: Multilevel governance and the "urban" politics of climate change. *Environmental Politics, 14*(1), 42–63. https://doi.org/10.1080/0964401042000310178.

Bunt, L., & Harris, M. (2010). *Mass localism: A way to help small communities solve big social challenges, National Endowment for Science, Technology and the Arts (NESTA).* London. http://camdencen.org.uk/Resources/Localism/MassLocalism_Feb2010.pdf.

Buzby, J. C., & Hyman, J. (2012). Total and per capita value of food loss in the United States. *Food Policy, 37,* 561–570. https://doi.org/10.1016/j.foodpol.2012.06.002.

Candel, J. J. L. (2019). What's on the menu? A global assessment of MUFPP signatory cities' food strategies. *Agroecology and Sustainable Food Systems, 44*(7), 919–946. https://doi.org/10.1080/21683565.2019.1648357.

Caprotti, F., Cowley, R., Datta, A., Broto, V. C., Gao, E., Georgeson, L., …, Joss, S. (2017). The new urban agenda: Key opportunities and challenges for policy and practice. *Urban Research and Practice, 10*(3), 367–378. https://doi.org/10.1080/17535069.2016.1275618.

Christis, M., Athanassiadis, A., & Vercalsteren, A. (2019). Implementation at a city level of circular economy strategies and climate change mitigation—The case of Brussels. *Journal of Cleaner Production, 218,* 511–520. https://doi.org/10.1016/j.jclepro.2019.01.180.

de Jesus, A., & Mendonça, S. (2018). Lost in transition? Drivers and barriers in the eco-innovation road to the circular economy. *Ecological Economics, 145,* 75–89. https://doi.org/10.1016/J.ECOLECON.2017.08.001.

UN DESA. (2019). *World urbanization prospects: The 2018 revision.* New York: United Nations. https://doi.org/10.18356/6255ead2-en.

Ellen MacArthur Foundation. (2013). *Towards the circular economy: Economic and business rationale.* Cowes, UK: Ellen MacArthur Foundation.

European Commission. (2014). *Communication from the Commission to the European Parliament, the Council, the European Economic and Social Committee and the Committee of the RegionsTowards a Circular Economy—A Zero Waste Programme for Europe*. Brussels: European Commission. https://doi.org/10.24264/icams-2018.xi.4.

European Commission. (2015). *An EU action plan for the circular economy*. Brussels: European Commission. https://doi.org/10.1017/CBO9781107415324.004.

European Commission. (2018). *Enhancing the contribution of the agri-food value chain to the circular economy*. Brussels: European Commission.

European Commission. (2019). *Communication from the Commission to the European Parliament, the Council, the European Economic and Social Committee and the Committee of the Regions. The European Green Deal*. Brussels: European Commission.

European Commission. (2019). *Report on the implementation of the Circular Economy Action Plan, European Commission*. Brussels: European Commission. https://doi.org/10.1259/arr.1905.0091.

European Commission. (2020). *Communication from the Commission to the European Parliament, the Council, the European Economic and Social Committee and the Committee of the Regions. A New Circular Economy Action Plan for a Cleaner and More Competitive Europe*. Brussels: European Commission.

FAO. (2014). *Definitional framework of food loss—SAVE FOOD: Global initiative on food loss and waste reduction*. Rome: Food and Agriculture Organisation of the United Nations.

Farla, J., Markard, J., Raven, R., & Coenen, L. (2012). Sustainability transitions in the making: A closer look at actors, strategies and resources. *Technological Forecasting and Social Change, 79*(6), 991–998. https://doi.org/10.1016/j.techfore.2012.02.001.

Fischer, A., Holstead, K., Hendrickson, C. Y., Virkkula, O., & Prampolini, A. (2017). Community-led initiatives' everyday politics for sustainability—Conflicting rationalities and aspirations for change? *Environment and Planning A, 49*(9), 1986–2006. https://doi.org/10.1177/0308518X17713994.

Fratini, C. F., Georg, S., & Jørgensen, M. S. (2019). Exploring circular economy imaginaries in European cities: A research agenda for the governance of urban sustainability transitions. *Journal of Cleaner Production, 228*, 974–989. https://doi.org/10.1016/j.jclepro.2019.04.193.

Geels, F., & Raven, R. (2006). Non-linearity and expectations in niche-development trajectories: Ups and downs in Dutch biogas development (1973–2003). *Technology Analysis Strategic Management, 18*, 375–392. https://doi.org/10.1080/09537320600777143.

Geissdoerfer, M., Savaget, P., Bocken, N. M. P., & Hultink, E. J. (2017). The circular economy—A new sustainability paradigm? *Journal of Cleaner Production, 143,* 757–768. https://doi.org/10.1016/J.JCLEPRO.2016.12.048.

Giampietro, M. (2019). On the circular bioeconomy and decoupling: Implications for sustainable growth. *Ecological Economics, 162,* 143–156. https://doi.org/10.1016/j.ecolecon.2019.05.001.

Gustavsson, J., Cederberg, C., Sonesson, U., Van Otterdijk, R., & Meybeck, A. (2011). *Causes and prevention of food losses and waste. Global Food Losses Food Waste*. Rome: Food and Agriculture Organisation of the United Nations.

Hargreaves, T., Hielscher, S., Seyfang, G., & Smith, A. (2013). Grassroots innovations in community energy: The role of intermediaries in niche development. *Global Environmental Change, 23,* 868–880. https://doi.org/10.1016/j.gloenvcha.2013.02.008.

Kirchherr, J., Piscicelli, L., Bour, R., Kostense-Smit, E., Muller, J., Huibrechtse-Truijens, A., et al. (2018). Barriers to the circular economy: Evidence from the European Union (EU). *Ecological Economics, 150,* 264–272. https://doi.org/10.1016/J.ECOLECON.2018.04.028.

Kirchherr, J., Reike, D., & Hekkert, M. (2017). Conceptualizing the circular economy: An analysis of 114 definitions. *Resources, Conservation and Recycling, 127,* 221–232. https://doi.org/10.1016/j.resconrec.2017.09.005.

Korhonen, J., Nuur, C., Feldmann, A., & Birkie, S. E. (2018). Circular economy as an essentially contested concept. *Journal of Cleaner Production, 175,* 544–552. https://doi.org/10.1016/J.JCLEPRO.2017.12.111.

Kovacic, Z., Strand, R., & Völker, T. (2019). *The circular economy in Europe: Critical perspectives on policies and imaginaries*. London: Routledge.

Linnér, B. O., & Wibeck, V. (2020). Conceptualising variations in societal transformations towards sustainability. *Environmental Science & Policy, 106,* 221–227. https://doi.org/10.1016/j.envsci.2020.01.007.

Mares, T., & Peña, D. (2010). Urban agriculture in the making of insurgent spaces in Los Angeles and Seattle. In J. Hou (Ed.), *Insurgent public space: Guerrilla urbanism and the remaking of contemporary cities* (pp. 241–254). London: Routledge.

Markard, J., Wirth, S., & Truffer, B. (2016). Institutional dynamics and technology legitimacy: A framework and a case study on biogas technology. *Research Policy, 45,* 330–344. https://doi.org/10.1016/j.respol.2015.10.009.

Marsden, T., & Smith, E. (2005). Ecological entrepreneurship: Sustainable development in local communities through quality food production and local branding. *Geoforum, 36,* 440–451. https://doi.org/10.1016/j.geoforum.2004.07.008.

Martin, C. J., & Upham, P. (2016). Grassroots social innovation and the mobilization of values in collaborative consumption: A conceptual model. *Journal of Cleaner Production, 134,* 204–213. https://doi.org/10.1016/j.jclepro.2015.04.062.

Martin, C. J., Upham, P., & Budd, L. (2015). Commercial orientation in grassroots social innovation: Insights from the sharing economy. *Ecological Economics, 118,* 240–251. https://doi.org/10.1016/j.ecolecon.2015.08.001.

Metabolic. (2018). *Monitoring voor een Circulaire Metropoolregio.* Amsterdam.

Moloney, S., Horne, R. E., & Fien, J. (2010). Transitioning to low carbon communities—From behaviour change to systemic change: Lessons from Australia. *Energy Policy, 38,* 7614–7623. https://doi.org/10.1016/j.enpol.2009.06.058.

Murray, A., Skene, K., & Haynes, K. (2017). The circular economy: An interdisciplinary exploration of the concept and application in a global context. *Journal of Business Ethics, 140,* 369–380. https://doi.org/10.1007/s10551-015-2693-2.

Neal, S. (2013). Transition culture: Politics, localities and ruralities. *Journal of Rural Studies, 32,* 60–69. https://doi.org/10.1016/j.jrurstud.2013.04.001.

Pact of Amsterdam. (2016). *Urban agenda for the EU: Pact of Amsterdam.* https://ec.europa.eu/regional_policy/sources/policy/themes/urban-development/agenda/pact-of-amsterdam.pdf.

Paül, V., & McKenzie, F. H. (2013). Peri-urban farmland conservation and development of alternative food networks: Insights from a case-study area in metropolitan Barcelona (Catalonia, Spain). *Land Use Policy, 30,* 94–105. https://doi.org/10.1016/j.landusepol.2012.02.009.

Petit-Boix, A., & Leipold, S. (2018). Circular economy in cities: Reviewing how environmental research aligns with local practices. *Journal of Cleaner Production, 195,* 1270–1281. https://doi.org/10.1016/J.JCLEPRO.2018.05.281.

Prendeville, S., Cherim, E., & Bocken, N. (2018). Circular cities: Mapping six cities in transition. *Environmental Innovation and Societal Transitions, 26,* 171–194. https://doi.org/10.1016/j.eist.2017.03.002.

Principato, L., Ruini, L., Guidi, M., & Secondi, L. (2019). Adopting the circular economy approach on food loss and waste: The case of Italian pasta production. *Resources, Conservation and Recycling, 144,* 82–89. https://doi.org/10.1016/j.resconrec.2019.01.025.

Raven, R. P. J. M., & Geels, F. W. (2010). Socio-cognitive evolution in niche development: Comparative analysis of biogas development in Denmark and the Netherlands (1973–2004). *Technovation, 30,* 87–99. https://doi.org/10.1016/j.technovation.2009.08.006.

Richards, T. J., & Hamilton, S. F. (2018). Food waste in the sharing economy. *Food Policy, 75,* 109–123. https://doi.org/10.1016/j.foodpol.2018.01.008.

Rosol, M. (2020). On the significance of alternative economic practices: Reconceptualizing alterity in alternative food networks. *Economic Geography, 96*, 52–76. https://doi.org/10.1080/00130095.2019.1701430.

Sauvé, S., Bernard, S., & Sloan, P. (2016). Environmental sciences, sustainable development and circular economy: Alternative concepts for trans-disciplinary research. *Environmental Development, 17*, 48–56. https://doi.org/10.1016/J.ENVDEV.2015.09.002.

Schot, J., & Geels, F. W. (2008). Strategic niche management and sustainable innovation journeys: Theory, findings, research agenda, and policy. *Technology Analysis & Strategic Management, 20*, 537–554. https://doi.org/10.1080/09537320802292651.

Seyfang, G., & Haxeltine, A. (2012). Growing grassroots innovations: Exploring the role of community-based initiatives in governing sustainable energy transitions. *Environment and Planning C: Government and Policy, 30*, 381–400. https://doi.org/10.1068/c10222.

Smith, A., Hargreaves, T., Hielscher, S., Martiskainen, M., & Seyfang, G. (2016). Making the most of community energies: Three perspectives on grassroots innovation. *Environment and Planning A: Economy and Space, 48*, 407–432. https://doi.org/10.1177/0308518X15597908.

Smith, A., Voß, J. P., & Grin, J. (2010). Innovation studies and sustainability transitions: The allure of the multi-level perspective and its challenges. *Research Policy, 39*(4), 435–448. https://doi.org/10.1016/j.respol.2010.01.023.

Springmann, M., Clark, M., Mason-D'Croz, D., Wiebe, K., Bodirsky, B. L., Lassaletta, L., ..., Willett, W. (2018). Options for keeping the food system within environmental limits. *Nature, 562*, 519–525. https://doi.org/10.1038/s41586-018-0594-0.

Stefani, G., Romano, D., & Cei, L. (2017). Grass root collective action for territorially integrated food supply chains: A case study from Tuscany. *International Journal of Food System Dynamics, 8*(4), 347–362. https://doi.org/10.18461/ijfsd.v8i4.847.

UNEP-DTIE. Sustainable Consumption and Production Branch. (2015). *Cities and buildings*.

Swilling, M., Hajer, M., Baynes, T., Bergesen, J., Labbé, F., Musango, J. K., ..., Tabory, S. (2018). *The weight of cities: Resource requirements of future urbanization*. Nairobi: UN Environment—International Resource Panel.

Tornaghi, C. (2014). Critical geography of urban agriculture. *Progress in Human Geography, 38*, 551–567. https://doi.org/10.1177/0309132513512542.

UNEP. (2011). *Decoupling natural resource use and environmental impacts from economic growth*. Nairobi: International Resource Panel.

UN-Habitat. (2016). *World Cities Report 2016; Urbanization and Development*. Nairobi, Kenya: UN-Habitat.

United Nations. (2015). *United Nations General Assembly Resolution A/Res/70/1: Transforming our world: The 2030 Agenda for Sustainable Development*. Resolution adopted by the General Assembly on 25 September 2015.

Van Oers, L. M., Boon, W. P. C., & Moors, E. H. M. (2018). The creation of legitimacy in grassroots organisations: A study of Dutch community supported agriculture. *Environmental Innovation and Societal Transitions, 29,* 55–67. https://doi.org/10.1016/J.EIST.2018.04.002.

Velenturf, A. P. M., Archer, S. A., Gomes, H. I., Christgen, B., Lag-Brotons, A. J., & Purnell, P. (2019). Circular economy and the matter of integrated resources. *Science of the Total Environment, 689,* 963–969. https://doi.org/10.1016/j.scitotenv.2019.06.449.

Wilson, C., Grubler, A., Bento, N., Healey, S., De Stercke, S., & Zimm, C. (2020). Granular technologies to accelerate decarbonization. *Science, 80*(368), 36–39. https://doi.org/10.1126/science.aaz8060.

Wolfram, M. (2018). Cities shaping grassroots niches for sustainability transitions: Conceptual reflections and an exploratory case study. *Journal of Cleaner Production, 173,* 11–23. https://doi.org/10.1016/j.jclepro.2016.08.044.

Ziskind, J., & Guna, D. (2018). *Circular economy in cities: Evolving the model for a sustainable urban future* (World Economic Forum White Paper).

CHAPTER 6

Taking Animals Out of Meat: Meat Industries and the Rise of Meat Alternatives

Malte B. Rödl

Introduction

Meat is a central element of many diets (e.g., Yates & Warde, 2015) and dining cultures (e.g., Joy, 2009). In western societies, it has grown from a luxury food to be enjoyed once a week to a staple food that essentially identifies a 'good' meal (e.g., Murcott, 1982; Smil, 2002). On a global level, meat consumption is similarly identified with luxury and it has been suggested that it has grown with the increasing level of global affluence (e.g., Machovina, Feeley, & Ripple, 2015; Smil, 2002). Although in many places extensive agriculture is still traditionally practiced—and is often the only means for farmers to save up or live off their land—a major portion of global meat production originates from intensive landless or mixed agriculture (Steinfeld et al., 2006). For this, fodder crops are grown, shipped, and fed to animals; they often originate from heavily fertilised agriculture, are mostly genetically modified crops, and are increasingly grown on newly claimed arable land, such as rain forests (Steinfeld et al., 2006).

M. B. Rödl (✉)
Sustainable Consumption Institute, University of Manchester, Manchester, UK
e-mail: malte.roedl@manchester.ac.uk

R. Bali Swain and S. Sweet (eds.), *Sustainable Consumption and Production, Volume II*,
https://doi.org/10.1007/978-3-030-55285-5_6

Rearing non-human animals for food has been identified as a major greenhouse gas emitter and thus contributor to anthropogenic climate change; it has also been identified as a major driver of local environmental issues such as deforestation or eutrophication (e.g., Nijdam, Rood, & Westhoek, 2012; Steinfeld et al., 2006). Furthermore, evidence has emerged that red and processed meats can cause cancer, heart disease, and other major impairments to human health (e.g., Battaglia Richi et al., 2015; Bouvard et al., 2015). Beyond these practical criticisms, there are objections to animal agriculture because of the conditions under which animals are raised, killed, and processed—or because people reject the idea of eating animals altogether (e.g., Armstrong & Botzler, 2016; Ruby, 2012; Verbeke & Viaene, 2000).

However, there are attempts to make animal agriculture and thus the production of meat more sustainable, ethical, or healthy: For example, a switch from intensive to extensive agriculture such as grass-feeding is suggested; but the efficacy of this depends on the underlying assumptions and local circumstances, as well as the sustainability indicators that one might look at (e.g., Haas, Wetterich, & Köpke, 2001; Nijdam et al., 2012; Tsutsumi, Ono, Ogasawara, & Hojito, 2018). Since ruminants are specifically responsible for high methane emissions because of belching, research is also concerned with the impact on emissions of various fodder mixes (e.g., Beauchemin & McGinn, 2006; Nkrumah et al., 2006). These attempts are nonetheless limited by conversion losses occurring through rearing animals: They have to grow, move, and keep up their body temperature, thereby reducing the productivity of any input such as fodder crops. It has been estimated that cattle need 36 kg of fodder for 1 kg of edible weight, whilst pigs need 9 kg, and poultry 4.2 kg per kg edible weight (Shepon, Eshel, Noor, & Milo, 2016). Although not all fodder would typically be consumed by humans, animal agriculture thus 'refines' one agricultural output to another at significant conversion losses.[1]

Parallel to the growing awareness about the negative externalities or side effects of animal agriculture, in the last three decades, some western

[1] Note that extensive agriculture may happen in regions that are otherwise deemed unsuitable for crops for economic reasons. This is often tied to geography, soil quality, labour, or transport costs (see e.g. Audsley et al., 2006; Garnett, 2011), and may be differently advantageous for the global climate and local ecosystems (e.g. Nijdam et al., 2012).

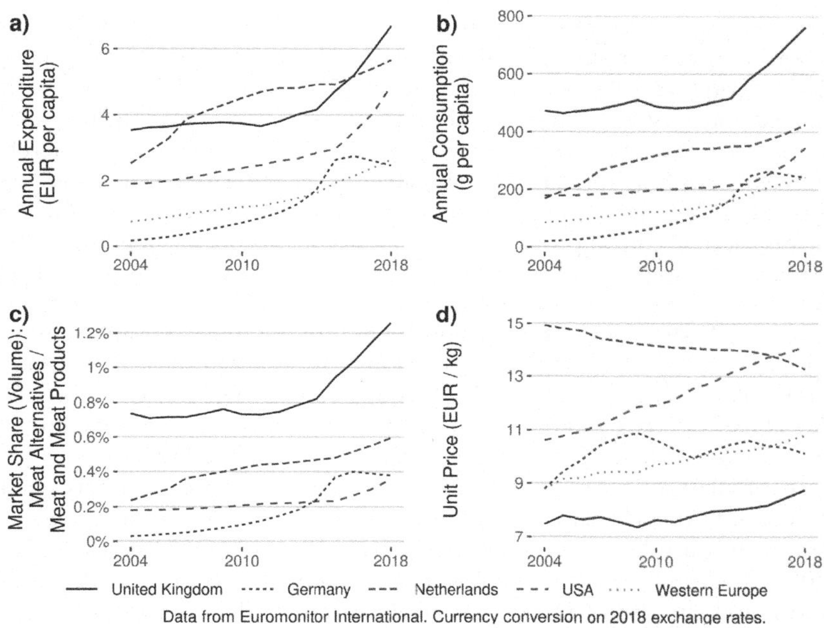

Fig. 6.1 Comparison of the markets for plant-based meat alternatives in UK, US, Germany, the Netherlands, and Western Europe. (a) annual expenditure per capita (based on Retail Service Price); (b) annual capita consumption (based on sold volume); (c) market value of sold meat alternatives relative to total volume of fresh and processed meats (including meat alternatives; no data for western Europe); (d) unit price of meat alternatives. All currencies were converted using 2018 exchange rates (*Source* Author's creation based on data from Euromonitor International, 2018a)

societies have seen the rise of plant-based meat alternatives (Rödl, 2019b, and Fig. 6.1)—a practice which has been established for many centuries in, for example East Asian cuisine through the use of tofu or seitan (Shurtleff & Aoyagi, 2014). Different from eating pulses or legumes directly,[2] meat alternatives are foodstuffs made to smell, look, and/or

[2] Legumes are said to be even better for the environment (cf. Clune, Crossin, & Verghese, 2017; Mejia et al., 2019), but are usually not understood to be 'meat alternatives' through their lacking similarity to meat (cf. Shurtleff & Aoyagi, 2014).

taste like meat to fulfil similar functions in diets (e.g., Hoek, van Boekel, Voordouw, & Luning, 2011; Rödl, 2019a; Shprintzen, 2012; Wild et al., 2014; Zorpette, 2013). From around 2015, global attention from both people and businesses to such products has increased, leading to rising sales and investments (e.g., CB Insights, 2017). And whilst still in development or not as ubiquitously available, other 'alternative proteins' are attracting interest. This covers, for example convenience products made from insects or algae protein, or animal tissue grown in cell cultures for human consumption (the latter is often called 'in-vitro meat' or 'cultured meat', e.g., CB Insights, 2017; Chiles, 2013; Sexton, Garnett, & Lorimer, 2019). All these new approaches promise more sustainable ways to eat 'meat'—even though some tensions remain about the ethics of such undertakings (e.g., Dilworth & McGregor, 2015; Gjerris, Gamborg, & Röcklinsberg, 2016), and how much animal is still needed for cell cultures to grow in the long term (Sexton, 2018; Stephens et al., 2018).

Regardless of these trends and stagnation in certain markets such as the UK or Germany, the global demand for meat is still growing, especially outside of developing countries (Euromonitor International, 2018b). Considering the increasing environmental awareness and pressures, and the rise of meat alternatives as nearly identical products, the question that arises is whether this poses a threat to, or an opportunity for, meat industries. Whilst meat alternatives can indeed be more sustainable than their model counterparts, I will argue that this expansion into meat alternatives is a coherent step within the industrialisation of the food system.

In the following section, I review the current state of plant-based meat alternatives taking the example of the UK—one of the most advanced markets for such products. Thereafter, the sustainability performance and resource efficiency of meat alternatives as compared to meat are discussed. Finally, I review the literature and evidence regarding meat industries' existing and potential involvement in meat alternatives from an economic and marketing perspective. The chapter closes with a summary of the reviewed evidence, and a cautionary note on the sustainability of a large-scale shift to meat alternatives.

What Are Meat Alternatives?

Plant-based meat alternatives, originally based on nuts or wheat gluten, have been available to western vegetarians since the late nineteenth century. They were understood as a convenient way to motivate meat eaters to adopt a meat-free diet—for example, for health or ethical/political reasons—as they facilitate dietary change without requiring a substantive change in food practices (e.g., Gregory, 2002; Shprintzen, 2012). Such products were particularly prominent in wartime when motivated by food or meat scarcity, or when in the 1960s and 1970s, worries emerged that a growing world population could not continue eating so much meat. In both these cases of perceived and/or actual scarcity, alternatives to meat were suggested as a palatable and protein-rich replacement for meat, as they generally require less land and other resources (Rödl, 2019b). Over the last few decades, meat alternatives have become popular with vegetarians and vegans. This was originally not motivated by ideas of scarcity, but by growing health and ethical concerns arising from an increasing intensification of animal agriculture (e.g., Beardsworth & Bryman, 2004). Through increasing awareness of the climate crisis, the notion of 'scarcity' found its way back into the motivations to reduce meat consumption, making meat alternatives a tool to achieve such change. In the 2010s, the increasing reduction of meat and dairy consumption (or the intention thereof) was thus motivated by health, environmental, or ethical reasons (e.g., Mintel, 2017, cf. 2004). With this growing consumer interest, alternatives to meat increasingly became attractive to global investors including traditional meat industries (e.g., CB Insights, 2017). The alternatives to meat that most commonly attract investment are improvements to already realised plant-based protein products, as well as still developed foods such as cultured meat or insect-based protein (e.g., Sexton, 2018). Specifically for cultured meat, it has been suggested that these could be seen as part of a historical process in which eating meat is increasingly detached from the animals they originate from (Buscemi, 2014).

Recent Market Developments (in the UK)

In many western countries, meat alternatives have been growing in popularity over the last decade. In some countries such as the UK or the Netherlands, this popularity increased from a high level, whereas in

Germany, a market emerged only recently (see Fig. 6.1). In the western world, the UK is the second largest marketplace for meat alternatives (after the US) in terms of sales and volume, with an estimated market value of £393 m in 2018. Based on retail volume, the average annual per capita consumption in 2018 was £5.93 (third after Israel and Sweden) or 764 g (second after New Zealand, Euromonitor International, 2018a). Using consumption-level data, Kantar Worldpanel (2016) estimated an average annual purchase of 4 kg for those households consuming meat alternatives in the first place. At £7–10 per kilo, prices of meat alternatives in the UK are roughly similar to those of meat, whilst some brands sell well below this price (Euromonitor International, 2017; Kantar Worldpanel, 2016).

Mintel (2018) has predicted that value sales for meat alternatives may grow by 44% between 2018 and 2023; nonetheless, meat alternatives made up only 1.2% of the total volume of meat products by weight (Euromonitor International, 2018a). Market research by Kantar Worldpanel (2016) suggests that increases in market value are related to both existing consumers buying more, and new consumers starting to buy meat alternatives. The general acceptance of meat alternatives in the UK is high—in research by Mintel (2018), 56% of respondents had eaten meat alternatives at least once in the six months preceding the survey. They also found that market-leading brand Quorn was consumed by 20% of respondents on a weekly or even more frequent basis.

Depending on the study, it is estimated that in the UK there are 3 to 13% vegetarians and vegans (The Vegan Society, 2016; Waitrose & Partners, 2018). These populations are more often young and/or female, with 25% of women between 16 and 24 not consuming meat (Mintel, 2017). The same consumer groups—vegetarians and vegans on the one hand, and the young and/or women on the other—were for long the primary consumers of meat alternatives (Hoek, Luning, Stafleu, & de Graaf, 2004; Mintel, 2013). However, according to Kantar Worldpanel (2016), in 2016, half of all meat alternatives were consumed by meat reducers. The proportion of meat reducers has increased from around 13% in 2004 to 28% in 2017, with another 17% now planning to decrease their meat consumption (Mintel, 2004, 2017). Meat reducers are most commonly motivated by concerns over health and weight management; vegetarians and vegans also frequently mention environmental and ethical reasons, as well as concerns about food quality and safety (Mintel, 2017; see also Izmirli & Phillips, 2011; Tobler, Visschers, & Siegrist, 2011).

Other reasons for the substitution of meat with meat alternatives are costs, concerns about the social acceptance of their own diet when meat is cut out, and meat alternatives as a transition aid to become vegetarian (Euromonitor International, 2017; Mintel, 2004, 2006, 2017).

Sustainability of Meat Alternatives

Conventional plant-based meat alternatives are usually based on protein crops. Feed such as peas or soybeans are harvested and, instead of feeding the crop to animals, protein is isolated or they are ground to flour, an emulsion is made, and a meat-like texture extruded, spun, or sheared (e.g., Davies & Lightowler, 1998; see also Krintiras, Gadea Diaz, van der Goot, Stankiewicz, & Stefanidis, 2016). Other available meat alternatives are based on 'single-cell protein' (Ugalde & Castrillo, 2002), such as the mycoprotein-based brand Quorn. For this, some feed is used to grow fungi (or other single-cellular organisms) in large fermentation vessels. The fibrous structures of the output are then aligned and stuck together, and can equally serve as a meat alternative. This feed might be a starch, which is a byproduct of producing wheat gluten, or some other carbohydrate (e.g., Davies & Lightowler, 1998; Trinci, 1992). Notably, since these single-cellular organisms are usually not considered food safe from the outset, lengthy certification processes might be needed to approve the products as a safe food (cf. Sadler, 1988).

Although some existing meat alternatives are based on or include milk protein, or use egg as a binder (e.g., Davies & Lightowler, 1998), a majority of the products are based on non-animal protein sources. Despite some ongoing use of animal products in otherwise plant-based meat alternatives, a majority of the meat alternatives available in supermarkets today require significantly less 'animal' than traditional meat products. Thus, there is a reduced need for growing animal organisms which, as discussed above, leads among others to excessive land use through grazing or producing fodder, and high carbon footprints through rumination and inefficient food conversion (e.g., Nijdam et al., 2012; Pimentel & Pimentel, 2003; Shepon et al., 2016).

Soy, an important ingredient in many meat alternatives, has been specifically criticised for its role in deforestation and other environmental issues. However, only 2% of the global soy harvest is used as flour or isolates—which is used for many processed meat alternatives—and another 6% is used for direct human consumption, largely in East Asia (e.g., plain, as tofu or tempeh). The remaining global harvest is used as fodder, to extract oil, or as fuel (WWF, 2014).

Other alternative proteins have been suggested to be similarly beneficial for the environment, although their use of animals is different. The growing of insects as a protein source relies inherently on animals; this causes different ethical, environmental, and social issues, but insects are nonetheless regarded as an alternative to traditional animal husbandry (e.g., Gjerris et al., 2016; House, 2019; Verbeke, 2015). Insects still need to be reared, fed, killed, ground up, and extruded. Yet, similar to single-cell protein, the feedstock does not need to be a protein source itself, thereby offering opportunities to use by-products of the food industry, such as beet pulp or manure—and even municipal organic waste may be used as feed for insects (Smetana, Palanisamy, Mathys, & Heinz, 2016).

For cultured meat too, animals are involved as stem cells of animals are required to grow meat. Furthermore, uncertainties persist on precise processes; it is yet unclear whether bovine muscle tissue, for example, can profitably be grown without foetal calf serum, which originates from animals (Butler, 2015). The identification of alternative sustainable, affordable, and animal-free growth media and their large-scale production is seen as one of the major challenges for cultured meat production (Stephens et al., 2018). However, as opposed to the previous technologies, cultured meat provides genuine animal muscle tissue, but without the animal organism.

Regarding the overall carbon intensity of plant-based meat alternatives, a median CO_2 footprint of 2.19 kg CO_2-eq/kg product has been estimated on data from three different factories (Mejia et al., 2019). This ranks similar to fruit and vegetables grown in heated greenhouses (2.13 kg CO_2-eq/kg) or rice (2.55), and is around a third better than animal products such as eggs (3.46), fish (3.49), or chicken (3.65)—but is considerably worse than dairy milk (1.29; all values are median values from across the food life cycle assessment literature collated by Clune et al., 2017). Looking at overall environmental footprints, it has also been suggested that apart from cultured meat, most meat alternatives (including those based on insects, soy, gluten, or mycoprotein) have a roughly equivalent or better overall environmental footprint than chicken. These values and precise rankings differ slightly depending on whether the focus is on digestible protein output or final product weight (Smetana, Mathys, Knoch, & Heinz, 2015). For cultured meat, it has been suggested that reliable data can only be presented on the basis of established production methods rather than experimental laboratory work, but it is generally assumed that land use would be much lower than for conventional meat, whilst industrial energy would be substantially greater (Mattick et al., 2015).

From a pure carbon-accounting and land-use perspective, replacing meat with meat alternatives is thus a reasonable choice. Benefits for the global climate may specifically arise when compared to ruminant meat (i.e. beef and lamb) and, to a lesser degree, to shrimp, pork, chicken, and some fish. It needs to be noted though, that compared to plain grains, vegetables, nuts, legumes, and other non-processed products, the environmental footprints of non-animal meats may be considerably worse (cf. Clune et al., 2017). Also, some other impacts and side effects of intensive animal agriculture, such as eutrophication or deforestation, may be eradicated through the removal of animal organisms from 'meat' (cf. Steinfeld et al., 2006).

Meat Alternatives as a Business Case

Plant-based meat alternatives have been available for a long time from smaller and specialised companies. But the global meat industries have only recently started investing in these alternatives on a larger scale, given their economic potential. Large agro-food companies including the US meat processor Tyson Foods, and food multinational Nestlé are increasingly investing in the market—either by own product developments or through investments in emerging companies as consumer demand is continuously increasing (e.g., CB Insights, 2017; Hartman, 2018). In the following sections, I will argue that there is a continuation of existing business for the meat industries, first, on the basis of increasing industrialisation of agriculture providing economic opportunities, and second, because of existing symbolic capital among those consumer groups which switch to more plant-based diets. For this argument to be valid, I have assumed, based on existing literature, that all 'meats' regardless of ingredients are close or similar substitutes to each other (e.g., Rödl, 2019a; Sexton et al., 2019).

Production and Supply Chains

Companies strive towards less risk and more profits. For agricultural industries in particular, with their dependence on crop yields and price variability, risk management is an important factor to maintain profitability (Just, 1975). Accordingly, Goodman, Sorj, and Wilkinson (1987) argue that agriculture is a production process bound by nature in its abilities and limitations of growth of organisms, and thereby subject to all uncertainties and inefficiencies of biological systems. This distinguishes agricultural industries from other industrial processes. According to the authors, two major risk management and profit maximisation strategies in the 'agri-industrial complex' are *appropriationism* and *substitutionism*. An expansion of animal-based meat industries to non-animal-based counterparts can suitably be analysed in these terms.

Appropriationism reduces 'the importance of nature in rural production' (1987: 3), so that the context of production is increasingly technologised in order to achieve higher productivity. This covers, for example, the use of tractors instead of horses, greenhouses instead of open fields, or mechanised instead of manual slaughtering. In all these cases, nature and its (seasonal) growth cycles remain the foundation of the production process.

Conversely, substitutionism describes the 'eliminat[ion of] the rural product' (1987: 4), thereby bypassing the limitation of growth itself. This covers clothing based on polyester instead of natural fibres (i.e. nylon instead of cotton or silk), synthetic instead of natural fertiliser, or the growth of single-cell protein (SCP) in fermentation vessels instead of growing protein crops. In these cases, the immediate natural source of the product is eliminated whilst other carbon molecules such as oil, gas, or starches take its place.

In both cases, limitations of nature are overcome: agricultural productivity is increased through mechanisation in the one case, and made obsolete in the other. As risk is reduced and resource efficiency increased, the overall operations promise more profit whilst minimising uncertainty. Goodman et al. (1987) see this process as a fundamental development of the agro-industrial complex as they increase capital accumulation.

Although some rural product is still required to produce alternatives to meat as outlined in the previous sections, animal metabolism and its growth is skipped as part of the ongoing development process. All risks of rearing animals, in a somewhat controlled natural environment such as stables and pastures, can be overcome through the use of meat alternatives; these environments include laboratories or clean rooms, factories, extruders, or fermentation vessels. However, in some cases the metabolism of livestock is replaced with that of other animals such as

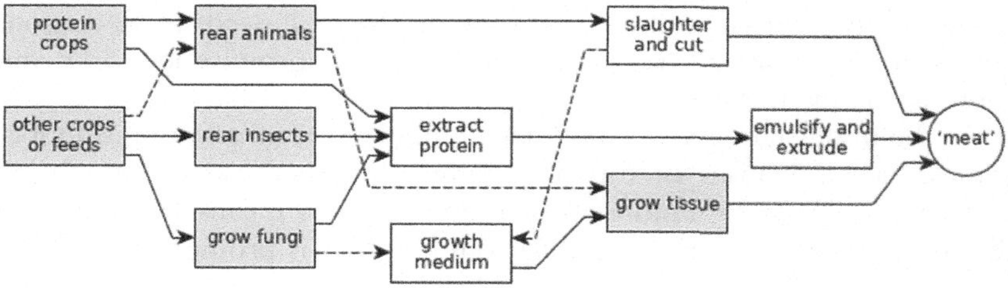

Fig. 6.2 Simplified visualisation of processes to produce conventional and alternative 'meat'. The coloured boxes involve organisms; dashed lines indicate considerably low or uncertain flows (*Source* Author's creation)

insects, with other cells such as fungi, or with cell cultures outside of a host animal. Compared to mammals or birds however, these metabolisms are still more efficient. A simplified account of the different uses of organisms and technology is displayed in Fig. 6.2.

In all of these cases, a rural product is still required as feed for the machines or cultures that make the textures we term 'meat alternatives' or 'alternative proteins'. Yet, the animal organism is ***substituted*** with technical equipment, thus lowering the risk and, in some way or another, overcome the barriers of animal metabolisms. Furthermore, through the domestication of fungus cultures or insects, some limitations of proteinaceous crops can be overcome—these feedstocks and their strain on soils can be substituted further, thereby using these single-cellular organisms or insects to refine certain agricultural or domestic outputs or 'waste streams' into protein matter (e.g., Smetana et al., 2016; Ugalde & Castrillo, 2002). In the case of cultured meat, cells are taken out of their context in the animal organism, which is replaced with petri dishes in sterile environments. Although in their conclusion, Goodman et al. understand tissue cultures as substitutionism (1987: 186), cultured meat is currently still constrained by 'nature' through the growing of (albeit disembodied) cells and the need to have an animal-derived growth serum (cf. Stephens et al., 2018).

As elaborated earlier, alternatives to meat are likely better for the environment than red meat; and compared to poultry, alternatives might be on par or slightly advantageous (Mejia et al., 2019; Smetana et al., 2015; cf. Clune et al., 2017). This means these products should also be more economical because less input and less land is used to produce a similar output—albeit for some alternative proteins, this still needs to be demonstrated at larger scales. Alternatives to meat thus promise less risky and more profitable business.

In the understanding of Goodman et al. (1987), substitutionism especially is a mechanism of capital accumulation, because investment in technology allows for a more efficient and less risky means of production for the same or a sufficiently similar output. This is promising for larger corporations, but excludes small-hold farmers who may lack the necessary capital and/or (access to) intellectual property (cf. Pechlaner, 2010); in turn, this might further centralise the agricultural and the meat industries, and farmers may be forced to alter their production methods due to cheaper competitor 'meat'. Of course, this presumes that these 'meat' products are identified as sufficiently similar by the target audiences to allow for seamless substitution, which will be elaborated in the following section.

Marketing and Consumers

Traditionally, most plant-based meat alternatives were manufactured by small businesses, often unrelated to meat industries.[3] However, the recent conjuncture of societal and environmental pressures has made meat alternatives increasingly popular among consumers, and thus created some interest by established companies. Previous literature suggests that this is commonly the case for sustainable business practices or sustainable innovations: the success of new market entrants motivates incumbents to follow up on such initiatives, which due to their influence and reach is often much more successful (Hockerts & Wüstenhagen, 2010). Through contagion within the market place, this may lead to even more competitors joining (Debruyne & Reibstein, 2005). Another strategy for incumbents to manage the threat of competing innovation in the market place is the investment of venture capital (e.g., Teppo & Wüstenhagen, 2009), which can also be observed in the market for alternative proteins (e.g., CB Insights, 2017).

Although incumbent actors are rarely found to take initiative regarding sustainability improvements, their established capital, including social, symbolic, and financial capital, makes it easier for them to catch up

[3] Note however, that some businesses may be part of food corporations. For example, Quorn was founded by a leading bread manufacturer in the UK (see Trinci, 1992).

with external developments (cf. Hockerts & Wüstenhagen, 2010). The remainder of this section will review the importance of the incumbents' capital with the example of Rügenwalder Mühle, a well-known German poultry processor and manufacturer of cold cuts. The brand joined the meat-free market in 2014, and five years later, a third of its revenue originated from meat-free produce (PETA Deutschland, 2019). Justifying why Rügenwalder Mühle produces meat-free meats, the FAQ on their website says:

> We welcome a varied and nutritional-physiologically balanced diet. Meat is still an important component—but not a must. More and more people in Germany live on a flexitarian diet, i.e., they eat meat and sausage at meals less frequently. For this reason, we offer our customers tasty meaty and vegetarian products, which are in the sense of a conscious diet. (Rügenwalder Mühle, n.d.-b)

Here, the company asserts that it is progressive and has acknowledged (but not affirmed) a zeitgeist in which excessive meat consumption is not environmentally affordable anymore. This may be understood as a strategy for corporate social responsibility, fostering consumer trust and brand identification even among those customers who do not normally choose animal-based meat products. Going beyond acknowledgement of trends, an earlier version of the company's German FAQ seemed to affirm food trends:

> We are the first and simultaneously last generation which has meat on their plates daily, ... [so that] on the long run, the global population cannot be fed with our current diets. This is why alternatives should be considered which are tasty and nutritionally valuable. (Rügenwalder Mühle, n.d.-a, translated by the author)

These sections have now disappeared from their FAQ, possibly recognising that this goes against their traditional business interests. Thus, in the recent version of the FAQ, the responsibility to argue for dietary change is outsourced to 'political consumers' (Ehgartner, 2018). In my earlier work based on interviews with manufacturers of meat alternatives, I identified similar patterns of outsourced individual consumer responsibility (Rödl, 2019a)—on the one hand, self-identified 'food activist' companies saw their mission as making changing diets more convenient for consumers enabling them in the first place through meat-free offerings; on the other hand, interviewees of more business-minded companies made clear that they were reactive to consumer demand by offering 'better' choices without relating this to dietary change. Rügenwalder Mühle clearly fits into the second category, as they refer to inadequate choice in the market:

> If anyone has the competence to produce vegetarian alternatives so that they taste like meat and sausage, then it should be us. (Rügenwalder Mühle, n.d.-b)

Here, the company invokes its established symbolic capital in the form of brand trust. This trust relies on the company targeting the same audiences, using the same brand, and manufacturing the 'same' products—just based on different agricultural outputs. Consumers can thus easily recognise products they have known and possibly eaten for long. Simultaneously, the brand vouches for a certain level of quality, although such expectations may not always be confirmed by all actors (e.g., Stiftung Warentest, 2016, an evaluation and comparison of meat alternatives by a German consumer organisation).

Recent research suggests that the marketing of existing meat and dairy alternatives seeks to appeal to the same social occasions and cultural concepts as their model counterparts, whilst distinguishing products sufficiently to function as alternatives rather than equivalents (Fuentes & Fuentes, 2017; Rödl, 2018, 2019a). Similarly, producer discourses and promises surrounding alternatives to meat have been found to alter notions of 'good' food, which are in line with and surpass what traditional meat can offer (Rödl, 2019a; Sexton, 2018; Sexton et al., 2019). A narrative of progress is thus inherent in these discourses (e.g., Chiles, 2013). For consumers of plant-based meat alternatives, such products can easily fit into the same social and cultural gatherings, thereby providing a sense of continuity and effortless change (e.g., Nath & Prideaux, 2011; Rödl, 2019a).

Even if not the same brands are used, meat businesses may still have advantages from an expansion into animal-free products: their social and financial capital. They can invest more and faster, do not have to convince potential lenders or venture capital of their undertaking, and because of their established relations with retailers, they may also have comparatively easy access to supermarket listings.

Although in some locations insect-based burgers can be bought (e.g., Reuters, 2018), and early versions of cultured meats have been sampled by consumers (e.g., Aymat, 2019), some uncertainties remain for these categories: technologies are still partially unclear (e.g., Mattick et al., 2015; Stephens et al., 2018), and consumer scepticism (Verbeke, 2015; Verbeke et al., 2015) and regulatory challenges persist (Halloran, Vantomme, Hanboonsong, & Ekesi, 2015; Johnson, 2018). Thus, whilst similar observations to plant-based meat alternatives can likely be made, there are no prominent references yet.

Conclusion

In the UK, overall consumption of animal and plant-based meats declined from around 66 kg per capita in 2010 to 60 kg in 2018; over the same period, the share of meat alternatives by volume increased from 0.7 to 1.2% (Euromonitor International, 2018a). Whilst these trends may not last and may not scale globally, the increasing interest in consuming less or no animals, together with potential environmental regulation, poses a risk to established meat industries. Although they may continue to grow through animal-based meats alone, it has been argued in this chapter that incumbents of the global meat industry can make profits and strengthen their businesses through non-animal meats. It has specifically been argued that first, replacing animals with more mechanised means of producing 'meat' is in line with historic trends of agro-industrial development as it reduces risks and increases profits whilst also serving capital accumulation; and second, existing social, symbolic, and financial capital enables these organisations to be key agents for large-scale sustainability change.

Taking a step back, it may be debated whether remaking meat is a reasonable strategy to engage with the emerging sustainability issues: These technological replacements of animal meat are a means of capital accumulation, and thereby have the potential of further centralisation. This may push small-hold and livestock farmers out of the market. The emergence of biodiversity issues such as the disappearance of traditional, regional livestock breeds or diverse ranges of legumes are equally plausible. Furthermore, non-animal alternatives to meat are considered a highly processed food with the attached negative image[4]; and whilst

[4] It may be argued that many animal-based meats are also highly processed foods, such as chemically cured meats based on animals from intensive farming.

plant-based meat alternatives have been found to be more healthy than animal meats (Sadler, 2004), diets free from animal meats may lack micronutrients which is not explicitly addressed by available meat alternatives (Seves, Verkaik-Kloosterman, Biesbroek, & Temme, 2017). It has also been argued previously that alternatives to meat further normalise the cultural and social concept of meat eating and thereby invisibilise or stigmatise other ways of eating (Rödl, 2019a); in this way, they would allow humanity to continue ignoring the moral injustice of industrial animal agriculture (Bramble, 2017).

Taking all things into account, alternatives to meat can be described as a technological fix to the sustainability issues associated with intensive animal agriculture; this technology is a profitable investment for existing agro-food industries and thus will not substantially alter the food system but only aid its further centralisation. Any alternative solutions to the meat crisis—such as a voluntary reduction in meat consumption or different governance systems to achieve that (Aleksandrowicz, Green, Joy, Smith, & Haines, 2016; Tilman & Clark, 2014; Vinnari & Tapio, 2012)—would require us to change what we eat, and would thus be considerably more difficult to achieve.

Acknowledgements The research presented in this article is based on work conducted with financial support of the Sustainable Consumption Institute's studentship. The funding had no impact on the views expressed in this work. I am grateful for the helpful comments made by the editors of this book, the reviewer and other participants at the book workshop, as well as my colleagues Ulrike Ehgartner, Shashwat Pande, and Godwin Chukwukelu.

References

Aleksandrowicz, L., Green, R., Joy, E. J., Smith, P., & Haines, A. (2016). The impacts of dietary change on greenhouse gas emissions, land use, water use, and health: A systematic review. *PLOS One, 11*(11), e0165797.

Armstrong, S. J., & Botzler, R. G. (Eds.). (2016). *The animal ethics reader*. London, UK: Routledge.

Audsley, E., Pearn, K. R., Simota, C., Cojocaru, G., Koutsidou, E., Rounsevell, M. D. A., … Alexandrov, V. 2006. What can scenario modelling tell us about future European scale agricultural land use, and what not? *Environmental Science & Policy*, *9*(2), 148–162.

Aymat, E. (2019, February 19). *SF Startup's lab-grown chicken nugget passes taste test*. https://sanfrancisco.cbslocal.com/2019/02/19/sf-startups-lab-grown-chicken-nugget-passes-taste-test/. Accessed 1 September 2019.

Battaglia Richi, E., Baumer, B., Conrad, B., Darioli, R., Schmid, A., & Keller, U. (2015). Health risks associated with meat consumption: A review of epidemiological studies. *International Journal for Vitamin and Nutrition Research, 85*(1–2), 70–78.

Beardsworth, A., & Bryman, A. (2004). Meat consumption and meat avoidance among young people: An 11-year longitudinal study. *British Food Journal, 106*(4), 313–327.

Beauchemin, K. A., & McGinn, S. M. (2006). Methane emissions from beef cattle: Effects of fumaric acid, essential oil, and canola oil. *Journal of Animal Science, 84*(6), 1489–1496.

Bouvard, V., Loomis, D., Guyton, K. Z., Grosse, Y., El Ghissassi, F., Benbrahim-Tallaa, L., ... Straif, K. 2015. Carcinogenicity of consumption of red and processed meat. *The Lancet Oncology, 16*(16), 1599–1600.

Bramble, B. (2017, December 14). Lab-grown meat could let humanity ignore a serious moral failing. *The Conversation*. http://theconversation.com/lab-grown-meat-could-let-humanity-ignore-a-serious-moral-failing-88909. Accessed 22 March 2019.

Buscemi, F. (2014). From killing cows to culturing meat. *British Food Journal, 116*(6), 952–964.

Butler, M. (2015). Serum and protein free media. In Mohamed Al-Rubeai (Ed.), *Animal cell culture* (pp. 223–236). London, UK: Springer.

CB Insights. (2017, November 9). Our meatless future: How The $90B global meat market gets disrupted. *CB Insights Research*. https://www.cbinsights.com/research/future-of-meat-industrial-farming/. Accessed 7 January 2019.

Chiles, R. M. (2013). If they come, we will build it: In vitro meat and the discursive struggle over future agrofood expectations. *Agriculture and Human Values, 30*(4), 511–523.

Clune, S., Crossin, E., & Verghese, K. (2017). Systematic review of greenhouse gas emissions for different fresh food categories. *Journal of Cleaner Production, 140*, 766–783.

Davies, J., & Lightowler, H. (1998). Plant-based alternatives to meat. *Nutrition & Food Science, 98*(2), 90–94.

Debruyne, M., & Reibstein, D. J. (2005). Competitor see, competitor do: Incumbent entry in new market niches. *Marketing Science, 24*(1), 55–66.

Dilworth, T., & McGregor, A. (2015). Moral steaks? Ethical discourses of in vitro meat in academia and Australia. *Journal of Agricultural and Environmental Ethics, 28*(1), 85–107.

Ehgartner, U. (2018). Discourses of the food retail industry: Changing understandings of "the consumer" and strategies for sustainability. *Sustainable Production and Consumption, 16*, 154–161.

Euromonitor International. (2017). *Plant-based protein: Assessing demand for sustainable alternatives* (Briefing).
Euromonitor International. (2018a). *Euromonitor statistics for the categories: Free from meat, meat, processed meat and seafood* (Database). Euromonitor International.
Euromonitor International. (2018b). *Global overview of agriculture* (Briefing).
Fuentes, C., & Fuentes, M. (2017). Making a market for alternatives: Marketing devices and the qualification of a vegan milk substitute. *Journal of Marketing Management, 33*(7–8), 529–555.
Garnett, T. (2011). Where are the best opportunities for reducing greenhouse gas emissions in the food system (including the food chain)? *Food Policy, 36*(Supplement 1), S23–S32.
Gjerris, M., Gamborg, C., & Röcklinsberg, H. (2016). Ethical aspects of insect production for food and feed. *Journal of Insects as Food and Feed, 2*(2), 101–110.
Goodman, D., Sorj, B., & Wilkinson, J. (1987). *From farming to biotechnology: A theory of agro-industrial development*. Oxford and New York: Basil Blackwell.
Gregory, J. R. T. E. (2002). *The vegetarian movement in Britain c. 1840–1901. A study of its development, personel and wider Connections* (Unpublished PhD Dissertation), University of Southampton, Southampton.
Haas, G., Wetterich, F., & Köpke, U. (2001). Comparing intensive, extensified and organic grassland farming in southern Germany by process life cycle assessment. *Agriculture, Ecosystems & Environment, 83*(1), 43–53.
Halloran, A., Vantomme, P., Hanboonsong, Y., & Ekesi, S. (2015). Regulating edible insects: The challenge of addressing food security, nature conservation, and the erosion of traditional food culture. *Food Security, 7*(3), 739–746.
Hartman, L. R. (2018, February 27). A bright future is germinating for alternative proteins. *Food Processing*. https://www.foodprocessing.com/articles/2018/bright-future-for-alternative-proteins/. Accessed 7 January 2019.
Hockerts, K., & Wüstenhagen, R. (2010). Greening Goliaths versus emerging Davids—Theorizing about the role of incumbents and new entrants in sustainable entrepreneurship. *Journal of Business Venturing, 25*(5), 481–492.
Hoek, A. C., Luning, P. A., Stafleu, A., & de Graaf, C. (2004). Food-related lifestyle and health attitudes of Dutch vegetarians, non-vegetarian consumers of meat substitutes, and meat consumers. *Appetite, 42*(3), 265–272.
Hoek, A. C., van Boekel, M. A., Voordouw, J., & Luning, P. A. (2011). Identification of new food alternatives: How do consumers categorize meat and meat substitutes? *Food Quality and Preference, 22*(4), 371–383.
House, J. (2019). Insects are not "the new sushi": Theories of practice and the acceptance of novel foods. *Social and Cultural Geography, 20*(9), 1285–1306.
Izmirli, S., & Phillips, C. J. C. (2011). The relationship between student consumption of animal products and attitudes to animals in Europe and Asia. *British Food Journal, 113*(3), 436–450.

Johnson, W. G. (2018, October 23). Lab-grown seafood and lab-grown meat might end up with different regulations. Thanks, bureaucracy! *Slate Magazine*. https://slate.com/technology/2018/10/lab-grown-meat-seafood-usda-fda-labeling.html. Accessed 17 April 2019.

Joy, M. (2009). *Why we love dogs, eat pigs, and wear cows: An introduction to carnism*. Berkeley, CA; Enfield: Conari Press.

Just, R. E. (1975). Risk aversion under profit maximization. *American Journal of Agricultural Economics, 57*(2), 347.

Kantar Worldpanel. 2016. *The meat reducer* (Custom Market Research).

Krintiras, G. A., Gadea Diaz, J., van der Goot, A. J., Stankiewicz, A. I., & Stefanidis, G. D. (2016). On the use of the Couette Cell technology for large scale production of textured soy-based meat replacers. *Journal of Food Engineering, 169,* 205–213.

Machovina, B., Feeley, K. J., & Ripple, W. J. (2015). Biodiversity conservation: The key is reducing meat consumption. *Science of the Total Environment, 536,* 419–431.

Mattick, C. S., Landis, A. E., Allenby, B. R., & Genovese, N. J. (2015). Anticipatory life cycle analysis of in vitro biomass cultivation for cultured meat production in the United States. *Environmental Science and Technology, 49*(19), 11941–11949.

Mejia, M. A., Fresán, U., Harwatt, H., Oda, K., Uriegas-Mejia, G., & Sabaté, J. (2019, March 28). Life cycle assessment of the production of a large variety of meat analogs by three diverse factories. *Journal of Hunger & Environmental Nutrition*. https://doi.org/10.1080/19320248.2019.1595251.

Mintel. (2004). *Meat-free foods—UK—December 2004* (Market Research). London, UK: Mintel Group.

Mintel. (2006). *Attitudes towards vegetarianism—UK—September 2006* (Market Research). London, UK: Mintel Group.

Mintel. (2013). *Meat-free and Free-from foods—UK—September 2013* (Market Research). London, UK: Mintel Group.

Mintel. (2017). *Meat-free foods—UK—May 2017* (Market Research). London, UK: Mintel Group.

Mintel. (2018). *Meat-free foods—UK—September 2018* (Market Research). London, UK: Mintel Group.

Murcott, A. (1982). On the social significance of the "cooked dinner" in South Wales. *Social Science Information, 21*(4–5), 677–696.

Nath, J., & Prideaux, D. (2011). The civilised burger: Meat alternatives as a conversion aid and social instrument for Australian vegetarians and vegans. *Australian Humanities Review, 51,* 135–151.

Nijdam, D., Rood, T., & Westhoek, H. (2012). The price of protein: Review of land use and carbon footprints from life cycle assessments of animal food products and their substitutes. *Food Policy, 37*(6), 760–770.

Nkrumah, J. D., Okine, E. K., Mathison, G. W., Schmid, K., Li, C., Basarab, J. A., … Moore, S. S. 2006. Relationships of feedlot feed efficiency, performance, and feeding behavior with metabolic rate, methane production, and energy partitioning in beef cattle. *Journal of Animal Science, 84*(1), 145–153.

Pechlaner, G. (2010). The sociology of agriculture in transition: The political economy of agriculture after biotechnology. *The Canadian Journal of Sociology, 35*(2), 243–269.

PETA Deutschland. (2019, July). *Rügenwalder Mühle: Wird der Fleischproduzent bald komplett vegan?* https://www.peta.de/ruegenwalder-muehle-vegan. Accessed 26 July 2019.

Pimentel, D., & Pimentel, M. (2003). Sustainability of meat-based and plant-based diets and the environment. *The American Journal of Clinical Nutrition, 78*(3), 660S–663S.

Reuters. (2018, April 22). Bug appetite: German supermarket sells insect burgers. *The Guardian*. https://www.theguardian.com/world/2018/apr/22/bug-appetite-german-supermarket-sells-burgers-made-from-worms. Accessed 1 September 2019.

Rödl, M. B. (2018). Marketing meat alternatives: Meat myths and their replication in advertising for plant-based meat. In D. Bogueva, D. Marinova, & T. Raphaely (Eds.), *Handbook of research on social marketing and its influence on animal origin food product consumption* (pp. 327–343). Hershey, PA: IGI Global.

Rödl, M. B. (2019a). *Categorising meat alternatives: How dominant meat culture is reproduced and challenged through the making and eating of meat alternatives* (Unpublished PhD Dissertation), University of Manchester, Manchester, UK.

Rödl, M. B. (2019b). What's new? A history of meat alternatives in the UK. In D. Bogueva, D. Marinova, T. Raphaely, & K. Schmidinger (Eds.), *Environmental, health, and business opportunities in the new meat alternatives market* (pp. 202–217). Hershey, PA: IGI Global.

Ruby, M. B. (2012). Vegetarianism. A blossoming field of study. *Appetite, 58*(1), 141–150.

Rügenwalder Mühle. (n.d.-a). FAQ zu vegetarischen Produkten. *FAQ zu vegetarischen Produkten | Rügenwalder Mühle*. http://www.ruegenwalder.de/unsere-produkte/fragen-vegetarisch/. Accessed 4 May 2016.

Rügenwalder Mühle. (n.d.-b). *Frequently asked question*. https://www.ruegenwalder.de/en/faq. Accessed 3 February 2019.

Sadler, M. (1988). Quorn case study: Enhancing the meat alternatives market by capitalizing on the health trend. *Nutrition & Food Science, 88*(3), 9–11.

Sadler, M. J. (2004). Meat alternatives—Market developments and health benefits. *Trends in Food Science & Technology, 15*(5), 250–260.

Seves, S. M., Verkaik-Kloosterman, J., Biesbroek, S., & Temme, E. H. (2017). Are more environmentally sustainable diets with less meat and dairy nutritionally adequate? *Public Health Nutrition, 20*(11), 2050–2062.

Sexton, A. E. (2018). Eating for the post-Anthropocene: Alternative proteins and the biopolitics of edibility. *Transactions of the Institute of British Geographers, 43*(4), 586–600.

Sexton, A. E., Garnett, T., & Lorimer, J. (2019). Framing the future of food: The contested promises of alternative proteins. *Environment and Planning E: Nature and Space, 2*(1), 47–72.

Shepon, A., Eshel, G., Noor, E., & Milo, R. (2016). Energy and protein feed-to-food conversion efficiencies in the US and potential food security gains from dietary changes. *Environmental Research Letters, 11,* 105002.

Shprintzen, A. D. (2012). Looks like meat, smells like meat, tastes like meat: Battle creek, protose and the making of modern American vegetarianism. *Food, Culture & Society, 15*(1), 113–128.

Shurtleff, W., & Aoyagi, A. (2014). *History of meat alternatives (965 CE to 2014): Extensively annotated bibliography and sourcebook.* Lafayette, CA: Soyinfo Centre.

Smetana, S., Mathys, A., Knoch, A., & Heinz, V. (2015). Meat alternatives: Life cycle assessment of most known meat substitutes. *The International Journal of Life Cycle Assessment, 20*(9), 1254–1267.

Smetana, S., Palanisamy, M., Mathys, A., & Heinz, V. (2016). Sustainability of insect use for feed and food: Life Cycle Assessment perspective. *Journal of Cleaner Production, 137,* 741–751.

Smil, V. (2002). Worldwide transformation of diets, burdens of meat production and opportunities for novel food proteins. *Enzyme and Microbial Technology, 30*(3), 305–311.

Steinfeld, H., Gerber, P., Wassenaar, T. D., Castel, V., Rosales M., M., & de Haan, C. 2006. *Livestock's long shadow: Environmental issues and options.* Rome: Food and Agriculture Organization of the United Nations.

Stephens, N., Di Silvio, L., Dunsford, I., Ellis, M., Glencross, A., & Sexton, A. (2018). Bringing cultured meat to market: Technical, socio-political, and regulatory challenges in cellular agriculture. *Trends in Food Science & Technology, 78,* 155–166.

Stiftung Warentest. (2016). Vegetarische Schnitzel & Co - Die besten Alternativen zu Fleisch. *Stiftung Warentest, 2016*(10), 20–29.

Teppo, T., & Wüstenhagen, R. 2009. Why corporate venture capital funds fail–evidence from the European energy industry. *World Review of Entrepreneurship, Management and Sust. Development,* 5(4), 353–357.

The Vegan Society. (2016, May 17). Find out how many vegans are in Great Britain. *The Vegan Society.* https://www.vegansociety.com/whats-new/news/find-out-how-many-vegans-are-great-britain. Accessed 8 March 2018.

Tilman, D., & Clark, M. (2014). Global diets link environmental sustainability and human health. *Nature, 515*(7528), 518–522.

Tobler, C., Visschers, V. H. M., & Siegrist, M. 2011. Eating green. Consumers' willingness to adopt ecological food consumption behaviors. *Appetite, 57*(3), 674–682.

Trinci, A. P. (1992). Myco-protein: A twenty-year overnight success story. *Mycological Research, 96*(1), 1–13.

Tsutsumi, M., Ono, Y., Ogasawara, H., & Hojito, M. (2018). Life-cycle impact assessment of organic and non-organic grass-fed beef production in Japan. *Journal of Cleaner Production, 172,* 2513–2520.

Ugalde, U. O., & Castrillo, J. I. (2002). Single cell proteins from fungi and yeasts. In G. G. Khachatourians & D. K. Arora (Eds.), *Applied Mycology and Biotechnology* (pp. 123–149). Amsterdam, NL: Elsevier.

Verbeke, W. (2015). Profiling consumers who are ready to adopt insects as a meat substitute in a western society. *Food Quality and Preference, 39,* 147–155.

Verbeke, W., Marcu, A., Rutsaert, P., Gaspar, R., Seibt, B., Fletcher, D., & Barnett, J. 2015. "Would you eat cultured meat?": Consumers' reactions and attitude formation in Belgium, Portugal and the United Kingdom. *Meat Science, 102,* 49–58.

Verbeke, W., & Viaene, J. (2000). Ethical challenges for livestock production: Meeting consumer concerns about meat safety and animal welfare. *Journal of Agricultural and Environmental Ethics, 12*(2), 141–151.

Vinnari, M., & Tapio, P. (2012). Sustainability of diets: From concepts to governance. *Ecological Economics, 74,* 46–54.

Waitrose & Partners. (2018). *Food and drink report 2018–2019* (Market Research). https://www.waitrose.com/content/dam/waitrose/Inspiration/Waitrose%20&%20Partners%20Food%20and%20Drink%20Report%202018.pdf. Accessed 5 March 2019.

Wild, F., Czerny, M., Janssen, A. M., Kole, A. P., Zunabovic, M., & Domig, K. J. (2014). The evolution of a plant-based alternative to meat. *Agro Food Industry Hi-Tech, 25(*1), 45–49.

WWF. (2014). *The growth of soy: Impacts and solutions*. Gland, Switzerland: WWF International.

Yates, L., & Warde, A. (2015). The evolving content of meals in Great Britain. Results of a survey in 2012 in comparison with the 1950s. *Appetite, 84,* 299–308.

Zorpette, G. (2013). Muscling out meat. *IEEE Spectrum, 50*(6), 64–70.

CHAPTER 7

Agencing Sustainable Food Consumers: Integrating Production, Markets and Consumption Through a Socio-Material Practice Perspective

Ingrid Stigzelius

Introduction

The aim of this chapter is two-fold: to better understand how the consumer becomes a sustainable actor across different moments of consumption, and

Parts of this text have previously been published in my dissertation titled "Producing Consumers: Agencing and Concerning Consumers to Do Green in Everyday Food Practices" (Stigzelius, 2017), Stockholm School of Economics, Sweden. The empirical data in this chapter, however, consist of previously unpublished material.

I. Stigzelius (✉)
Department of Marketing & Strategy and Center for Sustainability Research, Stockholm School of Economics, Stockholm, Sweden
e-mail: Ingrid.stigzelius@hhs.se

R. Bali Swain and S. Sweet (eds.), *Sustainable Consumption and Production, Volume II*,
https://doi.org/10.1007/978-3-030-55285-5_7

thereby to increase the understanding of the connections between production, markets and consumption in this process.

Current consumption patterns have been identified as a key contributor to several environmental and social problems. The so-called responsible, political, green and/or sustainable consumer has subsequently been promoted to solve societal problems by taking responsibility for the external effects of their purchase decisions (Boström & Klintman, 2009). By taking responsibility, consumers are expected to direct the markets, thus engendering a more sustainable production and consumption. Meanwhile, in order to become more sustainable, consumers are expected to need guidance from governmental agencies and interest organizations through, for example, information campaigns, eco-labelling and digital consumer apps (Fuentes & Sörum, 2019; Sadowski & Buckingham, 2007).

Critical voices, however, see this as an outcome of the neo-liberal agenda: where consumers must rely upon self-help tools that are provided by markets (Giesler & Veresiu, 2014). Moreover, critics voice their concern over the inability of individual consumers to change for the better, being trapped in unsustainable societal and market systems (Holt, 2012). Despite efforts to steer consumers in different ways, researchers have repeatedly noted that consumers are quite unwilling to follow suit (Solér, 2012). In a world of abundance that promotes products that primarily appeal to consumer tastes and identities (Dobers & Strannegård, 2005), consumers have been found to strategically avoid information about environmental benefits in their purchase decisions (Nordström & Thunström, 2015). This raises questions about the capacity of consumers to act sustainably and make a difference in production, markets and consumption. ***What is it that enables, or hinders, consumers to act sustainably in different moments of consumption? How can consumers themselves shape the courses of action in production, markets and consumption?***

To better understand what constitutes and shapes the consumer as an actor in different moments of consumption, such as in production, markets and usage, I argue in this chapter that there is a need to unpack the boxes of the all-too-often stereotypical and deterministic images of the sustainable consumer (for a similar argument, see Moisander, Markkula, & Eräranta, 2010; Reijonen, 2011). These images are connected to primarily two interrelated problems in previous research on the sustainable consumer.

First, the consumer will inevitably be ascribed with a certain set of capacities depending on which perspective is chosen to start with. In both *behavioural consumer research* as well as *socio-cultural consumer research*, consumers are on the one hand described as active, creative and powerful actors in the market (see for example Honkanen, Verplanken & Olsen, 2006; Thompson & Coskuner-Balli, 2007) and, on the other, they are presented as passive choice makers, controlled by more powerful actors, and duped into taking responsibility (see for example Giesler & Veresiu, 2014; Pickett-Baker & Ozaki, 2008). Second, previous research on the sustainable consumer in both behavioural consumer research and socio-cultural research tends to take the existence of consumer agency for granted (as also pointed out by Harrison & Kjellberg, 2016); this is seen in pre-existing situations where consumers get engaged with other market actors.

Thus, it seems as though consumers are pre-defined with a specific role—that of being active or passive—and act in accordance with the assumptions of the specific research perspective. It should rather be an open empirical question of how agency is awarded in specific situations than a priori assuming the existence of specific forms of agency.

Instead of assuming that the consumer is passive or active by default, this chapter, therefore, suggests that one should take a look at the interspaces between the dual poles and direct attention to the *practices* that work to produce consumers and their capacity to act. From this perspective, I argue that the sustainable consumer can fruitfully be regarded as a *result of collective efforts* by several socio-material actors in production, markets and consumption, being joined together to solve societal and environmental problems. Consumers are an integral part of this collective achievement; they are both produced by, and are part of producing sustainable consumption (Stigzelius, 2017). Consumers can from this perspective be seen as a *produced co-producer*. As such, consumers become practitioners in different practices related to production, market exchange and usage.

According to Kjellberg (2008) and Hagberg (2015), the research streams of practices related to consumption and markets have intellectual overlaps and possess much in common. However, there are relatively few studies that have actively *integrated* these perspectives (for notable exceptions, see Brembeck, Cochoy, & Moisander, 2015; Hagberg, 2015; Kjellberg, 2008; Shove & Araujo, 2010). This is especially true in relation to the processes of *agencing* consumers (for exceptions, see Fuentes

& Sörum, 2019; Stigzelius, 2017, 2018; Stigzelius, Araujo, Mason, Murto, & Palo, 2018). By bringing together markets and consumption through practices, and particularly *agencing practices* (Hagberg, 2015), it is possible to obtain a more holistic perspective and, thereby, identify important dimensions in the production of consumer agency to engage in practices of more sustainable consumption.

I thus rely upon the concept of *agencing* to study how agency becomes constructed in practical situations, which involves the *arranging* and *adjusting* of practice elements (Hagberg, 2015), in addition to the work of *putting them into motion* (Callon & Law, 1995, 1997; Cochoy, Trompette & Araujo, 2016). To illustrate how such practices are enacted, I will in this chapter attend to novel empirical material on situated practices performed in different moments of consumption, including *production, exchange* and *usage* situations related to green food practices.

The argument of the chapter is structured as follows. After an overview of the methodological and theoretical approach of this chapter, I review different conceptions of practice change within social science, and the relative weight practice perspectives place on materiality. I then introduce how a practice approach generally has been manifested within *consumption studies*, and how this perspective can be related to a view of socio-material practices within *market studies*. It is argued that different moments of consumption in both exchange and usage situations can become integrated through a focus on the practice elements of *objects, meanings* and *competence* and how these are adjusted to each other in the formation of new practices. The notion of *agencing* is then introduced to account for how practice change is taking place through the *arranging* of the practice elements and the *work to put these in motion*. The capacity of the consumer to engage in novel and more sustainable practices is thus a collective result of several socio-material actors that become integrated across production, exchange and use situations. Through empirical examples, the chapter then illustrates how this theoretical positioning is enacted in the area of food practices and consumption. The chapter concludes with a discussion on some theoretical implications of taking an integrated perspective on practices in markets and consumption, which calls for a wider understanding of the consumer's capacity to act and make a difference.

Approach

This chapter takes a practice approach related to consumption, wherein consumer competences and meanings for engaging in particular practices become important (Shove & Pantzar, 2005). This relates to, for example, the role consumers, as practitioners, can play both through reproducing practices and renegotiating meanings around different sustainability-related practices. Moreover, sustainable consumption is constituted by a range of socio-material actors that make up the capacity to act sustainably in different situations. The capacity of the consumer to become more sustainable can, thereby, be seen as constructed by the collective capacities of the involved actors in a practice; this includes both human and non-human actors, where all entities contribute to form its agency. Herein, socio-material consumer studies based upon a constructivist and an anti-essential approach (Moisander et al., 2010; Reijonen, 2011) provide the means to examine empirical situations under which consumers may, more or less, successfully engage in practices of green, political and sustainable consumption (Kjellberg & Helgesson, 2010).

The empirical material is based upon contemporary cases of what consumers do in everyday life when they engage in *green* forms of consumption. Data is collected through engaging with 25 individuals who have set out to learn and practise a different way of relating to nature in their food practices—ranging from producing their own food, buying or exchanging food according to environmental concerns, or by cooking climate-friendly food. The participants in this study were first recruited through engaging in participant observations in different study circles (growing your own food; cooking climate-clever food). People who showed an interest in taking part in this study were then asked to take their own pictures of what they did with their food during four subsequent weeks when they thought that they did something green, climate-friendly or sustainable. Afterwards, follow-up interviews were conducted in people's homes and kitchens, where we discussed the pictures and related food practices and how various environmental concerns have changed their courses of action.

Based on these empirical examples, I analyze the ongoing change processes of producing sustainable consumers as the *agencing* of consumers, whereby consumers get equipped and engaged to "do green" (Stigzelius, 2017). As a theoretical contribution, the chapter seeks to integrate studies on consumption with market practices: two separate, yet interrelated, streams of practice research that bear resemblance and that can be connected in how various practice elements and actors come together in the shaping of green, sustainable consumption and markets.

Theoretical Perspectives

Routines and Change in Practice Theories

Practices form the basis for a growing number of social science approaches that turn away from the individual versus structure dualism towards viewing social action as located in practices (Schatzki, Knorr, Cetina & von Savigny, 2001). According to Reckwitz (2002), the social is not placed in mere mental qualities, discourses or interaction; instead, it is found in practices. Although practice theories are quite dispersed and do not represent a unified body of thought, a shared interest among practice approaches lies in the performance or practical instantiation of mundane and everyday activities (Gronow & Warde, 2001; Reckwitz, 2002).

Practices consist of specific patterns composed of multiple and unique actions that together (re)produce them. The individual is seen as a bodily and mental agent who acts as a "carrier" of a practice, which should also be coordinated with many other practices that take place in everyday life (Reckwitz, 2002: 250). The individual performer of a practice, however, is not only a carrier of behavioural patterns, but also carries "certain routinized ways of understanding, knowing how, and desiring" (Reckwitz, 2002: 250). However, these elements are seen as traits of the practice, not of the individual participating in the practice.

Practice theories tend to stress the habits, routines and shared understandings that make up a practice (Reckwitz, 2002), rather than their dynamic character. Nevertheless, practice perspectives also acknowledge variations in the performance of practices, reflecting varying levels of commitment and competence on the part of practitioners (Warde, 2005). Some studies have shown how changes occur in practices (Bjørkeng, Clegg, & Pitsis, 2009; Pickering, 1993, 2001; Schatzki, 2013), but practice studies tend to favour human agency over other forms of agency. Meanwhile, Gherardi (2015) argues that processes of becoming, through which multiple human and non-human actors and resources become assembled into a practice, are largely lacking in practice research. In particular, the notion of *agencement* has proven to be a blind spot to practice theorists, which is suggested to help practice researchers better account for processes of becoming and involving both human and non-human actors (Gherardi, 2015). How, then, have practice theories accounted for the ***non-human, material*** dimension in the development of practices? And how can this help us to better understand the building of consumer capacities to make a difference?

A Socio-Material Practice Perspective

Even though human and non-human elements can, by definition, be seen as being given equal importance in practice theories (cf. Reckwitz, 2002), the significance of material elements is often stressed in different ways depending upon the chosen research perspective.

A *social science* practice approach would stress the human actors as carriers of practice (Reckwitz, 2002) by reproducing a set of established understandings, procedures and engagements. According to Halkier (2010), these work implicitly to govern the practice into routines. Practices are also generally viewed as being constructed and reproduced by the human actors involved in a practice: where collective learning and experience in the building of capacities become important (Warde, 2005).

A *socio-material* practice approach would conversely see competence not only as a human characteristic, but also as "distributed between practitioners and the objects they use" (Hagberg & Kjellberg, 2010: 1029). Similar to this, the material and social constitute each other and come into being as a single phenomenon entangled as "sociomaterial" (Orlikowski, 2007) where the material is social and vice versa (Gherardi, 2012). Thus, the social and material constitute each other in practice, through which agency also become configured (Gherardi, 2012).

Thus, a socio-material perspective would not view individual agency as an essential human characteristic built up through previous experience, but as configured through multiple acting entities, including material objects, that together construct a practice (Andersson, Aspenberg, & Kjellberg, 2008; Hagberg, 2010). Therefore, material objects are given an active role in enabling or obstructing practices. I adopt a socio-material perspective to practices in order to more fully understand what it is that constructs consumers' capacity to act and how various socio-material elements of a practice are involved in this process. To do so, I will primarily draw upon previous practice research developed in studies of *consumption* and *markets*, in order to combine them for a more complete understanding of how consumer agency comes into being in both markets and consumption.

Integrating Practice Theories in Consumption and Market Studies

Practice Perspectives on Consumption

Practice perspectives on consumption stresses the routine and mundane character of ordinary consumption, based upon practical competence, embodiment, materiality and meanings (Gronow & Warde, 2001; Shove & Pantzar, 2005; Warde, 2005). From this perspective, consumption is primarily seen as the practical organization and use of resources, rather than an expression of the self and identities in relation to specific consumer cultures involving certain consumption practices (cf. Holt, 1995). A return to consumption as using material and natural resources in mundane activities also held a particular interest for studies on environmental degradation and sustainability (Shove, 2010; Shove & Spurling, 2013). According to Warde (2005), consumption should not be viewed as a practice in itself; rather, it is an element in almost any type of practice in our everyday lives: for example, where practices of cleaning, cooking or keeping oneself warm or cool gives rise to moments of consumption. Therefore, consumption becomes an *effect* of the practices that consumers engage in throughout their everyday lives.

The view of consumption as an outcome of other practices is in line with the anti-essential stance within *market studies* that actors are results (Kjellberg, 2008) and conceived of as "provisional outcomes, as collectives, or networks of associated materials" (Araujo & Kjellberg, 2009: 207). This implies that acts of consumption adopt different forms depending upon the situation in which they are performed. Different forms of consumption would then need to be treated in relation to the practices that constitute them (Kjellberg, 2008). This makes it difficult to *à priori* define what it is of which consumption consists.

Such a perspective posits that processes of consumption in which the consumer acts, must acknowledge the contribution of other agents in consumption: such as material devices and tools in markets, marketing and consumption theories and so on. This way, studying consumption and the consumer should not be treated in the same way; as Cochoy et al. (2016) point out, this is done so often in consumer research. Rather, in order to better understand their complex integration, they must be treated as two distinct categories that mutually shape each other. The capacity of the consumer to engage in different forms of consumption could, thereby, be seen as distributed across *actor-networks* (Latour, 2005); this, in turn, are outcomes of different, and sometimes overlapping, practices that constitute forms of consumption (Fig. 7.1). This view of consumption and the consumer keeps the outcome of the process open for empirical inquiries, while necessitating constant questioning of how different categories—such as consumption, consumers and markets—become (re)produced (Canniford & Bajde, 2016).

One useful categorization, however, is the distinction Warde (2005) makes of practices related to consumption depending upon how it is performed: *consumption as purchase* and *consumption as usage*. The former notion of consumption has been relatively less researched within a practice approach to consumption: where consumption as usage and the notion of appropriation as non-market exchange has been stressed. Appropriation captures the domesticating and use of consumer goods in which items become incorporated in and used for practical purposes (Warde, 2014). Despite the divisions of different categories, these areas

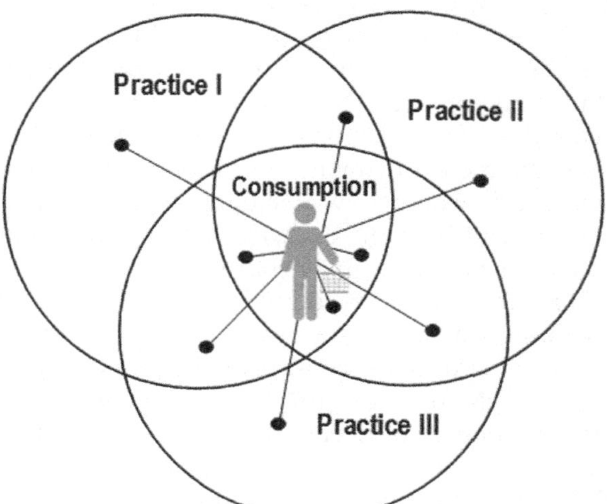

Fig. 7.1 Consumer actor-network in consumption as constituted by elements distributed in various practices (Stigzelius, 2017: 42)

are very much integrated in consumers' everyday life, which also involve several different socio-material actors.

Consumption as purchasing food, for example, is integrated with the practices of cooking as well as practices of travelling to the shop, in addition to the exchange practices in store. The capacity to make an in-store decision thus depends upon a number of heterogeneous elements that are involved in those practices: the recipes used for cooking, shopping lists designating what to buy, means of transportation that determine how to carry the food home, in addition to the various offerings in store. This calls for an integrated perspective on both consumption as purchase and consumption as usage. Therefore, I will turn next to practice theories in the field of ***market studies*** to better understand how especially market practices contribute to shape consumption.

A Practice Perspective on Markets

A practice perspective on markets stresses the emergent character of markets as being produced through various practices involving multiple socio-materially heterogeneous entities. As a market practice perspective brings in material agency as a possibility among many different heterogeneous actor assemblages, these work to decentre human subjects and their agency. What is important to note, however, is that this does not replace human agency; attention is instead directed towards agency as being distributed in the multiple possible agential configurations that become enacted through market practices (Araujo & Kjellberg, 2009).

Markets must be framed by multi-dimensional boundaries in order to function; these decide who and what should be part of the exchange, in addition to where and how the exchange takes place (Araujo & Kjellberg, 2009). The agential capacity of consumers to act in markets would, therefore, be ***a result*** of how markets are framed and enacted. Consumers, in addition to other (market) actors, may also be part of creating these boundaries in an effort to shape markets in different directions (Harrison & Kjellberg, 2016). Markets can thereby be seen as a collective device (Callon, 2007) to pursue different goals in society. Meanwhile, since consumption is a result of other forms of practices rather than a practice in itself (Warde, 2005), markets can also be employed to steer and engender different forms of consumption as a frame that challenges and redefines consumer agencies (Brembeck et al., 2015; Moisander et al., 2010). Consumers therefore, are both produced by and produce market practices. This perspective allows studies in which equipped consumers are seen as competent practitioners in the market, working to shape markets and consumption, while also being shaped by them.

Agencing Practices: Mutual Adjustment of Practice Elements into New Capacities

As a means of further the understanding of how consumption is shaped by various practices, I will attend to the central elements of practices, and the processes and places in which these elements are formed. Shove and Pantzar (2005) define practices as consisting of *materials, meanings* and forms of *competence* (Shove & Pantzar, 2005). The relationships between the different elements of a practice become important when considering how practices take shape and evolve. The elements thus provide a point of entry to study the co-constitution of practices and agencies based upon both markets and consumer studies. Moreover, the integration of the elements of practice can be studied through the conceptual lens of *agencing*, where the agencing of practices has been defined as "a process in which agency is acquired and sustained by the continuous *arranging* of the elements of practices, accompanied by continuous *adjusting* of these elements in relation to other elements of the practices in which they are included" (Hagberg, 2015: 2, italics in original).

The term agencing is the verb form of the concept of *agencement*, which has been defined as "arrangements endowed with the capacity of acting in different ways depending on their configuration" (Callon, 2007: 320). Agencement originally denoted both processes of assembling configurations and the resulting outcome. There is, however, a recent move within *market studies* to use the verb *agencing* to better capture the processes involved in arranging agencements, and how agency becomes constructed in practical situations (Cochoy & Trompette, 2013; Cochoy et al., 2016; Hagberg, 2015). This perspective paves the way for studying the processes in which consumers become equipped with agency being adapted to new situations through the arranging and adjusting of practice elements.

The notions of arranging and adjusting are similar to other notions proposed to account for the processes of becoming in practice approaches. For instance, Pickering (2001) argues: "*The only generally reliable and enduring feature of practice that I can discern is the pattern that I have so far called tuning, and elsewhere analyzed in detail as a dialectic of resistance and accommodation: 'the mangle' for short (Pickering,* 1993, *p. 1995a). And mangling is a temporally emergent process: its upshots are not given at all in advance*" (Pickering, 2001: 164).

Thus, the constant tuning and adjusting between elements of practices is in line with the notion of agencement and agencing to highlight that actors do not have stabilized natures or characteristics (MacKenzie, 2009). Actors should, instead, be seen as outcomes of the mutual adjustments between different elements involved in a practice. Moreover, in line with Callon and Law (1995, 1997), I support the important insight that agencies must also be *put in motion* to be able to act. This is a process whereby human and non-human entities—or combinations of these two—are converted into active agents, or rather actors (Cochoy et al., 2016). This conversion is in turn *mediated* by a number of different actors, places and spaces. Therefore, I will next consider possible forms of mediation of the agencing processes.

Mediating the Integration of Practices and Agencies in Junctions

Previous studies have revealed that different actors, places and spaces can mediate the work of integration of practices and agencies. These are commonly referred to as *junctions*: where different actors and practices meet and become integrated. Junctions constitute both physical places where the work of integration is performed—such as a kitchen—and more abstract spaces where different interest groups meet to negotiate the terms in markets and politics (Cowan, 1987; Hand & Shove, 2004).

Moreover, junctions also emerge in the overlapping of different agencies (Andersson et al., 2008). The junction is then constituted by an actor, or element, that is involved in several different actor-networks and that makes up the lowest common denominator for these agencements. This directs attention to agency as distributed and, at the same time, mediated. Consumer agency must, therefore, be seen in relation to the different mediators, places and spaces that integrate different elements and produce a capacity to act.

As Araujo and Brito (1998) suggest, the capacity of an actor must be seen in connection to the multiple games in which that they are involved. This can be compared to all the different situations that humans get involved in through the course of a single day: consider, for example, the different practices at home, at work, during shopping and travelling between places (cf. see Fig. 7.1). Even though these disparate networks have one entity in common—for example, an individual consumer—they constitute different agencies, which provide different capacities to act in different situations. This can help explain why one and the same actor sometimes performs contradictory actions. The challenge becomes how to converge and mediate the different actor-networks to act consistently across different practices and situations.

Connections between different practices can also be seen as facilitated in different junctions, which constitutes the lowest common denominator for the different acting entities. It is thus through the junction that specific actors emerge, which share certain characteristics that then can be subsumed under the same label (cf. Andersson et al., 2008). Junctions have also been referred to as *conduits* (Finch, Horan, & Reid, 2015), *crossing points* (Hagberg, 2015) or *nexus points* (Paddock, 2015); and they all work in different ways to bridge practices. Food practices have, for example, been identified as a form of junction to better understand how to disentangle practices in households towards more sustainable practices (Paddock, 2015).

In this chapter, I will attend to different forms of food consumption in order to examine the work of integration between various actors and practices where different matters of concerns related to the environment are raised and addressed. I will attend to food as a practice that is situated in specific junctions: *vegetable gardens*, *food stores* and ***kitchens***. These places correspond to different moments of consumption: ***production exchange***, and *usage*. As places of situated practices, these arenas constitute meeting spaces where multiple heterogeneous actors work to arrange, adjust and put into motion a capacity to act towards more green and sustainable food practices. Thus, food is here used as a space for studying situated practices in which sustainable consumption is produced.

Empirical Analysis

Taking Nature into Account as an Actor in Consumption

In line with a socio-material practice perspective, I set out to study the intermingling of social practices and material objects in the production of sustainable *green* consumption. As a method of inquiry, I "follow the actors" (Latour, 2005), more specifically how 25 consumers seek to take nature into account in different moments of consumption. In doing so, consumers indirectly or directly allow environmental concerns to take on a larger role in their lives and consumption, thus allowing nature to become an actor in their everyday life. As we will see through the consumers' own photographs and narratives, this sometimes steers consumers into new and sometimes unexpected practices in their consumption. The emergence of new practices takes place through the mangling and mediation of the different elements of practices, involving the intermingling of new meanings, objects and competences.

To study how new practices take shape, I have thus followed different *nature-objects* (Latour, 2004) and environmental representations, such as vegetables, weeds, natural seasons, and eco-labels, as they move from the garden, the store or any other place where food is purchased or collected and as they enter people's kitchens and their everyday life. I argue that these nature-objects, in conjunction with other *material objects* in the garden, market or kitchen, work in different ways together with the practice elements of *meanings* and *competences*, to mediate and shape the agency of the consumer to act more (or less) sustainable. The following empirical episodes focus on one of the practice elements in each turn (meanings, objects, competences) and as situated in different junctions (vegetable gardens, food stores, kitchens), although they are all integrated in practice.

Agencing New Meanings *to Food in Vegetable Gardens*

The vegetable garden constitutes an important place in which consumers come to renegotiate their relationship to food. As one consumer explains, when producing her own food, she had started to think differently about the food she buys in the store:

> From a societal perspective, it feels good that there is a growing interest in producing your own food, so that we do not totally lose contact with food [...] and get a better feeling for it. [...] It makes me think differently when I buy other food too: to realize, okay, how is chard produced? What sort of vegetable is it? What is demanded? To get to know the food a bit better. (woman, 28 years)

By producing your own food, the consumer becomes more dependent on the natural seasons and nature-objects that need to get enrolled, or expelled, to get vegetables to grow properly. In this way, nature comes to the fore as an actor that determines the forms of consumption. As exemplified by this quote:

> The potatoes could have been left [in the ground] if it was not because of all the worms in them. We had to take it all up at once. Then we had to eat a lot of potato salad! (Couple: woman 25 years, man 23 years)

The selection of what vegetables to grow and eat is thus depending on the success of growing them. However, the fact that people grow their own food does not make them independent of the market, but rather alters the objects of exchange in markets, which may need to be reformed over time depending on the provision from nature and the market. An illustrative example is of a woman who grows her own food, which she collects and carries home from the garden in a traditional shopping basket (Fig. 7.2):

> And there we have squash, which we got plenty of this year actually, and it is the first time I have yellow squash. Otherwise I have had green squash, but this year I took a yellow one because I had failed to pre-cultivate the green ones, and then I went to buy this instead at "Blomsterlandet" [a

Fig. 7.2 Shopping in the vegetable garden (Photo courtesy of an anonymous participant in the study)

> local plants and seeds shop] and they only had yellow squash. (woman, 62 years)

Thus, the garden becomes a crossing point for different elements of practice connected to both nature and the market, but primarily becomes a natural place that mediates a new *meaning* to food in which nature is taking a larger role. Herein, the forms and content of consumption is primarily determined by the natural seasons and different nature-objects involved. By acting together in the garden, nature becomes more vivid, which in turn is agencing the consumer into a new relationship with food that makes it easier to keep consumption in accordance with local and seasonal produce.

Agencing a Capacity to Do Green Through Objects *in the Food Store*

The close relationship to nature and food as fostered in the garden becomes more difficult to maintain when production and consumption become more separate, for example, as when buying food in the store. Trying to determine what is green is an ongoing negotiation for the consumer, which not only involves different varieties of products that can be seen as green, but is also determined by the consumer's own sentiments and freedom to choose what they want. Nature thus becomes less of an actor in determining their decisions. A woman, for example, exposes her dilemma in choosing what is environmentally friendly:

> This week I have thought about what really is the most environmentally friendly option, and have tried to cope with the fact that I want to have the least environmentally friendly one. (woman, 32 years)

She illustrates this dilemma by displaying two different packages of yoghurt: one organic traditional yoghurt and one made of soybean (Fig. 7.3).

As we will see, different tools and objects in the market can, however, be used to *mediate* a decision on what can be seen as sustainable. Green guides, for example on what is in season and what type of fish is sustainable to eat, can be used as a decision device (Fig. 7.4). One woman, for example, keeps the WWF red list of fish on her refrigerator door, together with a list of what food items she is currently missing in her household. However, what ultimately determines the decision in the store

Fig. 7.3 Dilemma of choosing between different shades of green (Photo courtesy of an anonymous participant in the study)

Fig. 7.4 Devices to agence sustainable decisions in the market (Photo courtesy of anonymous participants in the study)

is also other market mechanisms of price and availability, as one woman explains:

> With meat, fish etc., it is a bit improvized depending on what they have on offer and if they have any good prices. (woman, 62 years)

Nevertheless, prices can also be used as a device to determine if vegetables and fruits are in season, as one participant disclosed:

> I do not buy peppers when they cost 40 SEK per kilo, then you know that they are not in season. [...] You kind of know what the prices normally are, and if they are very much above that then you know that they are not in season. (woman, 25 years)

She has also posted a "season map" on her fridge, which illustrates the different vegetables that are in season every month (Fig. 7.4). However, according to this "season map" there are different food items in season everywhere around the globe, which then does not necessarily restrict the overall consumption to what is in season locally to your home.

Such different *agencing devices* are fragile arrangements that contain possible loopholes offered through the market, and which can be applied differently depending on the consumers' preferences and willingness to pay. Various objects offered through the market are, however, instrumental in order to carry out certain practices seen as environmentally friendly, such as picking your own berries:

> We have saved a lot in the freezer. We had to get a new one for the blueberries, lingonberries and such things. (Couple: woman 25 years, man 23 years)

Another participant had ordered a certain kitchen compost ("bokashi-compost") online, which enabled her to store her composted material in the kitchen, which later could be used at her allotment for food production.

In order to agence consumers to make more sustainable decisions, there is a need to better mediate different market offers and price mechanisms to accommodate environmental concerns, while also strengthening the competence of consumers to know what to choose and how to apply it in use. Here, the kitchen becomes another important crossing point where the different elements of practices come together in the formation of new practices, which we turn to next.

Agencing New Competences *as Integrated Practices in the Kitchen*

The different *meanings* of doing green and the various *objects* involved all depend on the *competences* that the consumer can apply in moments of usage. Importantly, competences rely on how well different elements of an agencement are assembled, which involves continuous mangling and mediation of multiple socio-material elements. Hence, in order to put these heterogenous elements in motion, they need to be adjusted to each other, which may take time and efforts to accommodate. For example, one participant explains her initial resistance to refrain from eating meat, and how she has gradually adjusted to a new, more climate-friendly diet:

> It was hard to know what to eat instead. To begin with, it was rather dull food and I missed meat. But it took maybe a couple of years, and now I think it is weird if I eat some meat, it does not taste any good. Now I don't need it any more. [...] I have eaten a bit different from time to time. In the beginning I ate a lot of quorn, which was what was available by then, but now I rarely eat it. Instead I buy these small beefs of soy. Now there are plenty to choose from, but before there were not that much good stuff. (woman, 28 years)

Thus, the competence of the consumer to eat more environmentally friendly food is distributed between the consumer and what is on offer in the market. Similarly, the capacity to accommodate for a non-meat diet is also dependent on the design and materials of the kitchen, which another woman who grows her own vegetables explains:

> I primarily miss a (cool) larder. Kitchens are still built for some sort of meat consumption. In my little fridge I can store some cheese and small beefs cuts, which takes up very little space. But my vegetables are so spacious, and I need this enormous space for it. The food cannot be stored properly. (woman, 54 years)

This often results in the harvested vegetables ending up in the hallway, waiting to get sorted out and stored where space is available (Fig. 7.5): "*The beets ended up in a plastic bag on the floor in the kitchen, since it's full in the fridge and cupboards.*" (woman, 54 years)

Fig. 7.5 Make space for the vegetables! (Photo courtesy of an anonymous participant in the study)

These moments of waiting and lingering nicely illustrate the *mangling of practices* (Pickering, 2001) and how these new nature-objects are entities with uncertain boundaries, entities that hesitate and induce complexity in consumers' everyday life (cf. Latour, 2004). Thus, in order to take nature into account and accommodate for greener consumption, there is a need to envision and agence how new green practices can work to integrate production, markets and consumption.

> If we want to make a transformation, what is it that we need to do? (…) Then you would need to think about how you build houses, and particularly how you build the kitchens. Things need to change. In this way it has been interesting to notice that there are obstacles in my everyday life when growing my own food. (woman, 54 years)

Conclusion

We will now return to the aim of this chapter, which has been on the one hand, *to better understand how the consumer becomes a sustainable actor across different moments of consumption*, and on the other, *to increase the understanding of the connections between production, markets and consumption in this process*. In addressing this aim, the overall argument of the chapter will be discussed in relation to the two research questions: *What is it that enables, or hinders, consumers to act sustainable in different moments of consumption? How can consumers themselves shape the courses of action in production, markets and consumption?* This is followed by a discussion of what theoretical and practical implications this perspective entails for the study of sustainable consumption.

Main Takeaway: Sustainable Consumption as a Collective Achievement

This chapter has provided a deeper understanding of how consumers become capable to act more sustainable in different moments of consumption. As seen from a socio-material practice theoretical perspective, the chapter goes to show how consumer capacity to act and make a difference is constituted through various socio-material arrangements, rather than being determined by the inherent capability of the individual consumer or the surrounding structures in markets or production. The main argument of this chapter is that sustainable consumption is a *collective achievement:* wherein sustainable practices become enacted through different forms of *mediation* involving multiple human and non-human actors, including the consumer, that in turn work to integrate different practices in production, markets and consumption. Thus, a practice perspective makes a move away from the individual agency of consumers to the complex socio-material entities that work to produce a capacity to act.

To support this argument, I have attended to food practices in production, exchange and usage, with a particular focus on situated practices and socio-material actors that have worked to modify and change food practices to become more sustainable. The empirical material illustrates how various *food practices* work to integrate and alter different moments of consumption with both production and market practices in the junctions of vegetable gardens, food stores and kitchens. I maintain that in order to better understand the formation of sustainable consumption, we cannot only look at one side (consumption, markets or production) if we want to see practice changes to sustainability; rather, we need to see them as integrated and entangled through *practices* (Ozaki & Shaw, 2014).

Enabling Consumers to Act Sustainable Through Agencing Practices

From the field of market studies, this chapter applies the notion of *agencing*, as the verb form of agencement (Callon, 2007), to the study of consumption. Agencing involves processes of *arranging entities* and *putting these into motion*, which work to convert people and non-human entities (Cochoy et al., 2016). Through different ways of agencing practices (Hagberg, 2015), the chapter thereby shows how food practices become rearranged through the mutual adjustment of *meanings*, *objects* and *competences* of a practice, whereby consumers become equipped and configured to act more (or less) sustainable. The assembled actor-network, that is the capacity to act, is situated across different moments of consumption in production, markets and usage, which gradually become arranged and rearranged into a new practice. The ability to put these new practices *into motion*, however, depends on how well the elements of practices in production, exchange and usage become integrated and thereby can act collectively as one actor.

The Role of the Consumer in Shaping Sustainable Production, Markets and Consumption

The consumer is an integral and important actor in this achievement. Yet, the consumer could merely be seen as the tip of the iceberg in relation to the wider network of actors that works to uphold and produce consumption. This iceberg of actors, however, should not be mistaken for any sort of hidden super structure or norm that is beyond the consumers' reach. By examining the consumers' practices, we can come to realize how the network is interconnected by socio-material entities in *chains of translations* (Helgesson, Kjellberg, & Liljenberg, 2004). Thus, by attending to ongoing practices that work to produce sustainable consumers, I have illustrated how consumers are an integral part of this collective achievement: as someone who is both produced and is part of producing green consumption.

An example can be found in an ordinary grocery store, where it is possible to detect multiple socio-material actors such as shelves, price tags, recommendations and advertisements that, along with the consumer, work to enact a decision. As a form of spokesperson for this actor-network, the consumer plays an important role in attributing and negotiating the *meaning* of the network. And as a carrier of the practices being performed as part of the network, consumers can bring in new forms of *competence* and *objects* that may change the course of action. However, it is only as a collective achievement, where the network acts as one actor (cf. Andersson et al., 2008), that it can become possible to move mountains in any given direction.

Implications: An Integrated and Wider Perspective on Sustainable Consumption

It, therefore, becomes paramount to take on an *integrated* and thus *wider perspective* on the building of sustainable consumer capacities, whereby consumption is integrated with markets and production. As illustrated in this chapter, the work of integration through *junctions* works to flatten markets and consumption (Bajde, 2013), which can contribute with a wider perspective to the study of markets and consumption. As Burr (2014) illustrates, a *market widening* takes place in how market demand is seen as created in the envisioning of new types of use-environments. For example, as a junction for production and consumption, *the kitchen* would need to be re-designed in order to accommodate for the large amounts of harvest when producing your own food (cf. Stigzelius et al., 2018). Envisioning such a new use-environment would, in turn, create an altered demand for products and services in the market (such as a new fridge/freezer, or complementary food products). Moreover, to be able to act as one actor, nature needs to be taken into account as an actor in re-envisioning and re-arranging different moments of consumption to become green. By envisioning what a new kind of sustainable consumption would look like in its use and produce environment, it would foster a different type of market demand and thus encompass a market-widening perspective (Burr, 2014).

Conversely, a similar form of *consumption widening* could be noted if we started to recognize the wider network of actors that collectively works to produce consumption in exchange, use and produce situations. The flattening and bridging of these perspectives can thereby widen the scope of the study of sustainable consumption: first, by including market practice as co-constituting consumer agency and, second, by including user environments in the production of markets. Thus, these perspectives are suggested to contribute towards a widening of both markets and consumption in the production of sustainable consumption.

Moreover, taking nature into account as an actor in the performance of production, markets and consumption could lead to a form of ***nature widening*** perspective: where the socio-material aspects of engaging with nature influence the performance of practices. What would production, consumption and markets look like if nature were given a more prominent role in determining the forms of consumption of what is produced, exchanged and consumed?

Returning to the metaphor of the consumer at the top of the (sadly, now melting) iceberg, we do not necessarily need to look so high for answers to the matters of increasingly mounting concern. In line with Asdal (2008), I would rather support a more down-to-earth approach where we only need to dig a little deeper to detect the numerous socio-material actors beneath the soil of green consumption (for example, nature-objects, producers, consumers, marketers, media magazines and politicians). These actors would now need to be assembled as one concerned actor to enable more efficient changes in the forms and levels of consumption, to enable a move towards sustainability.

References

Andersson, P., Aspenberg, K., & Kjellberg, H. (2008). The configuration of actors in market practice. *Marketing Theory, 8*(1), 67–90.

Araujo, L., & Brito, C. (1998). Agency and constitutional ordering in networks—A case study of the port wine industry. *International Studies of Management & Organization, 27,* 22–46.

Araujo, L. M., & Kjellberg, H. (2009). Shaping exchanges, performing markets: The study of marketing practices. In P. Maclaran, M. Saren, B. Stern, & M. Tadajewski (Eds.), *The Sage handbook of marketing theory* (pp. 195–218). London: Sage.

Asdal, K. (2008). On politics and the little tools of democracy: A down-to-earth approach. *Distinktion, 6,* 11–26.

Bajde, D. (2013). Consumer culture theory (re)visits actor-network theory: Flattening consumption studies. *Marketing Theory, 13,* 227–242.

Bjørkeng, K., Clegg, S., & Pitsis, T. (2009). Becoming (a) practice. *Management Learning, 40*(2), 145–159.

Boström, M., & Klintman, M. (2009). The green political food consumer: A critical analysis of the research and policies. *Anthropology of Food*, S5.

Brembeck, H., Cochoy, F., & Moisander, J. (2015). Moving consumption. *Consumption Markets & Culture, 18*(1), 1–24.

Burr, T. C. (2014). Market-widening: Shaping total market demand for French and American bicycles circa 1890. *Marketing Theory, 14*(1), 19–34.

Callon, M. (2007). What does it mean to say that Economics is performative. In D. MacKenzie, F. Muniesa, & L. Siu (Eds.), *Do economists make markets? On the performativity of Economics* (pp. 311–357). Princeton: Princeton University Press.

Callon, M., & Law, J. (1995). Agency and the hybrid collectif. *South Atlantic Quarterly, 94,* 481–507.

Callon, M., & Law, J. (1997). Agency and the hybrid collectif. In B. H. Smith & A. Plonitsky (Eds.), *Mathematics, science and postclassical theory* (pp. 481–507). Durham, NC: Duke University Press.

Canniford, R., & Bajde, D. (2016). *Assembling consumption: Researching actors, networks and markets*. London: Routledge.

Cochoy, F., & Trompette, P. (2013, September 17–20). *Agencing markets*. Proposal ESF exploratory workshop, Institut d'Etudes Scientifiques de Carge'se (IESC), France. http://www.pacte-grenoble.fr/wp-content/uploads/ESF_Exploratory_Workshop_Agencing_markets.pdf.

Cochoy, F., Trompette, P., & Araujo, L. (2016). From market agencements to market agencing: An introduction. *Consumption Markets & Culture, 19*(1), 3–16.

Cowan, R. S. (1987). The consumption junction: A proposal for a research strategy in the sociology of technology. In W. Bijker, T. P. Hughes, & T. Pinch (Eds.), *The social construction of technological systems* (pp. 261–280). London: MIT Press.

Dobers, P., & Strannegård, L. (2005). Design, lifestyles and sustainability. Aesthetic consumption in a world of abundance. *Business Strategy and the Environment, 14,* 324–336.

Finch, J., Horan, C., & Reid, E. (2015). The performativity of sustainability: Making a conduit a marketing device. *Journal of Marketing Management, 31*(1–2), 167–192.

Fuentes, C., & Sörum, N. (2019). Agencing ethical consumers: Smartphone apps and the socio-material reconfiguration of everyday life. *Consumption Markets and Culture, 22*(2), 131–156.

Gherardi, S. (2012). *How to conduct a practice-based study: Problems and methods*. Cheltenham, UK: Edward Elgar.

Gherardi, S. (2015). To start practice theory anew: The contribution of the concept of agencement and formativeness. *Organization, 23*(5), 680–698.

Giesler, M., & Veresiu, E. (2014). Creating the responsible consumer: Moralistic governance regimes and consumer subjectivity. *Journal of Consumer Research, 41*(3), 840–857. https://doi.org/10.1086/677842.

Gronow, J., & Warde, A. (2001). *Ordinary consumption*. London: Routledge.

Hagberg, J. (2010). Exchanging agencies: The case of NetOnNet. In L. Araujo, J. Finch, & H. Kjellberg (Eds.), *Reconnecting marketing to markets* (pp. 50–73). Oxford: Oxford University Press.
Hagberg, J. (2015). Agencing practices: A historical exploration of shopping bags. *Consumption Markets & Culture, 19*(1), 111–132.
Hagberg, J., & Kjellberg, H. (2010). Who performs marketing? Dimensions of agential variation in market practice. *Industrial Marketing Management, 39,* 1028–1037.
Halkier, B. (2010). *Consumption challenged: Food in medialised everyday lives.* Surrey, UK: Ashgate.
Helgesson, C-F., Kjellberg, H., & Liljenberg, A. (2004). *Den där marknaden. Om utbyten, normer och bilder*. Lund: Studentlitteratur.
Holt, D. (1995). How consumers consume: A typology of consumption practices. *Journal of Consumer Research, 22,* 1–16.
Holt, D. (2012). Constructing sustainable consumption: From ethical values to the cultural transformation of unsustainable markets. *The ANNALS of the American Academy of Political and Social Science, 644,* 236–255.
Hand, M., & Shove, E. (2004). Orchestrating concepts: Kitchen dynamics and regime change in good housekeeping and ideal home, 1922–2002. *Home Culture, 1*(3), 235–256.
Harrison, D., & Kjellberg, H. (2016). How users shape and use markets. *Marketing Theory, 16*(4), 445–468.
Honkanen, P., Verplanken, B., & Olsen, S. O. (2006). Ethical values and motives driving organic food choice. *Journal of Consumer Behaviour, 5*(5), 397–478.
Kjellberg, H. (2008). Market practices and over-consumption. *Consumption Markets & Culture, 11*(2), 151–167.
Kjellberg, H., & Helgesson, C.-F. (2010). Political marketing: Multiple values, performativities and modes of engaging. *Journal of Cultural Economy, 3*(2), 279–297.
Latour, B. (2004). *Politics of nature: How to bring the sciences into democracy.* Cambridge, MA: Harvard University Press.
Latour, B. (2005). *Reassembling the social: An introduction to Actor-Network-Theory.* Oxford: Oxford University Press.
MacKenzie, D. (2009). *Material markets: How economic agents are constructed.* Oxford: Oxford University Press.
Moisander, J., Markkula, A., & Eräranta, K. (2010). Construction of consumer choice in the market: Challenges for environmental policy. *International Journal of Consumer Studies, 34,* 73–79.
Nordström, J., & Thunström, L. (2015). *Styrning av konsumenter mot miljövänligare och hälsosammare produkter. Information och ekonomiska incitament.* Forskningsrapport, Handelns utvecklingsråd. http://www.handelsradet.nu/

wp-content/uploads/2010/05/2015-3-Styrning-av-konsumenter-mot-miljovanligare-och-halsosammare-produkter.pdf.

Orlikowski, W. J. (2007). Sociomaterial practices: Exploring technology at work. *Organization Studies, 28*(9), 1435–1448.

Ozaki, R., & Shaw, I. (2014). Entangled practices: Governance, sustainable technologies, and energy consumption. *Sociology, 48*, 590–605.

Paddock, J. (2015). Household consumption and environmental change: Rethinking the policy problem through narratives of food practice. *Journal of Consumer Culture, 17*(1), 122–139.

Pickering, A. (1993). The mangle of practice: Agency and emergence in the sociology of science. *The American Journal of Sociology, 99*(3), 559–589.

Pickering, A. (2001). Practice and posthumanism: Social theory and a history of agency. In T. Schatzki, K. Knorr Cetina, & E. von Savigny (Eds.), *The practice turn in contemporary theory* (pp. 163–174). London: Routledge.

Pickett-Baker, J., & Ozaki, R. (2008). Pro-environmental products: Marketing influence on consumer purchase decision. *The Journal of Consumer Marketing, 25*(5), 281–293.

Reijonen, S. (2011). Environmentally friendly consumer: From determinism to emergence. *International Journal of Consumer Studies, 35*, 403–409.

Reckwitz, A. (2002). Toward a theory of social practices. A development in culturalist theorizing. *European Journal of Social Theory, 5*, 243–253.

Sadowski, M., & Buckingham, F. (2007). Retail corporate responsibility—Retailers as choice editors. *European Retail Digest, 56*(Winter), 7–11.

Schatzki, T. R. (2013). The edge of change: On the emergence, persistence and dissolution of practices. In E. Shove & N. Spurling (Eds.), *Sustainable practices: Social theory and climate change*. Abingdon, Oxon: Routledge.

Schatzki, T., Knorr Cetina, K., & von Savigny, E. (Eds.). (2001). *The practice turn in contemporary theory*. London: Routledge.

Shove, E. (2010). Beyond the ABC: Climate change policy and theories of social change. *Environment and Planning A, 42*(6), 1273–1285.

Shove, E., & Araujo, L. (2010). Consumption, materiality, and markets. In L. Araujo, J. Finch, & H. Kjellberg (Eds.), *Reconnecting marketing to markets*. Oxford: Oxford University Press.

Shove, E., & Pantzar, M. (2005). Consumers, producers and practices: Understanding the invention and reinvention of Nordic walking. *Journal of Consumer Culture, 5*(1), 43–64.

Shove, E., & Spurling, N. (2013). *Sustainable practices: Social theory and climate change*. Abingdon, Oxon: Routledge.

Solér, C. (2012). Conceptualizing sustainably produced food for promotional purposes: A sustainable marketing approach. *Sustainability, 4*(3), 294–340.

Stigzelius, I. (2017). *Producing consumers: Agencing and concerning consumers to do green in everyday food practices* (PhD Dissertation). Stockholm School of Economics, Stockholm, Sweden.

Stigzelius, I. (2018). Representing the political consumer: Liquid agencies in the production of consumer voice. *Consumption Markets & Culture, 21*(5), 475–502.

Stigzelius, I., Araujo, L., Mason, K., Murto, R., & Palo, T. (2018). Kitchen concerns at the boundary between markets and consumption: Agencing practice change in times of scarcity (Husmodern, Sweden 1938–1958). *Consumption Markets & Culture, 21*(4), 347–372.

Thompson, C., & Coskuner-Balli, G. (2007, August). Countervailing market responses to corporate co-optation and the ideological recruitment of consumption communities. *Journal of Consumer Research, 34*, 135–151.

Warde, A. (2005). Consumption and theories of practice. *Journal of Consumer Culture, 5*, 131–153.

Warde, A. (2014). After taste: Culture, consumption and theories of practice. *Journal of Consumer Culture, 14*(3), 279–303.

CHAPTER 8

Tourism as (Un)sustainable Production and Consumption

Lin Lerpold and Örjan Sjöberg

Introduction

Sustainable and responsible tourism has long been on the agenda and rightly so. For while tourism is often hailed as a source of positive economic and social development, it is also a source of undesirable outcomes not only or even primarily because of the hedonism associated with mass tourism of the "sun, sand and sea" variety. From negative localised social and environmental impacts to global warming, tourism

The original version of this chapter was revised: This chapter is now published open access, and copyright holder has been updated. The correction to this chapter is available at https://doi.org/10.1007/978-3-030-55285-5_16

L. Lerpold (✉)
Department of Marketing & Strategy and Center for Sustainability Research, Stockholm School of Economics, Stockholm, Sweden
e-mail: Lin.Lerpold@hhs.se

Ö. Sjöberg
Department of Economics and Center for Sustainability Research, Stockholm School of Economics, Stockholm, Sweden
e-mail: Orjan.Sjoberg@hhs.se

R. Bali Swain and S. Sweet (eds.), *Sustainable Consumption and Production, Volume II*,
https://doi.org/10.1007/978-3-030-55285-5_8

contributes its share of adverse effects, some of which cannot be avoided even by the ethically conscious visitor (e.g., Hall, 2014; Weeden & Boluk, 2014). This is so not least because, at a time when "staycation" is gaining ground, tourism by definition requires some form of mobility. That mobility, often by car or air, does little to promote tourism as an alternative to the consumption of material goods that it is sometimes touted as (Gössling, 2000, for a critique). Similarly, while the recreation, pleasure and experiences that tourism provides might be a wiser way of spending increasing disposable incomes than the relentless accumulation of physical possessions, since to many shopping appears to be an important element of the rewarding trip, it is questionable whether tourism is part of the solution. Rather, in many respects it is a part of the problem.

Any such negative effects are compounded by the fact that, globally, tourism and hospitality is one of the fastest growing industries—as the World Tourism Organization points out it accounts for "10% of world GDP, 1 in 10 jobs and 7% of global exports" (UNWTO, 2017: 6). Yet the observation, by Lenzen et al. (2018), that global tourism and the transportation, consumption and shopping that goes with it also accounts for about 8% of all greenhouse gas emissions should give rise to sobering thoughts. Despite the recent "flight shame" movement and "Greta effect" linked to a decrease in air travel seen in Sweden during 2019, air travel, much of it leisure related, is projected to double over the next decade and a half. As such it does little to alleviate the concern that global trends point in the opposite direction to the one required by the Paris Agreement.

However, not all is gloom and doom. Important parts of the industry are labour intensive, and tourism and hospitality have a record of being inclusive. It often provides the entry point to labour markets and has a claim to being less discriminatory, allowing minority groups and newly arrived migrants better opportunities than is typically the case elsewhere (e.g., UNWTO, 2009). In addition to bringing pecuniary income at destination, tourism can also enhance our understanding of environmental issues, strengthen the appreciation of other cultures and bring people closer together. As such, it has the potential of being a vehicle for education and personal development.

This review of (un)sustainable tourism sets out to map both sides of the coin. As such it focuses on the shifts (and at times trade-offs) between different classes of sustainability concerns, and the variegated emphasis on the local versus the global. It concludes that the global significance of some local circumstances (indeed disorders) is yet to receive the attention it deserves.

Tourism in the Service of Economic Growth

It has long been recognised that tourism might help economic growth. As tourism is typically defined as including activities or trips "that take a traveller outside his/her usual environment for less than a year for a main purpose other than to be employed by a resident entity in the place visited" (UN, 2009: 9), this includes developments both at the national and sub-national levels. It is frequently the case that resource poor countries or peripheral areas, including rural ones with limited growth prospects in otherwise healthy economies, are encouraged to engage in tourism and leisure activities to attract visitors. To the extent that such inbound tourism, be it domestic or international in origin, is generated it is also expected to add to local earnings.

Indeed, there is no lack of official pronouncements to this effect (e.g., WTTC, 2019) and there is an extensive set of academic studies of national and regional economies starting with Ghali's (1976) study of Hawai'i. In a steady stream of reports, both direct and indirect effects on growth are recorded and detailed (e.g., Li, Jin, & Shi, 2018, for a review). It is also possible to relate the effect of the tourism and hospitality industry, delineated to "include that part of the economy which has a common function of supplying tourist needs" (Burkart & Medlik, 1974: 46) and understand the growth of the tourism development cycle (Butler, 1980), thereby capturing the structural transformation that tourism is often a part of and might contribute to. Summarising much of this work, Mihalič (2013: 660) notes that seen from the vantage point of economic growth, tourism brings development and reduces development gaps; generates foreign currency income; creates employment; and "valorises or adds value" to environmental goods.

It goes without saying that the effects of domestic and foreign tourism might differ along these various dimensions, as would also be the case depending on the purpose for travelling (be it leisure; business and professional; visiting friends and relatives or for religious, educational or medical reasons). Yet, the contribution of tourism to employment is invariably mentioned. It is often held forth as a major benefit not least for peripheral regions that have few other options available to them. As such, it may serve to reduce out-migration and help stabilise demographic change, at least to a degree. To the extent that small and medium-sized enterprises, including family firms, can capitalise on becoming suppliers, the effects on the local economy can be both positive and quite noticeable. The fact that jobs often are seasonal and temporary does have its own set of implications however, and may require locals to derive incomes from multiple sources beyond tourism or induce temporary in-migration, including the importation of labour from abroad.

The effects on poverty reduction can therefore be expected to be ambiguous. As with economic growth in general, which is not necessarily pro-poor, much depends on the type of jobs or other forms of income opportunities that tourism generates. For this reason, many discussions have also focused on the creation of backward and forward linkages in the (local) economy (e.g., Telfer & Wall, 1996). This can be done in quantitative terms, where the standard is to look both at tourism expenditure as such and suppliers' own spending, including local demand induced and resources spent on imports to the national or regional economy (Mihalič, 2013). These tourism income multiplier effects are often used to motivate concessionary terms for inward foreign direct investment (FDI).

In the context of sustainable consumption, also the final point on Mihalič's (2013) list is worth mentioning: the possibility that making the environment more valuable to the local community may serve to improve sustainability. If the surroundings of the local community can be preserved thanks to the fact that in its pristine state that environment represents a resource—be it an ecological or cultural heritage one—that in turn contributes to generating jobs and incomes, there is greater likelihood of it being better taken care of. That might serve ends as varied as biodiversity and the protection of valued cityscapes. It is also in line with the idea that the social and private costs and benefits need to be aligned to provide incentives not to over-use scarce resources.

Success might come at a cost, however. Also, confining the discussion to the realm of economic outcomes, high levels of net tourism receipts might lead to Dutch Disease and a hollowing out of other sectors of the economy (e.g., Capó, Riera Font, & Rosselló Nadal, 2007; Copeland, 1991; Inchausti-Sintes, 2015). If the hollowing out results in de-industrialisation, it is also likely to affect productivity growth negatively; already at the outset tourism-led growth includes the risk of leading on to lower levels of productivity growth than might otherwise be the case unless specialisation within tourism is embarked upon (e.g., Lanza, Temple, & Urga, 2003). Such structural distortions add to the problem of leakage, long considered to be a fallout of dependence on tourism for economic growth. Leakage results from high levels of reliance on imports in the tourism sector, but also from high rates of repatriation of profits in foreign owned tourism ventures. This not only reduces any positive multiplier effects as might exist but also erodes the capacity of capital accumulation at tourism destinations. As UNCTAD (2013: 13) somewhat bluntly states it,

> [t]he presence of transnational corporations (TNCs) in the tourism sector, together with the influx of FDI, leads to financial leakages. While such FDI provides important amounts of capital, TNCs repatriate profits, tend to be vertically integrated with suppliers outside the local economy and often bring in highly skilled international staff that take up the managerial positions. This raises concerns because it could hamper the potential for capital accumulation, integration with local suppliers, transfer of technology and knowledge, and the ability of local staff to upgrade their skills and take up higher value-added jobs.

It might seem, therefore, to be a fine balance between achieving growth through tourism and avoiding imbalances. Indeed, Ghali's (1976: 538) observation that rather than trying to find out how much tourism contributes "the more interesting but more difficult question of 'Was it worth it?'" is an appropriate one.

Tourism and the SDGs

A rapidly expanding industry, it is no surprise that tourism also features in the Agenda 2030 (UN, 2015). Accounting for as much as a quarter or even up to a third of the national GDP, not least small island states may rely on tourism and hospitality in ways that are inherently risky and unsustainable. But also, beyond such extremes, the Sustainable Development Goals adopted in 2015 points to the role of the industry under the headings of decent work and economic growth (SDG 8), responsible consumption and production (SDG 12) and life below water (SDG 14). Nowhere is this clearer than in target 8.9, which stipulates that UN members should "devise and implement policies to promote sustainable tourism that creates jobs and promotes local culture and products" and to do so by 2030. This is to be assessed as the share of jobs in sustainable tourism out of a total number of jobs in tourism. Meanwhile, target 12.b admonishes member states to "develop and implement tools to monitor sustainable impact for sustainable tourism" and to keep track of the "[n]umber of sustainable tourism strategies or policies and implemented action plans with agreed monitoring and evaluation tools" (all quotes in this paragraph from UN, 2017).

This has spawned a number of critical reviews setting sight on how the SDGs are framed and what is missing from Agenda 2030 as seen from the vantage point of tourism development. Gender issues, indigenous perspectives, ethical consumption and the possibilities of introducing circular economies are all either rather marginal or missing outright (Boluk, Cavaliere, & Higgins-Desbiolles, 2019). Furthermore, as is also true of the SDGs in general, there is no explicit general strategy for how these targets are to be reached or prioritised. Implementation is left to individual UN member states and, as Niklasson (2019) shows, the presumption is that economic growth is a necessity to achieve the SDGs irrespective of it being classified as environmental (including SDGs 12 and 14), social and economic (SDG 8). The World Tourism Organization report on tourism and the SDGs for its part notes, on the basis of a survey of a large number of CSR reports from different parts of the industry, that competitiveness and profitability is key to sustainability. This sounds very much like business as usual (Boluk et al., 2019: 855–856), and this despite the fact that it is explicitly noted that "the decoupling of tourism growth from the use of finite natural resources" is imperative (UNWTO, 2017: 35). As for SDG 8, in its efforts to "disentangl[e] tourism's connection with the SDGs in terms of public policy", the World Tourism Organization focuses on the need to create "decent work opportunities, particularly for youth and women". Furthermore, it suggests that "[b]y knowing their supply chain, companies can ask questions of their suppliers and help to ensure commitment to and compliance with the targets" (UNWTO, 2017: 16, 54). Even so, along with procuring local products, it is job creation rather than the safeguarding of decent work that comes to the fore.

Sustainable and Responsible Tourism

For those familiar with idea of sustainable tourism, this may well seem a tinge anaemic. Accepting the definition promoted by the UN system itself, namely that sustainable tourism is "[t]ourism that takes full account of its current and future economic, social and environmental impacts, addressing the needs of visitors, the industry, the environment and host communities" (UNEP & WTO, 2005: 12), it is clear that the scope of sustainability as relevant to the industry is wider than that hinted at by the specific SDGs that target tourism as such. The public policy actions outlined suggest as much and the more general provisions of Agenda 2030 are presumably seen as applicable to tourism and hospitality as well (compare UNWTO, 2004). Yet, it remains an empirical issue whether the industry may fly under the radar and escape the attention that would otherwise spur it into more determined and elaborate action. After all, the notion of "eco-tourism", much in vogue by the 1980s and into the 1990s, was widely perceived to be little else than a marketing device (e.g., Wight, 1993). Similarly, by the turn of the millennium, it could credibly be claimed that sustainable tourism had made its entry into "most strategic tourism planning documents" (Hardy, Beeton, & Pearson, 2002: 475), yet the effects remained uncertain.

The above might suggest that insight into sustainable tourism is lagging behind. Despite early assessments to the effect that little headway was being made (e.g., Wheeller, 1993), this is not quite the case, though there is neither any lack of research on unsustainable outcomes nor on the attempts to promote sustainable tourism. If anything, the list of undesirable effects as evidenced by the research literature has grown over time. By the point in time the flagship *Journal of Sustainable Tourism* was launched in the early 1990s, it was very clear that tourism, as a prominent consumer of resources, actively contributed to a number of adverse effects of a social, cultural and environmental nature (e.g., McKercher, 1993). Not least, the sheer scale of activities, as expressed in the notion of mass tourism—the "Golden Hordes" as Turner and Ash (1975) had described it—had come to the fore. In due time it induced scholars to discuss carrying capacity (O'Reilly, 1986) that, as Saarinen (2006: 1125) notes, was to carry over to the discussions of sustainable tourism where it "occupies a key position".

As a consequence, and long before responsible tourism became the watchword, alternative forms of tourism entered the agenda (e.g., Cazes, 1989). Butler (1992) usefully summarised the differences between conventional and alternative forms, while (Eadington & Smith, 1992: 3) thought the latter was "broadly defined as forms of tourism that are consistent with natural, social, and community values, and which allow both hosts and guests to enjoy positive and worthwhile interaction and shared experience".

At that point in time, in addition to emphasising long-term objectives and outcomes across all three major areas of sustainability, a move from conventional or mass tourism to alternative forms was thought to imply primarily taking the perspectives of the host communities rather than guests and tourism firms. As of today, community-based approaches have not gone out of fashion (e.g., Dangi & Jamal, 2016) and also more recent initiatives such as "inclusive tourism" (Scheyvens & Biddulph, 2018) belong here. Yet alternative forms, while possibly the thin edge of the wedge driving developments in a more sustainable direction, has not proven to be the panacea. It is clear that alternative tourism is unlikely to displace mass tourism in its various guises and if current numbers are anything to go by it would seem that the problem worsened over time. This also remains true as mitigation strategies have been developed (addressing issues such as enclave economies and currency leakage, e.g., Freitag, 1994) and as the range of tourism forms and destinations have expanded considerably. Had mass tourism not retained its hold, the notion of over-tourism would not have seen the light of day.

In fact, it seems that the latter phenomenon has been instrumental in allowing the local to make a comeback, as epitomised in the notion of responsible tourism (Boluk & Weeden, 2016). For while the focus on mass tourism was very much about localised impacts, with the emergence of concerns over climate change, the global commons, at least in part, changed the focus from solely that of impact at destination. This change was a stepwise one and early discussions on tourism and climate change were largely about the consequences to the tourism industry in those countries where the hospitality sector makes an important contribution to the economy (Scott & Becken, 2010; Wall & Badke, 1994). Before long, however, tourism as a source of climate change, not just a victim, became a mainstream concern, at least in research (Becken, 2004; Gössling & Hall, 2006).

By then the notion of green tourism had seen the light of day. With a pedigree that stretches back several decades, as part of his discussion on alternative forms of tourism, Butler (1992: 36) thus found it useful to address the differences between mass tourism and its green opposite number. The latter implied a focus on smaller scale, the prevalence of local ("native" as he had it) developers, development staying within the bounds of local capacity, proactive discussion and planning with respect to (all) conceivable issues of an economic, ecological and social nature. It was a while though before the first comprehensive review of the environmental impact of tourism, that of Gössling (2002), arrived. That review provides a long list of areas of impact, including land cover and land use; energy: greenhouse gas emissions; biotic exchange and extinction of species; the spread of disease; and a changing understanding of the environment. While yet other items can be added, including water use, increased use of consumables that are transported long distances and the average trip increasing in length distance-wise, it does point to problems that are of both local and global significance. All in all, it goes well with the idea of responsible tourism, one of the main champions of which (Goodwin, 2012: 8) claimed that:

> Responsible Tourism is not about creating long checklists; it is about identifying the economic, social and environmental issues which matter locally and tackling them. The only global issue is climate change.

Save perhaps for local loss of biodiversity potentially being also of global importance and that changing perceptions of the environment acquired in one place may carry over to other settings, this comes across as an apt way of summarising it. Or is it? There are in fact reasons to cast the net a little wider.

Socially Sustainable Tourism

The beginning of discussions on green tourism and on environmental impacts, more generally, has not been allowed to obscure the realisation that social sustainability is an important dimension of tourism development. As already noted, there are a number of economic and social benefits to be derived from tourism development, perhaps most easily seen in labour market developments, local earning capacity and its contribution to regional development. This is also a prominent justification for countries making an effort to expand this particular industry. It is also precisely here that we may see that the agenda of responsible tourism might benefit from scanning the horizon for global impact more carefully. This section, starting out with a topical aspect of tourism employment that of immigrant labour, is designed to substantiate that observation.

The Positive Side of the Tally: Labour Market and Related Effects

Integrating immigrants into the labour force of the tourism industry holds both opportunities as well as challenges for host countries and migrants alike. At the nation-state level, challenges of integrating immigrants into the labour force often dominate the debate overshadowing the potential positive impacts to further economic growth, enlarged tax base and ageing domestic population with challenges to future pension and health care costs.

For some, migration and tourism are perfect examples of blending production and consumption, as is the case of socio-economically strong youth working in hotels and restaurants abroad for a multi-cultural experience (Williams & Hall, 2000). For others, because of poverty and few work opportunities in their home country, or as refugees forced to flee because of conflict or climate-related changes, integrating into the host country's labour force is a necessity to survive. The International Labour Organization estimates the number of international migrant workers at 164 million (ILO, 2018). Although the number of these in the broadly defined tourism industry is less well documented, in many countries the tourism industry has been growing faster than the economy as a whole (UNWTO, 2009) and the share of international migrant workers in the sector in countries with available statistics has also grown (Joppe, 2012). International migrant workers have been seen as a solution to the growing demand for labour in the sector, as well as a source of population rejuvenation, labour market efficiency, entrepreneurship, dynamism and diversity (ILO, 2010).

At the nation-state level, both home and host country benefit and face challenges of international migration that are often posited against each other. Potential benefits to the host country include an enlarged tax base and larger employment pool for especially low-skilled labour, while challenges often associate immigration to "integration" problems and increased costs on social welfare, increased crime and populist politics. In tourism, migration presents opportunities and challenges related to labour shortages of both skilled and unskilled labour, along with the challenges of oftentimes temporal dimensions of seasonal demand. King (1995) defines tourism jobs into ranks—of skilled managerial jobs at the upper level of organisational hierarchies where migrants are recruited from high-income countries to locations where managerial experience is relatively lacking, the second rank as intermediate posts such as migrant tour guides and agency representatives with home and host country knowledge and language skills, and finally, the third and largest group involving unskilled migrants moving from low- to high-income countries.

The Other Side of the Labour Market Coin

Connecting to the SDG 8 on decent work and economic growth, tourism presents both opportunities in terms of economic growth but also considerable challenges in terms of decent work. Human resources issues are arguably one of the greatest challenges in tourism management (Baum, 2007, 2015), especially related to King's (1995) rank of unskilled migrant labourers. As Wood (1997: 198) once described work in hotels and catering,

> [h]ospitality work is largely exploitative, degrading, poorly paid, unpleasant, insecure and taken as a last resort or because it can be tolerated in light of wider social and economic commitments and constraints.

Though this bleak description of working conditions in the tourism sector may be overly generalised and historic, Baum (2015) argues that the working conditions have only marginally improved because of cheap mobile labour, over-education of school leaving population, de-skilling technologies, focus on cost cutting and higher unemployment has continued the shift towards employer power in developed countries.

Precarious work refers to the changing modes of differentiation of migrant workers that give them unequal chances in market competition (Castles, 2015). Though 1 in 10 jobs globally are said to be in tourism (UNWTO, 2017), compared to environmental issues, working conditions and human resource issues in the industry have been largely and surprisingly ignored by academic scholarship (Baum, Kralj, Robinson, & Solnet, 2016). In their overview of the literature on precarity in the work context, Alberti, Bessa, Hardy, Trappmann, and Umney (2018) characterise precarious work by lack of security and predictability and which manifests as material and psycho-social depravation. Robinson, Martins, Solnet, and Baum (2019) argue that the tourism industry sustains this precarity vis-à-vis its employment practices through the political and social neo-liberal market agenda, thus benefitting employers, especially in the tourism industry, to the detriment of workers.

Of largest academic concern seems to be the level of wages and working conditions. According to a study by APEC (2017), tourism workers earn on average less than half of the all-industries average in many countries, in both developed and developing nations, for instance, in Canada, New Zealand, Philippines and Indonesia. Women and young people are most marginalised. Though it is acknowledged that there are many tourism companies that commit to broad-based corporate social responsibility and have high standards on ethical employment, allegations of tourism work bordering on "modern slavery" have been documented. For instance, in a study of the UK hospitality sector, tourism work included child labour, sex work, trafficking and forced labour (Armstrong, 2016). Indeed, different forms of modern slavery in the tourism industry are well documented in ILO's case studies database, involving child labour, sex work, human trafficking and bonded labour, in both developing and developed nations. Cheer (2018) adds an aspect, linking the geographies of marginalisation and modern slavery to tourism research and includes the growing practice of so-called orphanage tourism in less developed contexts where good intentions are commodified by orphanages together with "do-good" experience tourists. In much of the extant literature on social sustainability challenges in the tourism industry, it is argued that the neo-liberal market or capitalist system is oftentimes responsible for sustaining deep social cleavages and economic inequalities, particularly in tourism, thereby extending the precarious nature of tourism work itself (Robinson et al., 2019).

Other Effects

Serious as the exploitation of labour is—and it is truly serious and often criminal—it is neither the beginning nor end of the social sustainability of tourism. Also, in addition to the effects on communities and the economics of leakage, that is, consumption of local vs non-local products and the effects on local business this implies, there are other phenomena that from a social sustainability point of view warrant consideration. One of the most basic is the relationship between tourism and forms of crime that do not primarily issue from or are part of labour relations (Jones, Barclay, & Mawby, 2012; Botterill & Jones, 2010a; Pizam, 1999; Ryan, 1993). Yet, despite research over several decades, there appears to be few truly conclusive and universally valid results as to the effects of tourism growth on crime rates. Save for the observation that tourists are more likely to be victims of acquisitive crimes than are locals, there is little systematic evidence to suggest that crime rates increase along with tourism growth or that either locals or tourists themselves suffer the most from any increased incidence as can be observed in several studies (e.g.,

Biagi & Detotto, 2014; Chesney-Lind & Lind, 1986; de Albuquerque & McElroy, 1999; Pizam, 1982).

Although tourists may be both offenders and victims, and the fact that crime at times and in specific places clearly does increase alongside the growth of tourism arrivals, this lack of clarity might be a result of criminologists (as opposed to tourism researchers) having "avoided discussion of tourism as a crime generator" (Mawby, Barclay, & Jones, 2010: 320). It also probably accounts for the observation that much of that research focuses on the real or perceived impact of crime on the reputation of destinations (e.g., Botterill & Jones, 2010b), just as security threats may also deter tourism (Fourie, Rosselló-Nadal, & Santana-Gallego, 2020). Corruption, for its part, may not just deter tourism (Papathanassis, 2019), but might also put visitors and locals at serious risk. This may include the violation of building codes, with the consequences of the 26 November 2019 earthquake in Albania only being the most recent example (at which point two hotels collapsed, a number of alleged perpetrators subsequently being brought before court; *KJ*, 2019). Likewise, it is easy to imagine that corrupt practices may negatively impact the natural environment or cultural heritage.

Another issue that has become increasingly salient is "touristification", gentrification and displacement (Cocola-Gant, 2018; Gotham, 2005; Ioannides, Röslmaier, & van der Zee, 2019; Sequera & Nofre, 2018). Often part of discussions on over-tourism, and not infrequently blamed on the advent of digital platforms such as Airbnb, the phenomenon is not as recent as one might be led to believe. By way of an example, it has long been recognised that the proliferation of second homes may contribute to gentrification (Coppock, 1977; Paris, 2009). Thus, while "[t]he perception of second-home landscapes as elite landscapes has dominated not least the literature originating from the Anglosphere" (Müller & Hoogendoorn, 2013: 359) and might not be applicable everywhere, also in egalitarian societies such as the Nordic ones "an increasing polarisation of second-home ownership reserving the most attractive spots to high-income households" can be observed.

That said, in metropolitan areas and at major tourist destinations, global tourists often act as "international gentrifying elites" (Gravari-Barbas & Guinand, 2017) that combine the pursuit of leisure activities with investment opportunities. This implies the conversion of residential space for the locals to accommodation for tourists with out-migration, at times also outright displacement, of the residents and a changing structure of local area services on offer as a result (e.g., Cocola-Gant, 2018; Yrigoy, 2019). Likely to be most severely felt in places of real or perceived over-tourism, the triggering events of such gentrification may of course differ—from "upscale culture consumption" to heritage restoration to various efforts to mimic the Bilbao effect with a view to harnessing global capital (Gravari-Barbas & Guinand, 2017; McNeill, 2000)—but the outcome is one where residents at destination start objecting to tourism and tourists.

The role of the digital economy in all of this is not always easy to disentangle. On the one hand, the role of new ways of coordinating demand and supply of accommodation might be an important factor in the continued growth of tourism (e.g., Dodds & Butler, 2019). On the other, renting out to holiday makers is not a new phenomenon (the ease with which it takes place might be though) and at the level of principle, the sharing economy and peer-to-peer exchanges of resources and assets else not used to capacity would be as favourable to tourism as to other domains. In short, it carries a promise of more sustainable consumption. However, as Gössling and Hall (2019: 90) argue, the sharing economy is often eclipsed by the collaborative economy with its stronger focus on entrepreneurial opportunities. This includes opportunities made use of by the large and distant "global corporations [that] 'collect' a share of revenue even from the smallest social entrepreneurs", thereby implying that "small and medium-sized enterprises now support the very structures the sharing economy was thought to overcome".

Conclusion

"Tourists are consumers, not anthropologists", McKercher (1993: 6) noted, and consumption is therefore integral to tourism. Tourism is also an industry that for the most part operates on the principles of profit maximisation; indeed, the UNWTO (2017) underlines that sound economic health of tourism industry firms is a *sine qua non* for the benefits that tourism delivers, chief among which is a dependable source of income at destination. Tourism provides much needed jobs and incomes not least in areas else potentially peripheral to the economic mainstream. Those else disadvantaged in the labour market—the young, the newly arrived, etc.—stand to gain from the expansion of tourism, and often do. In no small part, the capacity of tourism to offer such opportunities emerge from its sheer volume and its continued growth, which in turn is dependent on its apparent universal attraction to those who come to enjoy a measure of affluence or find tourism activities increasingly affordable.

Not all potential destinations might be so favoured. As the notion of a resort life cycle suggests formerly successful destinations run the risk of fading away. If rejuvenation cannot be engineered, the benefits as might have accrued are also likely to go into the reverse. Something similar can be said of developments at more aggregate levels: what happens to the national economy if a country, as a favoured tourist destination, falls from grace? And what might happen if, say, for reasons of climate change mitigation needs, tourism goes into global decline? Academic research, at least, appears to have given that scenario little thought.

Yet, with growth, a range of adverse effects often follow, several of which have been touched upon in this overview of sustainable tourism. It is important to underline that these effects rarely are only local in nature, but may have repercussions well beyond the site where these adverse effects are generated or immediately visible. Climate change impacts are the obvious example, affecting the global commons as greenhouse gas emissions do; the fact that tourism by definition requires mobility adds to the strain. Less obvious, but equally a matter of serious concern, is the social unsustainability implied by precarious work, including trafficking in humans and the bonded labour that is part of modern slavery. While research on issues of this kind has picked up, at least within tourism studies, the global implications of it remain less visible than the local dimension of the suffering it entails. Clearly more could be done, potentially building on the pioneering work on the tourism migration system by Hall and Williams (2002). The same could be said of the leisure-and-investment complex that results in touristification and gentrification. It is not that research on sustainable tourism has turned its back on international investment flows or the nature of financialisation, only that it has not been given the same level of attention as is the case, for instance, in island development (Clark, 2013) or urban change (Weber, 2010). It would, no doubt, be gratifying to prove Mitchell's (1997: 304) prescient observation wrong:

> by effectively masking the degree to which capital must be located, the ideology of globalization allows local officials, along with local business people and property owners, to argue that they have no choice but to

> prostrate themselves before the god Capital, offering not just tax and regulatory inducements, but also extravagant convention centers, downtown tourist amusements, up-market, gentrified restaurant and bar districts, and even occasional public investment in such amenities as museums, theatres and concert halls.

As this chapter bears witness to, it is doubtful whether the SDGs can help mitigate, let alone stamp out, the adverse effects observed. A lack of success on that score would be unfortunate, as tourism is not just a favourite pastime of a large and growing part of the world's population, as a product and as an object of consumption, it also has a number of positive traits that are well worth preserving.

Acknowledgements This work was partially funded by the Swedish government research council for sustainable development Formas in the project, "The tourist industry and its contribution to sustainable development: Social networks and social capital in the employment of immigrants".

References

Alberti, G., Bessa, I., Hardy, K., Trappmann, V., & Umney, C. (2018). In, against and beyond precarity: Work in insecure times. *Work, Employment & Society, 32*(3), 447–457.

APEC. (2017). *Developing the tourism workforce of the future in the APEC Region*. Singapore: Tourism Working Group, Asia-Pacific Economic Cooperation Secretariat.

Armstrong, R. (2016). Modern slavery: Risks for the UK hospitality industry. *Progress in Responsible Tourism, 5*(1), 67–78.

Baum, T. (2007). Human resources in tourism: Still waiting for change. *Tourism Management, 28*(6), 1383–1399.

Baum, T. (2015). Human resources in tourism: Still waiting for change? A 2015 reprise. *Tourism Management, 50,* 204–212.

Baum, T., Kralj, A., Robinson, R. N. S., & Solnet, D. J. (2016). Tourism workforce research: A review, taxonomy and agenda. *Annals of Tourism Research, 60,* 1–22.

Becken, S. (2004). How tourists and tourism experts perceive climate change and carbon-offsetting schemes. *Journal of Sustainable Tourism, 12*(4), 332–345.

Biagi, B., & Detotto, C. (2014). Crime as tourism externality. *Regional Studies, 48*(4), 693–709.

Boluk, K. A., Cavaliere, C. T., & Higgins-Desbiolles, F. (2019). A critical framework for interrogating the United Nations Sustainable Development Goals 2030 Agenda in tourism. *Journal of Sustainable Tourism, 27*(7), 847–864.

Boluk, K., & Weeden, C. (2016). Responsible tourism. In J. Jafari & H. Xiao (Eds.), *Encyclopedia of tourism* (pp. 794–795). Cham: Springer.

Botterill, D., & Jones, T. (2010a). *Tourism and crime: Key themes*. Woodeaton, Oxford: Goodfellow Publishers.

Botterill, D., & Jones, T. (2010b). Introduction: Tourism studies and criminology. In D. Botterill & T. Jones (Eds.), *Tourism and crime: Key themes* (pp. 1–18). Woodeaton, Oxford: Goodfellow Publishers.

Burkart, A. J., & Medlik, S. (1974). *Tourism: Past, present and future*. London: Heinemann.

Butler, R. W. (1980). The concept of the tourist area life-cycle of evolution: Implications for management of resources. *Canadian Geographer/Le Géograph canadien, 24*(1), 5–12.

Butler, R. W. (1992). Alternative tourism: The thin edge of the wedge. In V. L. Smith & W. R. Eadington (Eds.), *Tourism alternatives: Potentials and pitfalls in the development of tourism* (pp. 31–46). Philadelphian, PA: University of Pennsylvania Press.

Capó, J., Riera Font, A., & Rosselló Nadal, J. (2007). Dutch disease in tourism economies: Evidence from the Balearics and the Canary Islands. *Journal of Sustainable Tourism, 15*(6), 615–627.

Castles, S. (2015). Migration, precarious work and rights: Historical and current perspectives. In C.-U. Schierup, R. Munck, B. Likić-Brborić, & A. Neergaard (Eds.), *Migration, precarity, and global governance: Challenges and opportunities for labour* (pp. 46–67). Oxford: Oxford University Press.

Cazes, G. H. (1989). Alternative tourism: Reflections on an ambiguous concept. In T. V. Singh, H. Leo Theuns, & F. M. Go (Eds.), *Towards appropriate tourism: The case of developing countries* (pp. 117–126). Frankfurt am Main: Peter Lang.

Cheer, J. M. (2018). Geographies of marginalization: Encountering modern slavery in tourism. *Tourism Geographies, 20*(4), 728–732.

Chesney-Lind, M., & Lind, I. Y. (1986). Visitors as victims: Crimes against tourists in Hawaii. *Annals of Tourism Research, 13*(2), 167–191.

Clark, E. (2013). Financialization, sustainability and the right to the island: A critique of acronym models of island development. *Journal of Marine and Island Cultures, 2*(2), 128–136.

Cocola-Gant, A. (2018). Tourism gentrificaiton. In L. Lees & M. Phillips (Eds.), *Handbook of gentrification studies* (pp. 281–293). Cheltenham: Edward Elgar.

Copeland, B. R. (1991). Tourism, welfare and de-industrialization in a small open economy. *Economica, 58*(232), 515–529.

Coppock, J. T. (1977). Issues and conflicts. In J. T. Coppock (Ed.), *Second homes: Curse or blessing?* (pp. 195–215). Oxford: Pergamon Press.

Dangi, T. B., & Jamal, T. (2016). An integrated approach to "sustainable community-based tourism". *Sustainability, 8*(5), 475.

de Albuquerque, K., & McElroy, J. (1999). Tourism and crime in the Caribbean. *Annals of Tourism Research, 26*(4), 968–984.

Dodds, R., & Butler, R. (2019). The phenomenon of overtourism: A review. *International Journal of Tourism Cities, 5*(4), 519–528.

Eadington, W. R., & Smith, V. L. (1992). Introduction: The emergence of alternative forms of tourism. In V. L. Smith & W. R. Eadington (Eds.), *Tourism alternatives: Potentials and pitfalls in the development of tourism* (pp. 1–12). Philadelphia, PA: University of Pennsylvania Press.

Fourie, J., Rosselló-Nadal, J., & Santana-Gallego, M. (2020). Fatal attraction: How security threats hurt tourism. *Journal of Travel Research, 59*(2), 209–219.

Freitag, T. G. (1994). Enclave tourism development for whom the benefits roll? *Annals of Tourism Research, 21*(3), 538–554.

Ghali, M. A. (1976). Tourism and economic growth: An empirical study. *Economic Development and Cultural Change, 24*(3), 527–538.

Goodwin, H. (2012). Ten years of Responsible Tourism: An assessment. *Progress in Responsible Tourism, 2*(1), 4–33.

Gössling, S. (2000). Tourism: A sustainable development option? *Environmental Conservation, 27*(3), 223–224.

Gössling, S. (2002). Global environmental consequences of tourism. *Global Environmental Change, 12*(4), 283–302.

Gössling, S., & Hall, C. M. (2006). Uncertainties in predicting tourist flows under scenarios of climate change. *Climatic Change, 79*(3–4), 163–173.

Gössling, S., & Hall, C. M. (2019). Sharing versus collaborative economy: How to align ICT developments and the SDGs in tourism? *Journal of Sustainable Tourism, 27*(1), 74–96.

Gotham, K. F. (2005). Tourism gentrification: The case of New Orleans' Vieux Carre (French Quarter). *Urban Studies, 42*(7), 1099–1121.

Gravari-Barbas, M., & Guinand, S. (2017). Introduction: Addressing tourism-gentrification in contemporary metropolises. In M. Gravari-Barbas & S. Guinand (Eds.), *Tourism and gentrification in contemporary metropolises: International perspectives* (pp. 1–21). Abingdon: Routledge.

Hall, C. M. (2014). You can check out anytime you like but you can never leave: Can ethical consumption in tourism ever be sustainable? In C. Weeden & K. Boluk (Eds.), *Managing ethical consumption in tourism* (pp. 32–55). Abingdon: Routledge.

Hall, C. M., & Williams, A. M. (2002). *Tourism and migration: New relationships between production and consumption.* Dordrecht: Springer.

Hardy, A., Beeton, R. J. S., & Pearson, L. (2002). Sustainable tourism: An overview of the concept and its position in relation to conceptualisations of tourism. *Journal of Sustainable Tourism, 10*(6), 475–496.

ILO. (2010). *International labour migration: A rights-based approach*. Geneva: International Labour Office.

ILO. (2018). *Global estimates on international migrant workers: Results and methodology* (2nd ed.). Geneva: International Labour Office.

Inchausti-Sintes, F. (2015). Tourism: Economic growth, employment and Dutch Disease. *Annals of Tourism Research, 54,* 172–189.

Ioannides, D., Röslmaier, M., & van der Zee, E. (2019). Airbnb as an instigator of 'tourism bubble' expansion in Utrecht's Lombok neighbourhood. *Tourism Geographies, 21*(5), 822–840.

Jones, C., Barclay, E., & Mawby, R. (Eds.). (2012). *The problem of pleasure: Leisure, tourism and crime* . London: Routledge.

Joppe, M. (2012). Migrant workers: Challenges and opportunities in addressing tourism labour shortages. *Tourism Management, 33*(3), 662–671.

King, R. (1995). Tourism, labour and international migration. In A. Montanari & A. M. Williams (Eds.), *European tourism: Regions, spaces and restructuring* (pp. 177–190). Chichester: Wiley.

KJ. (2019, 16 December). Tërmeti tragjik, 9 të arrestuarit dalin sot përpara Gjykatës, *Koha Jonë*, Tirana. Retrieved from https://kohajone.com/termeti-tragjik-9-te-arrestuarit-dalin-sot-perpara-gjykates/. Accessed 16 December 2019.

Lanza, A., Temple, P., & Urga, G. (2003). The implications of tourism specialisation in the long run: An econometric analysis for 13 OECD economies. *Tourism Management, 24*(3), 315–321.

Lenzen, M., Sun, Y.-Y., Faturay, F., Ting, Y.-P., Geschke, A., & Malik, A. (2018). The carbon footprint of global tourism. *Nature Climate Change, 8,* 522–528.

Li, K. X., Jin, M., & Shi, W. (2018). Tourism as an important impetus to promoting economic growth: A critical review. *Tourism Management Perspectives, 26,* 135–142.

Mawby, R. I., Barclay, E., & Jones, C. (2010). Tourism and victimization. In S. G. Shoham, P. Knepper, & M. Kett (Eds.), *International handbook of victimology* (pp. 319–340). Boca Raton, FL: CRC Press.

McKercher, B. (1993). Some fundamental truths about tourism: Understanding tourism's social and environmental impacts. *Journal of Sustainable Tourism, 1*(1), 6–16.

McNeill, D. (2000). McGuggenisation? National identity and globalisation in the Basque country. *Political Geography, 19*(4), 473–494.

Mihalič, T. (2013). Economic impacts of tourism, particularly its potential contribution to economic development. In C. A. Tisdell (Ed.), *Handbook of tourism economics: Analysis, new applications and case studies* (pp. 645–682). Singapore: World Scientific.

Mitchell, D. (1997). The annihilation of space by law: The roots and implications of anti-homeless laws in the United States. *Antipode, 29*(3), 303–335.

Müller, D. K., & Hoogendoorn, G. (2013). Second homes: Curse or blessing? A review 36 years later. *Scandinavian Journal of Hospitality and Tourism, 13*(4), 353–369.

Niklasson, L. (2019). *Improving the sustainable development goals: Strategies and the governance challenge*. Abingdon: Routledge.

O'Reilly, A. M. (1986). Tourism carrying capacity: Concept and issues. *Tourism Management, 7*(4), 254–258.

Papathanassis, A. (2019). The impact of corruption on travelers' perceptions and preferences. *Tourism Review, 74*(4), 795–814.

Paris, C. (2009). Re-positioning second homes within housing studies: Household investment, gentrification, multiple residence, mobility and hyper-consumption. *Housing, Theory and Society, 26*(4), 292–310.

Pizam, A. (1982). Tourism and crime: Is there a relationship? *Journal of Travel Research, 20*(3), 7–10.

Pizam, A. (1999). A comprehensive approach to classifying acts of crime and violence at tourism destinations. *Journal of Travel Research, 38*(1), 5–12.

Robinson, R. N. S., Martins, A., Solnet, D., & Baum, T. (2019). Sustaining precarity: Critically examining tourism and employment. *Journal of Sustainable Tourism, 27*(7), 1008–1025.

Ryan, C. (1993). Crime, violence, terrorism and tourism: An accidental or intrinsic relationship? *Tourism Management, 14*(3), 173–183.

Saarinen, J. (2006). Traditions of sustainability in tourism studies. *Annals of Tourism Research, 33*(4), 1121–1140.

Scheyvens, R., & Biddulph, R. (2018). Inclusive tourism development. *Tourism Geographies, 20*(4), 589–609.

Scott, D., & Brecken, S. (2010). Adapting to climate change and climate policy: Progress, problems and potentials. *Journal of Sustainable Tourism, 18*(3), 283–295.

Sequera, J., & Nofre, J. (2018). Shaken, not stirred: New debates on touristification and the limits of gentrification. *City, 22*(5–6), 843–855.

Telfer, D. J., & Wall, G. (1996). Linkages between tourism and food production. *Annals of Tourism Research., 23*(3), 635–653.

Turner, L., & Ash, J. (1975). *The golden hordes: International tourism and the pleasure periphery*. London: Constable.

UN. (2009). Tourism satellite account: Recommended methodological framework 2008. Studies in Methods F 80/Rev. 1. New York: Statistics Division, Department of Economic and Social Affairs, United Nations.

UN. (2015). Resolution adopted by the General Assembly on 25 September 2015, 70/1. Transforming our world: The 2030 Agenda for Sustainable Development. General Assembly, A/RES/70/1. New York: United Nations.

UN. (2017). Resolution adopted by the General Assembly on 6 July 2017, 71/313. Work of the Statistical Commission pertaining to the 2030 Agenda for Sustainable Development. General Assembly, A/RES/71/313. New York: United Nations.

UNCTAD. (2013, 28 January). Sustainable tourism: Contribution to economic growth and sustainable development. Trade and Development Board, TD/B/C.I/EM.5/2. Geneva: United Nations Conference on Trade and Development.

UNEP & WTO. (2005). *Making tourism more sustainable: A guide for policy makers*. Paris and Madrid: United Nations Environmental Programme and World Tourism Organization, Trade and Development Board.

UNWTO. (2004). *Indicators of sustainable development for tourism destinations: A guidebook*. Madrid: World Tourism Organization.

UNWTO. (2009). *Tourism and migration: Exploring the relationship between two global phenomena*. Madrid: World Tourism Organization.

UNWTO. (2017). *Tourism and the sustainable development goals—Journey to 2030*. Madrid: World Tourism Organization.

Wall, G., & Badke, C. (1994). Tourism and climate change: An international perspective. *Journal of Sustainable Tourism, 2*(4), 193–203.

Weber, R. (2010). Selling city futures: The financialization of urban redevelopment policy. *Economic Geography, 86*(3), 251–274.

Weeden, C., & Boluk, K. (Eds.). (2014). *Managing ethical consumption in tourism*. Abingdon: Routledge.

Wheeller, B. (1993). Alternative tourism: A deceptive ploy. In C. P. Cooper & A. Lockwood (Eds.), *Progress in tourism, recreation and hospitality management* (Vol. 4, pp. 140–145). Chichester: Wiley.

Wight, P. (1993). Ecotourism: Ethics or eco-sell? *Journal of Travel Research, 31*(3), 3–9.

Williams, A. M., & Hall, C. M. (2000). Tourism and migration: New relationships between production and consumption. *Tourism Geographies, 2*(1), 5–27.

Wood, R. C. (1997). *Working in hotels and catering* (2nd ed.). London: Routledge.

WTTC. (2019). *Economic impact of travel and tourism*. London: World Travel and Tourism Council.

Yrigoy, I. (2019). Rent gap reloaded: Airbnb and the shift from residential to touristic rental housing in the Palma Old Quarter in Mallorca. *Spain. Urban Studies, 56*(13), 2709–2726.

CHAPTER 9

Consumers Practicing Sustainable Consumption: Value Construction in Second-Hand Fashion Markets

Jenny Yi-Chen Han and Susanne Sweet

Introduction

Although increasingly relevant to policy and academic debates, the concept of "sustainable consumption" remains elusive (Black & Cherrier, 2010; Schaefer & Crane, 2005). Several aspects relating to the consumer have been brought forward as important for a transformation towards a more sustainable consumption. One aspect of sustainable consumerism assumes the individual as the central unit of creating environmental impact, whose actions and values are expressed through their consumption choices (Bly, Gwozdz, & Reisch, 2015; Micheletti, 2003). Another aspect entails a rethinking of the cultural and social function

J. Y.-C. Han
Stockholm Environment Institute, SEI Asia, Bangkok, Thailand

S. Sweet (✉)
Center for Sustainability Research and Department of Marketing and Strategy, Stockholm School of Economics, Stockholm, Sweden
e-mail: susanne.sweet@hhs.se

R. Bali Swain and S. Sweet (eds.), *Sustainable Consumption and Production, Volume II*,
https://doi.org/10.1007/978-3-030-55285-5_9

of material consumerism (Black & Cherrier, 2010: 439; Joy, Sherry Jr., Venkatesh, Wang, & Chan, 2012), a view that reframes the normative conception of material possession as a symbol of well-being and calls for a holistic downscaling of consumption through an anti-consumption ethos (ibid.)

In the sustainable consumption literature, the common discourse associates sustainable consumption choices as linked to environmental and altruistic values and, to reach an impact on consumer behaviour, an increased consumer awareness of sustainability issues is suggested (Goworek, Fisher, Cooper, Woodward, & Hiller, 2012). While the studies of attitude and behaviour are indeed crucial, explaining consumer behaviour on the basis of individual choice is limited (ibid.; Warde, 2016: 185) We, therefore, suggest a sociological perspective to explore individual consumption embedded in particular social contexts and settings. Our study will, therefore, focus on the context and setting of consumption of fashion, and specifically second-hand fashion.

Within this discourse, "sustainable fashion" is typically used as an umbrella category that describes a certain set of practices that aims to reconsider how fashion production and consumption affect labourers, the communities they inhabit, and their environment (Moisander & Personen, 2002). The field of fashion is a fascinating place to investigate mechanisms of "sustainable consumption"—an industry that is responsible for the output of significant sources of pollution (Goworek et al. 2012). It is also an industry where discourse of sustainability has been increasingly central to its agenda and a concept that has been heavily marketed in recent years (ibid.). "Sustainable fashion" claims to offer a more thoughtful ways of producing and consuming fashion that is not bound by the resource-intensive methods and excessive impulses that characterize the dominant "fast fashion" paradigm (Clark, 2008).

Extending the life of a garment has been demonstrated to be the most effective way of reducing environmental impact (Sandin, Roos, Spak, Zamani, & Peters, 2019). With this goal in mind, business models with a stronger circular focus are emerging (Nielsen & Gwozdz, 2018; Sweet, Aflaki, & Stalder, 2019). The increased prevalence of and importance placed on sustainable business models within fashion assumes that business models have the potential to change ingrained consumption patterns (ibid.; Lüdeke-Freund, 2010: 23). However, despite the increasing prevalence of more circular business models, most garments are still disposed of prematurely, largely due to the planned obsolescence that characterizes much of the fashion landscape, as well as the "throwaway culture" that it perpetuates (Clark, 2008). Although new business models for prolonging the life of garments, such as leasing and commercial collection and resale of pre-used, has emerged, consumers have been slow in adopting these models (Sweet et al., 2019; Sweet & Wu, 2019).

To better understand the underlying motives and culture of second-hand consumption, we will therefore seek to explore the valuation mechanisms and symbolic associations that drive consumption practices within second-hand fashion markets. We argue that, while participants claim that they engage within second-hand markets primarily due to environmental considerations, the practice of second-hand shopping is one that is largely driven by gaining symbolic and cultural capital. These symbolic associations demonstrate that second-hand shopping is as much about responsible consumerism as it is about engendering concepts that transcend sustainability: individuality, authenticity, and distinction. Thus, increasing acceptance of alternative business models within fashion requires a stronger cultural narrative than simply a diluted notion of "green consumption." In this way, it is speculated that one aspect of prolonging the life of garments is to continuously create and recreate its symbolic value for consumers.

Background

Second-Hand Fashion Markets

The second-hand market has largely been dominated by non-profit actors, selling donated apparel items as part of their charity work, and by flea markets. However, with digitalization, new forms of re-selling clothes have emerged and online market places such as Tradera, online shops, and social media platforms have provided consumers with a new range of options to sell and buy used clothes (Sweet et al., 2019). In addition, fashion entrepreneurs have also entered the market to offer distinct services, such as pick-up and resale, rental, repair, and remake, in efforts to prolong the life of garments. However, it remains to be seen if this shift is a result of overall market growth or is due to increased awareness about and entrepreneurship around the potential of creating value for discarded clothes (ibid.). Studies on the potential of these new business models have proven hard to evaluate since they are fairly new and the actors are still experimenting on the value propositions; the volumes are small, and not enough consumers are as yet active in the pre-owned market to be able to significantly make an impact on fashion consumption (ibid.).

Sustainable Consumption and the Sustainable Fashion Consumer

Within the literature on promoting sustainable consumption, the common discourse associates sustainable consumption choices to "bio-spheric" and "altruistic" values, with the common approach to be increasing consumer awareness and knowledge of sustainability issues (Fashion Revolution, 2018; Gowerek et al., 2012). While bolstering consumer knowledge is indeed crucial, explaining consumer behaviour on the basis of individual choice is limited (ibid.; Warde, 2016: 185) A sociological perspective contends that individual consumption behaviour is not simply based on principles, but rather embedded within particular social contexts and settings. With its rising popularity in the United States and Western Europe, commercial second-hand markets are an intriguing space to explore how Western notions of consumerism intersects with the pursuit of sustainability (Dresner, 2008). When situated against proposed avenues for more sustainable modes of consumption, second-hand consumerism maintains a fascinating middle ground: it is not inherently a business model with roots in sustainable intentions, yet it holds the potential for sustainable outcomes while also contrasting with lifestyle approaches such as "voluntary simplicity" that hinges upon an anti-consumption ethic (Doherty & Etzioni, 2003). Thus, the second-hand market allows for a unique look at issues of sustainability while simultaneously considering the social significance of consumption (Elgin, 1993).

Studies on Swedish consumers show that Swedes express great willingness to be more environmentally friendly in their purchases of clothing (Nielsen & Gwozdz, 2017). However, while studying their willingness to use different modes of sustainable apparel consumption, a lack of consumer engagement could be seen in choosing second-hand shopping over buying new clothes (Nielsen & Gwozdz, 2018). This finding was also confirmed in a study by Sweet and Wu (2019).

In summary, we are, therefore, unclear if the availability of second-hand business markets as well as if the public awareness in the fashion arena is sufficient to make second-hand shopping the first choice of fashion consumption. Therefore, it is even more important to learn and understand the second-hand consumer in the context of a second-hand consumer practice. What is valued and how the individual engages in second-hand consumption could possibly give hints that could support the development of business models that can capture both consumer and business value in second-hand clothing.

Purpose

The purpose of this chapter is to explore consumers' ways of creating and interpreting value of second-hand clothing, with the empirical context being second-hand retail markets. In doing so, two central questions are asked:

1. How are notions of value established within second-hand consumer cycles?
2. What implications do insights into consumer value construction have for the engagement of alternative business models and sustainable consumption?

This work contributes to and builds on the previous literature on sustainable alternative business models in fashion. In the literature on this topic, several issues associated to consumer acceptance have been explored, including socio-demographic factors (Nielsen & Gwozdz, 2017, 2018), consumer perceptions (Goworek et al., 2012), consumer motivations (Guiot & Roux, 2008; Joung & Park-Poaps, 2013; Steg, 2015), and the influence of "human values" (Nielsen & Gwozdz, 2018; Poortinga, Steg, & Vlek, 2004; Tamir et al., 2016). This study is a significant addition—both academically and in terms of practical knowledge—to this body of literature.

First, this chapter uses a sociological perspective in elucidating consumption choices by exploring valuation mechanisms that drive consumption practices within second-hand fashion markets. Breaking from previous research on how human values determine sustainable choices, which largely interprets "value" from the angle of personal worldview (see Schwartz, 1994; Stern & Dietz, 1994), this study seeks to explore "value" from the angle of symbolic worth. By highlighting the cultural capital aspect of sustainable consumerism, the study is able to explore consumer motivation from a perspective that is not fettered by "ethical consumer ethos," but rather related to the ways in which sustainable consumption enables or reflects certain social structures within consumption.

Second, this study provides insights to understand the underlying drivers of shopping orientations. As the role of "business models" in promoting sustainable fashion is increasingly taking centre stage, an understanding of the social drivers of consumption within sustainable fashion systems is important for seeing potential barriers and opportunities in transforming towards more sustainable consumption practices.

Conceptual Framework

Second-Hand Spheres and Hierarchies of Taste

Our study draws upon Bourdieu's concept of habitus and social practice theory, which frames consumption as embedded behaviour and brings into light the unconscious schemata behind consumption choices that hold certain self-serving and rewarding social outcomes. Under this lens, the embodied cultural capital of consumers implicates that "sustainable consumption" within second-hand spheres becomes a site where hierarchies of taste are produced and reproduced.

Within the domains of sociological studies related to consumption and sustainability, scholars (Reckwitz, 2002; Schatzki, 2001, 2002; Shove, 2003; Shove, Pantzar, & Watson, 2012; Warde, 2005) have prominently used social practice theories to broaden understandings of "human action" beyond behavioural understandings. According to this postulation, a cultural theory model that puts emphasis on the symbolic aspects of consumption is limited in illuminating the structures that determine consumption routine (Warde, 2016). However, practice theory and cultural theory are not mutually exclusive. Exploring and understanding how value is interpreted and created by consumers in second-hand spheres, challenges default social organizations and interpretations of what is "good" and fashionable. While the unit of analysis in this study is the individuals, it seeks to draw attention away from individual choice and explores how individual choice is mediated by larger sociocultural norms.

This study zooms in on one particular practice within consumption that has significant bearing: valuation. Valuation is an interesting topic of study because the way "value" is assigned to commodities is often overlooked within the field of sustainable consumption, as it is commonly assumed that a commodity's environmental impact forms the basis of its value for consumers. To understand "valuation" as a social practice is to consider the built and social environment as key contextual elements of valuation, which also transcends the idea that individual preferences and rationality are the sole agents within valuation. By illuminating this, we are able to situate "sustainable consumption" within its larger sociocultural milieu.

The second-hand fashion market falls under what Aspers (2009) calls a "status market," meaning that the basis of value within this market is largely dependent on the social structures of the market. Knowledge, according to Aspers (ibid.: 120), is based centrally on interpretation and acts as the primary facilitator of valuation within such a market. In a status market like the fashion world, "knowledge" is about understanding the "social structure and how its 'game' of positioning and mobility in the market and the industry…is played and communicated" (ibid.: 124). This "knowledge" that is carried out via valuation can be interpreted as the basis of cultural capital within the second-hand market.

Valuation as Practice and Habitus

Within economics, value is commonly placed in the context of exchange or marginal utility (Richins, 1994: 505). However, it is worth considering that despite economic formulations of value that characterize much of commercial exchange, a pure economic understanding of value does not capture the whole picture of how and why certain objects are deemed more "valuable" than others. Within sociological theories of consumption, it has long been understood that consumption constitutes a crucial process of producing forms of capital for the consumer (Rey & Ritzer, 2012: 448; West, 2010; Wright, 2005). What this concept of "capital" assumes is that the essential value of a commodity lies within the "immaterial" aspect of its production and consumption (ibid.). Baudrillard (1998) has argued that commodities should be seen as exhibiting sign values, suggesting that "use value" and "utility" are in themselves an embedded part of the "reflexive symbolic repertoire of things" within consumer culture (Bardhi & Eckhardt, 2012: 890).

Perhaps more so than any other industry, the realm of fashion is driven primarily by symbolic value rather than functional value. Aspers and Beckert (2011: 13) discuss the "imaginative" nature of symbolic value, in which certain goods not only determine the position of their owners within a certain social space but are more importantly representations of "espoused ideals and values that can be imaginatively appropriated through the purchase of goods." For example, when considering the ways in which symbolic aspects of consumption are tied to environmental concerns, the symbolic value of the commodity is commonly derived from discourses such as pollution or resource scarcity (Neves, 2004; Rey & Ritzer, 2012; Wilk, 2006). In this sense, value is anchored within the social world, as it is not "intrinsic to the materiality of an object," but rather "inseparably connected to the concept of meaning." (Richins, 1994: 505)

Bourdieu's conception of the market as a sphere of symbolic goods suggests an understanding of value that reflect an interconnectedness between various aspects of cultural capital (Bourdieu, 1996; Wright, 2005: 305). In order for these symbolic goods to be meaningful within a market, there needs to be a mutual consensus among the actors of what is considered "valuable." According to Bourdieu (1996: 229), this can only be achieved when the actors within this market are "endowed with the aesthetic disposition and competence" to recognize its value. Exploring how actors perform judgement of value, or "taste," by negotiating the different valuation scales, as well as the frictions that emerge during the process, can be interpreted as expressions of distinction, or capital.

Methodology

The data collection took place in Stockholm, Sweden. In Sweden, second-hand consumerism exists within a de-stigmatized market and takes diverse forms such as retro shops, vintage boutiques, thrift stores, and flea markets (Appelgren & Bohlin, 2015: 149). Although much of the second-hand exchange occurs online or in informal settings such as flea markets, the scope of this study is limited to the context of fixed second-hand retail spaces, which limits the variability of the results.

Ten semi-structured interviews were conducted with consumers who self-identified as committed second-hand fashion shoppers motivated by ethical concerns and interpreted the—market as a space of sustainable consumerism. All interviews were conducted in English and lasted an average of one hour. The interviews followed a narrative approach characterized by open questions that invited the participants to tell stories of their engagement within second-hand fashion spaces. Due to the specificity of the study, purposive sampling was used to recruit participants.

Participants were selected based on self-identified commitment to shopping second-hand fashion and were recruited via social media groups and snowball sampling. It is acknowledged that the diverse reasons for shopping second-hand are by no means mutually exclusive. However, by speaking to participants who identified "sustainability" as their top priority for shopping second-hand, the study was able to explore how care for sustainability factors mediate other processes of valuation. All the interviews were audio-recorded, transcribed *verbatim*, and coded for thematic analysis.

Limitations

There are two main limitations to the study. First, the use of qualitative interviews relates to issues of participant subjectivity. A general challenge is that participants may either consciously or subconsciously withhold or manipulate responses to either fit into the perceived research agenda or preserve their self-image, especially if they detect that their "true" perspectives may be inconsistent with their stated intentions (Lambert & Loiselle, 2008: 229) To combat this, the researcher eliminated leading questions in the interview that may have elicited expected responses.

The second limitation is that of generalizability. Since participants were recruited through purposive sampling, the results of the study cannot be perceived as being representative of, or applicable to the broader population. It is also important to recognize that the study took place in a high-income, Western context. The interviews framed second-hand shopping as a matter of personal choice rather than necessity, thus negating the aspect of socio-economic class in the discourse. Additionally, the fact that nine out of ten interviewees were women also indicates the non-representative nature of the sampling.

Acknowledging these limitations do not invalidate the findings, but rather prevents the tendency to draw inaccurate conclusions. The aim of the study is not to produce generalized results but to explore the topic in greater depth than what quantitative methods may offer.

Understanding Value Creation in Second-Hand Clothing

Three central aspects of valuation are identified from the data: value creation through spatial narratives, value creation through social experiences, and value creation through savvy thrifting. The pursuit of "novelty," which, in this context, refers to an experiential phenomenon rather than material newness, is revealed to be a central impetus to second-hand consumerism (Campbell, 1992: 55). In the following section, the practices are defined and explored in relation to its relevant literature.

Perceiving Objects: Creating Value Through Perceptions of Space

The importance of the spatial narrative within second-hand spaces is that it is intrinsically connected to consumer perception and the consequent creation of commodity value. In the interviews, there was a prevailing consensus that in terms of spatiality, second-hand stores provide a creative and unique atmosphere that is often not found in first-hand retailers. However, contradictions among consumer narratives are common. Despite the consensus that a spontaneous environment is part of the appeal of second-hand shopping, there is also an overwhelming consensus that organization and ease of navigation are of central importance to the experience. As one of the consumers described: "[the store] has to be sorted in a way that makes it easier to make a decision about what you're interested in...I can't just go into a store and look through everything." Another consumer describes the following about her favourite second-hand store: "I like it because... there's no... t-shirts in a box, there's nothing like that, everything is neat and tidy." The desire for order within a second-hand consumer space is something that potentially contradicts another high priority of the second-hand shopping experience—that of the "treasure hunting" feeling. Consumer narratives suggest that the balance between authenticity and curation is delicate. In critiquing a second-hand store, one consumer mentions the following:

> "I feel like [the store] is capitalizing on the trend of second-hand and vintage... like, they would rather sell the image of second-hand... but they are just making it more normal, not more unique.
>
> Researcher: So, the element of spontaneity is important? Yeah... it is."

This conflicting desire for order and spontaneity within second-hand consumer spheres points to the central aspect of the contextualization of a used garment. A decontextualized garment easily becomes marginalized and eventually devalued.

Particularly with garments labelled as "vintage" that are decades removed from the initial market in which it existed, contextualization is vital. One consumer alludes to the importance of this:

> I love Beyond Retro... they have a focus on like...the 60s, 70s... They...-make it easy to imagine yourself in another era... it's quite expensive... but worth it... it's a nice experience.

Discussion on practices of display needs to be held in conjunction with the shift towards the "aestheticization" of social relations and how the emphasis on presentation affects the way of seeing, and thus valuation (Cronin, 2004; Featherstone, 1991; Parsons, 2007). Vatin (2013) argues that valuation studies must extend beyond simply evaluation, the activity of classifying whether something is valuable, but also valorizing—the process in which things are made more valuable (Heuts & Mol, 2013). The narratives provided by the consumers support this claim: when consumers discuss their favorite pieces of second-hand garments, only a fraction of that value derives from the piece itself, while a substantial part derives from the experience of acquiring it. The following section will delve further into this dynamic by discussing value creation through social experiences.

Socializing Objects: Creating Value Through Social Experiences and Storytelling

Previous studies have illustrated the ways in which second-hand consumption elicits various unique recreational pleasures that go beyond pragmatic needs (Appelgren & Bohlin, 2015: 151; Guiot & Roux, 2008). Sociality comprises a large part of the recreational value of the second-hand consumer experience, a theme that is consistently reflected in the data. A consumer highlights this social aspect, explaining how the rapport she develops with the business owners and other shoppers are central to her shopping experience:

> I like that when I do second-hand shopping, there is a possibility to interact with people who I think I would get along with... in a much different way than I would feel that I would get along with people that work in a regular store.

Other interviewees further elucidate how their experience with second-hand shopping differs distinctively from shopping in high-street chains by drawing on the spontaneous social relations that arise within second-hand spaces:

> I met...an older woman who was handing in some cloths [to sell at the second-hand store]... And then I realized [she] had a very nice pair of boots, and I said to her, 'maybe I'm interested in your boots'...and we started to talk...and we actually kept in contact after that. I think these are meetings I don't expect to find at an H&M.
>
> I get this anxiety in corporate shopping environments... stores like vintage shops are a bit more personal and you can often get recommendations from the staff. They're not trying to up-sell you on things. The fitting rooms are...genuine... I don't like it when there are too many mirrors in all directions.

By contrasting the experience with a high-street retailer, the above narratives illustrate the perceived ability for second-hand consumption spaces to hold human connection unlike its first-hand counterparts that are perceived to be devoid of it. The consumers' account suggests the second-hand consumption space to be one that is "authentic" and not simply driven by monetary interest. The perceived autonomy given to the customers to act freely within the space is part of establishing an authentic experience and one of the most recreationally fulfilling. As one consumer describes:

> [Sometimes] I don't even bother to cover myself with the curtains as much [when I try on clothing in a second-hand store] because... you're sort of engaged with the other people in the same store... someone will say, 'oh that looks nice' or 'I think you should try blue instead'... it becomes much more like an event.

Closely accompanying the social aspect of second-hand markets is the storytelling component that enhances the value attributed to second-hand garments. Rhetorical storytelling effectively frames second-hand garments as "clothing with a story," thus attributing a certain emotional value that is unable to be represented in monetary terms. This aspect is most evident in the consumer interviewees' narratives when asked about their favorite second-hand finds:

> I bought this dress… in a super nice neighborhood…It's very good quality. The price wasn't too high. I bought it on a very good day at a very nice place, everyone was friendly. I was very happy when I found it…I had a few occasions where I wore it which were all good occasions.
>
> I bought these pair of boots… and the lady who sold them… told me… that they were like handmade in a [Swedish town]… there's a tradition behind them… Every time I've worn them I think, I wonder if I'll run into her… it's like… a cozy feeling.

Similarly, a consumer describes her experience of acquiring clothing in a second-hand clothing swap:

> I came [to the swap] with three pieces and I left with seventeen…I have such a positive association with every piece…because I also know the backstory to it…one girl had this glittery sweater, and she said 'this is my job interview sweater. I always wear this when I go to job interviews and I've always gotten the job.' So for me…this is a success sweater.

Although the latter story did not take place in a retail context, it sufficiently illustrates how the value of a garment is enhanced by the story attached to it. Storytelling can be explained theoretically by the notion of circulation, a concept that is central to discussions of value of second-hand objects. Gregson and Crewe (2003) have contributed a comprehensive study of how second-hand commodities acquire a unique value via the act of circulation through different contexts. Various contributions within the field of waste and disposal studies explore the cultural and social processes involved when the value of a disposed object is resurrected in novel contexts of consumption (Appelgren & Bohlin, 2015: 148; Gregson, 2007; Hetherington, 2004). This process is illustrated through Kopytoff's (1986: 64) concept of "singularization," in which personal meaning is ascribed to commodities via social embedding. In other words, commodities are not simply produced materially as things, but must also be culturally marked in order to have symbolic value. The aspect of sociality within second-hand markets is part of the value creation processes of second-hand garments because it contributes to the emotional value acquired via the consumption experience. As demonstrated in the narratives, this also contributes to the cultivation of second-hand consumer spaces as distinct from mainstream high-street retailers. A consumer illustrates this notion through her narrative of finding her wedding dress in a second-hand store:

> I first went to an expensive wedding dress store…and you had this personal attendant following you…and you [can only] pick three items…The dresses costed… the equivalent to 3000 [US] dollars. Then I wonder, is this really better because it's this expensive? … Why don't we go to [a second-hand store] and just look there…then I found this…dress, and I tried it on, it just fits me [perfectly]. It was a really surreal experience…this is too good to be true. Then I looked at the price tag and we all laughed… It was [only] 299 kronor.

This spontaneity, in addition to the low price, is what constitute a "great find" as it both carries a good story and illustrates a triumph against the system. The next section will further discuss this intersection of the social experience and the act of finding by exploring value creation through "savvy thrifting."

Finding Objects: Creating Value Through Savvy Thrifting

The data overwhelmingly demonstrates that the major source of recreational value derived from second-hand shopping is the thrill of the hunt and the joy of finding something unexpected. Gabriel and Lang (1995: 67) assert that the concept of "the find" is central to consumerism within the non-new realm, and this feeling of triumph against the system is one that is mentioned in all the consumer interviews. The following accounts address this most vividly:

> It's a hunt. What's fulfilling is that I'm the only one who found this garment. For me fashion is… also like a sport… buy[ing] a piece when there are 500 pieces on the rack, it doesn't really trigger me… I want something that's hard to get…When I go to second-hand and I find something, I'm the only one to have it!
>
> I like my garments much more if I put a lot of hours into finding it…if I spend hours finding the perfect sweater or something, then that sweater becomes very valuable to me because there's so much work behind it. If I know the story…then I get more of a relation to it.

> The best part about these [second-hand clothes] is that I wasn't searching for them…' It was more of a treasure hunt thing, 'look at what I found' basically.
>
> I get a special rush when I find something really precious that I wasn't looking for.

Ultimately, "the find" underscores a sense of discovering something that has been overlooked or hidden away and relates to the notion of novelty. Thompson (1979: 10) goes so far as to suggest that the value of an object within a second-hand sphere is only created upon discovery: "[the discard] continues to exist in a valueless limbo where at some later date it has the chance of being discovered." In his book *A Theory of Shopping*, Miller (1998) argues that the two most important goals of shopping, whether intentional or not, is first, to create and reproduce social relationships, and second, to save. Miller (ibid.) further claims that even spending can be experienced as saving, a concept that succinctly defines much of the consumer narratives on their experience of thrifting.

However, Miller's theoretical explanations do not wholly account for the ways in which the *ability* to carry out a certain type of thrift is just as important to the consumption experience. A common source of pride among the consumer's narrative is their distinct ability to look beyond the obvious. In the consumer accounts, the ability "to find" is a prized trait that is key in distinguishing the second-hand consumer to the perceived mainstream consumer. Heavily coupled with the ability "to find" is the notion of exercising patience, creative vision, and expert knowledge in what is considered high quality or unique. The following consumer accounts illustrate this sentiment directly:

> [Second-hand shopping] is a thrill because you don't know what you'll find. It's …creative because sometimes you see something and think, is that really ugly or is it really cool…I always think that no cloths are ugly, it's just how you put them together, and that's a really creative process…also, you don't have a bad conscious.
>
> There's something extra to second-hand shopping…it's like I know something…I know this is a good piece and I'm only paying this [low price] because of my knowledge, you know? I have a sort of expert knowledge that this can be my perfect dress and it doesn't cost much.

The possibility of making a novel discovery among a heap of "discards" constitutes a big part of the excitement of second-hand consumerism—an object that has been deemed as rubbish can become valuable through the exercise of certain competencies. Gregson and Crewe (2003: 4) refer to this as "capturing value," a central component to the incentive structures of second-hand consumerism. The interview excerpts demonstrate that it is the act of thrifting—capturing value through "the bargain"—that constitutes value as much as, if not more than, the garment itself.

What can be considered in conjunction with the recreational value of thrifting among consumer narratives is the common critique of the "throwaway culture" of the mainstream market. One consumer puts it plainly: "there are so many perfectly good stuff you can find in second-hand stores… but companies still… produce, produce, produce… I think it's crap." Another consumer reflects a similar sentiment: "I found this really new sweater in the [second-hand store] … it's my favorite now. But I was like, 'why would anyone throw this away?" The prevalent concern around first-hand fashion markets is its normalization and even encouragement for individuals to consistently dispose of garments in favor of newer trends (Cooper, 2005). One of the appeals of the second-hand market is the perception that garments produced in the past are more durable and thus better quality:

> Most of the item I bought second-hand…I consider them better quality items than new ones.
>
> I find that when I buy something second-hand, it's either from the 1990 s or before, so it's something that's kind of proven its own durability.
>
> I think the quality of the shoes you can find second-hand, it's so difficult to find nowadays.

The shared emphasis on quality and longevity forms another distinguishing factor between second-hand consumer spaces and first-hand ones. By intentionally excluding themselves from the mass-produced first-hand market, the second-hand consumers interviewed not only deviated from the perceived low-quality goods, but their knowledge also allowed them to "cheat the system" by acquiring high-quality items at a lower cost.

Consumer narratives reflect this sentiment:

> It's all silk…I got these black and white silk pants, and it's probably 250 kronor or something… and my top… it's also silk, and I bought it for 85 kronor… So, it's a total of 350 kronor for pure silk, which is a joke.

> I found this really beautiful shirt... but it was only 39 kronor because people didn't recognize the brand... sometimes you can find... niche brands with really good fabric for really... cheap, because people don't know it. I found a jacket, I think it [costs] 150 kronor, and the new price was like 4000 kronor, and I don't think people even realize it.

As demonstrated by the data, the ability to perform "the find" is ultimately about exhibiting forms of savvy consumerism through capturing value. This expertise requires the consumer to have the creative eye or exclusive knowledge of fashion that others may not. The ability to identify status-conferring features of a garment (such as material quality and brand names) is ultimately founded on the consumer's display of cultural capital, a notion that will be described in-depth in the following section.

Discussion

The aim of this chapter is to explore consumer valuation within second-hand consumption spaces from the angle of cultural capital and to examine the ways in which this information can inform consumer engagement within alternative business models. The results have indicated the ways in which value is constructed and transmitted within the second-hand fashion market, alluding to the perception of the second-hand market as a space that holds novel experiences. In addition, the practices of value creation identified from the data, points to the bigger picture of how narrative constructs, across second-hand spaces, attempt to distinguish second-hand consumerism from the perceived homogenizing effects of mainstream mass consumerism. Thus, second-hand shopping, or rather, the know-how of "proper" second-hand shopping, is framed as a form of cultural capital. DeLong, Heinemann, and Reiley (2005: 24) describe the skill of value assessment within a second-hand context as essentially "the ability to discriminate the authentic product." It is this skill of valuation that serves as the embodiment of culture capital that transforms the average consumer into a connoisseur. This form of "savvy consumerism" effectively turns second-hand consumer spaces into spheres of performing cultural proficiency and leisure. Thus, the ability to conduct strategic shopping is an expression of individual capability and autonomy.

The narratives from the consumers suggest that second-hand shopping is interpreted as distinct from mainstream consumerism as a more thoughtful approach towards both personal style and consumption.

Among the narratives, there is a distinct need for the second-hand consumers to distinguish themselves from the average, mindless consumer culture in order to reassert their critical stance against mainstream fashion consumption. This aspect is especially evident when consumer interviewees describe their thriftiness in the second-hand realm. The undertone of pride that is prevalent among interviewees when discussing their mastery in this area subtly echoes a contemporary reflection of the Veblenian conspicuous consumer. Bourdieu (1984 [1979]) relates this to the notion of cultural capital in his conception of the discerning consumer. As the chapter shows, second-hand markets create a context in which consumers can shop under the assumption that they are separate from mainstream consumption and thus motivated by alternative "tastes" (ibid.). This observation draws attention to sustainable consumerism's more self-interested motivators of identity display, thus challenging the notion of individuals acting on behalf of their altruistic convictions (Black & Cherrier, 2010; Stern, Dietz, & Guagnano, 1995). Cherrier (2009) asserts this by discussing consumers who actively reject mainstream commercialization as a way of asserting their unique identity construction as well as "a desire to find meaning in their consumption practices" (Bly et al., 2015: 127). Thus, committing to sustainable consumerism (via shopping in second-hand markets) provides a sense of the distinguished self.

Understanding frameworks of valuation from the perspective of cultural capital suggests that, while second-hand markets are rhetorically and spatially constructed as alternative consumption spaces, the second-hand market itself is similarly created to accommodate and cultivate certain consumerist desires and practices. While consumers periodically refer back to sustainability as their point of departure in participating in the second-hand market, the data suggests that second-hand shopping is as much about reducing environmental and social impact as it is about engendering concepts that transcend sustainability: individuality, authenticity, and distinction.

Implications

This has implications f for business model implementation because instead of introducing models that appeal to the eco-consciousness or goodwill of the individual (whose effects are limited, see Warde, 2016, chapter 9), perhaps a more effective method is to challenge the convention or cultural narrative on what is perceived as valuable. For example, within fashion, instead of appealing to newness as a factor in good fashion, creativity, and scarcity can be one that is promoted. By situating "sustainable consumption" within its larger sociocultural milieu, one can better explore the underlying motivations that draw consumer engagement within a specific sustainable business model. Hence, current entrepreneurial efforts to engage with the second-hand consumers could be adapted to different value and cultural contexts of individuality, authenticity, and distinction, rather than solely lean on general information on consumers awareness, attitudes, and behaviour in relation to sustainability issues.

Acknowledgements We wish to thank our discussants at the book workshop, October 2019, at Stockholm School of Economics for their fruitful comments on our initial book draft and to the participants and discussants at the Mistra Center for Sustainable Markets on an early draft discussed at a WIP seminar during the spring of 2019.

References

Appelgren, S., & Bohlin, A. (2015). Growing in Motion: The circulation of used things on Secondhand Markets. *Culture Unbound, 7,* 143–168.

Aspers, P. (2009). Knowledge and theory in markets. *Theory and Society, 38*(2), 111–131.

Aspers, P., & Beckert, J. (2011). *The worth of goods: Valuation and pricing in the economy.* Oxford: Oxford University Press.

Bardhi, F., & Eckhardt, G. (2012). Access based consumption: The case of car sharing. *Journal of Consumer Research, 39*(4), 881–898.

Baudrillard, J. (1998). *The consumer society.* London: Sage Publications.

Black, I., & Cherrier, H. (2010). Anti-consumption as part of living a sustainable lifestyle: Daily practices, contextual motivations and subjective values. *Journal of Consumer Behavior, 9,* 437–453.

Bly, S., Gwozdz, W., & Reisch, L. (2015). Exit from the high street: An exploratory study of sustainable fashion consumption pioneers. *International Journal of Consumer Studies, 39,* 125–135.

Bourdieu, P. (1984). *Distinction: A social critique of the judgement of taste.* London: Routledge.

Bourdieu, P. (1996). *The rules of art.* Cambridge: Polity Press.

Campbell, C. (1992). The desire for the new: Its nature and social location as presented in theories of fashion and modern consumerism. In R. Silverstone & E. Hirsch (Eds.), *Consuming technologies: Media and information in domestic spaces* (pp. 48–64). London: Routledge.

Cherrier, H. (2009). Anti-consumption discourses and consumer-resistant identities. *Journal of Business Research, 62,* 181–190.
Clark, H. (2008). Slow + fashion—An oxymoron—Or a promise for the future? *Fashion Theory, 2*(4), 427–446.
Cooper, T. (2005). Slower consumption: Reflections on product life spans and the "throwaway society". *Journal of Industrial Ecology, 9,* 51–67.
Cronin, A. M. (2004). Regimes of mediation: Advertising practitioners as cultural intermediaries? *Consumption, Markets and Culture, 7*(4), 349–369.
Delong, M., Heinemann, B., & Reiley, K. (2005). Hooked on vintage! *Fashion theory. The Journal of Dress, Body & Culture, 9*(1), 23–42.
Dresner, S. (2008). *The principles of sustainability* (2nd ed.). London: Earthscan.
Doherty, D., & Etzioni, A. (2003). *Volontary Simplicity. Responding to consumer culture.* Oxford: Rowman & Littlefield Publishers, Inc.
Elgin, D. (1993). *Volontary Simplicity. Toward a way of life that is outwardly simple, inwardly rich.* Newyork: HarperCollins.
Fashion Revolution. (2018). *Consumer survey report: A baseline survey on EU consumer attitudes to sustainability and supply chain transparency in the fashion industry.* Retrieved from https://www.fashionrevolution.org/wp-content/uploads/2018/11/201118_FashRev_ConsumerSurvey_2018.pdf?fbclid=IwAR3MlghBIdIZa78Pu7LUh7XmDn0XY6lcOpcJyE5U9igErm5rgelC7Vk-SaY.
Featherstone, M. (1991). *Consumer culture and postmodernism.* London: Sage Publications.
Gabriel, T., & Lang, T. (1995). *The unmanageable consumer.* Thousand Oaks, CA: Sage Publications.
Goworek, H., Fisher, T., Cooper, T., Woodward, S., & Hiller, A. (2012). The sustainable clothing market: An evaluation of potential strategies for UK retailers. *International Journal of Retail & Distribution Management, 40*(12), 935–955.
Gregson, N. (2007). *Living with things: Ridding, accommodation, dwelling.* Wantage, UK: Sean Kingston Publishing.
Gregson, N., & Crewe, L. (2003). *Second-hand cultures.* Oxford: Berg Publishers.
Guiot, D., & Roux, D. (2008). Measuring secondhand shopping motives, antecedents and consequences. *Recherche et Applications En Marketing (English Edition), 23*(4), 63–91.
Hetherington, K. (2004). Secondhandedness: Consumption, disposal, and absent presence. *Environment and Planning D: Society and Space, 22*(1), 157–173.
Heuts, F., & Mol, A. (2013). What is a good tomato? A case of valuing in practice. *Valuation Studies, 1*(2), 125–146.

Joung, H.-M., & Park-Poaps, H. (2013). Factors motivating and influencing clothing disposal behaviours. *International Journal of Consumer Studies, 37*, 105–111.

Joy, A., Sherry, J. F., Jr., Venkatesh, A., Wang, J., & Chan, R. (2012). Fast fashion, sustainability, and the ethical appeal of luxury brands. *Fashion Theory, 16*(3), 273–296.

Kopytoff, I. (1986). The cultural biography of things: Commoditization as process. In A. Appadurai (Ed.), *The social life of things: Commodities in cultural perspective* (pp. 64–91). Cambridge: Cambridge University Press.

Lambert, S. D. & Loiselle, C. G. (2008). Combining individual interviews and focus groups to enhance data richness. *Journal of Advanced Nursing, 62*, 228–237.

Lüdeke-Freund, F. (2010, October). *Towards a conceptual framework of business models for sustainability*. Conference paper presented at the ERSCP-EMSU conference, Delft, The Netherlands.

Micheletti, M. (2003). *Political virtue and shopping*. New York: Palgrave Macmillan.

Miller, D. (1998). *A theory of shopping*. Cambridge: Polity Press.

Moisander, J., & Personen, S. (2002). Narratives of sustainable ways of living: Constructing the self and others as a green consumer. *Management Decision, 40*(4), 329–342.

Neves, L. M. P. (2004). Cleanness, pollution and disgust in modern industrial societies. *Journal of Consumer Culture, 4*(3), 385–405.

Nielsen, K. S., & Gwozdz, W. (2017). *Field report consumer survey* (A Mistra Future Fashion report Number: 2017:2). Stockholm. Retrieved from http://mistrafuturefashion.com/wp-content/uploads/2017/06/Nielsen-and-Gwozdz-Field-report-Consumer-Survey.pdf.

Nielsen, K. S., & Gwozdz, W. (2018). *Report on geographic differences in acceptance of alternative business models* (A Mistra Future Fashion Report 2018:3). Retrieved from http://mistrafuturefashion.com/wp-content/uploads/2018/05/Mistra-Future-Fashion-Report-3.1.2.1.pdf.

Parsons, E. (2007). Thompson's rubbish theory: Exploring the practices of value creation. *European Advances in Consumer Research, 8*, 390–393.

Poortinga, W., Steg, L., & Vlek, C. (2004). Values, environmental concern, and environmental behavior: A study into household energy use. *Environment and Behavior, 36*(1), 70–93.

Reckwitz, A. (2002). Towards a theory of social practices: A development in culturalist theorizing. *European Journal of Social Theory, 5*(2), 243–263.

Rey, P. J., & Ritzer, G. (2012). The sociology of consumption. In G. Ritzer & W. W. Murphy (Eds.), *The Wiley-Blackwell companion to sociology* (1st ed., pp. 444–469). Hoboken, NJ: Wiley Blackwell.

Richins, M. (1994). Valuing things: The public and private meaning of possessions. *Journal of Consumer Research, 21*(3), 504–521.
Sandin, G., Roos, S., Spak, B., Zamani, B. & Peters, G. (2019). *Environmental assessment of Swedish clothing consumption* (A Mistra Future Fashion Report No 2019:05). Retrieved from http://mistrafuturefashion.com/wp-content/uploads/2019/08/G.Sandin-Environmental-assessment-of-Swedish-clothing-consumption.MistraFutureFashionReport-2019.05.pdf.
Schaefer, A., & Crane, A. (2005). Addressing sustainability and consumption. *Journal of Macromarketing, 25*(1), 76–92.
Schatzki, T. (2001). *Social practices*. Cambridge: Cambridge University Press.
Schatzki, T. (2002). *The site of the social: A philosophical account of social life and change*. University Park: Penn State University Press.
Schwartz, S. H. (1994). Are there universal aspects in the structure and contents of human values? *Journal of Social Issues, 50*, 19–45.
Shove, E. (2003). *Comfort, cleanliness and convenience: The social organization of normality*. Oxford: Berg Publishers.
Shove, E., Pantzar, M., & Watson, M. (2012). *The dynamics of social practice: Everyday life and how it changes*. London: Sage Publications.
Steg, L. (2015). Environmental psychology and sustainable consumption. In L. Reisch & J. Thãgersen (Eds.), *Handbook of research on sustainable consumption*. Cheltenham, UK: Edward Elgar.
Stern, P. C., & Dietz, T. (1994). The value basis of environmental concern. *Journal of Social Issues, 50*, 65–84.
Stern, P., Dietz, T., & Guagnano, G. (1995). The new ecological paradigm in social-psychological context. *Environment and Behavior, 27*, 723–743.
Sweet, S., Aflaki, R., & Stalder, M. (2019). *The Swedish market for pre-owned apparel and its role in moving the fashion industry towards more sustainable practices* (A Mistra Future Fashion Report No 2019:01). Retrieved from http://mistrafuturefashion.com/wp-content/uploads/2019/02/Mistra-Future-Fashion-Report-2019_01-SRF-3.1.1-S.-Sweet.pdf.
Sweet, S., & Wu, A. (2019). *Second-hand and leasing of clothing to facilitate textile reuse: Identifying sources of value generation from the perspective of businesses and user* (A Mistra Future Fashion Report 2019:13). Retrieved from http://mistrafuturefashion.com/wp-content/uploads/2019/10/S.Sweet_.-second-hand-and-leasing-clothing-textile-reuse.-mistra-Future-fashion-2019.13.pdf.
Tamir, M., Schwartz, S. H., Cieciuch, J., Riediger, M., Torres, C., Scollon, C., … Vishkin, A. (2016). Desired emotions across cultures: A value-based account. *Journal of Personality and Social Psychology, 111*(1), 67–82.
Thompson, M. (2017 [1979]). *Rubbish theory: The creation and destruction of value*. Chicago: University of Chicago Press.

Vatin, F. (2013). Valuation as evaluation and valorizing. *Valuation Studies, 1*(1), 31–50.

Warde, A. (2005). Consumption and theories of practice. *Journal of Consumer Culture., 5*(2), 131–153.

Warde, A. (2016). *Consumption: A sociological analysis*. London: Palgrave Macmillan.

West, E. (2010). Expressing the self through greeting card sentiment. *International Journal of Cultural Studies, 13*(5), 451.

Wilk, R. (2006). Bottled water. *Journal of Consumer Culture, 6*(3), 303–325.

Wright, D. (2005). Commodifying respectability: Distinctions at work in the bookshop. *Journal of Consumer Culture, 5*(3), 295–314.

CHAPTER 10

Translation(s) of Circular Fashion: Production or Consumption?

Clara My Lernborg

Introduction

> *An app for selling your old used clothes, a for-profit clothing rental, a pair of trousers made of biomass, a clothing library, a dress made of plastic bottles, lending your ball gown to a friend or stranger, utilizing textile spill from the factory floor. All isolated examples of what could be considered the relatively novel concept of Circular Fashion. What is it and how is it translated to the Swedish fashion industry?*

An unsurmountable ecological crisis is no longer perceived to be merely at the horizon with mountains of waste accumulating, and industrial water depleting and polluting ground water; many claim that it is already knocking at our door. Cries for sustainable solutions in recent years have increasingly been answered with the implementing of a or *the* Circular Economy. With a global population of nine billion projected in 2050 and

C. M. Lernborg (✉)
Center for Sustainability Research, Stockholm School of Economics, Stockholm, Sweden

R. Bali Swain and S. Sweet (eds.), *Sustainable Consumption and Production, Volume II*,
https://doi.org/10.1007/978-3-030-55285-5_10

increased competition for resources, it is often argued that solutions are needed for addressing important environmental issues. Addressing these issues requires not only technical advances and transfers, but also societal shifts in terms of behaviour (Imaz & Sheinbaum, 2017).

Since its introduction in the 1960s, the idea and attraction of the Circular Economy has steadily increased, in academia and in the private sector, as well as at a policy level (EC, 2018; Schroeder, Anggraeni, & Weber, 2019). In particular, its potential for combining environmental and economic benefits is held forth (Geissdoerfer, Savaget, Bocken, & Hultink, 2017). Further, it is argued that hitherto, the concept has mainly been defined and developed by practitioners. Thereby, some find that the concepts of the Circular Economy, and in its continuation Circular Fashion, remain underdeveloped in research (Camacho-Otero, Boks, & Pettersen, 2018).

A wide range of actors engages in shaping the idea of Circular Economy and Circular Fashion. Overwhelmingly, the Circular Economy is presented as a win–win solution to overcome detrimental environmental impacts of business, whilst creating new business opportunities. However, the practical implementation of these ideas can be put into question; few practical examples exist of how companies have made use of them beyond efficiency measures (Haupt & Hellweg, 2019; Watson, Gylling, & Thörn, 2017). The context of study in this chapter is the Swedish fashion industry; therein, several companies now refer to circularity in its sustainability reports and consumer-oriented communication, and some claim to have implemented circular activities into its business models (Stål & Corvellec, 2018).

The global fashion industry has received poignant critique for its labour practices, but also engages in numerous detrimental environmental impacts contributing to overflows of waste, overuse of water and chemicals. In the past decade, one of several proposed sustainable solutions to these nefarious environmental impacts has been Circular Fashion. It often entails integrating the perspective of closed-loop systems, intended to reduce the need for finite resources. Similar to other sustainability-related concepts, this idea appears to be used interchangeably without a common definition (Merli, Preziosi, & Acampora, 2018), of course some definitions such as EMF's (2013) are influential (Schut, Crielaard, & Mesman, 2016). Given the importance bestowed upon circularity in order to achieve sustainability, it is herein considered relevant to unveil the different messages attached to the concept of Circular Fashion and from whom they stem. To this end, the concept of translation is used in order to allow further understanding of how the idea of Circular Fashion has and is still travelling across different sets of actors.

In this chapter, it is found that individual aspects of Circular Fashion are translated. Circular Economy, and Fashion, constitute typical examples of a management idea. In research on the travel of ideas, attention has been given to translation in order to capture how ideas flow and from whom. Actors promote certain ideas and discard others, further contributing to the institutionalization of ideas. The multitude of different actors, their different techniques and interconnectedness call for the need to understand their respective selective adaptations of Circular Fashion. Through a qualitative analysis of sustainability reports, governmental proposals, and social media messages, a case study of the studied actors' translation of the idea of Circular Fashion is presented.

Thus, this chapter investigates the translations of Circular Fashion, by analysing the circularity messages of the different actors contributing to the propagation of this idea in the Swedish fashion industry. This chapter will, therefore, review the numerous translations of this idea amongst cross-sectoral actors promoting its use. To this end, the fashion industry and its characteristics will be presented, followed by the historical background to the concepts of Circular Economy and Fashion. Thereafter, the methodological approach and theoretical framework of translation will be discussed. Subsequently, the empirics of the three key types of actors involved in the translation of this concept will be presented and analysed: companies, government, and NGOs. The chapter will conclude with a discussion of the findings.

The aim is to enhance the understanding of Circular Economy, and ultimately Circular Fashion, by addressing the following research question: How is Circular Economy and its practices translated by different actors to the Swedish fashion industry?

Circular Economy

Theories and definitions on Circular Economy (CE) are still relatively novel, yet appear to be prolific and overlapping, with definitions emanating from a wide range of actors. This section presents the background to the CE, a sample of its many definitions, and an overview of the general themes involved in related research.

Developing and Defining Circularity

> First, at its core, a circular economy aims to "design out" waste. Waste does not exist—products are designed and optimized for a cycle of disassembly and reuse. (EMF, 2013: 7)

The concept of CE was born in 1966, with the publication of Boulding's proposal of closed-loop systems, as opposed to traditional linear systems that exacerbate resource use and potential negative environmental impacts (Geissdoerfer et al., 2017). This idea has formed the basis for research and practice on the CE.

The interrelationship between sustainability, Corporate Social Responsibility (CSR), and circularity appears indisputable. Sustainability constitutes a wider perspective of addressing social, environmental, and economic issues to reach sustainable development. The need to integrate such concerns in turn is driven by the societal shifts in views of business-society relationships, globalized supply chains, and amplified sustainability impacts of business operations. However, the links between these concepts are seldom made explicit (Geissdoerfer et al., 2017; Kirchherr, Reike, & Hekkert, 2017) and thus how to achieve sustainable development remains blurred.

There is no commonly agreed upon definition of the CE, yet the focus is most frequently on closed-loop systems and reconnecting natural ecosystems with the economic systems (Kirchherr et al., 2017; Merli et al., 2018; Su, Heshmati, Geng, & Yu, 2013), see further Section Overview of CE Research. However, the circularity foci and its applications, appear to vary by region (Ghisellini, Cialani, & Ulgiati, 2016; Murray, Skene, & Haynes, 2017), consistent with a travel of ideas approach. In Europe, this development has been led by practitioners, through market demand and voluntary corporate initiatives (EC, 2015; EMF, 2013; Ghisellini et al., 2016).

The underlying assumption in the idea of CE is that the current resource usage is wasteful and unsustainable; thus, there is a need for a radical transformation of resource use in both production and consumption (Camacho-Otero et al., 2018; Urbinati, Chiaroni, & Chiesa, 2017). The subsequent practice and research foci in Europe are particularly intent on prolongation of product life through 'RECYCLING' and 'REUSE'

(Elia, Gnoni, & Tornese, 2017). Accordingly, the majority of definitions emphasize the importance of optimizing resource utilization, for example, value retention (CIRAIG, 2015; Kirchherr et al., 2017; Nasr et al., 2018) or prolonging resource productivity (Blomsma & Brennan, 2017) (Table 10.1).

Overview of CE Research

Many aspects of the CE relate to the importance of integrating sustainability concerns into the whole production and consumption chain: the supply chain. Unsurprisingly, the CE idea bases itself on supply chain research. It is tightly linked to theories of reverse logistics and of closed-loop systems (Witjes & Lozano, 2016) in which the supply chain constitutes a self-sufficient circular flow. Reverse logistics involves five key processes for CE: Product collection; Returns logistics; Sorting and disposal; Reuse alternatives; and Redistribution (Govindan, Soleimani, & Kannan, 2015; Krikke, Blanc, & van de Velde, 2004). Depending on the industry, these processes may have different orders of priority. The implications for the different stages of the fashion industry will be discussed in the Section titled 'Circular Fashion: Production & Consumption'.

In turn, the theory of closed-loop supply chains is derived from the reverse logistics research stream (Govindan et al., 2015). Therein, material or resource efficiency is essential, in that, no additional resource extraction is to be needed in such systems. The CE involves thinking of not only closing, but also slowing down resource loops. Slowing resource loops is of outmost importance in order to delay the creation of waste (Bocken, De Pauw, Bakker, & van der Grinten, 2016; Murray et al., 2017) (Table 10.2).

Circular Economy and Fashion

We will start by an overview of the global fashion industry, its characteristics as well as of the sustainability, and circularity, challenges involved before proceeding to an overview of the application of circularity in the fashion context, or Circular Fashion, for both production and consumption aspects.

Table 10.1 Definitions of circular economy

Author	*Definition*
EMF (2013: 7)	'An industrial system that is restorative or regenerative by intention and design'
Mistra Future Fashion (2019)	'Instead of today's linear structure where each business and production process is individually optimized, the circular economy focuses on how to maximize the processes collectively and secure as low environmental impact as possible. It means resource minimization and efficient resource use. Products and materials are designed to be upgraded or re-circulated and used again through as many cycles as possible. It implies intentionally designed systems where products are linked to materials cycles and designed for disassembly and re-purposing. The concept is closely related to Cradle-to-Cradle, Closed-Loop, Blue Economy and other similar concepts
Accenture (2014: 10)	'At its core, the circular economy is about creating new value chains that decouple growth from the use of scarce and linear resource inputs—i.e. inputs that cannot be returned and used in cyclical chains'
Deloitte (2016: 1)	'A circular economy is one that is restorative and regenerative by design—it is about optimisation of value circulation, not prevention of waste generation'
EY (2015)	Refers to EMF definition (2013)
EU Commission (2015: 1)	'The transition to a more circular economy, where the value of products, materials and resources is maintained in the economy for as long as possible, and the generation of waste minimised, is an essential contribution to the EU's efforts to develop a sustainable, low carbon, resource efficient and competitive economy. Such transition is the opportunity to transform our economy and generate new and sustainable competitive advantages for Europe'
Swedish Government (SOU 2017: 22:16)	'Circular economy is rather a metaphor for sustainable resource flows that can contribute to the development of economic theory and practice. (…) It is even more important how this metaphor can contribute to release innovation and enable a sustainable economic development'
Geng and Doberstein (2008: 231)	'mean the realization of a closed-loop of material flow in the whole economic system'
Geissdoerfer et al. (2017: 759)	'a regenerative system in which resource input and waste, emissions, and energy leakage are minimized by slowing, closing, and narrowing material and energy loops. This can be achieved by long lasting design, maintenance, repair, reuse, remanufacturing, refurbishing, and recycling'
Su et al. (2013: 216)	'to minimize the primary input of primary energy and raw materials'

Table 10.2 Overview of General, Particularly Production-oriented Concepts in Circular Economy & Circular Fashion Literatures

Concepts	*Authors*	*Summary explanation*
Reverse Logistics	Govindan et al., 2015; Guide & Van Wassenhove, 2002; Krikke et al., 2004	Involves five processes (Product collection; Returns logistics; Sorting and disposal; Reuse alternatives; and Redistribution) that are essential for reaching circularity.
Closed-Loop	Ashby, 2018; Elander & Ljungkvist, 2016; Fletcher, 2014;Masoudipour, Amirian, & Sahraeian, 2017; Niinimäki & Karell, 2020; Sandberg, Pal, & Hemilä, 2018; Sandin & Peters, 2018; Schmidt, Watson, Roos, Askham, & Brunn Poulsen, 2016	The goal of a closed-loop supply chain is to keep all materials used within the product life cycle and minimize the waste generated.
Slowing Resource Loops	Bocken et al., 2016; Murray et al., 2017	Contribute to delay the creation of waste generation
Product Service Design	Sakao, 2009; Seidman, 2007; Tukker, 2004, 2015; Widgren & Sakao, 2016	Reuse and recycle perspectives are integrated into the design stage
Cradle-to-Cradle	Krikke et al., 2004; McDonough & Braungart, 2002, 2009	Integrating an end-of-life perspective
3R	Choi, Lo, Wong, Yee, & Ho, 2012; Yuan, Bi, & Moriguichi, 2006	3R stands for REDUCE (resources), REUSE (prolong life), RECYCLE (reduce waste), Choi et al. (2012) add RE-IMAGINE, and REDESIGN.
Life Cycle Analysis	Kozlowski, Bardecki, & Searcy, 2012; Laitala & Klepp, 2015; Muthu, 2015; Roos et al., 2016; Schmidt et al., 2016	Life cycle analysis of products (i.e. clothing items) takes into account diverse environmental impacts

Fashion Industry Context

Between 2000 and 2015, global clothing consumption doubled (EMF, 2017). This increase is often connected with the increase and pace of the ‘fast fashion’ business model. The fast fashion industry is thus fast, not only in terms of its consumption and its production practices, but also its own growth rate (Khurana & Ricchetti, 2016; Vehmas, Raudaskoski, Heikkilä, Harlin, & Mensonen, 2018).

This pace is considered problematic as the fashion industry is associated with a range of complex environmental issues and is estimated to account for 6% of emissions in Europe, thereby ranking it the fourth largest after food, housing, and transport (Khurana & Ricchetti, 2016). Its production is also considered one of the most polluting global industries. 25% of global chemicals usage is used in textile production. The main environmental issues include energy, water, chemicals, colouring, as well as GHG emissions (Vehmas et al., 2018).

The fashion supply chain has indeed gone global and is heavily fragmented with asymmetric buyer–supplier power relationships between buyer and supplier (Gereffi, 1999). Management trends such as lean have led to shorter deadlines and low order predictability in the industry (Abernathy, Dunlop, Hammond, & Weil, 1999; Caro & Martínez-de-Albéniz, 2015; Lopez & Fan, 2009). The production of a single clothing item requires multiple processes in dispersed networks (Seuring, 2004) and often transportation between phases of production. The environmental impact of fashion is correspondingly dispersed around the globe.

Compared to 15 years ago, an average consumer today wears a clothing item for half as long, and buys 60% more (Remy, Speelman, & Swartz, 2016). 73% of the world's clothes end up in landfills, less than 15% is recycled and less than 1% is reused for new clothing items (LeBlanc, 2019).

The system described above is an example of the linear 'take-make-dispose' economy, in which textiles and clothing apparel are considered cheap and virgin raw materials thereby remain undervalued and underutilized. The linear fashion model thereby places increased pressures on valuable natural resource (i.e. water, energy) and materials usage. Considering the short product life of clothing, this is particularly wasteful. With an intensified cycle of clothing production and consumption observed, sustainability concerns abound in the environmental and social realm (Boström & Micheletti, 2016; EMF, 2017). Further, most garments are designed to last for a maximum of ten launderings (Niinimäki, 2018).

Further, few to no considerations of reuse and recycling in the prevalent system lead to large overflows of textile waste, with large swaths thereof going directly to landfill (Fuchs, 2016; Pal, Shen, & Sandberg, 2019). These are associated to the post-production and post-use phases. The sustainability challenges of the fashion industry are thus deeply embedded in the fast fashion sourcing model and the consumption habits it has brought about. Consequently, CE pertains to the need of addressing this system's shortcomings.

To note, the Swedish fashion industry is quite substantial and important for the Swedish economy. It is composed of approximately 60, 000 companies, of which a mere 0.1% of are large enterprises with 250 employees and above; the rest constituting small and medium-sized enterprises (SMEs). During the period between 2005 and 2015, echoing the global growth, Swedish clothing consumption increased on average by 24% (Roos, 2016) (Table 10.3).

Circular Fashion: Production and Consumption

The idea of the CE emphasizes the notions of circular production and of consumption; the two are linked in myriad ways. Notably, in order to achieve Circular Fashion (CF) consumption, circular production practices must be in place, including for textile collection. Thus, in practice applying the CE idea to fashion entails that companies must design, produce, distribute, and dispose of products in a way that minimizes environmental impact (Ashby, 2018), for example, reducing production and consumption through greater reuse rate of clothing items and subsequent fibre recycling (Vehmas et al., 2018).

These relate to the overarching idea of the 3R principles: 'REDUCE', 'REUSE', 'RECYCLE'. Table 10.4 presents the CF literature based on their inherent focus of the principles. The literature presents a siloed view of circularity, one in which principles and particular phases of the supply chain are analysed in turn. Predominantly, analyses of the CE integrate a 3R perspective in which it is seen as a combination of 'REDUCE', 'REUSE' and 'RECYCLE' activities. However, the need for a shift from linear to circular and its implications are seldom advanced, particularly the probable need for reduced consumption, with some notable exceptions (Bocken et al., 2014; Roos et al., 2016). Kirchherr et al. (2017) find in their analysis of CE definitions that the main aim considered is economic prosperity, thereafter environmental aspects. The effects of future generations are rarely considered.

Table 10.3 Sustainable or Circular Fashion concepts

Themes	*Authors*	*Associated concepts*
Circular Design	Cao et al., 2014; Curwen, Park, & Sarkar, 2013; Fletcher, 2014; Gam, Cao, Farr, & Heine, 2009; Goldsworthy, 2014; James, Reitsma, & Aftab, 2019; Laitala, Boks, & Klepp, 2015; Mendoza et al., 2017; Moorhouse & Moorhouse, 2017; Niinimäki, 2006; Zeng & Rabenasolo, 2013	Designing for circularity involves a closed-loop integration with concepts such as Design for Cyclability, Cradle-to-Cradle Apparel Design, and Adaptable Design
Sustainability Challenges in Fashion	Birtwistle & Moore, 2007; Boström & Micheletti, 2016; Curwen et al., 2013; Dahlbo, Aalto, Eskelinen & Salmenperä, 2017; Ekström & Salomonson, 2014; Henninger, Alevizou, & Oates, 2016; Khurana & Ricchetti, 2016; Vadicherla & Saravanan, 2014; Yang, Song & Tong, 2017	The main sustainability challenges in the fashion industry pertain to water, chemicals, and energy. Further challenges arise in terms of textile disposal and collection.
Environmental Impact of Fashion	Chen & Burns, 2006; Roos, Sandin, Zamani, & Peters, 2015; Sandin & Peters, 2018; Sandin, Roos, & Johansson, 2019; Sandin, Roos, Spak, Zamani & Peters, 2019a	The environmental impact of fashion is investigated and estimated in terms of environmental cost, possibilities of fibre recycling, and carbon footprint
Circular Business Models	Bocken et al., 2016; Bocken, Farracho, Bosworth, & Kemp, 2014; Evans et al., 2017; Geissdorfer, Morioka, de Carvalho, & Evans, 2018; Lewandowski, 2016; Lieder & Rashid, 2016; Nußholz, 2017; Pedersen & Netter, 2015; Urbinati et al., 2017	Circularity challenges relate to textile collection and technology; circular business models need to integrate both production and consumption aspects.

Table 10.4 Overview of themes related to circular fashion consumption

Consumption		
Themes	*Articles*	*3R application*
Consumer behaviour and attitudes, Consumer identity	Gwozdz, Steensen Nielsen, & Müller, 2017; Hustvedt & Dickson, 2009; James & Montgomery, 2017; James et al. 2019; Niinimäki, 2010; Røpke, 2009; van Weelden, Mugge, & Bakker, 2016; Vehmas et al., 2018; Wang, Hazen, & Mollenkopf, 2018	REUSE, REDUCE, & RECYCLE
Sharing economy; Collaborative fashion; Collaborative consumption	Becker-Leifhold & Iran, 2018; Demyttenaere, Dewit, & Jacoby, 2016; Pedersen & Netter, 2015	REUSE
Consumer post-purchase behaviour; Consumer care and repair;	Gwozdz et al., 2017; Sandin & Peters, 2018	REUSE & RECYCLE
Consumer disposal; Clothing disposal	Joung, 2013; Joung & Park-Poaps, 2013; Laitala, 2014	RECYCLE

Circular Production

Traditional forward supply chains end with the consumer purchase; however, CF is associated to a reverse supply chain, in which product disposal processes are included. The combination of a forward and a reverse supply chain is conceptualized as a closed-loop supply chain (Masoudipour et al., 2017).

REDUCE: Closed-Loop Systems

The goal of a closed-loop supply chain is to keep all materials used within the product life cycle and minimize the waste generated by the involved processes. Thereby, they can offer new business opportunities by minimizing or eliminating waste (Ashby, 2018; Urbinati et al., 2017).

In the fashion industry, particular efforts need to be made to avoid clothing items ending up in landfills, instead, these are to be returned to the supply chain to extract value to be reused in new products. One example thereof is the new focus on utilizing textile spill, thereby extracting value from parts that were previously considered worthless.

Nevertheless, there are numerous perceived obstacles to implementing such changes, particularly the perception that sustainability or circularity is too costly. Not all sustainability aspects are commensurate; the 'sustainable' choice can be perceived as inferior from different aspects thereof (Zacher, 2017). Thus, numerous circularity aspects and opportunities permeate the production of a clothing item. We proceed with an overview of these different stages.

Design. The design stage holds significance in determining the environmental impact of a product; it reflects 80% of a product's environmental impact (EC, 2012). All material choices have an environmental impact and are crucial for overall sustainability (Curwen et al., 2013). A large concern in textile recycling is, as noted, the multi-fibre composition of clothing items, render cost-efficient recycling of involved fibres difficult. Thus, it is *of* utmost importance to design with a life cycle approach (Roos et al., 2016). The HM Foundation's cooperation with *Hong Kong Research Institute of Textiles and Apparel* holds promising results thereto but upscaling remains an issue (HM, 2017). Given the numerous steps involved in the production of a clothing item, it is of *critical* importance to include and prioritize such sustainability issues in this phase in order to reach circularity (Hvass, 2016).

Product Collection. This process involves the collection of previously sold or used products. This constitutes the first step in order to extract added value from products. The lack of infrastructure for large-scale textile collection remains one of the main obstacles for its recycling (EMF, 2017; Hvass, 2014; Joung & Park-Poaps, 2013; Sandin & Peters, 2018). It is argued that this is a result of a lack of consumer awareness of adequate textile disposal processes. To note, during the past years, many Swedish fashion companies have established in-store product collection, with take-back processes based on economic incentives (Corvellec & Stål, 2019).

Sorting & Disposal. Post-textile collection, sorting is needed in order to determine its state by quality and composition, and course of action: reuse, recycling, or disposal by incineration. At this stage, a part of the original product value can be extracted; therefore, this stage is key in determining the possibility of extracting the remaining value (see discussion on downcycling and upcycling below).

RECYCLING

Recycling constitutes an activity that contributes to closing the resource loop. It entails the reprocessing of textile waste intended for use in new textile or non-textile products (Sandin & Peters, 2018). This holds great potential for improving circularity, yet, barriers for upscaling remain. Lack of technology, collection of textiles, and of economic viability, are some of those barriers identified by Elander and Ljungkvist (2016). For this reason, a majority of current textile recycling constitutes downcycling, rather than upcycling (EMF, 2017; Schmidt et al., 2016). Downcycling entails that the recycled textiles are transformed into lower-grade products than the original. (Fletcher, 2014; McDonough & Braungart, 2002). In contrast, upcycling entails that the recycled textiles are transformed into equal or higher-grade quality products. This means that downcycled textiles are transformed into materials such as upholstery and insulation materials (Schmidt et al., 2016). The technologies required for clothing items to be recycled into new ones, that is, textile-to-textile recycling, are still underdeveloped.

Recycling and reuse are argued to hold considerable potential in reducing negative environmental impacts of the fashion industry (EMF, 2015a; Sandin & Peters, 2018; Schmidt et al., 2016). According to the EU waste hierarchy, reuse is the best option in handling waste, followed by recycling, and lastly waste disposal (EC Waste Directive, 2008). The benefits involved in reuse are contingent upon several factors: replacement rates, as well as transportation modes of reused products (Sandin & Peters, 2018). Another environmental impact to be considered is that of the transportation mode used by consumers to and from the retail outlet (Gwozdz et al., 2017).

Calculating the respective environmental impacts involved in recycling and reuse involves the assumption of a 1:1 replacement rate. This assumes that each item reused or recycled will be used in equal measure as a new item. Thereby, the production of a new clothing item is assumed to have been replaced by the reused or recycled item (Sandin & Peters, 2018). This assumption has been shown to be unrealistic, in that the replacement rate remains unclear (Dahlbo et al., 2017). It is possible that it mainly contributes to creating new, second-hand, markets. Nevertheless, reuse presents clear benefits over recycling and incineration.

The clearest link between CF production and consumption occurs in the disposal phase; what consumers choose to do with a clothing item determines whether it can be reused or recycled in an upcycling or downcycling process.

Circular Consumption

The consumption literature related to CF is primarily focused on identifying factors promoting or hindering adoption of circular solutions, in relation to several consumer phases (Camacho-Otero et al., 2018; Pal et al., 2019). Few studies focus directly on an integrated circularity perspective. Rather, they tend to focus on one isolated aspect of closed-loop supply chain, e.g. waste (Dahlbo et al., 2017).

It is found in several literature reviews of circularity (Ghisellini et al., 2016; Kirchherr et al., 2017; Lieder and Rashid, 2016) that consumption aspects are important for CE, yet this perspective is frequently missing. Moreau, Sahakian, Van Griethuysen, and Vuille (2017: 498) finds that circularity entails 'rethinking [...] consumption' whilst Borrello, Caracciolo, Lombardi, Pascucci, and Cembalo (2017: 1) finds that 'little is known about consumers' willingness' to engage in circularity.

Gallaud and Laperche (2016) identify consumers as the central actor in circular business models. By focusing too much on 'circular production' or the supply-side, it may become more difficult to develop business models that cater to consumer demand (Repo & Anttonen, 2017).

However, most circularity-oriented consumption research remains focused on the purchase phase, taking little consideration of both the user- and disposal phases of this process (Ekström & Salomonson, 2014; Fletcher, 2014; Gwozdz et al., 2017; Stål & Jansson, 2017). To note, some researchers find that a decrease in consumption is necessary in order to achieve a circular, and thereby sustainable, fashion industry. Limiting or Reducing the number of clothing items produced and subsequently consumed would contribute to reduce the waste generated in the post-use phase and contribute to overcoming the remaining hurdles on recycling (Bocken et al., 2014; Elander & Ljungkvist, 2016; Roos et al., 2016).

Circular Consumer Attitudes

Changes in consumption practices include attitudes towards ownership and adoption of new services that pool resources (Ceschin, 2014; Demyttenaere et al., 2016) or what is sometimes called the 'sharing economy'. The move towards a circular model is thereby argued to entail a move from 'product' to 'system'. A circular consumer thereby no longer buys a particular product, but rather the result of a new circular system.

Despite the speedy turnover of clothing items, there is limited consumer awareness of the environmental impact of clothing items

(Harris, Roby, & Dibb, 2016). Consumer behaviour is essential in user and post-user (including disposal) phases. This bears implications on frequency, type and number of purchases, through their care and the means of disposal (Gwozdz et al., 2017). The largest energy consumption during the user phase emanates from washing and care behaviour, that is, consumer care practices greatly influence an item's environmental impact (Harris et al., 2016; Roos et al., 2015; Sandin, Roos, Spak et al., 2019).

The CE and CF concepts thereby imply the need for a shift in consumer behaviour and practices (Camacho-Otero et al., 2018) in terms of purchasing, use, and disposal. Product life of clothing items needs to be prolonged; the rates of reuse need to increase, recycling of clothes, fabrics, and fibres must be enabled at a large scale (EMF, 2017; Sandin & Peters, 2018).

REUSE: Prolongation of Product Life of Clothing Items

Fast fashion is often criticized for its detrimental impact on the environment, through reducing average product life. Prolongation of product life involves slowing resource loops; in terms of clothing items, product life may be prolonged by increasing the number of times a clothing item is used or worn. The Ellen MacArthur Foundation (2017) argues that this constitutes the most direct way of avoiding waste and negative environmental impact. Numerous reports highlight the need to make more durable clothing items, that also provide increased value for consumers and businesses alike (Ellen MacArthur Foundation, 2017; Mistra Future Fashion, 2019). Nevertheless, Gwozdz et al. (2017) nuance this proposal as they find that other factors determine the average product life length.

Other suggestions for prolongation of product life include reuse, repair, and re-make services (Sandin & Peters, 2018). If an average clothing item is used three times longer than currently, its environmental and water impact would diminish by 65% and 66% respectively. These calculations assume that the clothing item replaces another newly produced item made of virgin raw materials (Roos et al., 2015); see the above critique of the assumption of 1:1 replacement rate.

REUSE or RECYCLING: Textile Collection

As noted previously, a majority of textiles have hitherto ended up in landfills; this entails that the remaining value of textiles' remains unextracted and thereby wasted. Reuse involves prolongation of product life through transferral of clothing items to new users (Sandin & Peters, 2018), achieved through second-hand and vintage retailers (for-profit and non-profit charities), online marketplaces and applications, and clothing libraries (EMF, 2017). Consumers' disposal practices are thus key in prolonging product life.

Sustainable consumption research finds that consumer motivation for disposing of fashion items is frequently associated with making wardrobe space and the possibility to purchase new fashion items, second-hand or new (Gwozdz et al., 2017; Laitala, 2014; Morgan & Birtwistle, 2009; Norum, 2017). Given the critique of the 1:1 replacement rate, second-hand purchases of clothing items do not necessarily replace other (new) items in the Swedish fashion context.

In the Swedish context, consumers have several options for textile collection: independent second-hand shops including charities, vintage outlets, online communities, and consumer-to-consumer platforms as well as fashion retailers' in-store collection (Elander, Tojo, Tekie, & Hennlock, 2017; Sweet, Aflaki, & Stalder, 2019; Sweet & Wu, 2019). Most major fashion retailers in Sweden have implemented the latter (Stål & Corvellec, 2018). The clothing items collected through in-store systems are resold, reused, or recycled (EMF, 2017).

In 2017, the average Swedish consumption of clothes per person was estimated at 13.9 kg (SSNC, 2018) of which 7.5 kg ended up in residual waste. It is estimated that over half of the textiles found in residual waste are considered undamaged and could be reused (Schmidt et al., 2016). However, Gwozdz et al. (2017) find that a majority of Swedish respondents reported that they used environmentally friendly disposal methods for clothing items, with merely 14.1% discarded via residual waste. Comparative figures may differ given the observed behaviour-attitude gap in matters of sustainability (Öberseder, Schlegelmilch, Murphy, & Gruber, 2014) as well as a difference between textile and clothing items.

REUSE: Shifting Consumer Routine Care Practices

Routine clothing consumer practices tend to be taken-for-granted and unchallenged. Several routines relate to the different life cycle phases of clothing items with an environmental impact, particularly care practices and disposal practices. Washing and drying tend to decrease product life of clothing items (Granello, Jönbrink, Roos, Johansson, & Granberg, 2015; Roos et al., 2015) and hold negative environmental impacts in terms of energy usage (Fletcher, 2014).

Through economic incentives and corporate communication and marketing, disposal practices appear to have recently shifted in the Swedish context, from general waste disposal or conscious charity donations, to easily accessible in-store textile collection. However, these routine care practices, that is, washing and drying do not appear to have shifted (Gwozdz et al., 2017) and there are few examples of companies discouraging undue washing and drying.

Methodology

CF is presented as the solution to multiple sustainable production and consumption issues in the fashion industry. In the first part of this chapter, multiple definitions of and concepts related to CE and CF were presented. The proliferation of concepts shows evidence of the CE as a management idea adopted and adapted by different actors. This chapter takes an interest and attempts to answer how the idea of CF is translated across the Swedish fashion industry. Therein, it also identifies several new actors involved.

As a first step, the CE and CF literatures were reviewed in order to discover the dominant definitions and themes evoked. The following step involves coding the definitions and circularity-related statements in Swedish fashion companies' sustainability reports (Filippa K, 2018; Gina Tricot, 2018; HM, 2018; Kappahl, 2018; Lindex, 2018; Nudie Jeans, 2018) and in government reports. Finally, in relation to the SDG goal 12 of Responsible Production and Consumption, the importance of access to information is key; thereby, allowing consumers to make sustainable choices and achieve sustainable consumer behaviour pattern; it is therefore of interest to understand the messages diffused by organizations and particularly corporations in terms of circularity and CF. Consumer-directed messages in social media (i.e. Instagram) have thus been coded in order to derive the varying selective adaptations of the Circular Fashion idea and thereby its prevalent translations. These findings are summarized in Fig. 10.1.

As noted above, reaching the SDG goal 12 of Responsible Production and Consumption requires access to information in order to promote sustainable consumer behaviour. On a wide range of platforms, the identified actors promote and highlight the critical need for circularity and sustainability. Via such platforms, organizations can communicate and signal to consumers directly their particular take on circularity and CF.

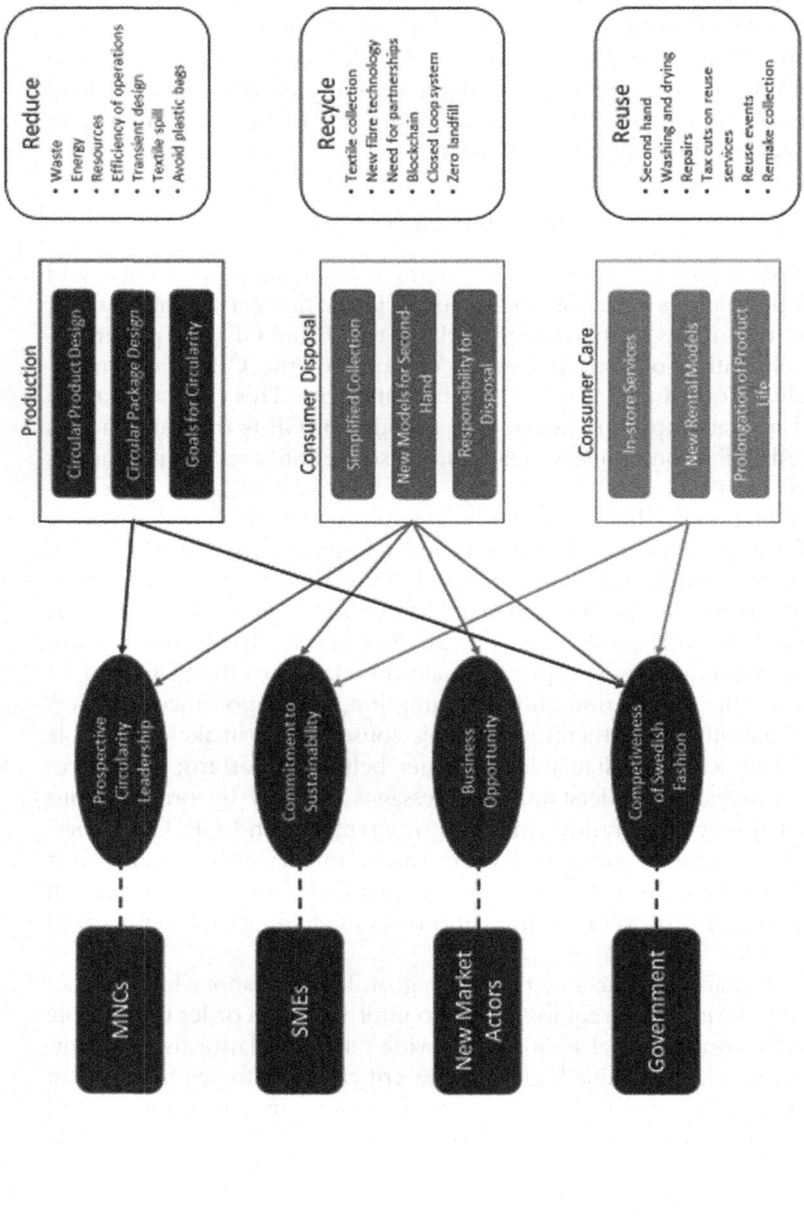

Fig. 10.1 Data structure: translations of circular fashion (*Source* Author's own illustration)

In this chapter, the communication studied contributes to identifying the circular aspects performed, as well as those considered most important. This illustrates the selective adaptations involved in the translation of the management idea of CE in the Swedish fashion industry context.

Theoretical Framework: Translating Ideas into Practice

Modern organizations cannot avoid demands placed on them by stakeholders; instead, they tend to react to a great extent to the institutional pressures in their environment in order to appear legitimate (DiMaggio & Powell, 1983; Meyer & Rowan, 1977). Pressures arise as ideas in the form of models, prototypes, and templates, circulate to such an extent that they are considered rational and necessary for organizations to adopt (Wedlin & Sahlin, 2017).

Early neo-institutional research investigated the diffusion of ideas in relation to institutional isomorphism with the outcome of homogeneity (DiMaggio & Powell, 1983). The Scandinavian institutionalization stream argues instead that ideas do not diffuse in a vacuum but are constantly translated as they travel between actors and settings. Thereafter, actors pick up, adopt, and incorporate new generalized and global ideas to fit different contexts (Czarniawska & Joerges, 1996; Wedlin & Sahlin, 2017). Reacting to institutional pressures in order to gain legitimacy is thereby explained as an act of both conformity and creativity (Czarniawska & Sevón, 1996).

Management ideas are in constant flux (Sahlin-Andersson & Engwall, 2002). Actors partake in the travel of ideas, taking on ever new forms and impacting which (management) ideas circulate and are popularized, and why certain ideas are retained, and others discarded (Meyer, 1996). The studied actors translate the international idea of CE or CF to the Swedish fashion industry and make selective choices for which aspects to integrate and promote, particularly instrumental aspects. In studies pertaining to the travel of ideas, it is argued that concepts are transformed by selective adaptation. The quest for legitimacy is often found to be the primary motivation of such translations (Czarniawska & Sevón, 1996; Røvik, 2000). Appearing to be up-to-date with the latest management ideas and in relation to the CE, or rather CF, also ensures alignment with societal expectations and management ideas of CSR and sustainability (Jutterström & Norberg, 2013).

Empirics: Translating Fashion Circularity

Practitioners are identified as key actors in the translation of the idea of CE (Geissdoerfer et al., 2017; Kirchherr et al., 2017; Schut et al., 2016), notably NGOs, including foundations (EMF, 2013, 2015a, 2015b, 2017), consultancies (Gartner, 2016; Hannon, Kuhlmann, & Thaidigsmann, 2016; Hestin, Chanoine, & Menten, 2016; Lacy et al., 2014) and individual companies.

The identified actors and their respective approaches to circularity are explained below in the following order: MNCs, SMEs, new circularity actors, government, Swedish Society for Nature Conservation (SSNC), Axfoundation, and Ellen MacArthur Foundation. Their explicit messages relating to circularity in reports, websites, and social media are presented.

MNCs

The MNCs identified as actors contributing to the translation of the CF idea were identified on the basis of size, the existence of a sustainability report, the content thereof, and the use of social media to communicate the idea. Subsequently, HM, Lindex, Kappahl, and Gina Tricot were identified as the main corporate actors involved in the translation of CF in the Swedish fashion industry.

In their respective sustainability reports, these companies show varying degrees of interest in the concept of circularity, as well as varying level of ambitions. An overview of their 2018 sustainability reports and social media messages shows the following themes relating to CF emphasized.

The particular circularity messages in the companies' respective sustainability reports involve the definition of circularity, as involving elements of circular production: 'RECYCLING' and 'REUSE', in the form of circular package and product designs. This involves aspects such as minimizing resource use and waste, and improving overall efficiency of operations, consistent with the definitions identified in Section on 'Developing and Defining Circularity'.

These companies tend to use a recycling terminology in consumer-oriented communication 'Recycle your closet' (Gina Tricot, 2019). This terminology appears to contribute to consumers' overrating of the possible positive environmental impact of such textile donation/collection.

Some companies, for example, Gina Tricot and Kappahl, also heavily emphasize the need for introducing and promoting circular consumption practices. The circular aspects mentioned primarily involve in-store textile collection, thereby allowing additional recycling efforts. Aspects of care and repair of fashion products, notably washing, are mentioned in Kappahl's sustainability report (2018). All companies emphasize its work on circular packaging, particularly the reduced use of plastic bags on the high-street. The introduction of a bag fee is also seen as contributing to CF.

The studied MNCs' sustainability reports more frequently refer to future goals, and needs for transitioning to 'Circularity', rather than the current level of circularity reached or actions undertaken. Certain companies do refer to current actions, albeit the messages frequently refer to the need for transitioning and taking leadership in the fashion industry: 'We thereby fully support the development of the new technology and innovation that is required to create a circular fashion industry' (HM, 2018).

The social media messages of the companies are consistent with those in the sustainability reports. To a large extent textile collection is emphasized as the key message of circularity; the messages highlight the practical means of doing so and the importance for circularity: 'Closed-loop (Lindex, 2019), 'That way, you can help to make fashion truly circular' (Kappahl, 2019), Do like @salemindrias and recycle your unwanted clothes 💪' (HM, 2019). However, those companies highlighting elements of circular consumption in its sustainability reports also do so in its social media. Kappahl (2019) for example provides messages of consumer care: 'Wash less. That means more time to do fun stuff. Win-win'. Gina Tricot (2019) highlights their temporary possibilities through clothing rental 'Rent your party look', and 'Gina Tricot Upcycle' selects certain unsold garments 'or garments that have been returned as defective' in order to re-make and create a new (limited) collection. The message is reinforced with green emojis of hearts and recycling.

SMEs

SME actors in circularity were also identified based on their established sustainability profile and sustainability reporting: Nudie Jeans and Filippa K. 'Our Circular Fashion principles keep us committed to the four Rs:

Reduce, Repair, Reuse and Recycle' (Filippa K, 2018). Nudie has even been described as an institutional entrepreneur in its attempts to implement a living wage for workers in its supply chain (Egels-Zandén, 2017). When it comes to circularity, they both heavily emphasize their long-term circularity activities and goals; similar to MNCs, these are often conflated with general sustainability or CSR goals.

Both refer to circularity explicitly in their social media messages, and Filippa K (2019); similar to the new circularity actors and MNCs, holds a category in its Instagram stories that emphasizes such activities. Filippa K (2019) emphasizes the raw materials used, new projects for reducing textile spill and waste, as well as temporary events such as second-hand pop-up stores. Nudie Jeans (2019) however informs of its circularity aspects through traditional posts such as 'RE-USE DROP 9 NOW ONLINE!', relating to a temporary collection.

New "Circularity" Actors

These constitute new actors, self-identified as contributing to CF in the Swedish context. Those included in this study are Sellpy, Tise, and Hyber. These are focused on consumer-to-consumer or consumer rentals promoting reuse of clothing in some form. Hyber favours a sharing economy, renting out children's clothing to consumers in order to promote circularity. The remaining three all constitute consumer-to-consumer platforms offering consumer services for selling their used clothing; thereby, prolonging life. Tise (2019), for example, does not specifically use the term circularity but claims that it will 'revolutionize the fashion industry'. Sellpy (2019) refers to circularity and informs consumers of a new application for calculating how much CO_2 and water consumers save through Sellpy purchases and attempt to launch new practices and culture through 'second-hand bragging'. Hyber (2019) mainly highlights the joint benefits of saving on costs and the environment: 'you save planetary resources and reduce CO_2 emissions'

Government

The importance of the CE in reaching the goals of Agenda 2030, particularly number 12, 'Responsible production and consumption' is recognized by the Swedish Government (2018). Its fashion counterpart, CF, is equally recognized as part of reaching the governmental ambition of enhancing Swedish fashion industry's sustainability and competitiveness (Swedish Government, 2017). This goal is consistent with the current governmental CSR objectives (Lernborg, 2019). The governmental interest is not only export-oriented but also relates to overarching EU directives: on waste hierarchy (EC Waste Directive, 2008) and CE principles (EC, 2015).

The Swedish Government refers to the CE in several tomes, two are particularly important for the fashion industry: a proposal for textile management (2016) and commissioned enquiry on the goals for a Swedish Circular Economy (Swedish Government, 2017). In the proposal by the Swedish Environmental Protection Agency (Swedish Government, 2016), it provides two alternative pathways for reducing the textile amount found in residual waste by 60% (between 2015 and 2025). Either a compulsory sorting requirement for textile collection, in which textiles become a separate waste stream, continuously managed by municipalities. The other involves the introduction of an Extended Producer Responsibility decree. These proposals are critiqued by Elander et al. (2017) as they merely address downstream production impacts. Furthermore, the Swedish Government (2017) cites the instrumental definitions of CE provided by the EU Commission (2015) and the Ellen MacArthur Foundation (2013), see further Table 10.1.

SSNC

SSNC is an influential Swedish actor in circularity promoting shifting production and consumption models. In particular, the need for reducing the level of virgin materials used is highlighted in order to reach a CE: increase reuse and recycling of materials, smarter product design and packaging, and utilize energy of non-recyclable products (SSNC, 2018). In their ideal model of CE, consumption decreases, and consumers place clothing items directly in the recycling loop, enabling them to become new materials. It is however not enough to recycle old clothing items; it is also held forth that consumption must diminish in order to achieve CE, and ultimately sustainable development.

Axfoundation

Axfoundation is an independent non-profit venture. However, it is connected to a large Nordic consortium of companies. It aims to use enterprising as an accelerator for driving sustainable change, and one of its four goals is to drive CE. It funds several corporate projects on improving circular practices in several industries, including fashion (Axfoundation, 2020b, 2020c, 2020d). These ventures are intended to promote the idea of a circular business case; it has funded projects with partner companies on textile collection, polyester recycling, and measuring the economic impact of ecosystem services. Focus is thereby on production, rather than consumption aspects.

Ellen MacArthur Foundation

The Ellen MacArthur Foundation is frequently linked to the development of the idea of the CE (2013, 2015a, 2015b, 2017); it has issued many publications in the area and collaborated with businesses, policymakers, and academia to promote the transition (Geissdoerfer et al., 2017). It is possible to argue that it is an important actor or carrier in the translation of the CE to the corporate world. Its reports focus on the key benefits for corporations and their products in an easy-to-understand and business-case manner; the reports are often focused on a particular industry, notably fashion (2017).

Discussion and Conclusions

The idea of the CE has been widely diffused in recent years. From the overview of literature presented in this chapter, it is corroborated that this idea has primarily been developed by practitioners: government, business actors, and even management consultants (Hannon et al., 2016; Hestin et al., 2016; Korhonen, Honkasalo, & Seppälä, 2018; Lacy et al., 2014; Remy et al., 2016). Multiple actors across different sectors thereby argue for the necessity of adopting more circular practices across industries to solve global environmental challenges (Kiørboe, 2015).

CF is a concept that has undergone selective adaptations and is considered particularly relevant for the particular phases of production and consumption involved in its life cycle. It is particularly salient in terms of the consumer disposal phase. The circular aspects of textile collection are emphasized in all company examples. It can thus be argued that as of yet, CF is primarily a management idea that is being translated to and by multiple actors: government and large MNCs. Other actors also contribute by seemingly seeking to challenge the status quo of linear production models: NGOs, SMEs, and new intermediaries, i.e. social entrepreneurs and consumer platforms.

In this chapter, actors from different spheres participating in and promoting the idea of CF have been identified: government, private sector, and civil society. An example of the latter, SSNC, highlights the incompatibility between production and consumption, and represents the sole identified actor primarily focussed on reducing consumption as the means to reach CF.

The Swedish Government (2017) highlights the need for a CE policy in order to increase the competitiveness of Swedish business. Regarding CF consumption, tax cuts on such services prolonging product life are proposed. The drivers of fast fashion-related production and consumption thereby remain unaddressed. The inherent possibilities of increasing the economic performance and competitiveness of the Swedish fashion industry remain at the helm of motivations. CE does not involve shifting the status quo of the current system, rather, it is viewed as a new resource-efficiency tool. Further, the proposal (Swedish Government, 2017) accentuates the Swedish dependence on innovations and the need to stay competitive. In terms of CF, it is seen as a possibility to improve its sustainability, and efforts should be placed on the designer and post-production phases.

The fashion industry currently faces pressures from multiple stakeholders demanding a transition to circularity. Large MNCs have long been targeted in name-and-shame campaigns for their lack of responsible labour practices. During the past years, fashion consumers have become more aware of sustainability issues (James & Montgomery, 2017), both social and environmental. Thereby, it can be argued that pressures to adopt the CF idea have also increased in order to restore and retain legitimacy. Furthermore, the current focus on collection and recycling of clothing items appears to lead to misunderstandings amongst consumers. Misunderstandings that are not necessarily corrected; consumers believe falsely that recycling involves a direct process in which the collected clothes turn into new clothes (Sandin & Peters, 2018; Schmidt et al., 2016). Indeed, with the use of economic incentives, it can be argued that consumers are discouraged from reducing their consumption (Stål & Jansson, 2017), all whilst companies appear to be promoting CF ideals.

As viewed in Fig. 10.1, the studied MNCs' adaptations of circularity are mainly reduced to production. The fast fashion mode of consumption can thereby continue. Circular leadership is conjugated in the future tense 'The fashion industry needs to embrace the circular economy and find new innovative solutions. Our role in all of this is to become more involved in research aimed at discovering climate-neutral production methods, fibres and resources' (Gina Tricot, 2018), a prospective leadership with lofty and abstract visions in which circularity will permeate the fashion industry. This echoes the moral decoupling of visionary procrastination of SMEs described in Sendlhofer (2019); the importance of being the circularity leader of tomorrow constitutes the main message. Selective adaptations of management ideas are indeed often associated to quests for legitimacy (Czarniawska & Sevón, 1996).

The studied SMEs make other adaptations of CF. Long-term commitment to circular aspects such as prolongation of life through repairs, and offering second-hand services are mentioned. Concrete actions were highlighted as well as past experimentations with new business opportunities were mentioned. The drawbacks, difficulties, or trade-offs involved in terms of financial models and consumer readiness were also transparent. The SME adaptation of CF can be summarized as emphasizing reuse and recycling in both consumption and production. To a lesser extent, the focus on prolongation of product life also accentuates reducing consumption. CF as an idea is herein aligned with a strong vision for sustainability and CSR, openness and frankness about the imperfect current model and the difficulties in reaching the ideal model.

The new actors identified provide sharing or consumer-to-consumer services; these all emphasize the environmental benefits of contributing to circularity through prolonged product life. However, their messages can be argued to support business-as-usual approaches in terms of the current linear production model. Despite the lack of consensus on the 1:1 replacement rate between used and new clothing items identified herein (Dahlbo et al., 2017; Sandin & Peters, 2018), Tise markets itself as a guilt-free means of consuming trends. Herein, circularity appears to be synonymous with 'REPLACE' rather than 'REDUCE' (see Fig. 10.1). In the case of rental service Hyber, 'REPLACE' may also be synonymous with 'REDUCE' in terms of resources. Hereby, a shift in disposal practices is encouraged, but not necessarily for other less lucrative practices such as care and repair.

The circular aspects of the purchase and use phases have received comparatively little attention in the studied communication materials. Particularly, the studied MNCs do not necessarily place much attention on circular consumption aspects, even those of care and repair. Especially, the circular aspects of slowing down loops and reducing certain aspects of consumption are rarely, if ever, emphasized. The discord between circular production and circular consumption is palpable; fashion items remain encouraged to be purchased and used in a linear manner, yet, there is promotion of circularity in the disposal phase of fashion items. It can be argued that companies choose to encourage the status quo of consumption in terms of purchasing, whilst potentially benefiting from the circular disposal aspects. The latter thereby would serve to legitimize the need and argument for circularity.

As is customary with management ideas, CF has been adopted and fitted to different contexts, in this case ranging from global companies to niche actors attempting to popularize new business models. Therein, there are multiple translations occurring simultaneously, emphasizing those aspects that contribute to gaining both legitimacy and improving profitability. The current efforts being made to encourage and adopt CF in various sectors and types of organizations point to its ongoing path of becoming institutionalized (Kiørboe, 2015; Murray et al., 2017). The goal adoption of CE by Axfoundation (2020a) points further to its acceptance, potentially legitimized by the potential for identifying new business opportunities and thereby sustained or increased profitability. However, similar to MNC adaptations, circularity actions mainly target production-related aspects.

MNC circularity messages tend to obscure the need for more circular or sustainable consumer care practices and focus on production aspects of recycle and reuse. The role of consumers in CF is largely reduced to textile collection and discarding plastic bags, rather than reviewing consumption patterns, or engaging in further care and repair of clothing items. SMEs to a larger extent include some consumer care practices but profess the need for governmental reforms and consumer awareness. New market actors are dependent on fast fashion flows stemming and rarely appear to challenge the underlying assumptions of linear production, rather, the contrary.

In line with Cullen (2017), circularity can be perceived as a theoretical ideal state of affairs rather than something that will be achieved in reality. This could be a reason for there being few examples of how and when precisely circularity is to be achieved. Rather, circular elements are parcelled together depending on chance and business opportunity. Circularity is also at times invoked for individual, often efficiency-oriented, corporate sustainability actions that do not necessarily contest the current system, i.e. challenge the status quo of the current linear production and consumption system. Circularity is also conjured when little substance, or rather substantive action, is taken or even suggested. A sense thus remains that Circular Fashion is or can be everything, or nothing.

References

Abernathy, F. H., Dunlop, J. T., Hammond, J. H., & Weil, D. (1999). *A stitch in time: Lean retailing and the transformation of manufacturing—Lessons from the apparel and textile industries*. New York: Oxford University Press.

Ashby, A. (2018). Developing closed loop supply chains for environmental sustainability: Insights from a UK clothing case study. *Journal of Manufacturing Technology Management, 29*(4), 699–722.

Axfoundation. (2020a). *Cirkulär ekonomi*. https://www.axfoundation.se/program/cirkular-ekonomi/. Accessed 20 January 2020.

Axfoundation. (2020b). *Filippa K Circle*. https://www.axfoundation.se/projekt/filippa-k-circle/. Accessed 20 January 2020.

Axfoundation (2020c). *Materialåtervinning av polyester*. https://www.axfoundation.se/projekt/materialatervinning-av-polyester/. Accessed 20 January 2020.

Axfoundation. (2020d). *Textilåtervinning på Åhléns*. https://www.axfoundation.se/projekt/textilatervinning-pa-ahlens/. Accessed 20 January 2020.

Becker-Leifhold, C., & Iran, S. (2018). Collaborative fashion consumption—Drivers, barriers and future pathways. *Journal of Fashion Marketing and Management: An International Journal, 22*(2), 189–208.

Birtwistle, G., & Moore, C. M. (2007). Fashion clothing—Where does it all end up? *International Journal of Retail & Distribution Management, 35*(3), 210–216.

Blomsma, F., & Brennan, G. (2017). The emergence of circular economy: A new framing around prolonging resource productivity. *Journal of Industrial Ecology, 21*(3), 603–614.

Bocken, N. M., De Pauw, I., Bakker, C., & van der Grinten, B. (2016). Product design and business model strategies for a circular economy. *Journal of Industrial and Production Engineering, 33*(5), 308–320.

Bocken, N. M., Farracho, M., Bosworth, R., & Kemp, R. (2014). The front-end of eco-innovation for eco-innovative small and medium sized companies. *Journal of Engineering and Technology Management, 31*, 43–57.

Borrello, M., Caracciolo, F., Lombardi, A., Pascucci, S., & Cembalo, L. (2017). Consumers' perspective on circular economy strategy for reducing food waste. *Sustainability, 9*(1), 141.

Boström, M., & Micheletti, M. (2016). Introducing the sustainability challenge of textiles and clothing. *Journal of Consumer Policy, 39*(4), 367–375.

Camacho-Otero, J., Boks, C., & Pettersen, I. N. (2018). Consumption in the circular economy: A literature review. *Sustainability, 10*(8), 2758.

Cao, H., Chang, R., Kallal, J., Manalo, G., McCord, J., Shaw, J., et al. (2014). Adaptable apparel: A sustainable design solution for excess apparel consumption problem. *Journal of Fashion Marketing and Management, 18*(1), 52–69.

Caro, F., & Martínez-de-Albéniz, V. (2015). Fast fashion: Business model overview and research opportunities. In N. Agrawal & S. A. Smith (Eds.), *Retail supply chain management* (pp. 237–264). Boston, MA: Springer.

Ceschin, F. (2014). Product-service system innovation: A promising approach to sustainability. In F. Ceschin (Ed.), *Sustainable product-service systems* (pp. 17–40). Cham, Switzerland: Springer.

Chen, H. L., & Burns, L. D. (2006). Environmental analysis of textile products. *Clothing and Textiles Research Journal, 24*(3), 248–261.

Choi, T. M., Lo, C. K., Wong, C. W., Yee, R. W., & Ho, H. P. Y. (2012). A Five-R analysis for sustainable fashion supply chain management in Hong Kong: A case analysis. *Journal of Fashion Marketing and Management: An International Journal, 16,* 161–175.

CIRAIG. (International Reference Centre for the Life Cycle of Products, Processes and Services). (2015). *Circular economy: A critical literature review of concepts*. Canada: Polytechnique Montréal.

Corvellec, H., & Stål, H. I. (2019). Qualification as corporate activism: How Swedish apparel retailers attach circular fashion qualities to take-back systems. *Scandinavian Journal of Management, 35*(3), 1–9.

Cullen, J. M. (2017). Circular economy: Theoretical benchmark or perpetual motion machine? *Journal of Industrial Ecology, 21*(3), 483–486.

Curwen, L. G., Park, J., & Sarkar, A. K. (2013). Challenges and solutions of sustainable apparel product development: A case study of Eileen Fisher. *Clothing and Textiles Research Journal, 31*(1), 32–47.

Czarniawska, B., & Joerges, B. (1996). Travels of ideas. In B. Czarniawska & G. Sevón (Eds.), *Translating organisational change* (pp. 13–47). Berlin: de Gruyter.

Czarniawska, B. & Sevón, G. (1996). *Translating organisational change*. Berlin: Walter de Gruyter.

Dahlbo, H., Aalto, K., Eskelinen, H., & Salmenperä, H. (2017). Increasing textile circulation—Consequences and requirements. *Sustainable Production and Consumption, 9,* 44–57.

Demyttenaere, K., Dewit, I., & Jacoby, A. (2016). The influence of ownership on the sustainable use of product-service systems: A literature review. *Procedia Cirp, 47,* 180–185.

DiMaggio, P. J., & Powell, W. W. (1983). The iron cage revisited: Institutional isomorphism and collective rationality in organizational fields. *American Sociological Review, 48*(2), 147–160.

EC. (2008). Directive 2008/98/EC of the European Parliament and of the Council of 19 November 2008 on waste and repealing certain Directives. *Official Journal of the European Union L, 312*(3). http://data.europa.eu/eli/dir/2008/98/oj/. Accessed 20 January 2020.

EC. (2012). *European Commission Report. Ecodesign your future—How eco design can help the environment by making products smarter*. http://ec.europa.eu/DocsRoom/documents/5187/attachments/1/translations/en/renditions/native. Accessed 15 March 2020.

EC. (2015). *European Commission Action Plan. Closing the loop: An EU action plan for the circular economy*. https://eur-lex.europa.eu/legal-content/EN/TXT/?uri=CELEX:52015DC0614. Accessed 15 March 2020.

EC. (2018). *European Commission. Circular economy package*. https://ec.europa.eu/commission/publications/documents-strategy-plastics-circular-economy_en/. Accessed 15 March 2020.

Egels-Zandén, N. (2017). The role of SMEs in global production networks: A Swedish SME's payment of living wages at its Indian supplier. *Business & Society, 56*(1), 92–129.

Ekström, K. M., & Salomonson, N. (2014). Reuse and recycling of clothing and textiles—A network approach. *Journal of Macromarketing, 34*(3), 383–399.

Elander, M., & Ljungkvist, H. (2016). *Critical aspects in design for fiber-to-fiber recycling of textiles*. Mistra Future Fashion Report 2016:1. Accessed 4 February 2020.

Elia, V., Gnoni, M. G., & Tornese, F. (2017). Measuring circular economy strategies through index methods: A critical analysis. *Journal of Cleaner Production, 142*, 2741–2751.

EMF. (2013). *Report. Towards the circular economy—Economic and business rationale for an accelerated transition*. Ellen MacArthur Foundation. https://www.ellenmacarthurfoundation.org/assets/downloads/publications/Ellen-MacArthur-Foundation-Towards-the-Circular-Economy-vol.1.pdf/. Accessed 19 October 2019.

EMF. (2015a). *Report. Delivering the circular economy—A toolkit for policymakers*. Ellen MacArthur Foundation. https://www.ellenmacarthurfoundation.org/assets/downloads/publications/EllenMacArthurFoundation_PolicymakerToolkit.pdf/. Accessed 19 October 2019.looseness-1

EMF. (2015b). *Report. Growth within: A circular economy vision for a competitive Europe*. Ellen MacArthur Foundation. https://www.ellenmacarthurfoundation.org/assets/downloads/publications/EllenMacArthurFoundation_Growth-Within_July15.pdf/. Accessed 12 December 2019.

EMF. (2017). *Report. A new textiles economy: Redesigning fashion's future*. Ellen MacArthur Foundation. https://www.ellenmacarthurfoundation.org/publications/a-new-textiles-economy-redesigning-fashions-future/. Accessed 10 January 2020.

Elander, M., Tojo, N., Tekie, H., & Hennlock, M. (2017). *Impact assessment of policies promoting fiber-to-fiber recycling of textiles*. Mistra Future Fashion Report, 3. Accessed 13 February 2020.

Evans, S., Vladimirova, D., Holgado, G., van Fossen, K., Yang, M., Silva, E. A., et al. (2017). Business model innovation for sustainability: Towards a unified perspective for creation of sustainable business models. *Business Strategy and the Environment, 26*(5), 597–608.

EY. (2015). *Are you ready for the circular economy? The necessity of an integrated approach*. http://kgk.uni-obuda.hu/sites/default/files/EY-brochure-cas-are-you-ready-for-the-circular-economy.pdf/.

Filippa K. (2018). *Sustainability Report*. https://www.filippa-k.com/globalassets/filippa-k-sustainability-report_2018_updated.pdf?ref=93A5B9A359/. Accessed 20 January 2020.

Filippa K. (2019). Instagram. https://www.instagram.com/filippa_k/. Accessed 20 January 2020.

Fletcher, K. (2014). *Sustainable fashion and textiles: Design journeys*. London: Taylor & Francis Ltd.

Fuchs, L. (2016). *Circular economy approaches for the apparel industry* (PhD dissertation). Universität St. Gallen. Switzerland.

Gam, H. J., Cao, H., Farr, C., & Heine, L. (2009). C2CAD: A sustainable apparel design and production model. *International Journal of Clothing Science and Technology, 21*(4), 166–179.

Gallaud, D., & Laperche, B. (2016). *Circular economy, industrial ecology and short supply chain* (Vol. 4). London: Wiley.

Gartner. (2016). *Market share analysis: Consulting services, worldwide*. https://www.gartner.com/doc/3317117/market-share-analysis-consulting-services/.

Geissdoerfer, M., Savaget, P., Bocken, N., & Hultink, E. (2017). The circular economy—A new sustainability paradigm? *Journal of Cleaner Production, 143*(1), 757–768.

Geissdoerfer, M., Morioka, S. N., de Carvalho, M. M., & Evans, S. (2018). Business models and supply chains for the circular economy. *Journal of Cleaner Production, 190*, 712–721.

Geng, Y., & Doberstein, B. (2008). Developing the circular economy in China: Challenges and opportunities for achieving 'leapfrog development'. *The International Journal of Sustainable Development & World Ecology, 15*(3), 231–239.

Gereffi, G. (1999). International trade and industrial upgrading in the apparel commodity chain. *Journal of International Economics, 48*(1), 37–70.

Ghisellini, P., Cialani, C., & Ulgiati, S. (2016). A review on circular economy: The expected transition to a balanced interplay of environmental and economic systems. *Journal of Cleaner Production, 114*, 11–32.
Gina Tricot. (2019). Instagram. https://www.instagram.com/ginatricot/. Accessed 22 January 2020.
Gina Tricot. (2018). *Sustainability Report*. https://www.ginatricot.com/cms/work/sustainability/policys/hållbarhetsredovisning_april_2018_webb.pdf/. Accessed 22 January 2020.
Goldsworthy, K. (2014). Design for cyclability: Pro-active approaches for maximising material recovery. *Making Futures, 3*, 1–12.
Govindan, K., Soleimani, H., & Kannan, D. (2015). Reverse logistics and closed-loop supply chain: A comprehensive review to explore the future. *European Journal of Operational Research, 240*(3), 603–626.
Granello, S., Jönbrink, A. K., Roos, S., Johansson, T., & Granberg, H. (2015). *Consumer behaviour on washing*. Mistra Future Fashion Report D4:5. Accessed 13 February 2020.
Guide, J. V., & Van Wassenhove, L. N. (2002). The reverse supply chain. *Harvard Business Review, 80*(2), 25–26.
Gwozdz, W., Steensen Nielsen, K., & Müller, T. (2017). An environmental perspective on clothing consumption: Consumer segments and their behavioral patterns. *Sustainability, 9*(5), 762–789.
Hannon, E., Kuhlmann, M., & Thaidigsmann, B. (2016). Developing products for a circular economy. *The Circular economy: Moving from theory to practice*, 22–25. http://www.mckinsey.com/business-functions/sustainability-and-resource-productivity/our-insights/developing-products-for-a-circular-economy/. Accessed 10 January 2020.
Haupt, M., & Hellweg, S. (2019). Measuring the environmental sustainability of a circular economy. *Environmental and Sustainability Indicators, 1–2*, 100005.
Harris, F., Roby, H., & Dibb, S. (2016). Sustainable clothing: Challenges, barriers and interventions for encouraging more sustainable consumer behaviour. *International Journal of Consumer Studies, 40*(3), 309–318.
Henninger, C. E., Alevizou, P. J., & Oates, C. J. (2016). What is sustainable fashion? *Journal of Fashion Marketing and Management: An International Journal, 20*(4), 400–416.
Hestin, M., Chanoine, A., & Menten, F. (2016). *Circular economy potential for climate change mitigation*. https://www2.deloitte.com/content/dam/Deloitte/fi/Documents/risk/Circular%20economy%20FINAL%20web.pdf/. Accessed 10 January 2020.
HM. (2019). Instagram. https://www.instagram.com/hm/. Accessed 19 January 2020.

HM. (2018). *Sustainability Report*. https://sustainability.hm.com/content/dam/hm/about/documents/en/CSR/2018_sustainability_report/HM_Group_SustainabilityReport_2018_%20FullReport_en.pdf/. Accessed 19 January 2020.

HM. (2017). Successful method found for recycling blend textiles into new fibres. https://about.hm.com/sv_se/news/general-2017/Successful-method-found-for-recycling-blend-textiles-into-new-fibres.html/. Accessed 16 March 2020.

Hustvedt, G., & Dickson, M. A. (2009). Consumer likelihood of purchasing organic cotton apparel. *Journal of Fashion Marketing and Management: An International Journal, 13*(1), 49–65.

Hyber. (2019). Instagram. https://www.instagram.com/hyber.sverige/. Accessed 27 January 2020.

Imaz, M., & Sheinbaum, C. (2017). Science and technology in the framework of the sustainable development goals. *World Journal of Science, Technology and Sustainable Development, 14*(1), 2–17.

James, A. M., & Montgomery, B. (2017). Connectivity, understanding and empathy: How a lack of consumer knowledge of the fashion supply chain is influencing socially responsible fashion purchasing. In S. Muthu (Ed.), *Textiles and clothing sustainability* (pp. 61–95). Singapore: Springer.

James, A. M., Reitsma, L., & Aftab, M. (2019). Bridging the double-gap in circularity. Addressing the intention-behaviour disparity in fashion. *The Design Journal*, 22(supl): 901–914.

Joung, H. M. (2013). Materialism and clothing post-purchase behaviors. *Journal of Consumer Marketing, 30*(6), 530–537.

Joung, H. M., & Park-Poaps, H. (2013). Factors motivating and influencing clothing disposal behaviours. *International Journal of Consumer Studies, 37*(1), 105–111.

Jutterström, M., & Norberg, P. (2013). *CSR as a management idea*. Cheltenham: Edward Elgar.

Hvass, K. K. (2016). *Weaving a path from waste to value: Exploring fashion industry business models and the circular economy* (PhD dissertation). Copenhagen Business School. Denmark.

Hvass, K. K. (2014). Post-retail responsibility of garments—A fashion industry perspective. *Journal of Fashion Marketing and Management, 18*(4), 413–430.

Kappahl. 2019. Instagram. https://www.instagram.com/kappahl/. Accessed 21 January 2020.

Kappahl, (2018). *Sustainability Report*. https://www.kappahl.com/en-US/about-kappahl/sustainability/responsible-fashion/sustainability-report/. Accessed 21 January 2020.

Kirchherr, J., Reike, D., & Hekkert, M. (2017). Conceptualizing the circular economy: An analysis of 114 definitions. *Resources, Conservation and Recycling, 127,* 221–232.

Khurana, K., & Ricchetti, M. (2016). Two decades of sustainable supply chain management in the fashion business, an appraisal. *Journal of Fashion Marketing and Management, 20*(1), 89–104.

Kiørboe, N. (2015). *Moving towards a circular economy: Successful Nordic Business Models—Policy Brief*. Nordic Council of Ministers.

Korhonen, J., Honkasalo, A., & Seppälä, J. (2018). Circular economy: The concept and its limitations. *Ecological Economics, 143,* 37–46.

Kozlowski, A., Bardecki, M., & Searcy, C. (2012). Environmental impacts in the fashion industry: A life-cycle and stakeholder framework. *Journal of Corporate Citizenship, 45*(Spring), 17–36.

Krikke, H., Blanc, I. L., & van de Velde, S. (2004). Product modularity and the design of closed-loop supply chains. *California Management Review, 46*(2), 23–39.

Lacy, P., Keeble, J., McNamara, R., Rutqvist, J., Haglund, T., Buddemeier, P., ...Pettersson, C. (2014). *Accenture Report. Circular advantage: Innovative business models and technologies to create value in a world without limits to growth.* Accent. Strateg. 24. https://www.accenture.com/t20150523T053139__w__/us-en/_acnmedia/Accenture/Conversion-Assets/DotCom/Documents/Global/PDF/Strategy_6/Accenture-Circular-Advantage-Innovative-Business-Models-Technologies-Value-Growth.pdf/. Accessed 10 January 2020.

Laitala, K., & Klepp, I. G. (2015). Clothing disposal habits and consequences for life cycle assessment (LCA). In S. Muthu (Ed.), *Handbook of life cycle assessment (LCA) of textiles and clothing* (pp. 345–363). Cambridge: Woodhead Publishing.

Laitala, K. (2014). Consumers' clothing disposal behaviour—A synthesis of research results. *International Journal of Consumer Studies, 38*(5), 444–457.

Laitala, K. M., Boks, C., & Klepp, I. G. (2015). Making clothing last: A design approach for reducing the environmental impacts. *International Journal of Design, 9*(2), 93–107.

LeBlanc, R. (2019). *Textile and garment recycling facts and figures*. http://www.thebalancesmb.com/textile-recycling-facts-and-figures-2878122/. Accessed 24 November 2019.

Lernborg, C. M. (2019). *Organising responsibility in the Swedish Fashion Market*. PhD dissertation: Stockholm School of Economics. Sweden.

Lewandowski, M. (2016). Designing the business models for circular economy—Towards the conceptual framework. *Sustainability, 8*(1), 43.

Lieder, M., & Rashid, A. (2016). Towards circular economy implementation: A comprehensive review in context of manufacturing industry. *Journal of Cleaner Production, 115,* 36–51.

Lindex. (2018). *Sustainability Report*. https://about.lindex.com/files/documents/lindex-sustainability-report-2018.pdf/. Accessed 22 January 2020.

Lindex. (2019). Instagram. https://www.instagram.com/lindexofficial/. Accessed 22 January 2020.

Lopez, C., & Fan, Y. (2009). Internationalisation of the Spanish fashion brand Zara. *Journal of Fashion Marketing and Management: An International Journal, 13*(2), 279–296.

Masoudipour, E., Amirian, H., & Sahraeian, R. (2017). A novel closed-loop supply chain based on the quality of returned products. *Journal of Cleaner Production, 151,* 344–355.

McDonough, W., & Braungart, M. (2002). Design for the triple top line: New tools for sustainable commerce. *Corporate Environmental Strategy, 9*(3), 251–258.

McDonough, W., & Braungart, M. (2009). *Cradle to cradle: Remaking the way we make things*. London: Vintage.

Mendoza, J. M. F., Sharmina, M., Gallego-Schmid, A., Heyes, G., & Azapagic, A. (2017). Integrating backcasting and eco-design for the circular economy: The BECE framework. *Journal of Industrial Ecology, 21*(3), 526–544.

Merli, R., Preziosi, M., & Acampora, A. (2018). How do scholars approach the circular economy? A systematic literature review. *Journal of Cleaner Production, 178,* 703–722.

Meyer, J. W. (1996). Otherhood: The promulgation and transmission of ideas in the modern organizational environment. In B. Czarniawska & G. Sevón (Eds.), *Translating organizational change* (pp. 241–272). Berlin: de Gruyter.

Meyer, J. W., & Rowan, B. (1977). Institutionalized organizations: Formal structure as myth and ceremony. *American Journal of Sociology, 83*(2), 340–363.

Mistra Future Fashion. (2019). *Sustainable Fashion*. http://mistrafuturefashion.com/sustainable-fashion/. Accessed 10 January 2020.

Moorhouse, D., & Moorhouse, D. (2017). Sustainable design: Circular economy in fashion and textiles. *The Design Journal, 20*(sup1), S1948–S1959.

Morgan, L. R., & Birtwistle, G. (2009). An investigation of young fashion consumers' disposal habits. *International Journal of Consumer Studies, 33*(2), 190–198.

Moreau, V., Sahakian, M., Van Griethuysen, P., & Vuille, F. (2017). Coming full circle: Why social and institutional dimensions matter for the circular economy. *Journal of Industrial Ecology, 21*(3), 497–506.

Murray, A., Skene, K., & Haynes, K. (2017). The circular economy: An interdisciplinary exploration of the concept and application in a global context. *Journal of Business Ethics, 140*(3), 369–380.

Muthu, S. S. (Ed.). (2015). *Handbook of life cycle assessment (LCA) of textiles and clothing*. Cambridge: Woodhead Publishing.

Nasr, N., Russell, J., Bringezu, S., Hellweg, S., Hilton, B., Kreiss, C., & Von Gries, N. (2018). *Report. Re-defining value: The manufacturing revolution-remanufacturing, refurbishment, repair and direct reuse in the circular economy*. IRP Reports.

Niinimäki, K. (2018). *Sustainable fashion in a circular economy*. Aalto University. https://aaltodoc2.org.aalto.fi/bitstream/handle/123456789/36608/isbn9789526000909.pdf/.

Niinimäki, K. (2010). Eco-clothing, consumer identity and ideology. *Sustainable Development, 18*(3), 150–162.

Niinimäki, K. (2006). Ecodesign and textiles. *Research Journal of Textile and Apparel, 10*(3), 67–75.

Niinimäki, K., & Karell, E. (2020). Closing the loop: Intentional fashion design defined by recycling technologies. In *Technology-driven sustainability* (pp. 7–25). Cham: Palgrave Macmillan.

Norum, P. S. (2017). Towards sustainable clothing disposition: Exploring the consumer choice to use trash as a disposal option. *Sustainability, 9*(7), 1187.

Nudie Jeans. (2018). *Sustainability Report*. https://cdn.nudiejeans.com/media/files/Nudie-Jeans-Sustainability-Report_2018.pdf/. Accessed 24 January 2020.

Nudie Jeans. (2019). Instagram. https://www.instagram.com/nudiejeans/. Accessed 24 January 2020.

Nußholz, J. L. (2017). Circular business models: Defining a concept and framing an emerging research field. *Sustainability, 9*(10), 1810.

Öberseder, M., Schlegelmilch, B. B., Murphy, P. E., & Gruber, V. (2014). Consumers' perceptions of corporate social responsibility: Scale development and validation. *Journal of Business Ethics, 124*(1), 101–115.

Pal, R., Shen, B., & Sandberg, E. (2019). Circular fashion supply chain management: Exploring impediments and prescribing future research agenda. *Journal of Fashion Marketing and Management: An International Journal, 23*(3), 298–307.

Pedersen, E. R. G., & Netter, S. (2015). Collaborative consumption: Business model opportunities and barriers for fashion libraries. *Journal of Fashion Marketing and Management, 19*(3), 258–273.

Remy, N., Speelman, E., & Swartz, S. (2016). *Style that's sustainable: A new fast-fashion formula*. McKinsey & Company, 1–6. Accessed 24 November 2019.

Repo, P., & Anttonen, M. (2017). Emerging consumer perspectives on circular economy. In *The 13th Nordic Environmental Social Science Conference HopefulNESS* https://www.researchgate.net/publication/317596538_Emerging_consumer_perspectives_on_circular_economy.

Roos, S., Sandin, G., Zamani, B., & Peters, G. (2015). *Report. Environmental assessment of Swedish fashion consumption. Five garments—Sustainable futures*. Mistra Future Fashion D2: 6.

Roos, S., Zamani, B., Sandin, G., Peters, G. M., & Svanström, M. (2016). A life cycle assessment (LCA)-based approach to guiding an industry sector towards sustainability: The case of the Swedish apparel sector. *Journal of Cleaner Production, 133,* 691–700.

Roos, S. (2016). *Advancing life cycle assessment of textile products to include textile chemicals. Inventory data and toxicity impact assessment* (PhD dissertation). Chalmers University of Technology. Sweden.

Røpke, I. (2009). Theories of practice—New inspiration for ecological economic studies on consumption. *Ecological Economics, 68*(10), 2490–2497.

Røvik, K. A. (2000). *Moderna organisationer: Trender inom organisationstänkandet vid millennieskiftet*. Liber.

Sandin, G., Roos, S., Spak, B., Zamani, B., & Peters, G. (2019a). *Environmental assessment of swedish clothing consumption—Six garments, sustainable futures*. Mistra Future Fashion Report 2019:05. Accessed 13 February 2020.

Sahlin-Andersson, K., & Engwall, L. (2002). *The expansion of management knowledge: Carriers, flows, and sources*. Stanford: Stanford University Press.

Sandin, G., & Peters, G. M. (2018). Environmental impact of textile reuse and recycling—A review. *Journal of Cleaner Production, 184,* 353–365.

Sakao, T. (2009). *Introduction to product/service-system design*. London: Springer-Verlag.

Seidman, D. (2007). *How: Why how we do anything means everything*. Hoboken: Wiley.

Sandberg, E., Pal, R., & Hemilä, J. (2018). Exploring value creation and appropriation in the reverse clothing supply chain. *The International Journal of Logistics Management, 29*(1), 90–109.

Sandin, G., Roos, S., & Johansson, M. (2019). *Environmental impact of textile fibers—What we know and what we don't know: Fiber Bible part 2*. Mistra Future Fashion Report 2019:03 Part II. Accessed 13 February 2020.

Schmidt, A., Watson, D., Roos, S., Askham, C., & Brunn Poulsen, P. (2016). *Report. Life Cycle Assessment (LCA) of different treatments for discarded textiles*. Denmark: PlanMiljo.

Schroeder, P., Anggraeni, K., & Weber, U. (2019). The relevance of circular economy practices to the sustainable development goals. *Journal of Industrial Ecology, 23*(1), 77–95.

Schut, E., Crielaard, M., & Mesman, M. (2016).*Circular economy in the Dutch construction sector: A perspective for the market and government*. https://rivm.openrepository.com/bitstream/handle/10029/595297/2016-0024.pdf/.

Sellpy. (2019). Instagram. https://www.instagram.com/sellpy/. Accessed 22 January 2020.

Sendlhofer, T. (2019). Decoupling from moral responsibility for CSR: Employees' Visionary Procrastination at a SME. *Journal of Business Ethics*, 1–18.

Seuring, S. (2004). Integrated chain management and supply chain management comparative analysis and illustrative cases. *Journal of Cleaner Production, 12*(8–10), 1059–1071.

Stål, H. I., & Corvellec, H. (2018). A decoupling perspective on circular business model implementation: Illustrations from Swedish apparel. *Journal of Cleaner Production, 171*, 630–643.

Stål, H. I., & Jansson, J. (2017). Sustainable consumption and value propositions: Exploring product—Service system practices among Swedish fashion firms. *Sustainable Development, 25*(6), 546–558.

Su, B., Heshmati, A., Geng, Y., & Yu, X. (2013). A review of the circular economy in China: Moving from rhetoric to implementation. *Journal of Cleaner Production, 42*, 215–227.

SSNC. (2018). *Fact sheet circular economy*. https://www.naturskyddsforeningen.se/cirkular-ekonomi?noredirect=true/. Accessed 20 January 2020.

Swedish Government. (2016). *Proposal. Förslag om Hantering av textilier Redovisning av regeringsuppdrag*. https://www.naturvardsverket.se/upload/miljoarbete-i-samhallet/miljoarbete-i-sverige/regeringsuppdrag/2016/redovisade/redovisning-regeringsuppdrag-hantering-textilier-2016-09-26.pdf/. Accessed 20 January 2020.

Swedish Government. (2017). *SOU 2017:22: Från Värdekedja till Värdecykel: Så får Sverige en mer Cirkulär Ekonomi*. Stockholm: Wolters Kluwers Offentliga Publikationer. https://www.regeringen.se/rattsliga-dokument/statens-offentliga-utredningar/2017/03/sou-201722/. Accessed 20 January 2020.

Swedish Government. (2018). *Action Plan Agenda 2030*. https://www.regeringen.se/49e20a/contentassets/60a67ba0ec8a4f27b04cc4098fa6f9fa/handlingsplan-agenda-2030.pdf/. Accessed 20 January 2020.

Sweet, S., Aflaki, R., & Stalder, M. (2019). *The Swedish market for pre-owned apparel and its role in moving the fashion industry towards more sustainable practices*. Mistra Future Fashion Report 2019:01. Accessed 13 February 2020.

Sweet, S., & Wu, A. (2019). *Second-hand and leasing of clothing to facilitate textile reuse*. Mistra Future Fashion Report 2019:13. Accessed 13 February 2020.

Tise. (2019). Instagram. https://www.instagram.com/tise.se/. Accessed 23 January 2020.

Tukker, A. (2004). Eight types of product—Service system: Eight ways to sustainability? Experiences from SusProNet. *Business Strategy and the Environment, 13*(4), 246–260.

Tukker, A. (2015). Product services for a resource-efficient and circular economy—A review. *Journal of Cleaner Production, 97,* 76–91.

Urbinati, A., Chiaroni, D., & Chiesa, V. (2017). Towards a new taxonomy of circular economy business models. *Journal of Cleaner Production, 168,* 487–498.

Vadicherla, T., & Saravanan, D. (2014). Textiles and apparel development using recycled and reclaimed fibers. In S. Muthu (Ed.), *Roadmap to sustainable textiles and clothing* (pp. 139–160). Hong Kong: Springer.

Van Weelden, E., Mugge, R., & Bakker, C. (2016). Paving the way towards circular consumption: Exploring consumer acceptance of refurbished mobile phones in the Dutch market. *Journal of Cleaner Production, 113,* 743–754.

Vehmas, K., Raudaskoski, A., Heikkilä, P., Harlin, A., & Mensonen, A. (2018). Consumer attitudes and communication in circular fashion. *Journal of Fashion Marketing and Management: An International Journal, 22*(3), 286–300.

Wang, Y., Hazen, B. T., & Mollenkopf, D. A. (2018). Consumer value considerations and adoption of remanufactured products in closed-loop supply chains. *Industrial Management & Data Systems, 118*(2), 480–498.

Watson, D., Gylling, A. C., & Thörn, P. (2017). *Business models extending active lifetime of garments: Supporting policy instruments*. Mistra Future Fashion 2017:7. Accessed 13 February 2020.

Wedlin, L., & Sahlin, K. (2017). The imitation and translation of management ideas. In R. Greenwood, C. Oliver, T. B. Lawrence, & R. E. Meyer (Eds.), *The Sage handbook of organizational institutionalism* (pp. 102–127). Singapore: Sage.

Widgren, M., & Sakao, T. (2016). Unanswered questions in conceptual design towards circular economy. In *DS 84: Proceedings of the DESIGN 2016 14th International Design Conference*: 571–578.

Witjes, S., & Lozano, R. (2016). Towards a more circular economy: Proposing a framework linking sustainable public procurement and sustainable business models. *Resources, Conservation and Recycling, 112,* 37–44.

Yang, S., Song, Y., & Tong, S. (2017). Sustainable retailing in the fashion industry: A systematic literature review. *Sustainability, 9*(7), 1266.

Yuan, Z., Bi, J., & Moriguichi, Y. (2006). The circular economy: A new development strategy in China. *Journal of Industrial Ecology, 10*(1–2), 4–8.

Zacher, L. W. (2017). *Technology, society and sustainability: Selected concepts, issues and cases*. Cham: Springer International.

Zeng, X., & Rabenasolo, B. (2013). Developing a sustainable textile/clothing supply chain by selecting relevant materials and suppliers. *Research Journal of Textile and Apparel, 17*(2), 101–114.

CHAPTER 11

A Generous Mindset Spells the Future for Sustainable Fashion

Jennie Perzon

Introduction

It is well accepted that the grand challenges of sustainability cannot be combated alone, and in line with a global call for collaboration, there is a recognized need for innovation and a disruption of our current trajectory. Academic discourse across disciplines often describes collaboration as the key to transformation and sustainable systemic change. Successful collaborations are also often considered a strategic advantage, particularly in uncertain market conditions. Extant literature on collaboration has evolved rapidly in the past decade and reflects practice with increasingly complex collaborations, from bilateral transactional relationships to broad multi-stakeholder collaborations with innovative ambitions.

However, collaborating is known to be difficult, and efforts to collaborate are often more costly and less effective than anticipated. Many of these failures are due to the complex and dynamic nature of alliancing

J. Perzon (✉)
Department of Marketing & Strategy and Center for Sustainability Research, Stockholm School of Economics, Stockholm, Sweden
e-mail: jennie.perzon@phdstudent.hhs.se

R. Bali Swain and S. Sweet (eds.), *Sustainable Consumption and Production, Volume II*,
https://doi.org/10.1007/978-3-030-55285-5_11

and collaborating (Mamédio, Rocha, Szczepanik & Kato, 2019), which is increasingly true for the types of complex partnerships that are now becoming the norm. These new collaborations include a collaboration between multiple stakeholders, often including start-ups, which span different sectors, and they set out to solve global and undefined challenges.

The fashion industry is often regarded as one of the highest polluting industries; however, it also has a huge potential for a sustainable transformation, and the interest in new, innovative, and circular approaches is increasing. In a recent press release, the HM Foundation stated that:

> By 2030, the global middle class is expected to have increased to 5 billion people and the consumption of textiles and shoes by 65% compared to 2015. The world is already using around 1.6 planet's worth of resources every year. But creativity and innovation can flip the numbers in our planet's favor and help enable the biggest transformation ever in the fashion industry. With a circular mindset, fashion can be designed, produced, sold, used, reused, and recycled in a way where resources are used and reused indefinitely in a closed loop. On 28 August 2019, the fifth round of Global Change Award opens.
>
> To win, the innovation should have the potential to make fashion circular and to scale. Maybe even more important than the 1-million-euro grant, the five winners embark on a one-year Innovation Accelerator Program taking them to Stockholm, New York and Hong Kong. In the accelerator, HM Foundation, Accenture and KTH support the winners in taking their ideas to the next level, with guidance on how to scale up quickly and maximize their impact on the industry (28th of August 2019).

This excerpt from the recent press release of the nonprofit foundation of one of the largest retailers in the world reflects a sense of urgency in terms of our sustainable future. At the same time, it illustrates optimism and exemplifies the high ambitions of all stakeholders, relying heavily on both innovation and collaboration for the much-needed transformation to a sustainable future.

The urgency is there; the ambition is there; and some have started to succeed. So, why is everyone not acting on it? Because it is complex and difficult. The central theme of this chapter takes a capabilities perspective of multi-stakeholder collaboration within the context of sustainability and competitive advantage. The theoretical lens of dynamic capabilities provide a useful starting point for exploring collaboration and responding to recent calls for increased focus and attention such as alliancing (Schilke, Hu & Helfat, 2018), and more specific calls for research on alliancing across sectors (Al-Tabbaa, Leach & Khan, 2019). While the emergence of these new types of complex partnerships is central to the investigation, the concept of sustainability adds an additional perspective to understand capabilities necessary for co-creating value for society (Al-Tabbaa et al., 2019). There is a large body of literature on the dynamic capabilities within strategy literature, and with the significant efforts that have been made for understanding the organizational antecedents of these capabilities, the role of culture has been underemphasized.

The case in focus in this chapter is a global multi-stakeholder collaboration of three different market actors spanning a five-year journey of collaborating, not only with each other but also with start-ups and other industry organizations, in their joint ambition to radically disrupt the fashion industry. Through deep access and an engaged scholarship approach, this case is uniquely positioned to provide insights into how collaborative capabilities are enacted, contributing to a better understanding of what capabilities underlie successful, particularly when considering the role of culture.

Setting the Context

Regardless of whether the motivation is based in sustainable development or in the new global complex operating environment and the need for organizational agility, there are calls for collaboration from both academia and practice. The following considerations are important for framing the discussion.

First, we are facing complex topics in a rapidly changing environment. The central reasoning in this chapter rests on the well-accepted assumption that the world is facing a crisis in terms of economic, social and environmental problems. At the same time, sustainability and sustainable development has gone mainstream, and there is movement away from damage control and do no harm towards driving a positive impact for both society and businesses (Waddock, 2013). There has been progress; however, we are clearly not there yet and need to disrupt our trajectory and chase sustainability in a more innovative and systematic way. At the same time, we also live in a world of volatility, uncertainty, complexity, ambiguity (VUCA) (Schoemaker, Heaton & Teece, 2018). The foundations of traditional business practices are increasingly being challenged in today's globalized and increasingly sustainability-minded society, where technological advancements mean that, for most organizations, their product or service advantage disappears quickly.

Second, academia and practice increasingly stress the importance of partnerships and collaboration for successfully solving social issues, as evidenced through the UN Sustainable Development Goals (General Assembly, United Nations, 2015, see goal 17 "Partnerships"). There is a growing awareness that successfully solving social issues in this new global landscape will require active participation from and collaboration between all sectors (Austin and Seitanidi, 2014; Bryson, Crosby, & Stone, 2006; Selsky & Parker, 2010). Research has moved on from concluding that a collaborative approach is necessary, to one of trying to understand what makes them work. Despite the fact that collaboration is at the core of organizational strategy, a large percentage of collaborations fail (Kale & Singh, 2009), which is often due to the complex and dynamic nature of the process of alliancing and collaborating (Mamédio et al., 2019). It is well established that leveraging the capabilities of actors from different sectors and operating across the traditional demarcations between geographies and sectors fosters innovation, as new ideas and points of view intersect and cross-fertilize; however, making these collaborations work is difficult.

There are multiple types of cooperative, inter-organizational relationships, which include strategic alliances, partnerships, coalitions, joint ventures, franchises, consortia and various forms of network organizations (Gulati and Kellogg, 1998); Kale & Singh, 2009; Ring & Van de Ven, 1994). While there are multiple names for these collaborations, extant literature arguably does not fully reflect the fast evolution of complex partnerships that we see in practice today, and we need to understand the dynamic nature of this evolution.

In a world where sustainable development is important, and strategies can no longer be developed based on predictable futures, there is an increased reliance on organizations' capabilities for managing and collaborating with others. The influence of organizations' dynamic capabilities on performance has been thoroughly articulated in the strategy literature. In order to develop dynamic capabilities, organizations increasingly engage in collaborations or alliances, but little focus is placed on the dynamic capabilities needed to make those collaborations work. Much of the existing collaboration literature focuses on the participating organizations' motivations, governance, or the process of collaboration. There is limited focus on the collaboration itself, where the capabilities are enacted. While culture has been identified, along with structure, experience, and process, as an antecedent to dynamic capabilities, there is little focus on how it is enacted in a collaboration. This case looks at the Global Change Award (GCA) collaboration, and specifically at the role of culture in making it work.

Capabilities

Organizational capabilities have long been considered a source of competitive advantage as part of the strategic logic in resource-based view (RBV), which relies on the concept of bundling resources for a sustained competitive advantage (Barney, 2001; Wernerfelt, 1984). The most basic definition of capabilities corresponds to those which allow an organization to function and make a living in the short term (Winter, 2003). Dynamic capabilities are a subset of organizational capabilities, and were originally conceptualized as an extension of RBV (Barney, 1991) and as an organization's strategy for constantly reconfiguring resources in response to dynamic market environments to obtain a competitive advantage (Teece, Pisano & Shuen, 1997). A large proportion of extant literature adds a layer of hierarchy to dynamic capabilities in an attempt to distinguish it from ordinary capabilities, where the former—with their higher order—can be used to modify ordinary capabilities (Schilke et al., 2018). To differentiate from operational capabilities, which are directed towards maintaining the current business and scope of activities, dynamic capabilities, which are defined as a strategic ability, are directed towards strategic change (Eisenhardt & Martin, 2000), and "specifically, they are those capabilities that can effect change in the firm's existing resource base, its ecosystem and external environment, as well as its strategy" (Schilke et al., 2018: 393). The ability to recognize and seize opportunities should also be considered (Teece, 2007) closely related to corporate foresight (Rohrbeck, Battistella & Huizingh, 2015). One is not better than the other. Both operational and dynamic capabilities are needed at different times and in different contexts (Qaiyum & Wang, 2018).

The most commonly cited reason for using dynamic capabilities and its stronghold in strategic management is for understanding capabilities under the conditions of change (Barreto, 2010), which is arguably also a reason for its increased attention in the past decade (Schilke et al., 2018). The capabilities required to generate a sustainable advantage have increased in importance in relation to other assets and are recognized in their speed and in the degree to which they manage organizational resources (Teece, 2012).

The broad span of perspectives within extant DC literature still has a stronghold in the functional and process areas of analysis (Schilke et al., 2018). For the purpose of this chapter, we rely on the definition of Eisenhardt and Martin (2000) for describing dynamic capabilities as key strategic processes within an organization: "*Dynamic capabilities consist of specific strategic and organizational processes like product development, alliancing, and strategic decision making that create value for firms within dynamic markets by manipulating resources into new value-creating strategies*" (Eisenhardt & Martin, 2000: 1106).

The unique access in the following case enabled an in-depth investigation of collaboration as a key strategic process. The findings from this study aim to contribute to a better understanding of what capabilities underlie success in multi-stakeholder collaborations, and aim to help managers manage their alliances better.

Capabilities are very difficult to observe, but previous research has identified several antecedents that can be linked to the existence of specific capabilities. A set of guiding principles, the details of which will be introduced later in the chapter, was developed based on the existing alliancing literature and was used for the analysis. The case and how it was studied will be explained in the next section.

The Global Change Award

A clear demonstration of a collaboration that aims at sustainable innovation is the GCA, a programme that was initiated by the HM Foundation,[1] working alongside Accenture[2] and the KTH Royal Institute of Technology. [3]The GCA takes on one of the biggest challenges facing today's fashion industry: how to meet a growing population's demand for fashion, while improving its impact on the environment. By catalyzing

[1] http://about.hm.com/en/about-us/hm-foundation.html.

[2] https://www.accenture.com.

[3] https://www.kth.se.

early innovations that can accelerate fashion's shift from a linear, disposable business to a creatively self-sustaining circular industry, the aim of the GCA is to protect the planet and improve living conditions.

Since its launch in 2015, the annual accelerator has seen more than 20,000 ideas applications, from over 180 different countries. Five winning ideas are selected each year by an expert panel as having the greatest potential to make a real difference to the industry's sustainability. Those selected are given access to a one-year innovation accelerator provided by the partners. The accelerator is designed to maximize the innovation's impact on the whole industry.

The partnerships that stand behind the GCA offer initial insights into the concept, and the multi-stakeholder collaboration works as the driver of sustainable innovation. The various partners collaborate and contribute leading expertise and thoughts within the circular economy and innovation, academic research and concepts surrounding innovation, and insights about the industry, funding and networks.

The collective structure that stands behind the collaboration has evolved over time. At its inception, the programme was reliant on a representative person from each participating organization to loosely ideate a plan to take the programme forward based on the HM Foundation's initial vision. In line with the rapid growth of the programme, the collaboration quickly expanded beyond the initiating organizations, and an overall approach with different work streams around application and selection, marketing and awareness and acceleration emerged (Fig. 11.1).

To find collaborative synergy and enable innovation, a lot of resources and hard work is required from all parties. The core teams managing the collaboration from each of the organizations grew organically, the processes for developing and managing the programme were truly co-created, and a genuine collaborative culture was quickly established. The programme continued to exceed expectations and grow exponentially in the number of applicants, global reach and content delivered. The innovation lead for the HM Foundation, said in his interview that "We can definitely say that GCA is a success and much much bigger than we dared to expect. I think we hoped for 200 applicants the first year...". The programme received more than 2500 applicants in year one.

Given the longitudinal perspective and deep access to all key stakeholders, the GCA is a fruitful case for providing additional insights into how dynamic capabilities play a role in multi-stakeholder collaboration.

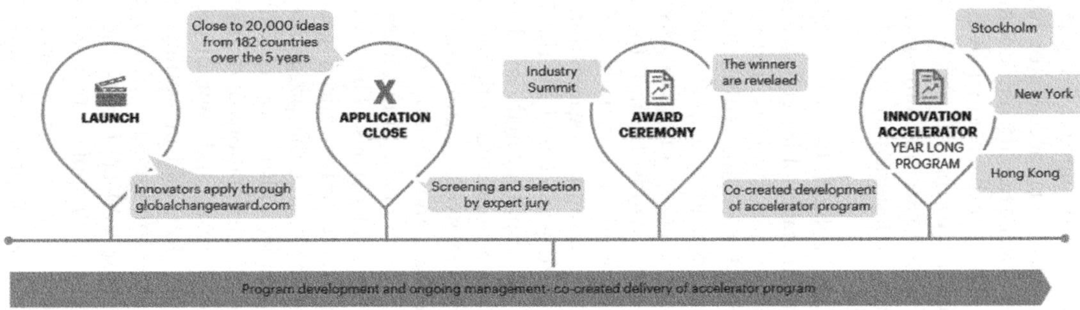

Fig. 11.1 Overview of the programme activities in focus for collaboration (*Source* Author's creation)

How I Studied the Case

The GCA is now in its fifth year of collaborating for sustainable change. Following the case since its inception has allowed for a close-up investigation of the inner workings and collaborative processes of a multi-stakeholder collaboration. A case-based methodology corresponds well with the engaged scholarship model of collaborative research with practitioners (Van de Ven, 2007), and using case studies provides rich descriptions of real-life context and was chosen as the method due to its ability to accommodate a variety of data sources, including interviews and observations (Eisenhardt & Eisenhardt, 1989; Yin, 2003). Based on the starting point where both the motivation and the desire to collaborate exists among the participating organizations, it is interesting to study the process and see how these interactions among organizational parties unfold, shape and modify the collaboration over time (Ring & Van de Ven, 1994).

Engaged scholarship is grounded in a participatory worldview (Reason & Bradbury, 2001), and it is an approach to integrating theory and action with the goal of addressing important issues together with those who experience them (Coghlan, 2016). As an active member of the Accenture team since the inception of the GCA, I have great access to all the people involved, and insight into details of the collaboration process, and my findings can impact how the project is designed going forward.

The empirical method for acquiring knowledge, in this case, relies on participation and careful observation throughout the programme, and observation notes are used for understanding the conceptual background in this chapter. For specific inquiries regarding capabilities, 10 in-depth interviews were held representing the project members from all the collaborating organizations. I am grateful for the candid responses in the interviews, which were accommodated based on deep relationships and a great sense of trust. The interviews took place in Stockholm and New York during May–September 2019, with some during the accelerator weeks. The interviews were recorded, transcribed and analyzed in Nvivo.

In the first stage of data analysis, I coded the interviews based on the attributes of the antecedents' collaborative capabilities that respondents expressed directly and indirectly using a primary set of codes based on the theoretical understanding and organizing framework developed by Schilke et al. (2018). An attempt was then made to relate the emerging themes with core concepts from literature to understand the collaborative process. The established dynamic capabilities, antecedents of experience, structure, process and culture were relied upon to understand how capabilities were enacted in this case.

Antecedents and Enactment

Dynamic capabilities in stable markets often rely on established structures, processes and prior experience. On the contrary, when the market conditions are more volatile, dynamic capabilities rely more on new and constantly changing knowledge and less formal routines and structures (Eisenhardt & Martin, 2000). The volatile context of the case in focus makes for an interesting setting for investigating what capabilities underlie success in multi-stakeholder collaborations and showcases who are less reliant on structure and experience, and more reliant on an informally established culture in the alliance. This section will first situate the investigation in extant literature of the organizational-level antecedents to dynamic capabilities, and second, it will reason around the enactment of these capabilities in the case of the GCA.

In order to provide a frame for analysis, this chapter relies on three comprehensive literature studies. We start by using the organizing framework developed by Schilke et al. (2008) based on a content literature review on dynamic capabilities where the organizational factors in regard to antecedents include experience, organizational structure, organizational culture, resources and information technology. Then, to set the scope of the alliance and narrow the focus of these antecedents to the specific alliance management process, we refine this list by leveraging the study by Kale and Singh (2009), which identifies the main drivers for positive firm-level alliance capabilities in various phases of the alliance lifecycle. Finally, the chapter draws on a review by Neisten and Jolink (2015) to reinforce the antecedents linked to the performance of structure, process, and alliance tools, as well as to set the scope for considering the capabilities that need to be considered both within the firm and within the alliance itself.

Drawing on the most relevant concepts from these authors, the enhanced list of organizational-level antecedents relevant for this chapter includes experience, structure, process and culture. Focus will be given to the formation and governance phase of the collaboration, as it is still a live case with little insight available for post-formation. Culture emerges as the strongest antecedent and how it is enacted in the alliance organization will be explored in greater depth.

Experience

It is understandable that prior alliance management experience is an important consideration; however, the relevance of previous experience varies with type, specificity and timing (Kale & Singh, 2009). In the present case, there was no prior experience as this type of collaboration had not been done earlier by any of the participating organizations (or anyone else in the world at the time of inception). It was new in terms of the number of partners, type of partners, and content of the collaboration—a joint endeavour to disrupt the fashion industry. Although the partners in this endeavour lacked similar prior experience at the outset, the experience they developed through the experience itself became very relevant as they learned from their successes and mistakes. A key part of this experience was to build a deeper understanding of what works and what is important to the other partners, and adjusting activities and behaviours accordingly.

These new types of alliances with multiple stakeholders and innovation as a goal are likely to increase, and as no one alliance is like another, relevant experience is hard to develop. As a result, it is necessary to expand the definition of experience, which could be extended to prior work in co-creation, relational experience, etc.

Structure

Structure has also been found to be an important consideration; leading scholars posit that having a dedicated alliance function is a critical mechanism for building alliance capability (Kale & Singh, 2009; Schilke et al., 2018). This structure can take many forms ranging from a dedicated organizational unit, alliance committees, and special taskforces to a single person or alliance manager (Niesten & Jolink, 2015). In this case, none of the core organizations in the collaboration had a formal alliance function or a dedicated alliance manager within their organization who was responsible for creating or managing alliances. All the people interviewed (particularly those in the university and the private sector) said that despite lacking a formal collaboration role as part of their employment, there was some level of flexibility and a mandate to act in the collaboration.

The collaboration structure in this case was an informal structure that emerged in the early stages of the project. While at first glance the case could appear to be completely unstructured, with a closer analysis one sees there are some rules and boundary conditions in place that enabled collaboration. For example, there were communicated prioritizations of key activities and common deadlines etc., factors which have been found in prior research to be key to success, particularly in volatile market conditions (Eisenhardt & Martin, 2000). This type of emergent structure is formed around the activities and looks different in terms of responsibilities and resources depending on activities. As the marketing lead from Accenture explains when asked about the structure, "We have a core team from each partner who are aligned around what we are doing".

It is of course always challenging to find the optimal amount of structure, especially since it is likely to look different for different organizations. The findings from this case, however, suggest that a flexible approach to structure may be the optimal one. These findings challenge earlier research (Kale & Singh, 2009; Schilke et al., 2018) which have argued that a dedicated alliance function is a predictor of alliance success; instead, we conclude that success lies in a flexible structure at role level.

All the core members perceived it as a central part of their role to drive the relationship and to manage the alliance; however, only two of the interviewees had this responsibility explicitly stated as part of their role of employment. What stood out in the team at Accenture was that all team members were engaged in the project unanimously based on their proactive desire to pursue a shared goal, rather than due to enforced formal structures and requirements. This is best illustrated by the following comment:

> You have to make an effort for something that you truly believe in for real. It is something we have actively chosen to engage in. I would almost go so far as to say that I had to fight to be able to dedicate time to this. (Trend report lead, Accenture)

It appears that the mindset in this case was more important than the formal structure of collaborating organizations, and this idea will be further explored in the section on Culture. A finding that was common across all interviews was the interviewees' personal conviction and belief that this was a relevant and important project to engage in. This mindset at the individual level of an undefined structure is consistent with previous findings, which showed that in contrast to traditional views on the necessity of a stable culture, alternative views have emerged to suggest that a structure is inherently temporary (Eisenhardt & Brown, 1999).

From this case, we can conclude that a dedicated structure for managing a collaboration is less relevant for these participating organizations, who are instead reliant on a collaborative structure and personal engagement. This reflects a trend for new types of alliances, which are becoming less reliant on an organizational-level formal structure, and more on creating space and possibility within individuals' roles. On a practical level, it becomes important for leaders to allow their employees to collaborate and have the room to manoeuvre within their roles to increase the overall flexibility of the structure.

Process

The process perspective within dynamic capabilities often includes information sharing, evaluation systems, training, routines that involve manuals, databases, and checklists and metrics. In the case of the GCA, no processes or tools existed at the beginning of the collaboration. What was interesting about this case was the process that quickly emerged at the core of the alliance. Without formal routines and tools, the collaboration process was very much a case of co-created learning by doing, where mistakes were allowed as a way to develop dynamic capabilities (Eisenhardt & Martin, 2000). This type of approach can be especially valuable when it comes to innovation. Successful requires participants who accept adaptive responsibilities and co-design mechanisms (Le Ber & Branzei, 2010).

Dynamic capabilities become particularly useful in high-velocity markets, where capabilities by nature are more iterative and "rely more on real-time information, cross-functional relationships and intensive communication among those involved in the process and with the external market" (Eisenhardt & Martin, 2000: 1112). Given that the GCA collaboration has a primary objective of innovation, it is of particular interest to look at prior studies which have shown that when working together in a process, allowing alteration of alliance objectives over time produces more innovations (Davis & Eisenhardt, 2011).

Culture

Culture can be even stronger than formal systems, and it is a powerful force that drives behaviour both at the individual and collective level. Organizational culture is often defined as the collective values, beliefs, rites and rituals of organizational members. It refers to shared assumptions, values and norms (Schein, 1985). Organizational culture is also a source of sustained competitive advantage (Barney, 1991). Culture is by its very definition an evolutionary concept. It represents something that a group has learned or adapted over time in efforts to survive and deal with its environment and organize itself (Schein, 2004). It can also get stronger over time (Schein, 2004). Corporate culture and leadership mindsets that focus on sustainability strategies are important factors for success (Baumgartner, 2009).

Culture, sometimes described as the social fabric of an organization, is a significant part of the foundation of dynamic capabilities (Fainshmidt & Frazier, 2017). In this study, the authors coupled dynamic capabilities with the organizational climate literature and found that trust was central to the discourse on the enhancement of dynamic capabilities. While trust is important, it is still a relatively broad term and arguably does not encompass the full construct of culture, and this case allowed for further refinement of the concept. When analyzed, the data revealed three subthemes which can best be described as Practice, Values and Mindsets. Refer to model below (Fig. 11.2).

It is difficult to observe culture and in order to fully understand it, it is necessary to deconstruct the idea. Culture manifests itself at different

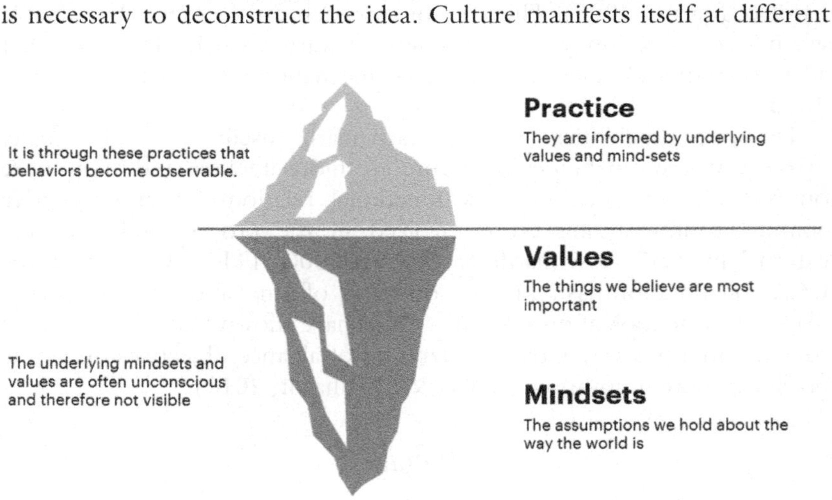

Fig. 11.2 Levels of organizational culture (Adapted from Schein's cultural model (Schein, 1985: 2004)

levels of observability (Schein, 2004). In this chapter, behaviour is interpreted as the outward sign of culture informed by underlying values and mindsets. Values are the things we believe are most important. Mindsets are the assumptions we hold about how the world functions.

Given the unique access to interview data, and the embedded relationship that were revealed in the interview process, this is a very suitable case to understand the nuances embedded in culture such as values and mindsets.

Values

Values can be observed through cultural expression and can range broadly (Schein, 2004), and often they are represented as principles rather than as products. Values reside in a deeper, often less visible level of culture, and they can persist over time, even when group members change (Wilson, 2001). The study of cultural values is closely related to that of ethics or religion, since ethical or spiritual outlooks similarly encompass states of mind or attitudes towards behaviour (de Lange, Armanios, Delgado-Ceballos & Sandhu, 2015).

In this case, all 10 interviewees highly valued enjoyment in their work and expressed a strong personal conviction in sustainability. With a multitude of projects to choose from, people engaged in the GCA because they thought it was not only important but also desirable to join this project. As the following testimonies will demonstrate, value was realized when conviction in sustainability—evidenced by bravery or tenacity, for example—met with personal enjoyment:

> To work with the GCA is like realizing my own values, what I think is important. So, in that sense, it is something very concrete ... I get to contribute to something I believe is very important. (Trend Report Lead, Accenture)

> Of course, you can show results when you can see the bigger picture, but on a personal level, it also comes down to...worth spending time on it, and fight for it, and really we should do. Then and there it is very important that it feels fun and good to work with these other people. I think the feeling and belief in something bigger has also been important, because then you know that even though it was not perfect from the beginning, and it takes time to get to know each other, but then it feels

> worthwhile to spend that time, because you feel that this can really be anything. (Accelerator Lead, KTH)

Among all members interviewed, personal conviction grounded in empathy and compassion—for people and for the planet—led to engagement and action. However, representatives from all three partnerships cited internal politics and structures as the major challenges to collaboration, and each pointed out that personal conviction needed to be exercised internally within their respective firms, not in the partnership organization.

Mindsets

A mindset is best described as a philosophy of life; it often refers to a set of assumptions or a worldview. Although no agreement exists on the conceptualization of mindset, within organizational leadership studies, mindsets are generalized as cognitive processes for filtering information (French, 2016), or in other words, a frame of reference. Similar to the *global* and *entrepreneurial* mindsets that have emerged over the past decades, a collaborative mindset has become an often-used term in practice. Despite broad and varied conceptualizations, they can provide interesting parallels, for example, they can refer to individual or collective attributes of capacities (French, 2016).

In this case, all interviewees expressed a strong personal commitment to the project and a continuous willingness to change. As the following testimonies will demonstrate, the collaboration worked well when strong relationships were established—evidenced by generosity and respect for differences—met with a common belief in "something bigger". When interviewees were asked how to collaborate with those different from them, the answers were revealing:

> For me, it is very much about giving and taking, that this is actually a partnership, not just a sponsorship where it is exchanged value in one direction, but where we all see these strengths and weaknesses of each player, and where together we find a platform where we can utilize the maximum of all the actors' strengths to create value for each organization that may have slightly different driving forces and where this value may look a little different, but where everyone understands that it is about give and take and to leverage the strengths to create value in our respective dimensions. (Marketing Lead, Accenture)

> All the parties involved, and perhaps especially the HM Foundation, have really opened up all their networks. You open up and try to help. (Accelerator Lead, KTH)

> It works because everyone feels needed. (Trend Report Lead, Accenture)

These findings indicate a mindset linked to the literature on ecosystems where successful depend on a broader consideration of value, where the value sits in the system instead of only within the participating organizations, and collaboration is based on interdependence. "When they work, ecosystems allow firms to create value that no single firm could create alone" (Adner, 2006).

Finally, common to all interviews about group dynamics was an overall willingness to change—on both individual and collective levels. While further investigation would be interesting to explore in more depth, based on this investigation, a collaborative mindset allows organizations to integrate respect for diversity with a generous mindset into their collaborative strategy.

Culture affects how people perceive and deliver their organization's strategy, and surprisingly little research exists to understand this process within the discourse of dynamic capabilities despite recognition of its importance in our current rapidly changing environment. "Managing innovation in a world of VUCA requires a strategic shifting of problem boundaries by challenging people's mental models" (Schoemaker et al., 2018: 34).

Studies on collaboration and capabilities are not new; however, most of the extant literature focuses on one or the other through simple parameters. This chapter has attempted to revisit the impact of culture on dynamic capabilities, particularly within the alliance itself (Niesten & Jolink, 2015). Arguably, we need a more dynamic perspective to understand collaborative capabilities where culture plays a strong role, in particular values and mindsets.

Although much of both values and mindsets inherently exist on the individual level, organizations often have their own institutionalized values and attributes. To bring the concept of collaborative culture to an organizational level, organizational leaders must steer individual or collective mindsets towards collaboration via leadership, training, and education. A value-driven organization depends on the establishment of a culture of shared core values among its employees. With a clearly stated purpose, value-driven organizations create work environments where workers can find meaning in their jobs and collaborate to deliver that organization's purpose.

During this longitudinal study, the proficiency of collaborative capabilities increased within the alliance and across each of the participating organizations, and it was evident that all the project members increasingly took risks, developed trust, and workshopped problems; as such, they arguably became more proficient in managing the collaboration.

Since I was able to monitor the development of this culture of collaboration, I can appreciate how much time it took to cultivate, and can recognize that its success depends on engaging people with strong personal convictions and generous mindsets.

When a lot of organizational resources and capabilities can be emulated, fostering a culture of supporting, the organizational strategy becomes even more important because these conditions are harder to replicate.

Conclusion

We live in a fast-changing world, and the need for advancement in sustainability has never been stronger; in the fashion industry, there is a clear burning platform for collaboration.

By observing and participating in the GCA since its inception, I was able to qualitatively capture insights about how collaborative processes were developed and enacted in this successful, multi-stakeholder collaboration. The alliance function within each of the collaborating partnerships was originally the unit of analysis for understanding collaborative capabilities at the organizational level. However, the GCA quickly evolved into a well-established programme with its own brand and virtual structure that was completely centred on collaborative activities and a common vision. This collaborative structure represented an extension of all the participating organizations where both strategic and operational activities were executed. For the purpose of this investigation, this collaboration therefore became the logical boundary for studying collaborative capabilities.

Collaborating for strategic change requires new types of skills and resources. Dynamic capabilities have become increasingly popular in management research (Schilke et al., 2018), and in this case they provided a useful lens for understanding collaboration. Capabilities are difficult to observe but the abundant literature within strategic management on organizational antecedents was helpful for guiding the investigation into the collaboration. The core concepts of experience, structure and process are well established as antecedents; however, they have most often been studied as mechanisms for managing single alliances or institutionalizing an alliance at the level of the firm. These antecedents remain relevant in instances where collaborative objectives are clear, the roles in the alliance are well defined, and the outcomes are predictable. However, new types of collaborations or alliances have emerged recently, where objectives are visionary, roles are undefined and composed of multiple actors from many sectors, and outcomes are highly unpredictable. The GCA represented such a case.

This study called into question the continued reliance on the established dynamic capability antecedents of experience, structure, and process. Instead, it stressed that the role culture plays should not be underestimated. Although there is no silver bullet, and building collaborative capabilities takes both time and effort, investing in and fostering a collaborative culture which allows for mistakes is key. The working culture established in this case was strongly grounded in a collective mindset of interdependence, generosity, and personal conviction.

The partners agreed that the programme was a success in its ambition to disrupt the fashion industry. Although not the focus of this study, the evolution of collaborative capabilities paralleled the improved performance of the collaboration itself, as each year the programme attracted more applicants, expanded its geographical reach, and caught more market attention. Of note, all the award winners and start-ups are still active and prosperous, which is not a common statistic in the start-up world. While the focus of this chapter was on the core partners of this collaboration, its conclusions extend far beyond them to include all the innovators and contributors involved in the GCA. Building on the initial insights of this chapter, I would like to consider this broader ecosystem of collaboration, and further investigate how these collaborations play a role in sustainable development.

Fostering a new mindset might disrupt our current trajectory and increase our chances for a more sustainable future. At the same time, looking back at the original concepts in RBV, it becomes clear that successful complex collaborations are harder to replicate; if managed well, they can greatly contribute to a competitive advantage. In a world where collaboration remains central to strategy, and organizations increasingly engage in complex alliances with more and new types of partners, we all stand to benefit from greater attention paid to collaborative capabilities. Based on this study, the future of both strategic success and sustainable development, at least in part, depends on individual people—their strong values and generous mindsets gives me hope.

References

Adner, R. (2006). Match your innovation strategy to your innovation ecosystem. *Harvard Business Review, 84*(4), 1–11.

Al-Tabbaa, O., Leach, D., & Khan, Z. (2019). Examining alliance management capabilities in cross-sector collaborative partnerships. *Journal of Business Research, 101*(8), 268–284.

Austin, J. E., & Seitanidi, M. M. (2014). *Creating value in nonprofit-business collaborations: New thinking and practice*. San Fransisco: Wiley.

Barney, J. B. (1991). Firm resources and sustained competitive advantage. *Journal of Management, 17*(1), 99–120.

Barney, J. B. (2001). Resource-based theories of competitive advantage: A ten-year retrospective on the resource-based view. *Journal of Management, 27*(6), 643–650.

Barreto, I. (2010). Dynamic capabilities: A review of past research and an agenda for the future. *Journal of Management, 36*(1), 256–280.

Baumgartner, R. J. (2009). Organizational culture and leadership: Preconditions for the development of sustainable corporation. *Sustainable Development, 17*(2), 102–113.

Bryson, J. M., Crosby, B. C., & Stone, M. M. (2006). The design and implementation of cross-sector collaborations: Propositions from the literature. *Public Administration Review, 66*, 44–45.

Coghlan, D. (2016). Retrieving a philosophy of practical knowing for action research. *International Journal of Action Research, 12*(1), 84–107.

Davis, J. P., & Eisenhardt, K. M. (2011). Rotating leadership and collaborative innovation: Recombination processes in symbiotic relationships. *Administrative Science Quarterly, 56*(2), 159–201.

de Lange, D. E., Armanios, D., Delgado-Ceballos, J., & Sandhu, S. (2015). From foe to friend: Complex mutual adaptation of multinational corporations and nongovernmental organizations. *Business and Society, 55*(8), 1197–1228.

Eisenhardt, K. M., & Eisenhardt, M. (1989). Building theories from case study research. *Academy of Management Review, 14*(4), 532–550.

Eisenhardt, K. M., & Brown, S. L. (1999). Patching. Restitching business portfolios in dynamic markets. *Harvard Business Review, 77*(3), 72–82.

Eisenhardt, K. M., & Martin, J. J. A. (2000). Dynamic capabilities: What are they? *Strategic Management Journal, 21*(10–11), 1105–1121.

Fainshmidt, S., & Frazier, M. L. (2017). What facilitates dynamic capabilities? The role of organizational climate for trust. *Long Range Planning, 50*(5), 550–566.

French, R. P. (2016). The fuzziness of mindsets: Divergent conceptualizations and characterizations of mindset theory and praxis. *International Journal of Organizational Analysis, 24*(4), 673–691.

General Assembly, United Nations. (2015). *Transforming our world: The 2030 agenda for sustainable development.*

Gulati, R. & Kellogg, J. L. (1998). Alliances and Networks. *Strategic Management Journal, 19*(4), 293–317.

Kale, P., & Singh, H. (2009). Managing strategic alliances: What do we know now, and where do we go from here? *The Academy of Management Perspectives, 23*(3), 45–62.

Le Ber, M. J. & Branzei, O. (2010). Value Frame Fusion in Cross Sector Interactions. *Journal of Business Ethics, 94*(1), 163–195.

Mamédio, D., Rocha, C., Szczepanik, D., & Kato, H. (2019). Strategic alliances and dynamic capabilities: A systematic review. *Journal of Strategy and Management, 12*(1), 83–102.

Niesten, E., & Jolink, A. (2015). The impact of alliance management capabilities on alliance attributes and performance: A literature review. *International Journal of Management Reviews, 17*(1), 69–100.

Qaiyum, S., & Wang, C. L. (2018). Understanding internal conditions driving ordinary and dynamic capabilities in Indian high-tech firms. *Journal of Business Research, 90*(9), 206–214.

Reason, P., & Bradbury, H. (2001). *Handbook of action research: Participative inquiry and practice.* London: Sage.

Ring, P. S., & van de Ven, A. H. (1994). Developmental processes of cooperative interorganizational relationships. *Academy of Management, 19*(1), 90–118.

Rohrbeck, R., Battistella, C., & Huizingh, E. (2015). Corporate foresight: An emerging field with a rich tradition. *Technological Forecasting and Social Change, 101*(12), 1–9.

Schein, E. H. (1985). *Organizational culture and leadership: A dynamic view.* San Francisco, CA: Jossey-Bass.

Schein, E. H. (2004). *Organizational culture and leadership* (3rd ed.). San Francisco, CA: Jossey-Bass.

Schilke, O., Hu, S., & Helfat, C. E. (2018). Quo vadis, dynamic capabilities? A content-analytic review of the current state of knowledge and recommendations for future research. *Academy of Management Annals, 12*(1), 390–439.

Schoemaker, P. J. H., Heaton, S., & Teece, D. (2018). Innovation, dynamic capabilities, and leadership. *California Management Review, 61*(1), 15–42.
Selsky, J. W., & Parker, B. (2010). Platforms for cross-sector social partnerships: Prospective sensemaking devices for social benefit. *Journal of Business Ethics, 94*(Suppl. 1), 21–37.
Teece, D. J. (2007). Explicating dynamic capabilities: The nature and microfoundations of (sustainable) enterprise performance. *Strategic Management Journal, 28*(13), 1319–1350.
Teece, D. J. (2012). Dynamic capabilities: Routines versus entrepreneurial action. *Journal of Management Studies, 49*(8), 1395–1401.
Teece, D. J., Pisano, G., & Shuen, A. (1997). Dynamic capabilities and strategic management. *Strategic Management Journal, 18*(7), 509–533.
Van de Ven, A. H. (2007). *Engaged scholarship: A guide for organizational and social research*. Oxford: Oxford University Press.
Waddock, S. (2013). The wicked problems of global sustainability need wicked (good) leaders and wicked (good) collaborative solutions. *Journal of Management for Global Sustainability, 1*(1), 91–111.
Wernerfelt, B. (1984). A resource based view of the firm. *Strategic Management Journal, 5*(2), 171–180.
Wilson, A. M. (2001). Understanding organisational culture and the implications for corporate marketing. *European Journal of Marketing, 35*(3/4), 353–367.
Winter, S. G. (2003). Understanding dynamic capabilities. *Strategic Management Journal, 24* (10), 991–995.
Yin, R. K. (2003). *Case study research: Design and methods*. Thousand Oaks: Sage.

CHAPTER 12

Towards Circular Economy: Enhanced Decision-Making in Circular Manufacturing Systems

Saman Amir, Farazee M. A. Asif, and Malvina Roci

Introduction

This chapter will provide an introduction to the different approaches to modelling and simulation and their importance in designing circular manufacturing systems (CMS). CMS refers to the recovery of value (i.e. material, embedded energy, and value that are added to products during

S. Amir (✉)
Department of Marketing & Strategy and Center for Sustainability Research, Stockholm School of Economics, Stockholm, Sweden
e-mail: saman.amir@phdstudent.hhs.se

F. M. A. Asif · M. Roci
Department of Production Engineering, KTH Royal Institute of Technology, Stockholm, Sweden
e-mail: aasi@kth.se

M. Roci
e-mail: roci@kth.se

R. Bali Swain and S. Sweet (eds.), *Sustainable Consumption and Production, Volume II*,
https://doi.org/10.1007/978-3-030-55285-5_12

manufacturing processes) through reusing, remanufacturing, and recycling in a systematic way (Asif, Roci, Lieder, & Rashid, 2018). The chapter will also show the importance of measuring the performance of circular systems and potential indicators. The case studies of circular systems simulation modelling are described to support the notion of simulation and performance measurement. Further, the future outlook of circular systems simulation and their role in enhancing the sustainability of production and consumption patterns is highlighted.

In recent years, production systems have been moving closer towards circular economy principles of resource efficiency. In this regard, closed-loop production systems where the products are brought back for recovery and repurposing is gaining momentum. Maximization of value recovery calls for innovation in business models and supply chains in an integrated manner. The adoption of circular transformation of production systems through an integrated approach of product design, business model, supply chain, and ICT will enable businesses to combine profit maximization and ecological impact reduction in one and the same approach. This approach will be substantially different from the linear thinking of business where the business secures profit only by selling the products and not necessarily by gaining back their ownership to exploit the material value embedded in the sold products.

In production systems, the most complex systemic effects arise between decisions in terms of the business model, product design and necessary supply chain considerations. If a product is designed in a way that it can be reused, it needs to be brought back and the resold product can cannibalize the traditional new product sales. These interactions need to be carefully discussed and analysed with all stakeholders and from a systemic perspective.

Interdependencies of Business Model, Product Design and Supply Chain

CMS essentially requires innovation in the business model, product design, and supply chains. To reap the implementation benefit of circular systems, a balance is needed between maximization of economic potential and a reduction in the environmental impact.

Business model innovation refers to the strategy based on which a firm generates revenue. The business model can either be direct sales, leasing, or a product-service system. Product design for circular systems looks into the role of modularity in products. Modularity aids in making the products conducive to reuse, remanufacture and recycle without loss of value carrying material, whereas the supply chain configuration is potentially required to support a new business strategy. The resulting supply chains can be centralized or decentralized supply chains with a corresponding leasing business model, or a service-based business model or a combination of both to improve the bottom lines of the companies.

Closed-loop supply chains as defined by Guide and Van Wassenhove refer to '*the design, control, and operation of a system to maximize value creation over the entire life cycle of a product with dynamic recovery of value from different types and volumes of returns over time*' (Guide & Van Wassenhove, 2009) and in addition to this definition include '*product return management, leasing and remanufacturing*' (Mishra, Hopkinson, & Tidridge, 2018).

In the classical closed-loop systems approach, the value of products is claimed only after they reach the end of useful life through reuse, remanufacturing or recycling. This means that the products that are returned to the manufacturers are not necessarily fit for repurposing through reuse or remanufacturing. This refers to the notion that the loop is closing by chance, and it is considered a reactive approach compared to a proactive approach as proposed in the concept of Resource Conservative Manufacturing (ResCoM).[1] In this concept, the interdependencies between the business models, product design, supply chains, and supporting ICT for circular value management are preconceived with loop-closure already in the design stage of products (Rashid, Asif, Krajnik, & Nicolescu, 2013a). The ResCoM concept includes the idea of multiple product lifecycles along with conservation of energy, material and added value with waste Prevention and environmental protection as integrated components of the product design and development strategy. The ResCOM concept of loop-closure through product design, business model, supply chain, and ICT has a far more significant impact on the operations in terms of timing, quantity and quality of product returns, as well as the mismatch between the supply and demand of product returns in remanufacturing scenarios (Asif, Bianchi, Rashid, & Nicolescu, 2012).

[1] ResCoM is a research initiative developed at the Department of Production Engineering at KTH Royal Institute of Technology with the vision to conserve resources in the context of manufacturing systems (Asif, 2017). This initiative was funded by the European Commission (EC) FP7 framework (website: www.rescoms.eu).

Performance of Circular Manufacturing Systems

Circular systems implementation in a systemic view poses certain complexities associated with the performance of supply chains from the perspective of business model and product design. Fluctuation in either the business model or the product design will require an adaptation in supply chain configuration. A cohesive picture of a potential circular supply network can only be obtained by addressing which parameters of performance shall be measured and what are the possible key performance indicators. Since the concept of circular manufacturing systems is in its infancy, specific performance measurement criteria, which has a clearly defined two-fold focus on environmental performance and economic performance of the system, does not currently exist in literature.

Let us take an example of circular supply chains performance criteria. To identify relevant performance criteria for circular supply/value chains, we only have performance indicators in linear supply chains which do not support the notion of circular manufacturing systems of loop-closure by design. Conventionally, linear supply chains are typically focused on business performance alone whereas closed-loop supply chains to a certain extent focus on a few environmental performance measures as well. Reverse logistics design, however, still leans towards profit maximization and less on environmental impact (Aras, Boyaci, & Verter, 2010). Performance measurement criteria can be further subdivided into functional criteria such as planning performance, sourcing performance, production performance, delivery performance, customer service performance (Gunasekaran, Patel, & Tirtiroglu, 2001). These measures can fall in the categories of strategic, tactical or operational. Strategic level measures include lead time against industry norm, quality level, cost saving initiatives, and supplier pricing against market. Tactical level measures include the efficiency of purchase order cycle time, booking, cash flow, quality assurance methodology, and capacity flexibility. Operational level measures include ability in day-to-day technical representation, adherence to developed schedule, ability to avoid complaints and achievement of defect-free deliveries (Gunasekaran, Patel, & Tirtiroglu, 2004).

Performance indicators encompassing economic feasibility and environmental sustainability is a prerequisite for circular systems implementation. For sustainable production and consumption patterns, these performance indicators should be embedded in business outcomes. Clear objectives and measurement indicators for economic and environmental performance will lead to enhanced decision-making and expedite the transition towards sustainable production.

Modelling and Simulation in Circular Manufacturing Systems

Complex systems theory develops principles and tools for making sense of the world's complexity and are defined as systems that are composed of multiple individual elements that interact with each other, yet whose aggregate properties or behaviour is not predictable from the elements themselves. Through the interaction of the multiple distributed elements an 'emergent phenomenon' arises. The phenomenon of emergence is characteristic of complex systems (Wilensky & Rand, 2013).

Models can be used to come up with the best possible solutions in different scenarios. It provides a possibility to envisage real-world problems in a simplified manner to establish a sound basis for decision support with measurable parameters and indicators. A simulation model is an extended version of reality where the results and analysis can be simulated and forecast over a period of time. Modelling and simulation help in understanding the dynamics of complex systems and how the underlying attributes behave over time. The choice of modelling method depends on the questions to be answered, the underlying phenomenon to be studied, or to test different scenarios in a simulation and find out the best solution to be implemented in the real world. The major benefit of simulation models is the aspect of scalability, flexibility in introducing the levels of abstraction and modularity, that is, the system can be analysed in part or as a whole. Furthermore, it allows one to experiment in a 'risk-free' environment (Borshchev, 2013).

Simulation models allow for identifying and understanding the propagation of the consequences of any potential decision, in order to develop an environmentally and economically viable system (Merkuryev, Merkuryeva, Piera, & Guasch, 2009).

However, simulation models have their limitations with regard to factors such as modelling rationale, data acquisition, modellers' expertise and external validation of the model. Representing the modelling boundary accurately can result in a robust model. Input data used in the model may affect the modelling accuracy, the rationale, modelling boundary and assumptions for the problem or aspect to be modelled. The expertise of the modeller also plays a role in the outcomes of the simulation while accurately representing the reality. External validation of the model poses another limitation to replicate the results of the model for other types of data or input parameters which in most cases is difficult to achieve.

In simulation modelling, there are three methods namely, System Dynamics, Discrete Event and Agent-Based, with each method serving a particular range of abstraction levels. System dynamics operates at high abstraction level and is mostly used for strategic modelling. Discrete event modelling with the underlying process-centric approach supports medium and medium-low abstraction. Agent-based modelling uses a bottom-up approach, where the system is described as interacting objects with their own behaviours. Agent-based models can vary from being very detailed where agents are modelled as physical objects, to highly abstract where agents are competing companies or governments (Borshchev, 2013).

The benefits of modelling and simulation as highlighted in the above section have enormous applicability in the domain of circular manufacturing systems. Conventional closed-loop systems already represent a high level of complexity in terms of product flows, information flows and financial flows. Closing the loop by design as in CMS, adds another layer of complexity. Modelling and simulation can be used to capture the dynamics of such complex systems by connecting the aspects of business model, product design and supply chain.

Different business model strategies that can enable economically viable ways to continually reuse products and materials have been proposed in literature. Modelling and simulation can help in choosing the right strategy by assessing the economic and environmental potential of new circular business models. It can be employed to determine new revenue streams, define payment schemes, propose pricing and marketing strategies, estimate market share and profit margins over the course of time. Business model is a primary driver in CMS dictating both the design of products and supply chain. Different design strategies and supply chain configurations have been proposed in literature for closing the loop. Further work is being carried out to develop these concepts in an EU-funded project, ReCiPSS.[2] However, it is very challenging to choose the right strategy at an early design stage since the economic and environmental impact of different strategies depend heavily on the chosen

[2] ReCiPSS is an EU-funded project composed of two industrial large-scale demonstrators from the automotive and white goods industries. The project is co-funded by the European Commission's Horizon 2020 research and innovation programme under grant agreement No. 776577-2 (website: www.recipss.eu).

business model and the associated supply chain. Therefore, modelling and simulation can support in quantifying design efforts for different circular business configurations and optimize the associated circular supply chain necessary to ensure product returns and redistribution.

A multimethod modelling approach combining system dynamics, agent-based and discrete event is necessary to capture the complex and systemic nature of CMS as different levels of abstractions are needed to model the mutual interaction of the elements of the system.

Modelling and simulation allow experiment in a 'risk-free' environment by quantitatively analysing the implications of certain business model strategies on product design and supply chain to propose solutions that are economically feasible and environmentally sustainable.

The Case Studies of Circular Manufacturing Systems Modelling

In the previous sections, the importance of designing, analysing and implementing CMS using simulation models is outlined. It has also been highlighted that there are inherent systemic dependencies among the business model, product design and supply chain aspects of the CMS. These interdependencies make analysis of the CMS complex, and decision-making becomes troublesome. Furthermore, due to the diversity in the aspects of business model, product design and supply chain, it is hard to capture the true nature of a CMS using a single modelling approach. Therefore, multimethod modelling is considered to be an appropriate approach to systematically design and analyse the complexity as well as the dynamics of the CMS. This section presents four industrial cases of CMS that are modelled using multimethod simulation approach between 2015 and 2017 as part of an EU-funded research project called ResCoM.[3]

Introduction to the Industrial Cases

The ResCoM project dealt with four industrial cases. All four companies were interested in designing and analysing (in a virtual environment)

[3] www.rescoms.eu.

the economic and environmental performance of the CMS that is envisaged by the case companies. Although all companies had the same goal, that is, to assess the economic and environmental performance, the scope of the CMS for each company was different. As a result of this, the models developed for these companies were different in their form and the implementation approach. The following sections provide an overview of the CMS that are envisaged by two of the companies in the ResCoM project. To maintain confidentiality, details of the case companies are not disclosed; they are named as company A and B.

A. Circular manufacturing system of company A

Let us assume that company A is a manufacturing company that produces bicycles for children between the ages of 4 and 7 years. The manufacturing system they use is a typical linear system shown in Fig. 12.1, where most of the materials used for manufacturing the bicycles come from primary sources acquired through material extraction. The bicycles are manufactured in China and the complete assembled products are shipped to the European markets. The bicycles are typically sold through the local retailers spread all over Europe with limited online selling. The company also sells spare parts through its retailers. Typically, the bicycles are returned (by the users) to the local recycling centres after use, where the bicycles are shredded. The shredded bicycles are recycled, incinerated and disposed off as per the character of the materials used in the first place. Since the bicycles are suited for children ages 4–7, typically they are in use for three years. Due to the short use-span, the bicycles are traded multiple times in the second-hand market by the users. This is considered

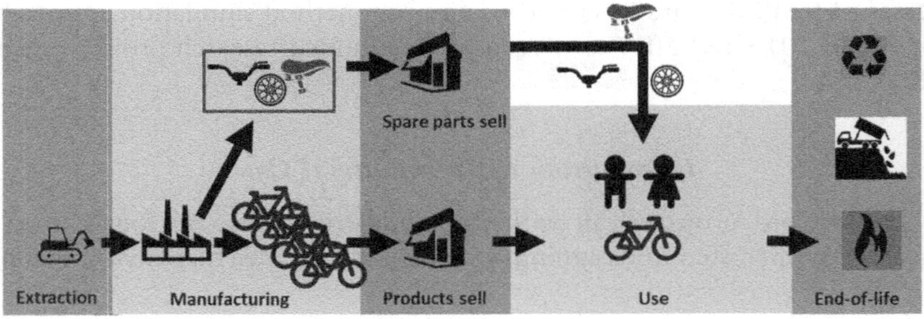

Fig. 12.1 A depiction of Company A's current linear manufacturing system (Inspired by and modified from Mihelič et al., 2017)

a lost opportunity by the company. Furthermore, the bicycles can be categorized as high-end products, which are made out of non-conventional materials. Due to the use of these non-conventional materials, the recyclability of the bicycles is rather low. Therefore, the company is also interested in improving design features in order to increase recyclability, and thereby reduce the bicycles' lifecycle impact.

The envisaged CMS for company A is leasing of products with the purpose of using the same products throughout multiple lifecycles as shown in Fig. 12.2.

In this leasing model, customers can lease the bicycles for a duration of 6 to 36 months. The contract includes the possibility of exchanging the bicycles for a newer model whenever a customer wants. The bicycles go through refurbishment operations before they are leased to new customers. In an ideal case, the bicycles are leased for 36 months and refurbished at the end of the first leasing contract. After refurbishment the bicycles enter into a second lease contract for another 36 months. The second round of refurbishment takes place when the second leasing period is over. These second-time refurbished bicycles are then sold in the second-hand market. The company plans to establish the refurbishment operations in Europe. The leasing offer is to be introduced in two markets (locations) in Western Europe, which the company has identified as the most favourable markets for leasing. To facilitate this leasing with the refurbishment model, company A is considering improving the design of its products in order to make refurbishment operations efficient, and redesigning supply chain networks to make the reverse operations

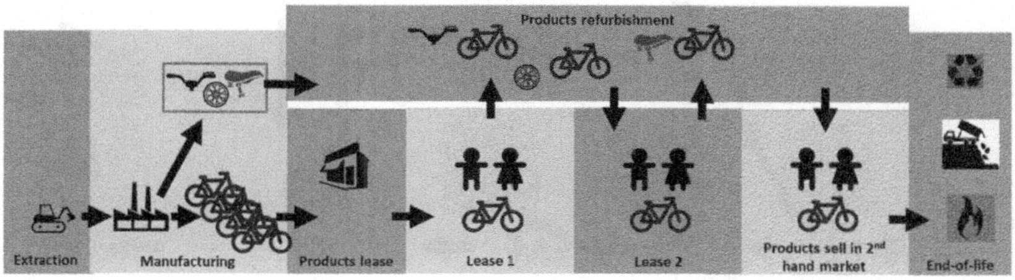

Fig. 12.2 A depiction of circular manufacturing system envisaged by company A (Inspired by and modified from Mihelič et al., 2017)

agile. The company is also considering mixing new and refurbished bicycles to fulfill the demand for leasing in case the demand is higher than the number of refurbished bicycles available at any given time. This new business model set-up is expected to influence the forward and reverse supply chains in terms of return, refurbishment and supply activities. These activities are expected to result in additional costs, a new pricing structure and different environmental impacts at different stages of the product lifecycle. The company also sees an opportunity for new revenue streams through leasing and entering the second-hand market.

B. Circular manufacturing system of company B

For the purpose of a representative case study description, let us assume that company B is one of the major household appliance manufacturers the world. The company among other appliances also produces high-end dishwashers for both Business to Business (B2B) and Business to Consumer (B2C) markets. The manufacturing system they use is a typical linear system shown in Fig. 12.3, which has remained the same since the company was established.

In this linear system, the company is mainly dependent on materials from primary sources. The dishwashers are manufactured and assembled in Europe and shipped to both B2B and B2C customers all over the world

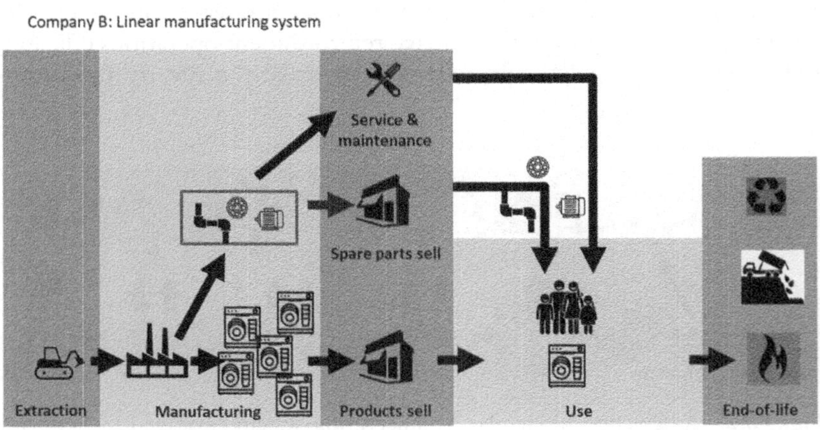

Fig. 12.3 A depiction of Company B's current linear manufacturing system (Inspired by and modified from Mihelič et al., 2017)

through both the company's own and local dealers. The company also provides after-sales support in the form of maintenance, repair and spare parts through their own and third-party service providers. According to the information of the company's service division, a dishwasher is in use for seven years on average before it turns up at the local recycling centre. The current design of the dishwashers is optimized for material recycling for secondary applications. From this conventional linear system, the company is aiming to move towards a circular system through the approaches described below.

For company B, CMS implies a service/function-oriented product-service system where customers obtain the dishwashers in a pay-per-use scheme as shown in Fig. 12.4.

In this scheme, the ownership of the dishwashers remains with company B and full maintenance service is included in the offer. In an ideal case, the customers will sign a five-year contract with the company and they will be billed monthly for the number of washes they perform in that month. This pay-per-use scheme is to be introduced in both B2C and B2B markets. To make the pay-per-use scheme affordable to a wide range of customers, the company plans to categorise the scheme into three segments—offering brand new, one-time, and two-times remanufactured products, respectively. This means a brand new dishwasher serves a customer for five years and after that the machine goes through remanufacturing operations before it enters a new contract. After serving another five years, the dishwasher goes through another round of remanufacturing operations, and is entered into the final contract for its last years. In this approach, in an ideal case, a dishwasher will serve up to three customers

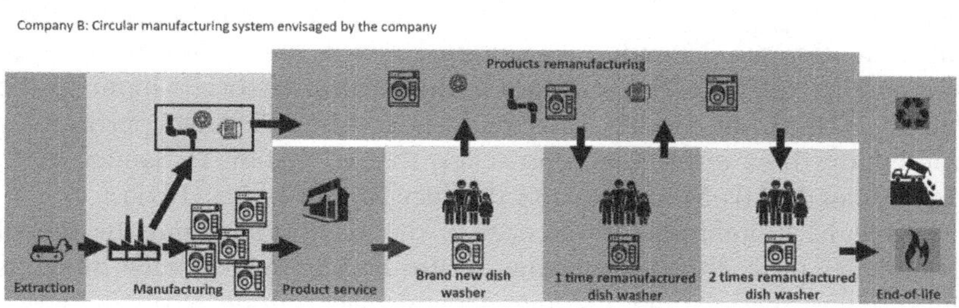

Fig. 12.4 A depiction of circular manufacturing system envisaged by company B (Inspired by and modified from Mihelič et al., 2017)

for total 15 years and will be remanufactured twice before it is shredded for recycling.

This new approach is to be tested in several locations in Northern and Central Europe, and remanufacturing operations are to be performed in Eastern Europe. To facilitate this, company B foresees product design improvement to make products modular in order to make remanufacturing efficient, and redesigning supply chain networks to make the collection as well as redistribution of dishwashers efficient. Also, to meet demand, the company plans to mix new, one-time and two-times remanufactured dishwashers, depending on their availability. This will also influence the forward and reverse supply chain in terms of return, remanufacturing, and supply activities. This new business approach will initiate new activities, which will require additional investments, new pricing, and will have different environmental impacts at different stages. The company also sees this as an opportunity to ensure new streams of revenue.

The sections above present an overview of the CMS of two companies. Both companies analyse the economic and environmental performance of the envisaged CMS through modelling and simulation. The overview of the cases also confirms that different companies or industries set different levels of ambition and therefore, the CMS of each company and industry varies. Due to these differences, two simulation models are developed and different simulation implementation approaches are adopted for the companies. However, there are some critical commonalities in these two models. First, both companies are interested in measuring two critical performance indicators of CMS, that is, economic and environmental performance with reference to the business as usual (existing linear manufacturing system) scenario. Second, all models have considered the inherent systemic dependencies among business model, product design and supply chain aspects by incorporating critical factors as input to the models. Third, all models used multi-method modelling approach by combining three modelling approaches, that is, System Dynamics (SD), Agent-Based (AB) Modelling and Product Design Index (PDI).[4]

Table 12.1 highlights differences in the assumptions and the model boundaries for each case company. It also highlights how each model is appreciating the inherent systemic dependencies among business model, product design and supply chain.

[4] Product design index is a novel approach to create and analyse different design options and their associated economic and environmental implications (Asif, Lieder, & Rashid, 2016).

Table 12.1 Summary of the differences in the case company simulation models (Modified from Asif, 2017)

	Company A	*Company B*
Purpose of the decision support tool	Measuring the economic and environmental performance of the circular manufacturing system	
Business model	• Conventional sales of new products • Leasing of new and refurbished products • Sales of refurbished products	• Conventional sales of new products • Sales of product-service contracts (pay-per-use)
Target segment	• Current segment	• Current B2C (high-income) segment • B2C high, medium- and low-income segment • B2B high, medium- and low-income segment
Product design	• Design for refurbishment and improved recyclability	• Modular design • Design for remanufacturing
Strategy for multiple lifecycles	• Two-times refurbishment	• Two-times remanufacturing
Sources of used products	• Own products returning from the end of leasing contracts	• Own products returning from the end of service contracts
Supply chain	• Leasing in two locations in Western Europe • Refurbishment in one location in Western Europe	• Service contracts in Northern and Central Europe • Remanufacturing in Eastern Europe
Elements of the tool	• 23 stocks • 16 flows • 68 input and auxiliary variables	• 29 stocks • 19 flows • 59 input and auxiliary variables

The Scope of the Models and the Modelling Approach

The models developed for the case companies evolved around the conceptual model captured through two causal loop diagrams (CLD) shown in Fig. 12.5

The CLD (R1) shown in Fig. 12.5 is a reinforcing loop implying that if demand for leasing (here it is assumed that leasing is an appropriate business model to implement CMS) increases, so does the demand for

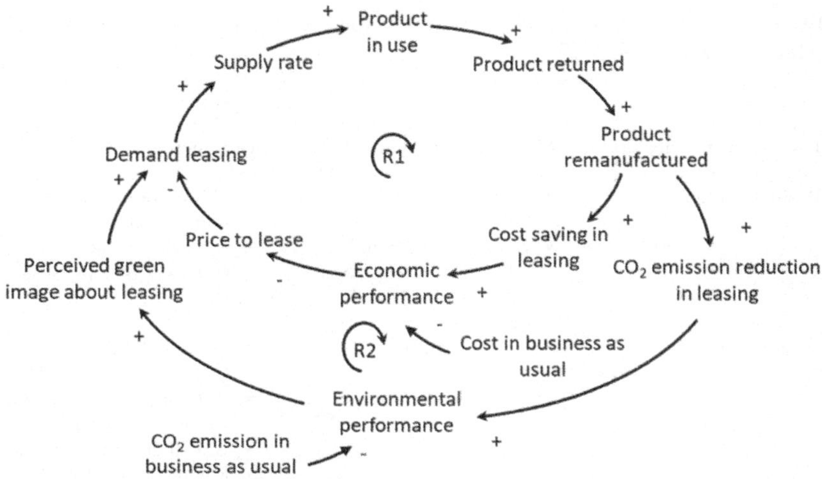

Fig. 12.5 CLD to capture the dynamics of economic and environmental performance (Modified from Asif et al., 2016)

more products that need to be supplied. As more products are supplied, more products are expected to return after use, which also means more products can be remanufactured. If it is assumed that remanufacturing operations cost less than manufacturing a new product, the overall costs of operations are expected to decrease. Reduced costs in this context means better economic performance in comparison to the situation where demands of leasing are fulfilled by producing only new products. If overall manufacturing costs are lower, the manufacturer will have the possibility of leasing at a lower cost, which may attract more customers and, as a result, the demand is expected to increase.

Following the same logic, the reinforcing loop (R2) shown in Fig. 12.5 implies that, if it is assumed that remanufacturing causes less CO_2 emissions, the environmental performance of leasing will be better. This may improve the perceived environmental image of the leasing offer, causing customers to prefer leasing over buying new products.

The positive relationship described in the above CLDs regarding cost saving and CO_2 emissions reduction is based on research done in the area of remanufacturing. Case studies such as Sundin and Lee (2012) and Lund (1996) suggest that remanufacturing has a positive impact on both cost and emissions reduction. The positive relation between price and demand is a known phenomenon in economics and it is generally perceived that the green image of a product/offer tends to (assuming that the product performance, price and other preferred utilities are not compromised) impact customers' decision-making positively.

Although the two CLDs mentioned above show the main dynamics that drive the performance of the envisaged CMS, many other aspects of the business model, product design and supply chain need to be included. Each element in the CLDs represents part of the complexity of the entire CMS. For example, the element ***demand*** in the CLD is represented by a complex customer decision-making process built on AB models. To capture all the complexity and dynamics a multimethod modelling approach combining SD, AB and PDI (Product Design Index) methods is taken. The interactions between these modelling approaches as well as an overview of the associated critical parameters used in the models are shown in Fig. 12.6.

The figures show that the SD model of the supply chain takes input from the PDI and AB business model and market. The PDI and AB model takes several critical inputs and processes them to generate outputs such as manufacturability, reusability, recyclability index demands, etc. The supply chain model is producing outputs such as the number of products supplied, used, returned, remanufactured, etc. These outputs are then fed in as inputs to the supply chain extension model to generate two main outputs, that is, economic and environmental performance. The economic and environmental performance outputs are fed back to the AB model, thus closing the loop of information.

The Utility of the Models in Decision-making

The models developed for case study companies are capable of measuring the economic and environmental performance of CMS. Although these are the two key performance indicators that are of interest to the case companies, the model can do much more than just measuring these. The models are basically comprehensive analysis methods that allow users to create different scenarios and compare them. Such analyses can aid companies in their decision-making and in setting policies for successful implementation of CMS. The models also support in exploring the critical aspects of CMS, which influence economic and environmental

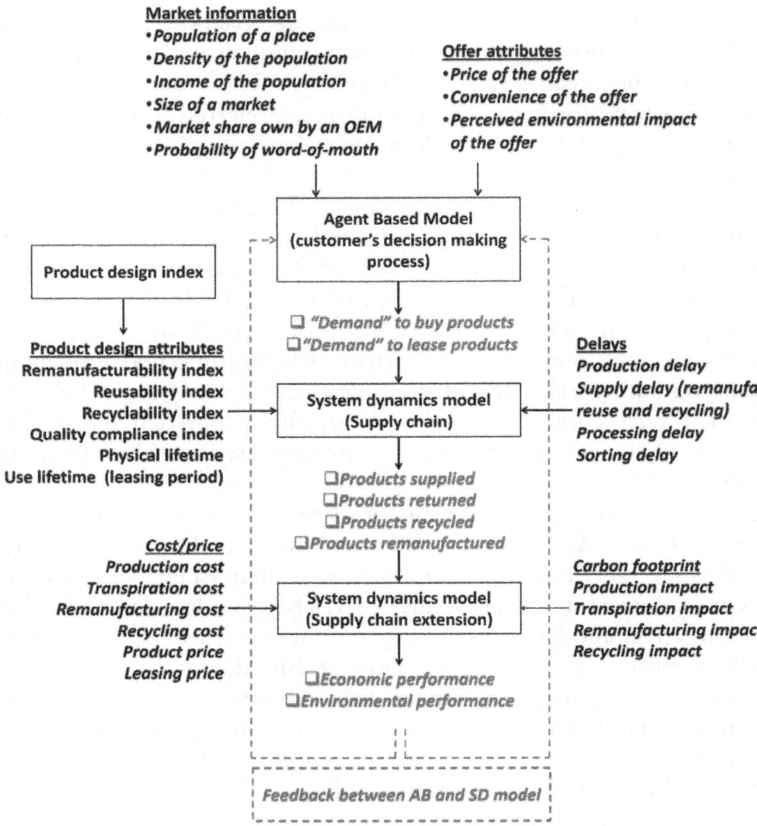

Fig. 12.6 An overview of the critical parameters used in the models (Modified from Asif et al., 2016)

performance. For instance, case company B identified that remanufacturing success rate is one of the key factors in influencing the economic and environmental performance of their CMS. Using the model, the company could also explore how remanufacturing success rate is influencing reverse supply chain, remanufacturing operations market demand, etc. This would allow the company to decide where to place focus to improve economic and environmental performance. In advanced cases, the users can also use the model to optimize the performance of the CMS.

The Role of Modelling and Simulation for Enhanced Decision Support

As mentioned above, a concurrent approach considering business model, product design and supply chains are essential for the successful implementation of circular manufacturing systems as these elements interact dynamically in a systemic manner. When it comes to a decision, supporting the development of simulation models that can capture the dynamics of CMS by connecting aspects of business models, product design and supply chain is needed.

The business model is a primary driver in CMS, dictating both the design of products and supply chains. Different business models have been proposed in the literature on circular economy implementation (Bocken, Pauw, Bakker, & Grinten, 2016; Tukker, 2015; Urbinati, Chiaroni, & Chiesa, 2017). Modelling and simulation can be used to assess the economic and environmental potential of introducing new circular business models. These tools can support decision-makers in estimating new revenue streams, cost impact, and investment potential of different business approaches, and identifying the most promising business models from both economic and environmental perspectives. Lieder, Asif, and Rashid (2017) have developed an agent-based simulation model to analyse customer behaviour in terms of their acceptance of circular business models such as leasing or functional sales. The tool is based on socio-demographic factors of a population (e.g. income, age, education, and geographic location) and customers' relative preferences of a product attribute, price, environmental friendliness and service-orientation. As a result, revenue streams, profit margins and market shares of the new business approaches over different time horizons can be assessed. The tool is capable of identifying marketing and pricing strategies to obtain best-fit demand behaviour for the chosen business model and can, therefore, serve as decision support for companies willing to move towards circular systems. This agent-based model can be extended and combined with other modelling techniques such as discrete event and systems dynamics to link to aspects of product design and supply chain while keeping an optimal profit strategy when changing the business model.

Designing products for multiple lifecycles is an essential step in implementing CMS as it allows for prolonging the functional life of products. (Rashid, Asif, Krajnik, & Nicolescu, 2013b) propose the notion of multiple lifecycle products of predefined lifecycles, encompassing manufacturing, distribution, use, return, recover, and reuse. In this approach, the entire life of the product is divided into multiple lives of the predefined period (time or performance). After each lifecycle, the products are taken back for remanufacturing to the original performance or upgrading to new specifications. In this context, modular design is an important approach for increasing performance in every lifecycle process such as disassembly, maintainability, upgradeability, reusability, and recyclability (Umeda, Fukushige, Tonoike, Kondoh, & Yoshikawa, 2008). After each lifecycle, the product is disassembled and its components are either reused, remanufactured, or recycled. A product can be given an additional lifecycle by reusing and upgrading some components of the product from the previous lifecycle, as well as replacing other components with newly manufactured ones. The number of lifecycles a product can have in this context is constrained by economic and environmental feasibility. Choosing the right strategy at the design stage is a challenging task since the economic and environmental impacts of adapting these strategies depend on the chosen business model and associated supply chain. Therefore, modelling and simulation can help assign appropriate value-recovery strategies (e.g. reuse, remanufacture, recycle) to the product over its multiple lifecycles. In this way, solutions that aim at optimizing the lifecycle as a whole can be found. Lieder, Asif, Rashid, & Mihelič, 2017 have developed a systematic method to quantify design effort for different circular design options through a multimethod simulation approach. The simulation model combines an agent-based product architecture and a discrete event circular supply chain. The tool is able to quantify design efforts for reuse, remanufacturing and recycling.

Moreover, costs, CO_2 emissions, and material savings of different design options can be explored with different business model configurations. The tool can be used for optimization purposes to identify the most cost-effective combination of reused, remanufactured, and recycled components for a chosen business model. Further developments could result in extending the model and linking it to aspects of marketing and customer demand variation to include potential revenue streams in order to consider the profitability of CMS. Rather than looking at specific economic and environmental performance, a system dynamics model was developed by Franco, 2019 to analyse the general dynamics present in closed-loop value chain covering issues related to product design, product use and replacement, product discard, and collection and processing for product recycling.

Circular systems require products to be returned for value recovery through reuse, remanufacturing or material recycling depending on the circular business approach adopted. Uncertainty in quality, quantity, and timing of product returns affect the performance of circular business models significantly. Therefore, well-designed circular supply chains are necessary to ensure product returns and redistribution. Modelling and simulation can support in circular supply network design and optimization. For example, if a company decides to adopt service-based business models, simulation models can help in locating the collection centres and remanufacturing facilities in a way that both economic and environmental aspects are taken into account. Moreover, fluctuation in either the business model or the product design will require an adaptation in the supply chain configuration. By using simulation modelling, different scenarios can be built to analyse different configurations.

Traditional methods and tools are not suitable for decision-making in circular manufacturing systems as they fail to capture the dynamics of such systems. Complex modelling of CMS is needed to connect to aspects of business model, product design and supply chain, and capture their mutual interactions. It allows experimenting in a risk-free environment, to find answers to 'what if' questions, and propose optimal solutions.

Conclusion

Circular manufacturing systems that are designed intentionally for closing the loop of components or products preferably in their original form, through multiple lifecycles, are indispensable for sustainable development. For a successful implementation of CMS, business model, product design and supply chain need to be considered simultaneously as these elements of the system influence each other in diverse ways. When it comes to decision support, traditional methods and tools are not suitable in circular manufacturing systems as they fail at capturing the dynamics of such systems. This chapter provides an overview of the importance of modelling and simulation for enhanced decision-making towards the implementation of circular manufacturing systems. An overview of system modelling methods relevant for modelling and simulation of CMS is given. These methods include system dynamics, discrete event and agent-based, each of which serves a particular range of abstraction levels.

System dynamics operates at a high abstraction level and is mostly used for strategic modelling. Discrete event modelling with the underlying process-centric approach supports medium and medium-low abstraction. Agent-based models can vary from very detailed to highly abstract. In order to understand the dynamics of CMS and how the underlying elements of the system behave over time, multimethod modelling (i.e. a combination of systems dynamics, agent-based and discrete event) is considered as an appropriate approach to systematically design and analyse the complexity as well as the dynamics of the CMS.

This chapter describes two industrial cases that are modelled using a multimethod simulation approach as part of the EU-funded ResCoM project. The first company aims at introducing leasing in addition to conventional sales. The second is interested in introducing functional sales (i.e. pay-per-use) in addition to conventional sales and considers introducing remanufacturing. Each industrial case has been modelled using a combination of system dynamics and agent-based modelling to evaluate the economic and environmental performance of the circular business approaches considered by the case study companies with respect to their linear approach. Specifically, the agent-based model includes the business model and the market aspects to provide product demand as output. As a supplement to the tool, a method to determine the product design index has been developed to define different product design attributes. The system dynamics model takes the market demand as input and combines the product design attributes to assess the economic and environmental performance.

Based on the analysis of prevailing research in the context of modelling and simulation of circular manufacturing systems, there are few examples that have employed simulation modelling to analyse circular systems. Agent-based modelling can be used to assess customer behaviour in terms of their acceptance of circular business models. As a result, pricing and marketing strategies can be identified to obtain best-fit demand behaviour for the chosen business model. This agent-based model could be developed further and combined with other modelling techniques such as discrete event and systems dynamics to link to aspects of product design and supply chain while keeping an optimal profit strategy when changing the business model. This will allow quantifying design efforts for reuse, remanufacturing and recycling for a chosen business model. Moreover, since fluctuation in either the business model or the product design will require an adaptation in supply chain configuration, simulation modelling can support in optimizing the design of circular supply networks.

It can be concluded that multimethod simulation modelling is capable of capturing the complexity and dynamics of circular manufacturing systems by taking into consideration mutual interactions among critical factors of business model, product design and supply chain.

References

Aras, N., Boyaci, T., & Verter, V. (2010). Designing the reverse logistics network. In M. E. Ferguson & G. C. Souza (Eds.), *Closed-loop supply chains: New developments to improve the sustainability of business practices* (pp. 67–97). https://doi.org/10.1201/9781420095265.

Asif, F. M. A. (2017). *Circular manufacturing systems: A development framework with analysis methods and tools for implementation*. KTH Royal Institute of Technology. http://www.diva-portal.org/smash/get/diva2:1096938/FULLTEXT01.pdf.

Asif, F. M. A., Bianchi, C., Rashid, A., & Nicolescu, C. M. (2012). Performance analysis of the closed loop supply chain. *Journal of Remanufacturing, 2*(1), 1. https://doi.org/10.1186/2210-4690-2-4.

Asif, F. M. A., Lieder, M., & Rashid, A. (2016). Multi-method simulation based tool to evaluate economic and environmental performance of circular product systems. *Journal of Cleaner Production, 139,* 1261–1281.

Asif, F. M. A., Roci, M., Lieder, M., & Rashid, A. (2018). A practical ICT framework for transition to circular manufacturing systems. *Procedia CIRP, 72,* 598–602. https://doi.org/10.1016/J.PROCIR.2018.03.311.

Bocken, N. M. P., Pauw, I. D., Bakker, C., & Grinten, B. V. D. (2016). Product design and business model strategies for a circular economy. *Journal of Industrial and Production Engineering, 33*(5), 308–320. https://doi.org/10.1080/21681015.2016.1172124.

Borshchev, A. (2013). *The big book of simulation modeling, Multimethod modeling with AnyLogic 6.* https://doi.org/10.7551/mitpress/9610.003.0011.

Franco, M. A. (2019). A system dynamics approach to product design and business model strategies for the circular economy. *Journal of Cleaner Production, 241,* 118327. https://doi.org/10.1016/j.jclepro.2019.118327.

Guide, V. D. R., Jr., & Van Wassenhove, L. N. (2009). The evolution of closed-loop supply chain research, *Operations Research*, 10–18. https://doi.org/10.1287/opre.1080.0628.

Gunasekaran, A., Patel, C., & Tirtiroglu, E. (2004). A framework for supply chain performance measurement. *International Journal of Production Economics, 87*(3), 333–347. https://doi.org/10.1016/j.ijpe.2003.08.003.

Gunasekaran, A., Patel, C., & Tirtiroglu, E. (2001). Performance measures and metrics in a supply chain environment. *International Journal of Operations and Production Management, 21*(1–2), 71–87. https://doi.org/10.1108/01443570110358468.

Lieder, M., Asif, F.M.A. & Rashid, A (2017). Towards circular economy implementation: An agent-based simulation approach for business model changes. *Autonomous Agents and Multi-Agent Systems,* 31(6): 1377–1402. https://doi.org/10.1007/s10458-017-9365-9.

Lieder, M., Asif, F. M. A., Rashid, A., & Mihelič, A. (2017). Towards circular economy implementation in manufacturing systems using a multi-method simulation approach to link design and business strategy. *International Journal of Advanced Manufacturing Technology, 93*(5–8): 1953–1970. https://doi.org/10.1007/s00170-017-0610-9.

Lund, R. T. (1996). *The Remanufacturing Industry: Hidden Giant*. Boston University.

Merkuryev, Y. Merkuryeva, G., Piera, M. A., & Guasch Petit, A. (2009). *Simulation-based case studies in logistics: Education and applied research*. https://doi.org/10.1007/978-1-84882-187-3.

Mihelič, A., Kotnik, S., Roci, M., Asif, F. M. A., Lieder, M., Ye, X., …, de Pauw, I. (2017). *Market Pilot and validated virtual model for Gorenje case study, Internal report of ResCoM, Resource Conservative Manufacturing—Transforming waste into high value resource through closed-loop product systems*. EU-funded project from the European Union's Seventh Programme for research, technological development and demonstration under grant agreement No. 603843.

Mishra, J. L., Hopkinson, P. G., & Tidridge, G. (2018). Value creation from circular economy-led closed loop supply chains: A case study of fast-moving consumer goods. *Production Planning and Control, 29*(6), 509–521. https://doi.org/10.1080/09537287.2018.1449245.

Wilensky, U., & Rand, W. (2013). *An introduction to agent-based modeling modeling natural, social, and engineered complex systems with NetLogo*. Cambridge, MA: MIT Press.

Rashid, A., Asif, F. M. A., Krajnik, P., & Nicolescu, C. M. (2013a). Resource conservative manufacturing: An essential change in business and technology paradigm for sustainable manufacturing. *Journal of Cleaner Production, 57,* 66–177. https://doi.org/10.1016/J.JCLEPRO.2013.06.012.

Rashid, A., Asif, F. M. A., Krajnik, P., & Nicolescu, C. M. (2013b). Resource conservative manufacturing: An essential change in business and technology paradigm for sustainable manufacturing. *Journal of Cleaner Production, 57,* 166–177. https://doi.org/10.1016/J.JCLEPRO.2013.06.012.

Sundin, E., & Lee, H. M. (2012). "In what way is remanufacturing good for the environment?." *Design for Innovative Value Towards a Sustainable Society*, (pp. 552–557). Dordrecht: Springer.

Tukker, A. (2015). Product services for a resource-efficient and circular economy—A review. *Journal of Cleaner Production, 97*, 76–91. https://doi.org/10.1016/j.jclepro.2013.11.049.

Umeda, Y., Fukushige, S., Tonoike, K., Kondoh, S., & Yoshikawa, H. (2008). Product modularity for life cycle design. *CIRP Annals—Manufacturing Technology, 57*(1), 13–16. https://doi.org/10.1016/j.cirp.2008.03.115.

Urbinati, A., Chiaroni, D., & Chiesa, V. (2017). Towards a new taxonomy of circular economy business models. *Journal of Cleaner Production, 168*, 487–498. https://doi.org/10.1016/j.jclepro.2017.09.047.

CHAPTER 13

Social Sustainability from Upstream: Important Takeaways from DBL Group's *People* Programmes in the Bangladeshi Apparel Supply Chain

Enrico Fontana

Introduction

> If it was only coming from buyers, then we probably wouldn't have thought about sustainability, right? It's not really like that. People's mindset is changing. There is a next generation of business in Bangladesh. This is much more aware about sustainability and collaborations. Everything is here. (Project Manager—Phulki)

E. Fontana (✉)
Sasin School of Management, Chulalongkorn University, Bangkok, Thailand
e-mail: enrico.fontana@sasin.edu

Mistra Centre for Sustainable Markets (MISUM), Stockholm School of Economics, Stockholm, Sweden

R. Bali Swain and S. Sweet (eds.), *Sustainable Consumption and Production, Volume II*,
https://doi.org/10.1007/978-3-030-55285-5_13

> DBL[1] is by far one of the most advanced factories in terms of sustainability programmes in Bangladesh. They are very committed to sustainability as a core part of their business rather than something driven by buyers. (Corporate Social Responsibility Specialist—UNICEF)

With the purpose of improving labour conditions in developing countries, Global Value Chain (GVC) literature has gradually shifted attention from dyadic buyer-manufacturer[2] compliance codes (Lim & Phillips, 2008; Locke & Romis, 2010; Mamic, 2005) to multi-stakeholder initiatives (MSIs) (Arora, Kourula, & Phillips, 2019; Baumann-Pauly, Nolan, van Heerden, & Samway, 2017; Soundararajan & Brown, 2016). These voluntary governance regimes for social sustainability include the participation of buyers and manufacturers with non-market stakeholder organizations, such as development agencies and nongovernmental organizations (NGOs) (O'Rourke, 2006; Rodríguez, Giménez Thomsen, Arenas, & Pagell, 2016). MSIs have been praised for releasing a number of new programmes and certifications (de Bakker, Rasche, & Ponte, 2019; Dolan & Opondo, 2005) to help overcome the inefficiencies of extant auditing procedures through collaboration (Fransen & Kolk, 2007; Hughes, Buttle, & Wrigley, 2007). Despite the emergence of MSIs, GVC scholars portray international buyers such as apparel retailers (buyers) as 'lead' change agents, crediting them with spurring social sustainability programmes in the chain from downstream (Gereffi, Humphrey, & Sturgeon, 2005; Gimenez & Tachizawa, 2012; Ponte & Sturgeon, 2014; Soundararajan & Brown, 2016). Alexander (2019: 17) for instance, underscores that 'despite input from multiple stakeholders, often lead firms [buyers] decide what type of sustainability issues they want to address and what approach they want to use'.

In this chapter, I problematize the inherent notion of buyers' change agency perpetuated by GVC literature. I argue that this largely overshadows the contribution of manufacturers in the Global South to MSIs and their ability to advance the United Nations Sustainable Development Goals (SDGs) from upstream. For this purpose, I convey a compelling counternarrative that draws on a case study of DBL Group (hereafter

[1] DBL is an acronym for Dulal Brothers Limited.

[2] In line with Ponte and Sturgeon (2014), this chapter defines "buyers" as global firms that place merchandise orders outside their home country, and "manufacturers" as export-oriented supplier firms operating in the developing world.

DBL)—an apparel manufacturer operating in the Bangladeshi apparel supply chain—and specifically on an analysis of its approach in articulating its *People* programmes for social sustainability. These programmes hold underlying relevance for GVC scholars in that they symbolize a distinctive attempt to create change for workers from upstream, independently from buyers' demands. Importantly, DBL's *People* programmes primarily hinge on DBL's participation in MSIs and contribute to the advancement of SDG 1 (No Poverty), SDG 3 (Good Health & Well-being), SDG 4 (Quality Education), SDG 5 (Gender Equality), SDG 8 (Decent Work & Economic Growth) and SDG 10 (Reduce Inequalities).

This case study follows a qualitative trajectory while triangulating between a pool of secondary data (e.g., sustainability reports and publicly available information) and interviews that I conducted, recorded and analysed since 2014. These are part of a wider project with market and non-market stakeholder organizations operating in the Bangladeshi apparel supply chain. While drawing on DBL's approach, including its opportunities and challenges, this chapter conceptualizes a three-step and MSI-focused governance process based on (1) learning, (2) integrating and (3) scaling. This process, equally relevant for GVC scholars and practitioners, puts the spotlight on how developing countries' manufacturers can participate with MSIs to lead and diffuse social sustainability programmes in the chain that can support achievement of the SDGs.

The chapter is structured in three sections. First, it provides a descriptive overview of the Bangladeshi apparel supply chain and a case study of DBL. It then delves into the process and presents the findings. It concludes with a discussion that compares the implications of buyers' change agency assumed in GVC literature and the evidence from DBL's analysis. This helps formulate five different takeaways for both GVC scholars and practice.

The Bangladeshi Apparel Supply Chain as Relevant Context of Scholarly Inquiry

Bangladesh is classified by the United Nations (2019) as a least developed country, and its people are among the poorest in South Asia. Despite a period of prolonged instability after the end of the liberation war with Pakistan in 1971, Bangladesh's gross domestic product has grown roughly 6% since 2005 (CIA, 2019). More precisely, its apparel supply chain has been the largest contributor to its growth. It accounted for more than 80% of the country's exports in the 2016–2017 financial year, including more than 4500 first-tier manufacturing firms officially recognized by the Bangladesh Garment Manufacturers and Exporters Association, the local industrial association (BGMEA, 2019a). Their US $30.6 billion worth of exports make the Bangladeshi apparel supply chain the second largest worldwide (BGMEA, 2019b). The industry offers employment opportunities to approximately 4.4 million workers, predominantly women from rural backgrounds (Ahmed, Greenlead, & Sacks, 2014; Rahim, 2017). Despite the potential to lift millions of workers from poverty while helping to reach gender equality goals, the Bangladeshi apparel supply chain also represents a major source of workplace risk and difficulty. The shocking images of the Rana Plaza factory collapse in 2013 that 'killed and injured at least 1135 and 2500 people respectively' helped uncover the fragility of workplace conditions in Bangladesh, diffusing anger and sorrow across the world (Chowdhury, 2017: 1111). Ever since Rana Plaza, GVC scholars have focused on gleaning empirical evidence from buyers' social sustainability programmes for better working conditions, often labelling manufacturers in the developing world as unethical, corrupted, harmful and opportunistic (Bird & Soundararajan, 2018; Huq, Chowdhury, & Klassen, 2016; Jiang, 2009).

The Case of DBL in the Bangladeshi Apparel Supply Chain

Founded in 1991 by four brothers—Abdul Wahed, M. A. Jabbar, M. A. Rahim, M. A. Quader—DBL is a 1st tier and export-focused manufacturer operating in the Bangladeshi apparel supply chain. Although its product range is diversified and involves packaging, ceramic tiles, telecommunications, dredging, VLSI semiconductor design and pharmaceuticals, DBL specializes in apparel—knitwear—production and sales. Its major buyers include large international retailers such as Hennes & Mauritz AB (H&M), Walmart, Clemens et August (C&A), Puma and Target, among many others (DBL Sustainability Report, 2019). Due to its steady growth, it currently employs more than 35,000 people spread across 23 concerns, and had a turnover of US $575 million during the year 2018–2019 (DBL, 2019).

Since 2014,[3] DBL has released five sustainability reports in line with the Global Reporting Initiative, structuring them along five pillars—People, Process, Product, Community and Environment (DBL Sustainability, 2019). Each of them includes a large number of innovative programmes that break conventional wisdom around apparel manufacturing in Bangladesh.

Although DBL has received a number of awards for its pioneering work in various sustainability fields—such as water conservation (Yee, 2013)—what is perhaps most striking is DBL's emphasis on improving workers' welfare. Ensuring high standards of working conditions lies 'at the centre of DBL's interest...and particular attention is given to the employees and surrounding communities' (Salvetti & Nijhof, 2018: 188). Additionally, in 2013, DBL started the Matin Jinnat Foundation, a charitable trust that looks after the welfare of the poorest (Matin Spinning, 2019). As indicated in Table 13.1, these programmes are achieved both in-house and through MSIs, helping DBL attain SDGs 1, 3, 4, 5, 8 and 10.

Findings

As displayed in Table 13.1, DBL carries out several *People* programmes for social sustainability, both in-house and through MSIs. In structuring them, DBL uses a three-step governance process. This stems from *learning* (transferring knowledge from non-market stakeholder organizations through MSIs by voluntarily piloting and testing social sustainability programmes), *integrating* (reframing these programmes into in-house programmes that can survive long term, without external support) and *scaling* (teaming up with non-market stakeholder organizations to promote its social sustainability programmes along the apparel supply chain). This section provides an overview of each of these steps.

[3] DBL publishes its annual sustainability reports with reference to the year before (e.g., the first 2013 Report was published in 2014. The 2015/16 report is the only exception where DBL published one report in two consecutive years).

Table 13.1 An overview of DBL's *People* programs for social sustainability since 2014[a]

Year	*Type*	*Sustainability programmes*	*SDGs*[b]
2013	In-House	– Bandhan Fair Price Shop	1, 8
		– Women Health Program Initiative	3, 8
		– In-House Garments Training Centre	4, 8
		– Future Leaders Development Program	4, 8
	MSIs	– Pillars in Practices & Social Fingerprint (with: *Social Accountability International*, *the Danish Institute of Human Rights* and *CSR Centre*)	10, 8
		– Promotion of Female Line Operator to Line Supervisor Program (with: *GiZ* and *University of Warwick*)	5, 8
		– Global Women's Economics Empowerment Initiative (with: *Walmart Foundation*, *CARE Bangladesh* and *Sheva*)	5, 8
		– Reproductive Health (with: *The Embassy of the Kingdom of the Netherlands* and *Phulki*)	3, 8
		– Tuberculosis Screening (with: *Centre for Woman and Child Health*)	3, 8
2014	In-House	– Bandhan Fair Price Shop	1, 8
		– Women Health Program Initiative	3, 8
		– In-House Garments Training Centre	4, 8
		– Future Leaders Development Program	4, 8
	MSIs	– Nirapod: Saving women from unwanted pregnancies (with: *The Embassy of the Kingdom of the Netherlands* and *Phulki*)	3, 5, 8
		– Women in Factories Initiative (with: *Walmart Foundation*, *CARE Bangladesh* and *Sheva*)	5, 8
2015–2016	In-House	– Bandhan Fair Price Shop	1, 8
		– Women Health Program Initiative	3, 8
		– Female Supervisors Leadership Program	5, 8
		– Children Education Support Initiative	4, 8
	MSIs	– Women in Factories Initiative (with: *Walmart Foundation*, *CARE Bangladesh* and *Sheva*)	5, 8
		– Breastfeeding in the Workplace Initiative (with: *UNICEF* and *BRAC*)	3, 8
		– Financial Literacy Program (with: *VISA Worldwide Inc. USA* and *CARE Bangladesh*)	4, 5, 8

(continued)

Table 13.1 (continued)

Year	*Type*	*Sustainability programmes*	*SDGs*[b]
		– Nirapod: Saving women from unwanted pregnancies (with: *The Embassy of the Kingdom of the Netherlands* and *Phulki*)	3, 5, 8
		– Rice Fortification Program (with: *World Food Program*)	3, 8
2017	In-House	– Bandhan Fair Price Shop	1, 8
		– Women Health Program Initiative	3, 8
		– Female Supervisors Leadership Program	5, 8
		– Children Education Support Initiative	4, 8
	MSIs	– Nirapod: Saving women from unwanted pregnancies (with: *The Embassy of the Kingdom of the Netherlands* and *Phulki*)	3, 5, 8
		– Disability Inclusion Program (with: *Centre for Disability in Development*)	10, 8
		– Mothers@Work (with: *UNICEF* and *BRAC*)	3, 8
2018	In-House	– Bandhan Fair Price Shop	1, 8
		– Women Health Program Initiative	3, 8
		– Female Supervisors Leadership Program	5, 8
		– Children Education Support Initiative	4, 8
	MSIs	– Shobola: Empowerment for Better Business (with: *Amfori* and *CSR Centre*)	5, 8
		– Mothers@Work (with: *UNICEF* and *BRAC*)	3, 8
		– Better Business for Children (with: *UNICEF* and *Phulki*)	
		– Family Planning Corner (with: *Marie Stopes Bangladesh*)	3, 5, 8
		– Disability Inclusion Program (with: *Centre for Disability in Development*)	10, 8

[a]In addition to the above social sustainability programmes, DBL workers receive a wide range of social trainings that range from worker rights and responsibilities to trainings against child labour, forced labour, discrimination, harassment and abusive behaviour

[b]The SDGs were rolled out by the UN in 2015. However, DBL was working on similar objectives prior to their official release

Source Author's summary based on DBL sustainability reports

Step One: Learning

Although some of DBL's *People* programmes for social sustainability are initiated in-house, such as the Bandhan Fair Price Shop,[4] started in 2014 (Table 13.1), a major element of DBL's approach involves continuous learning by participating in MSIs with non-market stakeholder organizations such as development agencies and NGOs. As DBL points out, relying solely on its internal decision making would largely hamper its ability to innovate and continuously grow.

> What we do is that we learn from others. One of our important say is that 'learning is growing'. So, the more we learn, the more we can share our knowledge. Then others share their knowledge as well. Overall this becomes a holistic improvement. Not just for us as a company, but for the entire country. (Manager Sustainability—DBL)

An example of this is the very innovative *Mothers@Work*[5] programme started in 2016 with UNICEF and BRAC. Due to the composition of its workforce, DBL places great emphasis on co-piloting social sustainability programmes that can explicitly benefit female workers and mothers. *Nirapod*[6] (commenced in 2013 with the Embassy of the Kingdom of the Netherlands and Phulki), *Promotion of Female Line Operator to Line Supervisor Program* (with GiZ and University of Warwick until 2014), *Women in Factories Initiative* (with Walmart Foundation, CARE Bangladesh and Sheva between 2012 and 2014) and *Disability Inclusion Program* (started in 2016 with the Centre for Disability in Development) are other examples of DBL's activities in building relationships with MSIs to improve working conditions in their factories. Part of DBL's approach in creating these programmes through MSIs involves co-piloting through active testing, with the support of development agencies and NGOs. It also requires developing a normative understanding of these programmes as an opportunity to enhance workers' welfare.

[4] DBL created the *Bandhan Fair Price Shop* programme as in-factory point of sale to provide basic commodities to workers at a non-market rate.

[5] The *Mothers@Work* programme aims to provide facilities and expert personnel to support pregnant and lactating female workers and their infants.

[6] The *Nirapod* programme promotes awareness on health and sexual reproduction issues through peer education.

> Then DBL is the factory that, having heard our initiatives and concepts, immediately jumped and they told us "this is something we need" ... We didn't pick them. Rather, they came to us with sincere commitment and interest. And we found them suitable and this is how they have been selected. (Senior social compliance advisor—GiZ)

> DBL was cooperative from the beginning. After our orientation and training to the factories, we always got that kind of support from them. I mean, their management, senior mid-level, they were also involved...they actually had that kind of interest in doing better for their workers. (Senior Sector Specialist, Health Nutrition and Population Program—BRAC)

Step Two: Integrating

DBL attempts to integrate the knowledge acquired while co-piloting MSIs by crafting and defining in-house social sustainability programmes. Development agencies and NGOs usually operate through MSIs for fixed terms. Through integration, DBL sustains MSI programmes long term without necessitating external support. For instance, DBL was able to integrate the expertise gained during the execution of the *Women in Factories Initiative*, which ended in 2014, to design its own *Female Supervisor Leadership Program*. This is currently running and has been praised for transforming female workers' lives, not only monetarily, but also in terms of increasing women's social status in the industry and their communities (SDG Action Awards, 2019).

> We started one programme of CARE Bangladesh, funded by the Walmart Foundation and implemented by a local NGO called Sheva. That programme helped in training female workers... It started in 2012 and ended in 2014. This programme inspired us to have our own programme. That's when we started our Female Supervisor Leadership Program from 2014. The programmes by NGOs are project-based, so they run for a limited amount of time. So, after CARE's programme was over, they moved to newer programmes. We had developed the Female Supervisor Leadership Program to sustain this programme. (Manager Sustainability—DBL)

The importance of DBL's transfer and integration of knowledge into in-house programmes following its involvement in MSIs was often highlighted during fieldwork. Take for example the ongoing *Mothers@Work* programme—BRAC explained DBL's efforts in co-piloting and testing it, but also disclosed its expectations for DBL to 'fully own' the knowledge transferred after the completion of orientations and trainings, integrating it into new in-house programmes.

> Our main target was to establish a function, a daycare centre or breastfeeding corner. The breastfeeding corner is now functional. The mothers are going there. They're having their babies in the community, and they now know how to use breast milk. How to treat it. How to store it. This is remarkable. I feel this is what we wanted... That has improved a lot. Previously there was just a room for breastfeeding of the babies. That was not up to the standards. So, we trained them [DBL staff]. We did an orientation with them, advocacy meetings and then we got our breastfeeding corner... They can still improve by engaging more staff from their headworkers and welfare workers in Mothers@Work. Now we are still doing that type of intervention for the female workers ourselves. So, when BRAC will not be there anymore, their staff should be capable to take over those responsibilities. (Senior Sector Specialist, Health Nutrition and Population Program—BRAC)

UNICEF similarly clarified the importance of DBL's knowledge acquisition for the *Mothers@Work* programme, emphasizing the importance of internalizing it long-term through new and in-house social sustainability programmes.

> The programme is designed to give DBL capacity on this to be able to maintain it for the long term. We're always very clear that to really do this, you're not talking about a one off and then you forget about it forever. This is something that you integrate into your business on an ongoing basis, regularly, reminding employees about the maternity support policies and offers. But then also the upgrading and renovation of facilities regularly. Because establishing a day care facility or breastfeeding corner once is one thing, but ensuring it remains fit for purpose over many, many years is another thing. DBL will be expected to maintain this going forward. (Corporate Social Responsibility Specialist—UNICEF)

Step Three: Scaling

In partnership with MSI development agencies and NGOs, DBL scales its newly crafted and in-house social sustainability programmes to create greater change in communities. This involves attempting to shift mindsets and prompting other manufacturers operating in the Bangladeshi apparel supply chain to follow in DBL's footsteps. Although other firms might be sceptical of social sustainability, the examples below indicate that DBL's reputation is often used to inspire the adoption of its programmes.

> When we approach different factories, initially we make presentations for them and we cite the good programmes of DBL. This is evidence that we share in different workshops and trainings with the factories. Initially the factories disagree or are very demotivated. But DBL is one of the most reputed apparel factories in Bangladesh. When other factories see that DBL is doing this, in most of the cases they are motivated to take this as a good example or as a good preference. This is the most convincing instrument for us. (Manager Corporate Affairs—CDD)

> DBL has been working in Bangladesh for a very long time, and with the amount of good work they have earned the name of a model factory in Bangladesh. So, in terms of their work, they are, their activities, their styles are very much replicated in other garment factories as well. So, considering their work, most of the people take their work as an inspiration. They feel more participative if DBL is doing such work. (Project Manager—Phulki)

The evidence also highlights that DBL's engagement in social sustainability helps generate a word-of-mouth effect not just among manufacturers, but also among buyers, who speak to each other about what DBL does.

> Seminars that we did for the factory owners, we invited them to come and hear about the programme implemented by DBL. Then we invited them to express interest in participating in the programme. So, that's what's been happening. We've had three sorts of awareness raising seminars. We've had good results from that. Now we're getting to the stage where there's a bit more external visibility on the initiative thanks to DBL. Word of mouth is starting to kick in as well. So, you know, it's not unusual for us to be contacted now by businesses that have been speaking to DBL and that have mentioned you should talk to UNICEF about this. Yeah. That is happening. (Corporate Social Responsibility Manager—UNICEF)

> What we see is that buyers are also getting interested in learning from our female supervisors. Because gender equality is not only a local issue, it is a global issue. And our female supervisor programme is something

that is very appealing to them. So, we feel we are inspiring them as well. (Manager Sustainability—DBL)

DBL's success also motivates other development agencies and NGOs to engage and foster similar social sustainability programmes and solutions with other manufacturers.

We have initiated a project called Shobola which in Bangla means "empowerment". So, this project focuses on women's empowerment. The basis of this project was a programme that DBL Group had already initiated in a small way—engaging women from frontline workers as supervisors and in managerial positions. DBL initiated this and now they have convinced us that productivity increases if there are female supervisors on the production floor. So, we decided to work with DBL on a project which was shared with Amfori—formerly known as "Foreign Trade Association". The CSR Centre is the training partner. The Shobola project hopes to build awareness among factory management and factory workers to encourage factory owners to increase female representation at the supervisory level to enhance productivity and profits. (CEO—CSR Centre)

After we scaled up the female supervisory leadership programme in our own facilities, we got involved with the ILO Better Work programme, which had an initiative called GEAR, i.e., Gender, Equality and Returns. That particular programme focuses on development of female supervisors as well. So, now we are moving into a partnership focusing on women's empowerment. The objective is the same, creating female supervisors. (Manager Sustainability—DBL)

Opportunities and Challenges for DBL

During the interviews on its *People* programmes for social sustainability, DBL revealed it was able to achieve direct opportunities such as higher visibility and appreciation from buyers, and indirect benefits from workers ranging from superior retention rates in factories to greater productivity because of greater workplace satisfaction.

I have been in the industry for almost 20 years. We started this business in 1991. Since then until say, 2003, we had the same set of buyers, and we were working in the same building. Then we brought in direct change through sustainability. Because of our standards and our reputation, since

2003, buyers have always have been coming after us and asked us for space. (Chief Sustainability Officer, DBL)

The indirect consequences of some of DBL interventions are things such as higher numbers of women returning to work after pregnancy. Efficiency gains in terms of reductions in the number of faulty garments which are being produced by female workers who are able to bring their children to the factory for breastfeeding or have their children attending the daycare centre. And, you know, factories are aware UNICEF works with some of the big international brands. Eventually the brands will get to hear about this [project with DBL] as well, even though they're not always directly involved. (Corporate Social Responsibility Specialist—UNICEF)

On the contrary, DBL also warned about market challenges. One of the main difficulties was to ensure an innovative and growing social performance while keeping costs low. A recurring element of vulnerability faced by DBL was increasingly low price demanded by buyers that typifies the Bangladeshi apparel supply chain. Although buyers' low price could potentially restrain the development of its *People* programmes, the importance DBL attributes to being a social leader prevents it from reducing its engagement in social sustainability.

Sustainability is more like market value rather than just financial value. Finance works in a different way. In fact, that is one of the challenging parts. Global apparel prices tend to move down while compliance and production costs go up. That is the particularly challenging part. But if we did not have the direct and indirect sustainability benefits, we would move downward. So, this is actually what is keeping us up. Sustainability does produce business value. I mean, the modern articles that tend to come up, whether they are from McKinsey or whether it comes from the UN Global Compact, they talk about the financial value of sustainability. Even when we are sharing the different information, what we are trying to do is sharing about the financial value. Earlier we stated that we have done a particular programme and so many numbers of people have been trained. Then as we saw that the absenteeism rates, turnover and other factors, we are now talking about financial value. Once other companies in Bangladesh realize it, they will be adopting sustainability as well. (Manager Sustainability, DBL)

Volumes are increasing, we are increasing in capacity. But margins are not increasing. They are going down. Prices are going downwards. Margins are

> going down in spite of our investments in sustainability. But if you do not expand, your company collapses. You will lose your position. Others are going ahead of you. If you don't expand, if you don't invest in sustainability, you don't grow. We believe in continuous growth. I joined this company since 2003 and every year I have seen business expansion (Chief Sustainability Officer, DBL)

Discussion, Takeaways and Conclusion

Despite the gradual shift from dyadic compliance towards MSIs, GVC literature assumes that social sustainability programmes are driven by buyers as 'lead' change agents (Alexander, 2019; Ponte & Sturgeon, 2014). On the one hand, this has prompted scholars towards greater empirical scrutiny of social sustainability programmes and transnational engagement in the chain from downstream. On the other, it has neglected the positive efforts of manufacturers in the Global South, often emphasizing cases of regulatory violation and selfishness rather than innovation and success (Bird & Soundararajan, 2018; Jiang, 2009; Lim & Phillips, 2008). In this chapter, I have demonstrated the problems inherent in the notion of the buyers' change agency in GVC literature, arguing that it underplays the contribution of developing countries' manufacturers to MSIs and their ability to achieve the SDGs from upstream. The analysis of DBL's approach in articulating its *People* programmes for social sustainability helped conceptualize a three-step governance process based on (1) learning, (2) integrating and (3) scaling. In short, this unveils how the voluntary participation of developing countries' manufacturers in MSIs can help them acquire and integrate knowledge from government agencies and NGOs into in-house social sustainability programmes. What is more relevant is that it also indicates how participation in MSIs can help manufacturers lead and diffuse these programmes in the chain, ultimately supporting the achievement of the SDGs. In the case of DBL's *People* programmes and as highlighted in its sustainability reports, this achievement particularly concerned SDG 1 (No Poverty), SDG 3 (Good Health & Well-being), SDG 4 (Quality Education), SDG 5 (Gender Equality) SDG 8 (Decent Work and Economic Growth) and SDG 10 (Reduce Inequalities).

In this final section, I include a discussion on the underlying implications of the assumed buyer's agency in GVC literature alongside the evidence from the case study analysis. There are five main takeaways and suggestions for theoretical and practical actions going forward, (1) *Co-creating knowledge from upstream*, (2) *Scaling through horizontal dynamics*, (3) *Examining unethical pricing and demonstrating responsibility*, (4) *Ensuring national in addition to transnational governance through MSIs*, (5) *Redefining assumptions of resource asymmetry*.

The first takeaway from the DBL case is *co-creating knowledge from upstream*. In accordance with the view that they are change agents, buyers are credited with the fundamental ability to spread knowledge of social sustainability programmes in the chain from downstream. While buyers are often deemed to be repositories of knowledge, manufacturers rely on them to transfer and implement expertise that can enable change for workers (Gereffi et al., 2005; Ponte & Sturgeon, 2014). Nonetheless, the analysis of DBL's approach in articulating its *People* programmes in the Bangladeshi apparel supply chain indicates that manufacturers can acquire knowledge by voluntarily participating in MSIs beyond buyers' decision making, becoming a relevant source of knowledge themselves on social sustainability programmes. Understanding how different sources of knowledge flow and consolidate in the chain from both downstream and upstream can significantly speed up the advancement of the SDGs. This has important implications for GVC literature and practice.

GVC scholars can benefit by examining in detail the process of knowledge co-creation and transfer between developing countries' manufacturers, development agencies and NGOs. This requires teasing out how these partners establish their iterative and overtime interactions, how they frame and test social sustainability programmes collectively, and are able to translate them into in-house programmes that are sizeable and transferable in the chain.

Likewise, this can help manufacturers become aware of the importance for developing countries' manufacturers to partner with development agencies and NGOs. Although manufacturers often lack the necessary knowledge to structure standalone social sustainability programmes, collaborating with development agencies and NGOs can represent an additional way to acquire this knowledge on top of their traditional relationships with buyers. This also represents a way to gain a reputational advantage in their chain as social sustainability pioneers and points of reference.

The second takeaway that the DBL case highlights is *scaling through horizontal dynamics*. The notion of buyers' change agency has brought much attention to the vertical diffusion of social sustainability programmes in the chain from downstream up to developing countries' manufacturers. In adherence with the vertical perspective, buyers frame social sustainability programmes—whether independently or as part of MSIs—and ask developing countries' manufacturers to adopt them in exchange for better contractual conditions (e.g., better volumes) or just stronger trust (Mamic, 2005; Ponte & Sturgeon, 2014). Although buyers' vertical diffusion of social sustainability programmes remains an undoubtedly important point of reference, the analysis of DBL's approach in articulating its *People* programmes in the Bangladeshi apparel supply chain determines that additional diffusion exists at the horizontal level among manufacturers. Top manufacturers in developing countries that invest in social sustainability programmes—such as DBL—are often mimicked by their peers, who communicate with each other in groups and share awareness. Arguably, manufacturers' reputation and size are particularly influential in prompting horizontal diffusion.

While GVC literature has systematically neglected this horizontal diffusion among manufacturers, it can largely benefit by examining it. Specifically, understanding how manufacturers exert pressure on each other—directly or indirectly—can uncover important information on how to accelerate the adoption of social sustainability programmes and achieve success in the SDGs. In turn, this might also show how different manufacturers' roles and features explain their ability to facilitate or prevent the diffusion of these programmes.

Analogously, manufacturers keen to improve workers' welfare might explicitly benefit from interacting and establishing ongoing communication on social sustainability with other and top-performing manufacturers in their chain. This would help them stay abreast of new programmes, and also understand the feasibility of these programmes and their potential advantages for themselves and their workers.

The third takeaway from the DBL case relates to *examining unethical pricing and demonstrating responsibility*. Buyers' assumed change agency in promoting social sustainability in the chain originates from the imperative to overcome expected and unethical behaviours of developing countries' manufacturers. In the Bangladeshi apparel supply chain, disasters such as the 2013 Rana Plaza collapse have contributed to strengthen this view (Chowdhury, 2017; Huq et al., 2016). Despite the latter, the analysis of DBL's approach in articulating its *People* programmes helps uncover the problems related to buyers' unethical pricing policies. As indicated by the interviews with DBL and its stakeholders, these often reduce the ability of developing countries' manufacturers to invest in social sustainability programmes. Although prices are not always correlated with the decision to invest or not in social sustainability, manufacturers are expected to take responsibility for the increasing cost of social sustainability while being charged progressively less. This raises numerous responsibility questions, for example, who should really be held accountable for impoverished workers' welfare? What would buyers really need to give up to support change? How could buyers and manufacturers find a financial compromise while reinforcing their ability to benefit workers?

While stressing the relevance of adopting social sustainability programmes, GVC literature has focused less on providing quantifiable evidence of the correlation of these programmes with costs, remuneration and/or financial support. GVC scholars would greatly benefit from a deep examination of how and to what extent the financial situation of developing countries' manufacturers and the trade-offs they face due to buyers' unethical pricing steers their decisions on whether to invest in social sustainability. This is particularly relevant for the advancement of the SDGs as it could provide a suitable tool to determine the barriers that prevent manufacturers from advancing them.

Analogously, buyers should reflect upon their profit imperative in light of workers' welfare and well-being. They should reflect upon how to better frame pricing policies that can support more balanced economic and social growth in developing countries. Arguably, a small trade-off in buyers' pricing policy might not only reinforce the already fragile trust with their manufacturers, it might also help advance the SDGs and improve the quality of employment and life for thousands of workers.

Ensuring national in addition to transnational governance through MSIs is the fourth takeaway from the DBL case. The notion of buyers' change agency has brought much attention on MSIs as a transnational form of governance. Hence, social sustainability programmes are framed by development agencies and NGOs globally—in terms of standards and certifications and in line with buyers' final approval—before being adopted by manufacturers in different developing countries (Alexander, 2019; Arora, Kourula, & Phillips, 2019). On the contrary, only a few organizations participating in transnational MSIs are familiar with the context of implementation. DBL's approach in articulating its *People* programmes from the Bangladeshi apparel supply chain demonstrates the relevance of creating MSIs that are contextual and geographically bounded. Arguably, one of the reasons social sustainability programmes fail to be implemented correctly is the implementing organizations' lack of understanding of contextual differences. Developing countries are not a uniform block, but vary widely in religious beliefs, social norms and institutions that explain the local dynamics between people and organizations. Social sustainability programmes in the Bangladeshi apparel supply chain, for instance, focus more on female workers' welfare, and have been largely shaped by disasters such as the one at Rana Plaza. As DBL's *People* programmes tell us, examining social sustainability programmes that draw on MSIs at the national level in addition to the transnational level can be particularly valuable.

GVC scholars might take advantage of the familiarity of their organizations in national MSIs to understand the elements facilitating the implementation of social sustainability programmes, delving deeper into studying why some programmes are easier to implement than others within specific developing countries, and why some are more conducive to achieving the SDGs than others. This might help tease out root causes of failure and success behind the implementation of social sustainability programmes within specific contexts.

Buyers might similarly leverage national MSIs to understand the opportunities and challenges related to executing social sustainability programmes within one specific context before choosing which programmes to introduce in that context, for how much time and with what supporting organizations.

The fifth and final takeaway from the DBL case is *redefining assumptions of resource asymmetry*. The notion of buyers' change agency stems from a generic assumption of switching costs and resource asymmetry along the chain that originated in the 1990s. Developing countries' manufacturers are often believed to suffer from poverty, requiring incentives or being compelled by legislation to not behave unethically (Gereffi et al., 2005; Jiang, 2009). Although shortage of resources remains an undeniable barrier to growth for many manufacturers in the Global South, DBL's approach in the Bangladeshi apparel supply chain demonstrates that this assumption in the literature is increasingly less generalizable. Many manufacturers are undergoing major economic upgrades. Some of them enjoy greater availability of resources, and also capitalize upon them to gain a leading position in their chain, taking initiative and investing extensively in social sustainability programmes to achieve the SDGs. In other words, there is ongoing change in the upstream positions of the chain that scholars are largely failing to observe.

GVC literature would largely benefit by delving into the decision making and perspective of developing countries' manufacturers at the more general organizational dimension, for example, what they do, why they do it and how they do it. This also requires scholars to elevate themselves beyond the focus on manufacturers' compliance and violations, and rather understand whether they have programmes and structures in place that can inform others along the chain. More examples of excellence and innovation from upstream—rather than additional cases of failure—would help better achieve the SDGs among peer manufacturing companies, shifting mindsets and even inspiring institutional change in the Global South.

Likewise, buyers might benefit by detecting leaders among the manufacturers in their chain, as well as examining the programmes they are implementing. Understanding who these leaders are, what they do and how they have achieved a competitive position in social sustainability, might help others learn from them, leveraging their programmes to foster and improve their own social sustainability programmes.

Acknowledgements I am very thankful to Mr. Mohammed Zahidullah, Chief Sustainability Officer at DBL, and his team for their transparency and willingness to share insights. I am particularly grateful to Mr. Mashook Mujib Chowdhury, Manager Sustainability at DBL, for his continuous cooperation and visionary efforts. It came as no surprise to me he has been selected as the 2019 Global Compact Network Bangladesh SDG Pioneer for his contribution in advancing the SDGs, especially in relation to improving female workers' welfare. I am also indebted to a large number of experts from development agencies and nongovernment organizations (e.g. GiZ, UNICEF, Phulki, BRAC, CDD) in Bangladesh who shared their insights and viewpoints with me. Part of this research was conducted while I was a post-doctoral fellow at the Centre for Social and Sustainable Innovation (CSSI) at the Gustavson School of Business, University of Victoria, British Columbia, Canada. CSSI receives funding from Newmont Goldcorp Inc.

References

Ahmed, F. Z., Greenlead, A., & Sacks, A. (2014). The Paradox of export growth in areas of weak governance: The case of the ready made garment sector in Bangladesh. *World Development, 56*, 258–271.

Alexander, R. (2019). Emerging roles of lead buyer governance for sustainability across global production networks. *Journal of Business Ethics, 162*(2), 269–290.

Arora, B., Kourula, A., & Phillips, R. A. (2019). Emerging paradigms of corporate social responsibility, regulation, and governance: Introduction to the thematic symposium. *Journal of Business Ethics, 162*(2), 265–268.

Baumann-Pauly, D., Nolan, J., van Heerden, A., & Samway, M. (2017). Industry-specific multi-stakeholder initiatives that govern corporate human rights standards: Legitimacy assessments of the Fair Labor Association and the Global Network Initiative. *Journal of Business Ethics, 143*(3), 771–787.

BGMEA. (2019a). *About garment industry of Bangladesh*. Retrieved October 21, 2019, from http://www.bgmea.com.bd/home/about/AboutGarmentsIndustry.

BGMEA. (2019b). *Trade information*. Retrieved October 10, 2019, from http://www.bgmea.com.bd/home/pages/tradeinformation.

Bird, R., & Soundararajan, V. (2018). The role of precontractual signals in creating sustainable global supply chains. *Journal of Business Ethics*. Retrieved November 1, 2019, from https://doi.org/10.1007/s10551-018-4067-z.

Chowdhury, R. (2017). Rana Plaza fieldwork and academic anxiety: Some reflections. *Journal of Management Studies, 54*(7), 1111–1117.

CIA. (2019). South Asia: Bangladesh. Retrieved October 21, 2019, from https://www.cia.gov/library/publications/the-world-factbook/geos/bg.html.

DBL. (2019). *About us*. Retrieved October 23, 2019, from http://www.dbl-group.com/about-us/#about-dbl.

DBL Sustainability. (2019). *Our pillars of sustainability*. Retrieved October 23, 2019, from http://www.dbl-group.com/sustainability.

DBL Sustainability Report. (2019). *Sustainability report 2018: Progress towards prosperity*. Retrieved October 15, 2019, from http://www.dbl-group.com//wp-content/uploads/2019/07/DBL-Sustainability-Report-2018.pdf.

de Bakker, F. G. A., Rasche, A., & Ponte, S. (2019). Multi-stakeholder initiatives on sustainability: A cross-disciplinary review and research agenda for business ethics. *Business Ethics Quarterly, 29*(3), 343–383.

Dolan, C. S., & Opondo, M. (2005). Seeking common ground: Multi-stakeholder processes in Kenya's cut flower industry. *Journal of Corporate Citizenship, 18*, 87–98.

Fransen, L. W., & Kolk, A. (2007). Global rule-setting for business: A critical analysis of multi-stakeholder standards. *Organization, 14*(5), 667–684.

Gereffi, G., Humphrey, J., & Sturgeon, T. J. (2005). The governance of global value chains. *Review of International Political Economy, 12*(1), 78–104.

Gimenez, C., & Tachizawa, E. M. (2012). Extending sustainability to suppliers: A systematic literature review. *Supply Chain Management: An International Journal, 17*(5), 531–543.

Hughes, A., Buttle, M., & Wrigley, N. (2007). Organisational geographies of corporate responsibility: A UK–US comparison of retailers' ethical trading initiatives. *Journal of Economic Geography, 7*(4), 491–513.

Huq, F. A., Chowdhury, I. N., & Klassen, R. D. (2016). Social management capabilities of multinational buying firms and their emerging market suppliers: An exploratory study of the clothing industry. *Journal of Operations Management, 46,* 19–37.

Jiang, B. (2009). Implementing supplier codes of conduct in global supply chains: Process explanations from theoretic and empirical perspectives. *Journal of Business Ethics, 85*(1), 77–92.

Lim, S. J., & Phillips, J. (2008). Embedding CSR values: The global footwear industry's evolving governance structure. *Journal of Business Ethics, 81*(1), 143–156.

Locke, R. M., & Romis, M. (2010). The promise & perils of private voluntary regulation: Labor standards and work organizations in two Mexican factories. *Review of International Political Economy, 17*(1), 45–74.

Mamic, I. (2005). Managing global supply chain: The sports footwear, apparel and retail sectors. *Journal of Business Ethics, 59*(1–2), 81–100.

Matin Spinning. (2019). *Matin Jinnat Foundation.* Retrieved October 23, 2020, from https://www.matinspinning.com/index.php?option=page&id=6&Itemid=21.

O'Rourke, D. (2006). Multi-stakeholder regulation: Privatizing or socializing global labor standards? *World Development, 34*(5), 899–918.

Ponte, S., & Sturgeon, T. J. (2014). Explaining governance in global value chains: A modular theory-building effort. *Review of International Political Economy, 21*(1), 195–223.

Rahim, M. M. (2017). Improving social responsibility in RMG industries through a new governance approach in laws. *Journal of Business Ethics, 143*(4), 807–826.

Rodríguez, J. A., Giménez Thomsen, C., Arenas, D., & Pagell, M. (2016). NGOs' initiatives to enhance social sustainability in the supply chain: Poverty alleviation through supplier development programs. *Journal of Supply Chain Management, 52*(3), 83–108.

Salvetti, N., & Nijhof, A. (2018). From sustainable sourcing to sustainable consumption: The case of DBL Group in Bangladesh. In C. Becker-Leifhold & M. Heuer (Eds.), *Eco-friendly and fair: Fast fashion and consumer behaviour* (pp. 183–194). New York, NY: Routledge.

SDG Action Awards. (2019). *Female Supervisor Leadership Program (FSLP): A project by DBL Group*. Retrieved October 1, 2019, from https://sdgactionawards.org/initiative/1689.

Soundararajan, V., & Brown, J. A. (2016). Voluntary governance mechanisms in global supply chains: Beyond CSR to a stakeholder utility perspective. *Journal of Business Ethics, 134*(1), 83–102.

United Nations. (2019). *The least developed country category: 2018 country snapshots*. Retrieved August 21, 2019, from https://www.un.org/development/desa/dpad/wp-content/uploads/sites/45/Snapshots2018.pdf.

Yee, A. (2013). Special report: Business of green. Conservation pays off for Bangladeshi factories. *New York Times*. https://www.nytimes.com/2013/03/22/business/energy-environment/conservation-pays-off-for-bangladeshi-factories.html.

CHAPTER 14

The Return on Sustainability Investment (ROSI): Monetizing Financial Benefits of Sustainability Actions in Companies

Ulrich Atz, Tracy Van Holt, Elyse Douglas, and Tensie Whelan

Introduction

Managers struggle with how to assess the financial return on their own sustainability-centred business decisions, despite wide-ranging evidence showing that solving sustainability challenges can lead to higher corporate financial performance (CFP) (Orlitzky, Schmidt, & Rynes, 2003; Peloza

U. Atz (✉) · T. Van Holt · E. Douglas · T. Whelan
NYU Stern Center for Sustainable Business, New York University, New York City, NY, USA
e-mail: uatz@stern.nyu.edu

T. Van Holt
e-mail: tvanholt@stern.nyu.edu

E. Douglas
e-mail: edouglas@stern.nyu.edu

T. Whelan
e-mail: twhelan@stern.nyu.edu

R. Bali Swain and S. Sweet (eds.), *Sustainable Consumption and Production, Volume II*,
https://doi.org/10.1007/978-3-030-55285-5_14

& Yachnin, 2008; Margolis, Elfenbein, & Walsh, 2009; Fulton, Kahn, & Sharples, 2012; Clark, Feiner, &Viehs, 2014; Friede, Busch & Bassen, 2015). Our Return on Sustainability Investment (ROSI) methodology aims to close that gap and support researchers, managers, or those evaluating companies (investors, analysts, insurers, etc.) to quantify potential and realized financial benefits of sustainability strategies and practices. Indeed, the business case of corporate sustainability (Reed, 2001; Salzmann, Ionescu-Somers, & Steger, 2005; Steger, 2006) is critical within organizations to overcome organizational inertia or the perception that sustainability does not pay off (Garavan, Heraty, Rock, & Dalton, 2010). In a survey with 60,000 respondents from companies around the world, Kiron et al. (2017) found that only a fourth have developed a clear business case for sustainability, even though 90% of the executives viewed sustainability as important.

We apply our methodology to two industries. First, we assessed potential benefits of deforestation-free beef for two Brazilian supply chains (with a forward-looking view). Second, we worked with three automotive companies and developed a financial model to monetize sustainable practices in manufacturing operations, using data from 2015 to 2016 (realized cash earnings). Through ROSI, we focus on the mediating factors or drivers of financial performance such as customer loyalty that drive profitability, company valuation, and/or lower cost of capital (Fig. 14.1). Including mediating factors in our framework is essential for analyzing the business case of sustainability because we can: (1) explain conceptually how sustainability drives intermediate state CFP measures (e.g., improved cash flow, reduced cost or higher revenue); (2) capture benefits beyond tangible outcomes (e.g., car manufacturers saved money by reducing water use and pollution, but also lowered their risk of a reputational scandal); and (3) focus on metrics that are more practical than end state measures such as stock price because the results of sustainability investments may get lost across different business units or are "owned" by different managers. Our overall objective is to develop a methodology that supports researchers, managers, and practitioners by helping them formulate the business case for sustainability through a framework, tools, and concrete examples of how to monetize sustainability benefits. First, we provide an integrative literature review; second, we outline the steps conceptually; and third, we apply the methodology in the two industries.

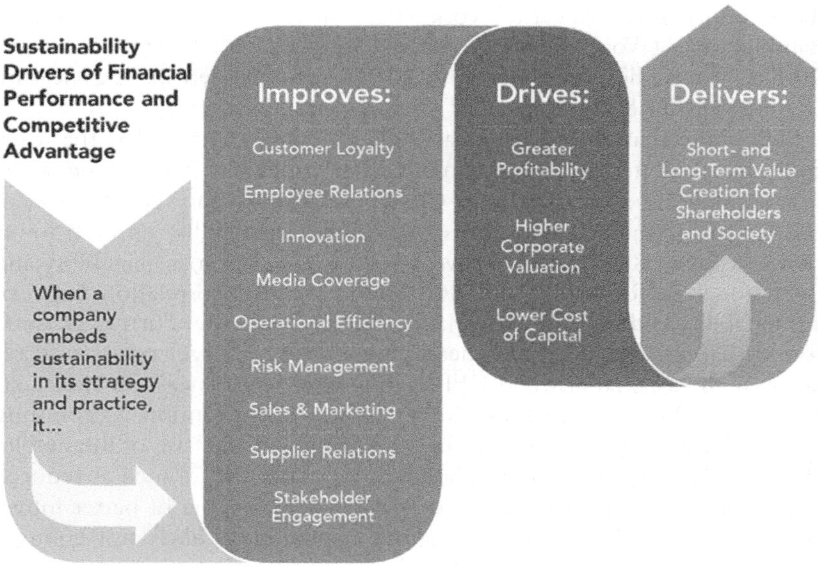

Fig. 14.1 Benefits emerge when companies embed sustainability. The mediating factors can be identified, quantified, and monetized to assess financial benefits of sustainability actions

Literature Review

Corporate Financial Performance

Review studies and meta-analyses from academia and industry have shown a positive relationship between corporate financial performance (CFP) and sustainability measures (Clark et al., 2014; Friede et al., 2015; Fulton, Kahn, & Sharples, 2012; Margolis et al., 2009; Orlitzky et al., 2003; Peloza & Yachnin, 2008). This relationship appears robust, as similar findings are reported considering national cultures (Miras-Rodríguez, Carrasco-Gallego, & Escobar-Pérez, 2015), supply chains (Golicic & Smith, 2013), and firm performance in developing countries (Desai, Kharas, & Amin, 2017), as well as studies that consider nonlinear relationships (Barnett & Salomon, 2012), materiality (Khan, Serafeim, & Yoon, 2016), and causality (i.e., whether there is a bidirectional relationship between CFP and sustainability) (Endrikat, Guenther, & Hoppe, 2014).

These efforts build on earlier work where the relationship was considered "ambiguous" (Wood & Jones, 1995), "mixed" (McWilliams & Siegel, 2000), "contradictory" (Albertini, 2013), or depended on the measure of CFP (Griffin & Mahon, 1997).

The more than 2000 empirical studies (Friede et al., 2015) that exist today have elevated the discussion of CFP beyond market-based measures. For example, in a meta-analysis, Clark et al. (2014) showed that 90% of the reviewed studies found firms with high sustainability enjoyed lower cost of capital; 88% had a positive correlation between sustainability and operational performance; and 80% had a positive correlation between sustainability and superior financial market performance. Further research found that accounting-based measures may have a larger positive correlation with sustainability and CFP than market-based measures (Margolis et al., 2009; Peloza & Yachnin, 2008). However, conventional accounting has also been criticized for keeping up poorly with the rise of intangibles (Lev, 2001; Lev & Gu, 2016; Haskel & Westlake, 2017) such as reduced risk, improved customer loyalty, or the long-term value of better infrastructure. Market-based measures alone are therefore likely not enough, and monetizing intangibles needs to be at the forefront when making the business case for sustainability.

Factors That Mediate Financial Performance

Additional work on corporate financial performance and sustainability has focused on mediating factors, which are essentially drivers of CFP: Peloza and Yachnin (2008) found 15 such studies in total. This work builds on academic research that evaluates how sustainability efforts may drive financial value in corporations (e.g., Rappaport, 1986; Schaltegger & Figge, 2000; Steger, 2006), The positive relationship between CFP and sustainability is explained through various theories and concepts. For example, ***instrumental stakeholder theory*** (Cornell & Shapiro, 1987; Freeman, 1984; Orlitzky et al., 2003) suggests that CFP is driven by the satisfaction of various stakeholder groups because their implicit claims can have costs and benefits that are larger than direct cash impacts. Others have introduced the idea of a ***virtuous circle***, where sustainability is both a predictor and consequence of CFP (Waddock & Graves, 1997). More recently, the concept of ***shared value*** (Porter & Kramer, 2006, 2011) defined value as benefits relative to cost and moved beyond Milton Friedman's profit maxim (*The New York Times Magazine*, 1970) as the firm's prime responsibility because profit alone does not meet fundamental societal needs nor enhance competitive advantage.

Some mediating factors are easier to monetize, establish causal linkages, and conceptualize than others. Operational efficiency (similar to eco-efficiency [United Nations ESCAP, 2009]) aims to reduce the use of materials, water, and energy to operate sustainably. It can drive profitability directly, for example, through energy savings in green buildings (Eichholtz, Kok, & Quigley, 2010) or lower the cost of capital (Chava, 2014; Schneider, 2011). Better employee relations, on the other hand, are difficult to associate with a sustainability initiative because companies are not collecting data on its relationship with employee engagement. There is, however, much cross-sectional research that explains how sustainability and employee relations are related. In general, sustainability makes an organization more attractive to prospective employees (Turban & Greening, 1997), reduces voluntary turnover (Vitaliano, 2012), and increases productivity (Delmas & Pekovic, 2013, 2018). Studies also show how specific actions such as diversity programmes improve sales and profits (Herring, 2009; Hunt, Prince, Dixon-Fyle, & Yee, 2018), or how nondiscrimination spurs innovation (Gao & Zhang, 2017). Studies have also tried to investigate whether firms with greater sustainability were less likely to be sued (Barnett, Hartmann, & Salomon, 2018), because sustainability efforts may act as a buffer from harm (Godfrey, 2005).

Our approach applies conventional accounting to sustainability practices and monetizes tangible and intangible assets (Lev, 2001; Lev & Gu, 2016). Others are also working to monetize sustainability. For example, the *PRI-UN Global Compact LEAD's Value Driver Model* (Lubin & Krosinsky, 2013) monetizes sustainability benefits according to growth, productivity, and risk management categories. We propose nine mediating factors that explain why, when companies solve sustainability challenges, financial performance may change. They include: customer loyalty, stakeholder engagement, employee relations, innovation, operational efficiency, risk management, sales and marketing, media coverage, and supplier relations (Fig. 14.1). Which of these factors drive corporate financial performance is chiefly an empirical question depending on industry and firm. When we interviewed sustainability professionals and coded 251 sustainability actions in the automotive industry according to mediating factors, we found that all nine mediating factors were mentioned at least four times. We empirically tested how these factors are related to corporate financial performance in this research.

Five Steps to Monetize Sustainability Actions

We propose to capture the benefits of sustainability by looking at the potential effects and interactions of sustainability actions through *mediating factors* (Fig. 14.1). The methodology requires an iterative process of five steps that reflects inputs from multiple stakeholders. For example, what we learn in step 4, documenting assumptions, may influence step 2, generating a comprehensive list of benefits.

Step 1: Identify Material Sustainability Strategies and Actions

Sustainable practices (similar to corporate social responsibility [CSR]) at minimum do not harm people or the planet and at best create value for stakeholders (Whelan & Fink, 2016). Ideally, a company's sustainability strategy and actions respond to material environmental, social, and governance (ESG) issues outlined in accounting standards such as the Sustainability Accounting Standards Board (SASB) or the Global Reporting Initiative (GRI). Guidance also exists in broad frameworks: Almost 10,000 companies subscribe to the UN Global Compact principles (Voegtlin & Pless, 2014). Information on sustainability actions can be gathered from the company's own assessment, rankings, or sustainability report, as well as interviews across the organization to generate a comprehensive list of actions, benefits, and metrics.

Step 2: List Potential Benefits That Might Drive Financial and Societal Value from Sustainability Actions

Identify the sustainability benefits that come from sustainability actions or practices through the lens of mediating factors (Fig. 14.1), which include greater customer loyalty, better employee relations, more innovation, better media coverage, higher operational efficiency, better risk management, improved sales and marketing, improved supplier relations, and more value-adding stakeholder engagement. Depending on the sustainability action, supply chain target area, business units, or materiality, different benefits will emerge. Some benefits may relate to more than one mediating factor.

Step 3: Quantify Costs and Benefits Associated with Sustainability Actions

Gather specific data, inputs, and assumptions for each benefit (step 2). Each benefit may be project- or company-specific. Individual benefits, however, should not be treated in isolation because this increases the possibility of double-counting the financial benefits and could inflate the aggregate figures. Calculating net benefits also requires an estimate of the cost (sometimes these costs are investments) of the sustainability action.

Step 4: Build Scenarios, Document Assumptions, and Iterate Research

In reality, data are often incomplete, missing, or rely on future value projections. Practitioners must come up with a credible set of assumptions guided by academic publications, business reports, and specialist interviews. All assumptions should be transparent and clearly documented. Even where estimates rely on assumptions, we argue that any valid measurement reduces uncertainty (Hubbard, 2014). Scenarios or sensitivity analyses may help mitigate some of the inevitable uncertainty. This may be done from the outset (e.g., as a simulation model) or as an intermediate step with different input values. The project scope should allow time to include learnings during the monetization process.

Step 5: Monetize and Calculate the Value for All Benefits

We do not prescribe using a specific economic or accounting measure so long as they show the benefits impact or impacted financial results. For a corporation, this could be, for example, proxies for cash flow such as Earnings Before Interest & Taxes (EBIT). Valuing future benefits can be shown through a net present value (NPV) model. We recommend weighting uncertain benefits, such as reducing the risk of regulatory fines, by probability. A further step could be to estimate probability-based outcomes with a Monte-Carlo simulation, as does a valuation tool developed by the International Finance Corporation for extractive companies (IFC & Deloitte, 2014). This requires users to be highly confident in their assumptions. Like most budgeting, forecasting, and analysis, it is often more art than science, but findings at the least ought to be directional and proximate, assisting managerial and investor decision-making.

Methods

Case Selection

Within the Brazilian beef supply chain, we focused on ranches, slaughterhouses, and retailers. One large ranch, Fazendas São Marcelo (FSM) and Projeto Novo Campo (PNC), a group of smaller ranches, invested heavily in more sustainable ranching. These ranches supplied the Marfrig and JBS slaughterhouses, which supplied retailers Carrefour and McDonald's, respectively. In the automotive case, three international companies of different sizes and complexity agreed to participate. The monetization model was generated through discussions with the three companies, a survey of 15 senior executives, and a detailed exchange of financial and non-financial data. We provide the financial outcomes for one company in the results section.

We relied on extensive interviews in both cases. In the beef case, we developed a model and relied on published literature for many data points; for the automotive work, we developed the model and asked the companies to gather the appropriate data for a given year. The goal of the interviews was to ensure our methodology generated a comprehensive list of costs and benefits of sustainability actions as well as input on how best to monetize benefits.

In the beef case, we conducted over 20 interviews including field visits to gather primary data on the benefits and assumptions for applying our methodology. With the help of the consulting firm A. T. Kearney, we interviewed non–governmental organizations (Imaflora, The Nature Conservatory [TNC], Instituto Centro de Vida [ICV], organizations part of the Grupo de Trabalho da Pecuária Sustentável [GTPS], Antea Group, Sustainable Agriculture Network [SAN] and Pecsa Pecuária Sustentável da Amazônia), public institutions devoted to agricultural research and development (Empresa Brasileira de Pesquisa Agropecuária [Embrapa]), large retailers (Carrefour, Arcos Dourados [McDonald's franchisee], and McDonald's) and small retailers (Gran Beef), slaughterhouses (Marfrig and JBS), and ranches (Fazenda do Bugre, São Marcelo, São Matheus, and CMA) about their business practices. We completed the data collection between 21 November and 20 December, 2016 and between 10 January and 20 January, 2017.

For the automotive case, we developed a semi-structured questionnaire to guide the telephone interviews with the respondents of two companies; the third company opted to respond to the questionnaire in writing. People interviewed in each company included CFOs, sustainability officers, and other middle and senior management professionals ($N = 13$ total). Among the questions we asked were: Which environmental, social, and governance factors are most material to the company and stakeholders; how does the company address these issues in its business strategies; and what product, process, or service innovation occurred? We also asked them to provide examples of investments in sustainability initiatives and information on their approach to track and calculate return on investment.

In both cases, we asked respondents to identify sustainability strategies and how they were linked to mediating factors as described in the *Harvard Business Review* article "The Comprehensive Business Case for Sustainability" (Whelan & Fink, 2016) and in Fig. 14.1.

Monetization Methodology

In both industries, we applied the framework and followed the proposed steps on how to derive the financial benefit of sustainability actions. We allowed the companies to identify which actions they viewed as addressing sustainability and placed no value judgment on whether these actions were the most appropriate or effective. Notable differences exist in the scope and financial metrics that were used in step five (monetize and calculate the value for all benefits). For the beef project, we were predominantly interested in the potential benefits over a 10-year horizon and in comparisons across the three main stakeholders in the supply chain. Therefore, we calculated and analyzed the respective net present values. In contrast, for the automotive project we estimated the cash earnings contribution from all sustainability strategies for a given year. Our analysis calculated the EBIT value related to the respective margin increase from 2015 to 2016. For a comprehensive view of how the financial benefits impact overall company value, we also calculated a net present value. In most cases, we assumed the 2016 results could be replicated for a five-year period. In reality, the benefits may be achievable over longer periods, but at either an accelerating or decelerating pace. We reviewed these assumptions with participating companies, which confirmed this to be a reasonable forecast period. In both cases, the financial benefits are "net" figures, meaning we took into account all direct costs. Further details follow in the next section.

Applying the Methodology to Monetize the Benefits of Sustainability Actions

Deforestation-Free Beef

Material sustainability actions. The material sustainability actions for ranches at FSM and PNC were required for Rainforest Alliance and EMBRAPA's (Brazilian Agricultural Research Corporation) Good Agricultural Practices (GAP) certification. Examples of changed practices included intensification (moving from 2 to 10 head of cattle per hectare) to pasture rotation to management of water sources, biodiversity and forestlands, to reduced use of agrichemicals. The slaughterhouses JBS and Marfrig committed to deforestation-free beef: they monitored suppliers with satellite imaging tools to track forest cover and excluded suppliers that had violations for environmental, labour, and indigenous rights. Different organizations and government agencies generate such lists: The Ministry of Labour (Ministério do Trabalho) collects information for farms that have been associated with slave labour conditions; Fundação Nacional do Índio (FUNAI) and/or Instituto Nacional de Colonização e Reforma Agrária (INCRA) record farms associated with indigenous issues; and the Ministry of the Environment (Ministério do Meio Ambiente) records farms associated with deforestation. McDonald's and Carrefour selected or black-listed suppliers and promoted sustainable products (e.g., via certification logos).

Potential benefits. We first identified the benefits associated with the changed practices, and then classified benefits according to the mediating factors (Table 14.1). In total, we gathered 21 benefits across the three supply chain levels for the beef industry associated with sustainable agriculture and deforestation-free beef. Not all benefits applied to all levels of the supply chain. Sustainable ranches may benefit, for example, from greater customer loyalty because ranches with GAP or Rainforest Alliance certification had higher quality beef because of the sustainable agriculture practices and were able to sell more beef at full price. In periods of excess supply, slaughterhouses were buying higher quality beef first and generally purchased uncertified, often low-quality beef at a discount (Table 14.1, benefit 2.2). Slaughterhouses that worked with sustainable ranches benefited because they had better quality beef, better risk management and avoided deforestation-focused fines (Table 14.1, benefit 3.3). Slaughterhouses must comply with the regulation or face fines if they are caught

Table 14.1 The material benefits for sustainability actions in two Brazilian beef supply chains categorized according to ROSI's mediating factors

Mediating factors	*Benefits in the beef in Brazil case study*	*Monetization method (listed examples apply to ranches only)*
Greater customer loyalty	2.2. Selling at full price (no discounts)	Avoided total sales loss based on the current percentage of sales of low-quality beef sold at a discount, weighted by probability
Better employee relations	5.1. Talent attraction	Incremental revenue that top performing employees generate and potential to attract top performing employees
	5.2. Talent retention	Turnover reduction and costs associated with turnover (e.g., training cost)
More innovation	1.2. Innovation and better agricultural techniques	Cost reduction per kg of beef derived from better technology by comparing average cost per kg before and after sustainable practices are implemented
Better media coverage	3.4. Reputational risk avoidance	Revenues at risk after 5 years, weighted by probability (avoided revenue loss from reputational damage, e.g., activist campaign, scandals)
Higher operational efficiency	1.1 Better cost management (inputs)	Production input costs before and after implementing sustainable agricultural initiatives (to calculate NPV, costs were weighted per kg of beef produced, and applied to expected forecasts)
	1.3. Higher land productivity	Total rented area that no longer needs to be rented, multiplied by cost of rental

(continued)

Table 14.1 (continued)

Mediating factors	*Benefits in the beef in Brazil case study*	*Monetization method (listed examples apply to ranches only)*
Better risk management	3.1. Operational risk avoidance	Revenues at risk after 5 years, weighted by probability (avoided revenue loss from operational complications that reduce production and sales—e.g., pasture exhaustion, water shortage, cattle diseases)
	3.2. Market risk avoidance	Revenues at risk after 5 years, weighted by probability (avoided revenue loss from a decreasing market demand for unsustainable beef)
	3.3. Regulatory risk avoidance	Revenues at risk after 5 years, weighted by probability (avoided revenue loss from future changes in regulation that disqualify producers)
Improved sales and marketing	2.1. Price premiums	Revenue increase from premiums paid by slaughterhouses for sustainable beef (i.e., price increase multiplied by total expected production)
	2.3. Increase in demand for sustainability	Revenue increase from a forecasted increase in consumer demand of sustainable beef over the medium- and long-term
	2.5. New revenue stream - additional land	Percentage of ranch that can be reallocated to other activities (e.g., planting soy), and estimated revenue from new activity per ha

(continued)

Table 14.1 (continued)

Mediating factors	*Benefits in the beef in Brazil case study*	*Monetization method (listed examples apply to ranches only)*
Improved supplier relations	5.4. Corporate ecosystem: reduced volatility	Avoided revenue loss from missing economy of scale (applied to forecasted purchases, weighed by probability—slaughterhouse and retailer only: They may buy beef from a large number of suppliers, but some concentrate a significant part with volatile suppliers resulting in higher procurement costs)
More value-adding stakeholder engagement	5.5. Environment: Emission avoidance	Reduced greenhouse gas emissions (GhG) per ha from sustainability based on a cost per ton of GhG, weighted by probability (for a future carbon tax based on Mexico's benchmark)
	5.6. Environment: Carbon sequestration	Carbon sequestration by forest or pasture recuperation based on a cost per ton of GhG, weighted by probability (for a future carbon tax based on Mexico's benchmark)

The numeric classification references the monetization spreadsheet in Whelan, Zappa, Zeidan, and Fishbein (2017) and is available for download

sourcing from suppliers associated with deforestation. By commercializing and tracking sustainably sourced beef, slaughterhouses likely avoided fines. Of the 21 potential benefits, one-third were incremental revenue (31%), one-quarter reduced cost (25%), 44% were avoided cost, and five benefits were excluded from the monetization model.

Quantify costs and benefits associated with sustainability actions. To quantify costs and benefits, we (1) gathered inputs on cost; (2) estimated inputs for benefits; (3) modelled future market behaviour; and

(4) assigned probabilities to certain events occurring. Productivity data for ranches were obtained from previous studies. For example, Marcuzzo (2015) found that the GAP at the PNC ranch yielded 161 kg/ha, with sustainable ranching compared to 68 kg/ha for traditional ranching. We used proxies when data were not available, such as using PNC ranch's values for FSM's investment cost for sustainable infrastructure. From an interview with ICV, we learned that PNC's infrastructure investment was approximately $635 per ha. Overall, based on the size of the ranches, we estimated that PNC ranches invested $4.9 million and FSM ranches $20 million in infrastructure. The estimated cost to monitor deforestation by slaughterhouses and retailers was derived from the cost to licence monitoring software priced at $320,000 per year for JBS. Also, since fewer suppliers provided deforestation-free beef, with less competition, the increased cost per kg of deforestation-free beef was higher.

We collected all inputs and assumptions, market estimates, and costs and benefits in a spreadsheet, and quantified them separately for each benefit and company. Broman and Woo (2018) guide practitioners on how to best organize spreadsheets. For example, we separated input data and calculations, and, for inputs, we tracked where each assumption originated. The final spreadsheet included over 300 inputs of assumptions and metrics as basis for our calculations. Table 14.1, column 3 lists examples of how we operationalized the benefits, net of costs.

Build scenarios, document assumptions, and iterate research. From academic publications, business reports, and interview with specialists, we gathered information such as forecast values for the inflation rate. We continued to refine our estimates of these model parameters. For example, our initial value for the discount rate was set at 8% based on the market standard. We revised this to 15% after consulting with our project partner, The Nature Conservancy, which had on-the-ground experience. This meant that the revised estimates of financial benefits were considerably lower. We addressed uncertain benefits, such as a future revenue increase from premiums paid by slaughterhouses for sustainable beef, using probability weighting, to reflect an expected NPV. We considered two scenarios: For each benefit with uncertainties attached, we estimated a low (conservative) and high (aggressive) probability of occurrence. The two different scenarios presented us with a range in outcomes. To reduce complexity, we chose to report the low scenario in the results section because it is the more conservative scenario.

Monetize and calculate the value for all benefits. Since most of this work concerned potential benefits, we calculated overall costs and benefits as the NPV of estimated future values with a 10-year horizon using a discount rate of 15%.

$$\text{Net Present Value} = \sum_{i=\text{year1}}^{10} \frac{\text{Future value for year}i}{(1+\text{discount rate})^{i}}$$

Tangible benefits were relatively straightforward: to monetize the benefit of cost reduction from the sustainability investments, for example, we compared the total cost per kg of beef on land with and without higher productivity. ICV estimated the PNC ranch pilot saved R$1 per kg of meat as a result of improvements to ranching practices. We multiplied the total cattle production with that cost difference and arrived at how much potential savings the sustainability investment created.

Intangible benefits such as reduced employee turnover required additional work to monetize. To quantify turnover for JBS, for example, we estimated the number of new employees per year needed to replace turnover. This value was based on the average number of employees, the turnover percentage, and the expected reduction in turnover. We also included the time and cost to train an employee. To monetize this, we multiplied the total training time avoided with the cost of training. In the final monetization calculation, we weighted the expected reduction in turnover by probability (50% likelihood of occurring) and calculated the net present value. We expected that employees were more likely to stay with an operation that produced sustainable and good quality beef, as a result of better operations and overall better working conditions.

The Automotive Industry

Material sustainability actions. In the automotive case, we used SASB as a guide to gather information on company-specific sustainability strategies that were material to the company's financial performance. In contrast to the beef case, we focused on the auto manufacturers, rather than on the supply chain. The material sustainability strategies identified for automotive companies by SASB were materials efficiency and recycling, product safety, labour relations, fuel economy and use-phase emissions, and materials sourcing. In the interviews, the three companies described 18 sustainability strategies, of which 16 were feasible to monetize.

Potential benefits. The automotive companies identified 34 benefits derived from the 16 strategies (Tables 14.2–14.5). Operational efficiencies from sustainability actions included benefits from reducing resource consumption, improving waste management, reducing carbon emissions, reducing VOC emissions, and recycling and recovering materials from end of life products. Benefits that reduced risks included reducing dependency on critical materials, avoiding the use of conflict minerals, and minimizing recalls. Benefits that emerged from innovations stemmed from increasing sustainable product presence, long-term improved sustainability technologies, engaging consumers with sustainability through services, and incorporating more sustainable materials into product design. Other benefits from stakeholder engagement included: increasing the percentage of suppliers that are compliant with sustainability standards, efficacy of marketing spend on sustainable products, and improving employee retention. Of the 34 potential benefits, two-thirds (23) were classified as cost savings, 15% (5) as increased revenues, and 18% (6) as avoided cost.

Quantify costs and benefits associated with sustainability actions. From the monetization methods (Tables 14.2–14.5, column 4), we saw that benefits emerged in various financial accounts and across different cost centres. For each benefit, we developed formulas to calculate the financial impact for a single year, between 2015 and 2016. We created a spreadsheet to collect the required data inputs (with over 400 inputs in total) from the companies. We made a concerted effort to capture data across all cost centres by organizing the data input tool by department (R&D, sales, HR, manufacturing, etc.).

An example of a benefit that was relatively straightforward to calculate was lower resource consumption. Automotive companies often report cost savings from reduced energy consumption in their sustainability reports; data on the amount and per unit cost of energy or water use and amount consumed are readily available.

Automotive companies also track annual waste reduction, but rarely report on financial impact. Data to capture the benefits were difficult to collect, given there are various forms of waste (water, raw materials, packaging waste, paper products) and waste exists throughout all company locations (administrative, factories, and warehouses). Savings related to reduced waste disposal costs or revenues gained by selling waste to recyclers were easy to track and quantify. However, more efficient material use not only reduces waste but also results in lower raw materials that need to be purchased. Without a process in place, it is difficult to track this benefit by material. We therefore used the weighted average unit price of comparable virgin materials and applied it to the increase in amount of materials recovered and reused in the manufacturing process to estimate the benefit. Similarly, we also calculated the difference in energy intensity using untouched versus recovered and reused material to capture the full benefits of waste reduction.

Build scenarios, document assumptions, and iterate research. We incorporated the ability to provide sensitivity analysis for the growth in units and unit prices of electric and hybrid vehicles. For instance, if volume and prices vary by 10% from the forecast, we found an impact to company operating margins of plus or minus five basis points. Similarly, we sensitized the NPV model for growth in sustainable services, namely car sharing and subscription-based services such as car communications, security and emergency services, and navigation systems.

For changes in regulations, we also included calculations that tested sensitivities. When evaluating disposal of end-of-life vehicles (EOLV), European regulations mandate that the original manufacturer bears this responsibility, but this is not the case in the United States. As a result, car companies with European manufacturing operations have agreements in place with third parties to handle much of the process. To assess the savings in using EOLV materials in current production volumes, we used the weighted average cost of pristine materials along with the weighted average selling price of EOLV materials to recyclers, less the costs associated with recovering and recycling materials. The amount today of EOLV materials used in new car manufacturing and amounts sold to recyclers was small (2.5 and 10% respectively of the actual weight of treated materials—and only related to European operations where this is tracked). At some point, these regulations could arrive at the United States. Hence, if the same percentages of weight were applied to total metric tons of cars sold in a given year (proxy for the material available from EOLVs), the benefits would have increased by a multiple of 20. The large range of financial value showed us that if manufacturers decide to invest in improving EOLV value, there might be potential for substantial net revenues.

Monetize and calculate the value for all benefits. The benefits we assessed fell into three main categories: cost savings, avoided cost, and incremental revenues, which were netted against cost to achieve the benefits. Primarily, we monetized the impact on operating earnings (EBIT) as a proxy for cash savings. This is because our analysis of actual company outcomes included only one year and because cash flows are of immediate relevance to managers.

In addition, to estimate the financial benefit on company value, including investments, we calculated a NPV for each strategy using the company's assumed cost of capital as the discount rate (ranging from 10 to 12.5%). Using the company's cost of capital versus a risk- or sustainability-adjusted one is a simplifying assumption given we did not have this information available.

$$\text{Net Present Value} = \sum_{i=\text{year}1}^{5} \frac{\text{Future value for year}i}{(1+\text{cost of capital})^{i}}$$

For assessing the financial benefit of new and evolving technologies, such as electric and hybrid vehicles, we included five years of forecasted sales, costs, and investments (conservatively assumed to accrue every year) to derive the benefits. For all other benefits, we assumed the annual benefit identified in 2016 accrued for five years because this simplified the calculations and established a reasonable estimate of company valuation. While some of the benefits, such as waste reduction, will have diminishing returns over time, we believe they are likely to extend beyond five years. For instance, as the company makes progress in reducing waste, the opportunity for savings may decline over time. But as the company expands into new technologies, material use may change, creating new challenges, such as a need for EV battery disposal or refurbishing.

In Tables 14.2, 14.3, 14.4, and 14.5 we provide a comprehensive list of the benefits and monetizing methods used for the reviewed strategies and benefits for the automotive sector.

Results

Potential Net Benefits in the Deforestation-Free Beef Supply Chains

We found that the potential net benefits from sustainable ranching practices for ranches ranged from $1.4 million (9% of revenues) for PNC to $16.6 million (12% for FSM) (Fig. 14.2). For slaughterhouses and retailers (Brazilian operations), the net benefits ranged from $1.3 million (0.01% revenues) for Marfrig, $18 million (0.02%) for JBS, $6.8 million (0.01%) for Carrefour, to $5.7 million (0.13%) for McDonald's (Whelan et al., 2017).

Table 14.2 Operating performance strategies to achieve operational efficiencies and generate new revenues

Strategies	*Benefits*	*Mediating factor*	*Monetization methods*
Reduce resource consumption	Reduced electricity or water cost	Higher operational efficiency	The reduced per unit cost of energy or water on current year production. Subtract any costs to achieve the benefit for operating income impact. Calculate NPV assuming 5-year forecast of net operating income benefits and upfront investments
Improved waste management	Revenue from selling recycled materials	Improved sales and marketing	Average selling price per ton of solid waste on amount sold less the cost to recover (calculated as $/per ton) less cost per ton to recycle
	Savings from using recovered waste	Higher operational efficiency	Savings from using less virgin material and lower disposal costs associated with the recovery and reuse of solid materials (weighted average per price per metric ton)
	Savings from using recycled water		Savings from reduced spend on freshwater due to using recycled water net of costs to recycle plus the savings unless waste water disposal cost using average disposal price per M3
	Cost avoided from traditional waste disposal		Per unit disposal cost per ton of waste to the amount of material recovered/reused or recycled
	Energy savings in manufacturing		Energy savings by comparing the weighted average energy intensity per ton using virgin material to the energy intensity using recovered/recycled material
Reduce emissions—carbon	Savings from reduced need for carbon credits	Higher operational efficiency	Reduced spending on carbon credits due to the reduction in emissions in manufacturing subtract costs incurred to achieve the reduction for net operating income benefit

(continued)

Table 14.2 (continued)

Strategies	*Benefits*	*Mediating factor*	*Monetization methods*
Reduce emissions—VOC	Savings from reducing/recycling solvent	Higher operational efficiency	Savings from the overall reduction in solvent used. Amount of solvent recovered and reused and multiplied by the weighted average virgin solvent unit cost. Reduce savings cost of recovery by multiplying the amount of solvent recovered by the cost of recovery per kg
	Savings from Using Substitutes for Solvent		Amount of substitute solvent multiplied by the difference in weighted average cost of virgin solvent per kg versus substitute solvent cost per kg
	Savings from avoided treatment costs		Percentage reduction in VOC emissions per metric ton, per car produced multiplied by total treatment cost to derive treatment cost savings
	Savings related to reduction in other costs		Saving in employee-related health and safety expenses and the savings related to the reduction in average number of fines received times the average regulatory fine for VOC emissions incidents
Recycle and recover from end of life products	Savings from using recovered materials from EOL vehicles versus virgin material	Higher operational efficiency	Savings in virgin materials by multiplying the weighted average value of virgin materials by the amount of material weight reused from treated material form captured at the end of the vehicle's useful life
			Process savings (energy, logistics, etc., using recovered material/components from EOL vehicles)
			Cost of recovery (recycling) derived from multiplying the per unit cost of recovery (recycling) by the amount recovered (recycled) and net against the savings for the net benefit

Strategies	*Benefits*	*Mediating factor*	*Monetization methods*
	Revenue from selling EOL materials to recyclers	Improved sales and marketing	Revenues from selling EOL vehicle materials derived from multiplying the product weight of material sold by the weighted average price of recycled EOL materials sold
	Reduction in disposal cost from reusing/recycling materials from EOL vehicles	Higher operational efficiency	Savings in disposal costs related to amounts reused/recycled

Table 14.3 Risk reduction strategies to reduce susceptibility to resource scarcity, natural disasters and regulatory non-compliance as well as reduce quality errors and improve safety features

Strategies	*Benefits*	*Mediating factor*	*Monetization methods*
Reduce dependency on critical materials	Savings from reduced use of critical materials	Higher operational efficiency	Reduction in spending on critical materials derived from multiplying the percent of reduction in amount of critical material per vehicle by the annual volume of critical materials used. Amount of reduction due to less use of critical materials multiplied by the weighted average price of critical materials
	Savings from substituting critical materials with other products		Reduction in critical materials due to substitute product and multiplied by the conversion rate and by the cost differential in price of material
	Savings related to lower energy consumption using substitute materials		The sum of: (i) savings from a reduction in use of critical materials derived from multiplying the reduced material used by the weighted average spend on energy used in manufacturing using critical materials per ton; and (ii) the savings from substituting materials derived from multiplying the material substituted by the differential in the weighted average cost of energy per ton using critical materials and the weighted average cost of energy per ton using substitute materials

Strategies	*Benefits*	*Mediating factor*	*Monetization methods*
	Savings related to lower water consumption using substitute materials		The sum of: (i) the savings from a reduction in use of critical materials derived from multiplying the reduced material used by the weighted average spend on water used in manufacturing using critical materials per ton; and (ii) the saving from substituting materials derived from multiplying the material substituted by the differential in the weighted average cost of water per ton using critical materials and the weighted average cost of water per ton using substitute materials
	Avoided costs related to supply shortages	Better risk management	Cost of a short supply incident by the average annual incidents of short supply
Avoid use of conflict materials	Savings from reduced use of conflict minerals	Higher operational efficiency	Spending reduction on conflict minerals derived from multiplying the percent reduction in amount of conflict minerals per vehicle by the annual volume of conflict minerals used. Reduction due to less use of conflict minerals multiplied by the weighted average price of conflict minerals
	Lower costs associated with substitute materials		Reduction in conflict minerals due to substitute product multiplied by the conversion rate and by the cost differential in price of material

(continued)

Table 14.3 (continued)

Strategies	*Benefits*	*Mediating factor*	*Monetization methods*
	Savings related to lower energy consumption using substitute materials		The sum of: (i) the savings from a reduction in use of conflict minerals derived from multiplying the reduced material used by the weighted average spend on energy used in manufacturing using conflict minerals per ton; and (ii) the saving from substituting materials derived from multiplying the material substituted by the differential in the weighted average cost of energy per ton using conflict minerals and the weighted average cost of energy per ton using substitute materials
	Savings related to lower water consumption using substitute materials		The sum of: (i) the savings from a reduction in use of conflict minerals derived from multiplying the reduced material used by the weighted average spend on water used in manufacturing using conflict minerals per ton; and (ii) the saving from substituting materials derived from multiplying the material substituted by the differential in the weighted average cost of water per ton using conflict minerals and the weighted average cost of water per ton using substitute materials
	Avoided costs related to supply shortages	Better risk management	Estimated cost of a short supply incident by the average annual incidents of short supply
	Avoided costs related to regulatory fines		Estimated cost from multiplying the average annual number of incidents of conflict mineral related fines by the average fine per incident less additional compliance costs incurred

Strategies	*Benefits*	*Mediating factor*	*Monetization methods*
Minimize recalls	Avoided cost of recalls	Better risk management	Estimated average cost of avoided recalls related to reduced number of recalls by using the average cost of repair per vehicle times the average number of vehicles per recall plus the average legal and image repair costs (PR, advertising, etc.), net of costs incurred to improve quality, use premium parts (COGS), and additional spend on quality training

Table 14.4 Innovation to develop new sustainability products, services or processes

Strategies	*Benefits*	*Mediating factor*	*Monetization methods*
Increase sustainable product presence	Incremental sales from new sustainable products	Improved sales and marketing	Incremental sales from the number of zero emission and low emission models sold using the weighted average price per unit. Incremental margin on zero emission and low emission vehicles, sold assuming an average cost of goods sold (COGS)
Innovate to provide long-term improved sustainability technologies	Increased pricing on products with enhanced sustainability features	More innovation	Differential in average price per vehicle with and without innovative sustainability features. minus the sales weighted average COGS of sustainability features and multiplied by the number of non-zero and low emission vehicles sold that include the added sustainability features
Engage consumers with sustainability through innovative services	New revenue streams	Improved sales and marketing	Annual revenue stream from sustainable services (e.g., car sharing, in-vehicle security or emergency services) less wages and other SG&A costs associated with the services
Incorporate more sustainable materials into product design	Savings from substituting sustainable materials in product design (i.e., recycled and renewable materials)	Higher operational efficiency	Raw material purchased that is renewable/recycled/lightweight materials in tons multiplied by the differential in weighted average price of traditional versus renewable/recycled/lightweight materials per ton less any additional operating costs required

(continued)

Table 14.4 (continued)

Strategies	*Benefits*	*Mediating factor*	*Monetization methods*
	Lower costs on energy and resources used in manufacturing when using renewable/recycled lightweight materials	Higher operational efficiency	Differential in weighted average spend on energy and resources in traditional manufacturing versus the weighted average spend on energy and resources in manufacturing using renewable/recycled/lightweight materials multiplied by the amount of substituted sustainable material less any additional amount of operating costs incurred on using the substitute materials

We can understand the benefits better if we look at them through the lens of the framework, that is, by mediating factors (Fig. 14.3). It now is apparent that the benefits for ranches (PNC and FSM) accumulated through *more innovation* and *higher operational efficiency*. Cost reduction came because of innovation and better agricultural techniques, such as pasture recuperation, water distribution system, and fencing and rotation of pastures.

The slaughterhouses (Marfrig and JBS) and the retailers (Carrefour and McDonald's) accrued potential benefits mostly through *better risk management* and *improved sales and marketing*. We can operationalize market risk for slaughterhouses, for example, by estimating the decreased market demand for unsustainable beef and its potential impact on revenues. Given the size of the companies, even small risks can have a large financial ramification. Note that in comparing total benefits, we did not account for the different amounts of cost and investments that occurred in the different stages of the supply chain (nor the size in revenue).

Realized Net Benefits in the Automotive Industry

In the automotive example, we estimated that sustainability actions between 2015 and 2016 led to incremental revenues, cost savings, and avoided cost and a positive impact of $5.7 billion (or 3.6% of annual

Table 14.5 Other stakeholder engagement strategies

Strategies	*Benefits*	*Mediating factor*	*Monetization methods*
Increase % of suppliers/carriers/dealers that are compliant with high sustainability standards	Savings from closed—loop recycling	Improved supplier relations	Savings from closed-loop recycling by adding rebates and discounts from suppliers to the decrease in spending due to reduced volume of material needed lower operating costs associated with closed-loop recycling
Efficacy of marketing spend on sustainable products	Savings from incremental sales and operating income from dedicated marketing spend on sustainable products	Greater customer loyalty	Estimated annual sales attributable to dedicated marketing from annualized marketing spend ROI (sales over one dollar of marketing spend, or any internal metric to evaluate marketing/PR returns) and the marketing/advertising spending on zero-emission and low-emission vehicles (including internal person-hours and third-party fees such as agencies, production, and media distribution fees). Average gross margin on zero and low emission vehicles used for profit impact

Strategies	*Benefits*	*Mediating factor*	*Monetization methods*
Improve retention	Cost avoidance related to reduced voluntary turnover	Better employee relations	Reduction in number of employees lost to voluntary turnover versus a historical average and multiplied by number and margin on lost sales per person plus the average new worker training cost per person. Operating income impacted by reducing the saving of annual SG&A costs to improve working conditions and annual wage increase for existing workers

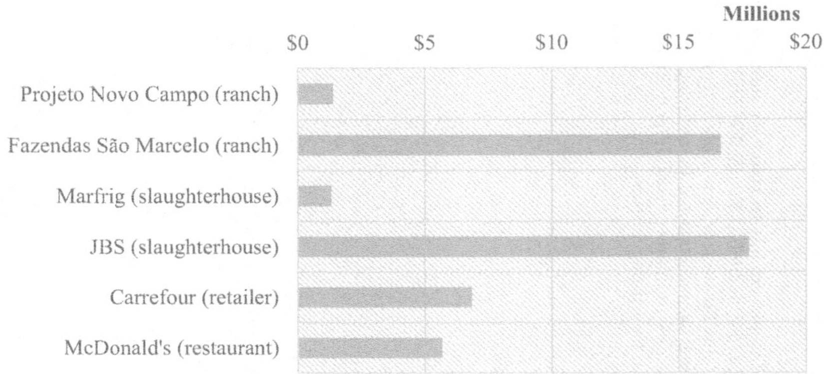

Fig. 14.2 Net benefits in USD million for sustainability actions across the Brazilian beef supply chain based on the net present value projected over 10 years. Note that for ranches, the cost of sustainability actions are investments in infrastructure, while for slaughterhouses and retailer/restaurant the estimates are an increased cost of working with deforestation-free beef suppliers

revenue) on EBIT for one company. Only direct costs were included in the net figures. Since these earnings estimates were a proxy for cash savings net of costs, we did not count depreciation and allocated overheads. By examining the benefits by their mediating factor (Fig. 14.4), we found that the benefits, unlike in the beef case, did not accrue predominantly through operational efficiency and risk management. The largest financial benefit came from *more innovation*, more specifically, increased pricing on products with enhanced sustainability features (Table 14.4, row 2). The total EBIT increase for more innovation was $3.0 billion, which represented 1.7% of annual revenue. In one mediating factor, greater customer loyalty (operationalized as efficacy of marketing spend), calculating net benefits meant that the impact on EBIT was actually negative (-$6 million). The cost of marketing spend on sustainable products (electric vehicles and hybrids), outweighed earnings in 2016, but the net benefits would turn positive in year five as volumes ramp up. That is why we also calculated NPVs over five years (Fig. 14.5). As innovation here was the most material mediating factor, we split the associated strategies into three categories: product (zero emission, hybrids), product safety features, and services (e.g., car sharing). We identified none of the potential benefits (Tables 14.2–14.5, column 2) as better media

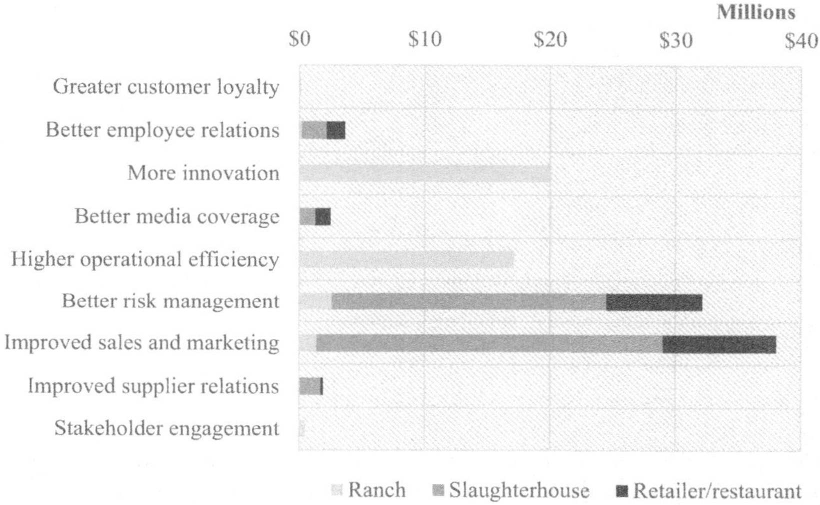

Fig. 14.3 Total benefits (in USD million) across the Brazilian beef supply chain based on a net present value projected over 10 years and split by mediating factor from the ROSI framework. Total benefits do not account for the different amounts of cost and investments

coverage or stakeholder engagement because they were either not salient to manufacturing or there was no proxy measure available from traditional accounting measures. Thus, these two mediating factors remained at $0.

Discussion

When Sustainability Improves Corporate Financial Performance

We introduced a novel methodology, ROSI, that emphasizes nine ***mediating factors*** when monetizing tangible and intangible benefits of sustainability actions such as innovative sustainable agricultural techniques or innovation in electric vehicles. We showed empirically which factors likely drove corporate financial performance in our two cases. In the deforestation-free beef example, efficiencies and innovation provided financial benefits for the ranches, whereas higher up in the supply chain the greatest potential benefits came from better risk management and improved sales and marketing. In the automotive example, innovation

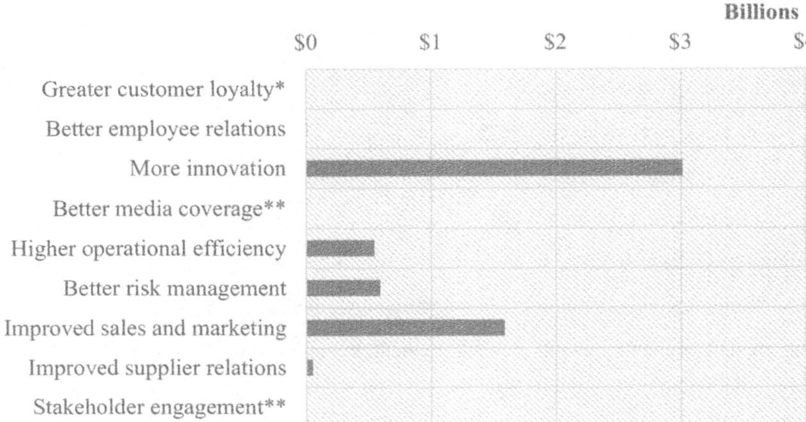

Fig. 14.4 Total net benefits (in USD billion) for one automotive company based on EBIT as proxy for cash flow from 2015 to 2016 and split by mediating factor from the ROSI framework (*Greater customer loyalty was −$6 million because earnings would outweigh cost only over a period of five years. **Operationalizing better media coverage and stakeholder engagement was not feasible and benefits are hence not available [$0])

drove much of the financial benefit, with improved sales and marketing, reduction in risk, and operational efficiencies capturing a smaller portion of the value. In all cases, we were able to quantify the financial benefits, potential or realized. Using the mediating factors allowed us to capture tangible and intangible benefits for a diverse range of sustainability actions that otherwise can be ignored. Drivers that captured the least value included greater customer loyalty and stakeholder relationships, in part because there were no systems in place to collect data on these measures. Our findings show that these nine factors should be considered in research that monetizes the benefits of sustainability efforts so we can begin to understand mechanistic linkages better. We also show that focusing on operational efficiency alone, for example, tells an incomplete story.

Not everyone agrees that we should monetize sustainability actions in the first place. Some academics argue that monetizing sustainability simplifies diverse values into a single metric, lacks academic rigour, or is difficult to interpret because there are too many assumptions. In public decision-making these issues may be even more prominent (Anderson,

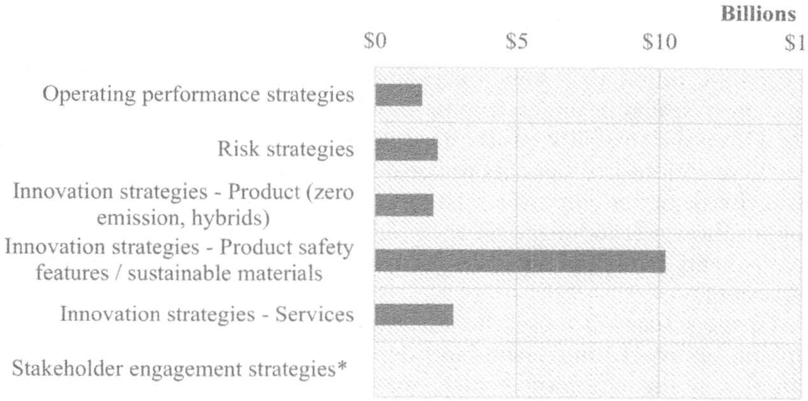

Fig. 14.5 Total net benefits (in USD billion) for one automotive company based on an NPV over five years split by the most salient sustainability strategies (*Sustainable stakeholder engagement strategies [suppliers, employees, customers] were negative with −$45 million because for all benefits we conservatively assumed investment cost accrue every year)

Teisl, Noblet, & Klein, 2015). Others argue that monetizing sustainability enables decision-making to be focused on data, not opinions, and to be more transparent (Bebbington, Brown, & Frame, 2007). We assert the latter: Making the financial case for sustainability speaks the language of business managers and is necessary (yet not sufficient in itself) to change their mindsets.

Considerations for Practitioners

We encourage companies to use this approach as a tool to better incorporate sustainability into corporate business strategy. With the financial case in hand, it becomes easier to embed sustainability into daily business operations. Managers could focus on a single sustainability strategy, identify and monetize corresponding benefits, and use that learning process to then analyze additional sustainability strategies. It is possible to evaluate all concurrently, but the effort needed to monetize many benefits across many strategies is substantial. In addition, managers will find that in the case of missing or incomplete data, they will need to work with proxy estimates. Providing a range of estimates may mitigate uncertainty and give directional guidance.

We have found that sometimes simply listing the full set of benefits stimulates a different understanding of why sustainability actions are valuable. Often sustainability efforts start out with operational efficiencies and end there. Additional benefits under different mediating factors, such as lower risk or better employee relations, are often not acknowledged. Our monetization methodology shines a light on those neglected and intangible benefits and allows a richer discussion of the return on sustainability investment.

Managers may also use the methodology to encourage a systems-thinking approach and encourage departments to work together. For example, in the automotive case, we gathered and analyzed information pertaining to the disposal of vehicles at end of life. While in some ways this is a basic question (number of vehicles, percentage of material recycled, etc.), it also became a technical question (how are vehicles designed, who sources materials), and a strategic one (what happens if a new regulation is introduced into the United States). Critical data are typically sequestered in multiple departments. Without a systematic way to collect data and monetize it, managers may not be able to justify investment expenses, higher procurement costs, or strategic changes to pursue sustainability actions. As a result, actors in a supply network or within one company may not invest in sustainability, even if the benefits are positive for all stakeholders. Especially for sustainability actions that span a supply chain or require collaboration, we hope that our framework introduces a shared vocabulary and a deeper understanding of how sustainability leads to short- and long-term value creation. We encourage practitioners to continuously test inputs, assumptions, and outcomes of quantifying and monetizing the benefits in order to maintain credibility. Common pitfalls include: (1) double-counting the benefits from a single sustainability action; (2) missing a substantial benefit, cost or action; (3) technical errors in working with complex spreadsheets; (4) omitting the opinions of important stakeholders; and (5) not documenting critical assumptions such as the discount rate, among other issues.

Mainstream Adoption

The ROSI methodology has been successfully field tested in two complex industries, complete with examples of benefits and monetization methods.

We will continue this work with further case studies in other sectors to make the research even more rigorous, valid, and applicable in other industries. Researchers and practitioners are typically faced with a simpler scenario, perhaps looking at one sustainability action or investment. Therefore, we expect that the ROSI methodology can be applied in different industries and domains. This flexibility carries a limitation: We are not able to, nor could we, prescribe specific benefits or monetization methods as each industry will have different material ESG factors and thus different sustainability strategies and actions.

While some researchers provide highly generalized requirements for measuring corporate sustainability (Searcy, 2012, 2016), we emphasize the current lack of using company-internal financial data and a misalignment of sustainability and financial disclosure (The World Business Council for Sustainable Development, 2017, 2019). External data and analytics providers are tracking the performance of corporations on ESG. ESG metrics range from greenhouse gas emissions to board-member diversity to human-rights efforts, depending on what is material for an industry—yet these efforts are rarely monetized. And even when ESG efforts are monetized, the information generally is not publicly available (Douglas, Van Holt, &Whelan, 2017). Sustainability is more, though, than disclosing on some ESG indicators. Voluntary and self-referential reporting has been criticized as insufficient (Milne & Gray, 2013), ignoring wider thresholds such as climate targets, that is, the "sustainability context" (Haffar & Searcy, 2018; McElroy & van Engelen, 2012), and being irrelevant or counter-productive (Gray, 2010; Joseph, 2012). ESG indicators, moreover, miss monetizing how sustainability actions affect, for example, employee or supplier relations because these data are difficult to monetize or are not available.

Tools to monetize sustainability actions can help those interested in evaluating opportunities and risks in a company. For example, insurance agencies may focus on the financial impacts of risk; investors may be interested in the value of strategic innovations; and sell-side analysts may evaluate cash wrung from operational efficiencies. Corporate managers can use monetization tools to understand the value of sustainability actions, guide strategy, recognize risks, and explore how solving sustainability challenges can create new revenue streams. Beyond identifying potential or realized benefits, monetization efforts may foster cross-departmental collaboration, through gathering and assessing relevant data, for example.

In the ideal scenario, the methodology gets embedded within an organization and leads to changes that incorporate sustainability into long-term strategic planning. In fact, there is already evidence that sustainability is a long-term corporate strategy ***and*** common practice (Ioannou & Serafeim, 2019).

Conclusion

Our research aims to support researchers, practitioners, and investors who want to monetize the tangible and intangible benefits that companies obtain (or may obtain) when implementing sustainability strategies and practices. The framework systematically examines opportunities for reducing costs, increasing revenues, and avoiding risks among other benefits through what we call ***mediating factors***. We presented and applied a monetization methodology, ROSI, and its five steps on how to calculate the return on sustainability investment.

In our two Brazilian case studies of the beef supply chain, the material sustainability actions for ranches, slaughterhouses, and retailer/restaurant were fundamentally different, but we were able to cover them in one unifying methodology. Projeto Novo Campo and Fazendas São Marcelo ranches invested to make their operations more sustainable; Marfrig, JBS, Carrefour, and McDonald's set commitments to buy deforestation-free beef. Being able to value an investment is crucial for decision-making, and cattle ranchers in Brazil are no exception. As one rancher said: "We might take loans in the future now that we know it pays back".

In the automotive industry, across three companies, we identified 16 sustainability strategies that included strategies to achieve operational efficiencies and generate new revenues; risk reduction strategies to reduce exposure to resource scarcity, natural disasters, and regulatory non-compliance; innovation to develop new sustainability products, services, or processes; and other stakeholder engagement strategies such as improving retention. Sustainability-driven innovation was the greatest source of financial benefit for the companies, though operational efficiencies, reduction in risk, and improved sales and marketing also produced value.

Using the ROSI methodology can help managers champion sustainability investments, improve decision-making, and foster a culture that embeds sustainability core to business strategy. Actors in a supply network or across departments may not invest in sustainability, even if the benefits are positive for each step of the value chain due to the lack of financial information. By monetizing the tangible and intangible benefits of sustainability actions, companies may overcome one of the barriers for scaling up sustainability and trigger a virtuous circle.

Acknowledgements This research was originally published in Atz, U., Van Holt, T., Douglas, E., & Whelan, T. (2019). The Return on Sustainability Investment (ROSI): Monetizing Financial Benefits of Sustainability Actions in Companies. *Review of Business: Interdisciplinary Journal on Risk and Society, 39*(2), 1–31.

This paper has been selected to receive an honorarium underwritten by Munich Re, a leading advocate of sustainable business strategies.

This research was funded in part by the Investindustrial Foundation and the Gordon and Betty Moore Foundation. We thank Bruno Zappa and Rodrigo Zeidan for their contributions in the deforestation-free beef project. For part of the work, we also received pro bono support provided by AT Kearney.

Appendix A: Implementing Monetization Methods Illustrated with an Example

The details of all calculations for the first case study (beef supply chain) are available in a spreadsheet for download (Whelan et al., 2017).[1] For the automotive industry, we released only the spreadsheet template[2] because of the confidential nature of internal company data. To guide practitioners further on how to implement their own ROSI analysis, we walk through one example, conflict materials, from Table 14.3. Risk Reduction Strategies (below).

Excerpt from Table 14.3. Risk Reduction Strategies

[1] The download link is at the bottom of the page: https://hbr.org/2017/09/how-to-quantify-sustainabilitys-impact-on-your-bottom-line.

[2] The Excel download link is available at http://bit.ly/rosi-auto and on the CSB website.

Strategy	#	*Benefits*	*Mediating factors*	*Monetization methods*
Avoid use of conflict materials	1	Savings from reduced use of conflict minerals	Higher operational efficiency	Spend reduction on conflict minerals derived from multiplying the per cent reduction in amount of conflict minerals per vehicle by the annual volume of conflict minerals used. Reduction due to less use of conflict minerals multiplied by the weighted average price of conflict minerals
	2	Lower costs associated with substitute materials		Reduction in conflict minerals due to substitute product multiplied by the conversion rate and by the cost differential in price of material
	3	Savings related to lower energy consumption using substitute materials		The sum of: (i) the savings from a reduction in use of conflict minerals derived from multiplying the reduced material used by the weighted average spend on energy used in manufacturing using conflict minerals per ton; and (ii) the saving from substituting materials derived from multiplying the material substituted by the differential in the weighted average cost of energy per ton using conflict minerals and the weighted average cost of energy per ton using substitute materials
	4	Savings related to lower water consumption using substitute materials		The sum of: (i) the savings from a reduction in use of conflict minerals derived from multiplying the reduced material used by the weighted average spend on water used in manufacturing using conflict minerals per ton; and (ii) the saving from substituting materials derived from multiplying the material substituted by the differential in the weighted average cost of water per ton using conflict minerals and the weighted average cost of water per ton using substitute materials

(continued)

(continued)

Strategy	#	*Benefits*	*Mediating factors*	*Monetization methods*
	5	Avoided costs related to supply shortages	Better risk management	Estimated cost of a short supply incident by the average annual incidents of short supply
	6	Avoided costs related to regulatory fines		Estimated cost from multiplying the average annual number of incidents of conflict mineral related fines by the average fine per incident less additional compliance costs incurred

The U.S. Securities and Exchange Commission (SEC) had required publicly traded companies to annually report use of conflict minerals (tin, tantalum, tungsten, or gold) in their products (the rule was suspended in April 2017). Regardless, SASB, who standardizes voluntary disclosure, identifies the management of risks associated with critical materials in their materiality map. Automotive companies have worked towards this goal by, for example, signing a declaration of support for the Responsible Raw Materials Initiative or using algorithms to ensure tier 3 and 4 supplier compliance. In the manufacturing process, using less material for achieving the same output has obvious implications for improved resource consumption and using substitute materials may also lead to efficiencies. However, the latter is a less clear financial benefit as the substitute material may cost more or be required in larger quantities.

When companies avoided sourcing and using conflict minerals, they generated value through two mediating factors: operational efficiency and risk management. Operational efficiency benefits were a combination of savings from: (1) reduced use; (2) using cheaper substitute materials—both of which led to (3) lower energy consumption and (4) lower water consumption according to the companies. On the risk side, the benefits were: (5) avoided cost related to supply shortages, and (6) avoided regulatory fines. Above, the monetization method (last column) describes the following calculations. The calculations in Table A1 and A2 follow a similar logic: We gathered the realized inputs for 2015 and 2016, adjusted for vehicle production (so that a change is independent of how many cars were produced), and monetized the changes with average weighted cost.

Table A1 and A2 show how we simplified calculations by using aggregate data. Other benefits, for instance, managing manufacturing material waste, were also included as a total category (by using the average weighted cost of disposal instead of breaking it down). Some analyses may require an even more granular level of data. If the mix of manufactured vehicles were to have an impact on year-on-year changes, including it would yield more precise estimates. Regardless of the level, however, the framework provides solid directional guidance for forecasting investments and likely outcomes.

Table A3 takes a simplified approach to assessing risk because of the overall complexity resulting from many sustainability strategies. The companies provided estimates for the incident rate and average cost for supply shortage and regulatory fines related to conflict minerals. We postulated that the sustainability strategies would mitigate the potential

Table A1 Reduction and substitutes for conflict materials sourcing (1, 2). Cells in yellow are company inputs. Note that substitution was a net loss and so the overall benefit resulted in $14,950,952. Figures were obscured with a random perturbance term to preserve confidentiality that maintained the scale in magnitude

Benefits	Unit	Value	Explanation
2016			
Total Raw Materials Weight	Metric Tons	4,266,909	
% of the Raw Materials that Confirmed Conflict Materials -by Weight	%	2.0%	
Total Annual Volume of Conflict Materials Used in Mfg.	Metric Tons	84,911	Multiply two rows above
Per vehicle Total Annual Volume of Conflict Materials Used in Mfg.	Metric Tons per vehicle	0.0084	Above divided by annual vehicle count
2015			
Total Raw Materials Weight	Metric Tons	4,525,901	
% of the Raw Materials that Confirmed Conflict Materials -by Weight	%	2.1%	
Total Annual Volume of Conflict Materials Used in Mfg.	Metric Tons	96,402	Multiply two rows above
Per vehicle Total Annual Volume of Conflict Materials Used in Mfg.	Metric Tons per vehicle	0.0100	Above divided by annual vehicle count
Compare improvement from 2015 to 2016			
% Reduction of Conflict Materials Used in Mfg.	%	16.4%	% change 2015—2016 based on Per vehicle Total Annual Volume
Reduction of Conflict Materials Used in Mfg.	Metric Tons	15,841	Delta 2015—2016 adjusted for vehicle production
Reduction as a result of reduced use of Materials	%	34%	
Reduction as a result of substituting Conflict materials with Others	%	25%	
Weighted Average Price of Conflict Materials - 2016	USD/Metric Ton	$3,590	Includes materials, logistics, handling, and taxes
Weighted Average Price of Substitute Materials - 2016	USD/Metric Ton	$3,443	Includes materials, logistics, handling, and taxes
Weighted Average Substitute to Conflict Material Weight Conversion Constant	#	1.34	For example, 1 ton tin may require 1.2 tin alternatives to replace
Savings from Reduced Use of Material	USD	$19,059,657	Multiply reduction of conflict materials, reduced use of materials, and weighted avg price of conflict materials
Amount of substitution	USD	4,015	Multiply reduction of conflict materials with % of substitution
Savings from substitution before cost of substitute materials	USD	$14,413,351	Multiply amount of substitution with weighted avg price of conflict materials
Cost of substitute including conversion	USD	$18,522,056	Multiply amount of substitution with weighted avg price of substitute materials and conversion factor
Savings from Using Substituted Materials	USD	$(4,108,705)	Delta two rows above

Table A2 Savings for energy and water consumption impact (3, 4). Cells in yellow are company inputs. The overall benefit resulted in $593,181. Figures were obscured with a random perturbance term to preserve confidentiality that maintained the scale in magnitude

Benefits	Unit	Value	Explanation
Weighted Average Spend on Energy in Mfg. for Conflict Materials per Ton	USD/Metric Ton	$52	
Weighted Average Spend on Energy in Mfg. for Substitute Materials per Ton	USD/Metric Ton	$29	
Energy Savings from Reduced Use of Material	USD	$276,055	Multiply amount of reduction (from Table A1) with spend above
Energy Savings from Using Substituted Materials	USD	$92,336	Multiply amount of reduction (from Table A1) with delta of spend above
Weighted Average Spend on Water in Mfg. for Conflict Materials per Ton	USD/Metric Ton	$31	
Weighted Average Spend on Water in Mfg. for Substitute Materials per Ton	USD/Metric Ton	$16	
Water Savings from Reduced Use of Material	USD	$164,571	Multiply amount of reduction (from Table A1) with spend above
Water Savings from Using Substituted Materials	USD	$60,219	Multiply amount of reduction (from Table A1) with delta of spend above
Savings from Changes in Energy and Water Consumption	USD	$593,181	Sum all four rows with savings

Table A3 Avoidance of short supply and regulatory fines (5, 6). Cells in yellow are company inputs. The overall benefit resulted in $21,321,739. Figures were obscured with a random perturbance term to preserve confidentiality that maintained the scale in magnitude

Benefits	Unit	Value	Explanation
Avoidance of Short Supply			
Historic Average Annual Incidents of Conflict Material Short Supply	#	0.95	2011—2016 Annual Average
Average Cost of Conflict Material Short Supply Per Incident	USD	$21,039,489	2011—2016 Annual Average
Total Impact of Short Supply	USD	$20,049,647	Multiply rows above
Avoidance of Regulatory Fines			
Historic Average Annual Incidents of Conflict Material Related Fines	#	0.35	2011—2016 Annual Average
Average Fines for Conflict Material Issues per Incident	USD	$3,682,211	2011—2016 Annual Average
Annual Potential Fines	USD	$1,272,093	Multiply rows above

cost in the long-term. For a risk assessment approach, an extended analysis may choose to model the incident rate and cost as a distribution with, for example, a truncated lognormal distribution. The simulation outputs based on such parameters might then provide more than a point estimate and inform the analyst further on extreme values.

Tables A1–A4 provided the information required to calculate the net financial benefit of the sustainability strategy. The annual additional operating income was $35,944,801 (i.e., $36,865,873 minus the cost of $921,072). Lastly, we wanted to know the value of these benefits if they were to continue over the next five years and calculated the NPV as shown in Table A5.

Table A4 Annual costs and investments for Avoid Use of Conflict Materials. Cells in yellow are company inputs. Figures were obscured with a random perturbance term to preserve confidentiality that maintained the scale in magnitude

Costs	Unit	Value
Additional Annual Operational Costs for Reducing Use of Material	USD	$ 448,744
Additional Annual Operational Costs for Using Substitutes	USD	$ 238,220
Additional Compliance Costs	USD	$ 234,108
Total Costs	USD	$ 921,072

Investments	Unit	Value
Total Existing Equipment/Hardware Modification Investment	USD	$ 2,115,220
Other One-Time Capitalizable Spends	USD	$ 131,237
Total Investments	USD	$ 2,246,458

Table A5 Net present value (NPV) analysis with an assumed discount rate of 10%. We conservatively assumed that all investments (including so-called one-time spends) accrued every year. The total NPV for this strategy over five years was $125,496,776. Figures were obscured with a random perturbance term to preserve confidentiality that maintained the scale in magnitude

Total Financial Impact	0	1	2	3	4	5
Incoming - Benefits		$36,865,873	$36,865,873	$36,865,873	$36,865,873	$36,865,873
Outgoing - Investment	$2,246,458	$2,246,458	$2,246,458	$2,246,458	$2,246,458	$2,246,458
Outgoing - Additional Operational Costs Required		$921,072	$921,072	$921,072	$921,072	$921,072
Total	($2,246,458)	$33,698,343	$33,698,343	$33,698,343	$33,698,343	$33,698,343
NPV	($2,246,458)	$30,634,858	$27,849,870	$25,318,064	$23,016,422	$20,924,020
Total NPV	**$125,496,776**					

Appendix B: How the Return on Sustainability Investments (Rosi) Framework May Be Applied in the Insurance Industry

Companies that focus on a sustainable business model and related risk management might incur short-term costs and investments, but benefit from mid- and long-term benefits. Some of the benefits materialize right away in reduced insurance premiums as underwriters ought to take the risk management of companies into consideration. Companies and their insurance coverage have similar interests to prevent potential losses, to mitigate losses, and to find innovative solutions. Investments in sustainable solutions have therefore a direct monetary impact as they will be reflected in reductions of insurance premiums. ROSI and its associated data can be used to provide transparency and can be applied in the underwriting process. Identifying, quantifying, and monetizing the value of these sustainability strategies can help insurers further understand how a company is mitigating material risks such as recalls for the automotive industry, which may be used, for example, in assessing price premiums (Table B1).

In Table B1, we list three sustainability benefits that were monetized in our study based on the automotive industry:

- *Water use reduction*: Insurance companies are already modelling the growing risk of water, its cost implications, and how droughts and floods can both affect operations. We showed how to monetize the automotive companies' efforts to improve water consumption, which affected the amount of water used, recovered and reused, and disposed.
- *Critical materials*: The automotive companies aimed to reduce their dependency on critical and conflict minerals (e.g., tin, tantalum, tungsten, and gold, which have been regulated in the past). The ROSI metrics we used show how companies are either reducing or substituting critical materials, the scale of these efforts, and how they generated a positive net return because of reduced costs associated with the new approaches and the reduced risk from supply chain disruptions (see Appendix A).
- *Recalls*: Recalls have been increasing in the automotive industry, and addressing recalls are material to the automotive industry (see the SASB materiality map). The ROSI metrics we used show the

Table B1 Examples of how metrics captured in the ROSI may be used by insurers for underwriting and asset management

Data from ROSI framework	*Interest to insurers*	*Potential use to underwriters*	*Potential use to asset managers*
Water use reduction			
Per unit cost of water Water usage per unit of production Amount of water recovered & reused Per unit cost of wastewater disposal	Trends over time Comparison to peers Investment in new technologies to reduce water use Forecast future impacts	Pricing on property and business interruption insurance—for drought and/or flooding	In assessing relative value of investment vs alternatives
Critical materials			
Amount of critical materials per unit Amount of substitute materials used Differential in price of critical & substitute materials Number of incidents of supply shortage Estimated cost of a supply shortage	Trends over time Comparison to peers Investment to reduce critical material use Forecast future impacts	Pricing on business interruption insurance coverage	In assessing relative value of investment vs alternatives
Recalls			
Number of recalls Average cost of recalls	Trends over time Comparison to peers Investment to improve quality or reduce defects Forecast future impacts	Pricing on coverage related to recalls and assessing manufacturers management of the supply chain	In assessing relative value of investment vs alternatives

scale of the recalls and the associated cost for a recall. For example, in one company, recalls were reduced likely because they incorporated more systems thinking into the manufacturing process, so that the design process spanned multiple departments that were previously isolated in their sustainability efforts. The company's ability to improve quality in manufacturing along with working closer with their supply chain partners, ought to mitigate the number of recalls. Insurers, during their due diligence, can ask clients about their manufacturing improvements, request that companies begin to track and monetize necessary information, or engage in a collaborative discussion on sustainability strategies that reduce risk exposure.

When a company monetizes its sustainability actions, others can evaluate how they are innovating and investing to minimize risk. People can see, and quantitatively value, robust contingency plans to mitigate future losses, and they can create opportunities for procuring cost-effective insurance coverage. Insurers may be able to capture insights into the long-term prospects of a company that are otherwise hidden. This is useful for assessing risk, gaining customer loyalty, and improving underwriting performance.

Insurance underwriting performance depends on appropriately assessing the risk profile of a company (and industry). The ROSI framework and associated data can enhance analyzing a company's exposure to risks and the potential impacts of events that they are underwriting, such as catastrophe (floods, hurricanes), business interruption (supply chain disruptions), or product liability (recalls, accidents) losses. These analyses may also open the dialogue on what companies are doing to mitigate these challenges. For example, public company information on manufacturing and other critical locations can be mapped to drought-prone regions. Select ROSI data in our analysis, such as historical incidents in production disruptions or number of recalls along with the associated costs, can be the basis of forecast models that assess the likelihood and severity of losses under various future assumptions. Better assessments of probable outcomes and losses improves underwriting practices for insurers. Measuring the return of sustainability investment can contribute towards these improved practices and more sustainable businesses.

Originally published in: Sezgi, F., & Mair, J. (2010). To control or not control: A coordination perspective to scaling. In G. Dees, P. Bloom, & E. Skloot (Eds.), *Scaling social impact—New directions in research* (pp. 34–60). New York: Palgrave Macmillan.

References

Albertini, E. (2013). Does environmental management improve financial performance? A meta-analytical review. *Organization & Environment, 26*(4), 431–457. https://doi.org/10.1177/1086026613510301.

Anderson, M. W., Teisl, M. F., Noblet, C., & Klein, S. (2015). The incompatibility of benefit–cost analysis with sustainability science. *Sustainability Science, 10*(1), 33–41. https://doi.org/10.1007/s11625-014-0266-4.

Barnett, M. L., Hartmann, J., & Salomon, R. M. (2018). Have you been served? Extending the relationship between corporate social responsibility and lawsuits. *Academy of Management Discoveries, 4*(2), 109–126. https://doi.org/10.5465/amd.2015.0030.

Barnett, M. L., & Salomon, R. M. (2012). Does it pay to be really good? Addressing the shape of the relationship between social and financial performance. *Strategic Management Journal, 33*(11), 1304–1320. https://doi.org/10.1002/smj.1980.

Bebbington, J., Brown, J., & Frame, B. (2007). Accounting technologies and sustainability assessment models. *Ecological Economics, 61*(2–3), 224–236. https://doi.org/10.1016/j.ecolecon.2006.10.021.

Broman, K. W., & Woo, K. H. (2018). Data organization in spreadsheets. *The American Statistician, 72*(1), 2–10. https://doi.org/10.1080/00031305.2017.1375989.

Chava, S. (2014). Environmental externalities and cost of capital. *Management Science, 60*(9), 2223–2247. https://doi.org/10.1287/mnsc.2013.1863.

Clark, G. L., Feiner, A., & Viehs, M. (2014). From the stockholder to the stakeholder: How sustainability can drive financial outperformance. *SSRN Electronic Journal*. https://doi.org/10.2139/ssrn.2508281.

Cornell, B., & Shapiro, A. C. (1987). Corporate stakeholders and corporate finance. *Financial Management, 16*(1), 5. https://doi.org/10.2307/3665543.

Delmas, M. A., & Pekovic, S. (2018). Corporate sustainable innovation and employee behavior. *Journal of Business Ethics, 150*(4), 1071–1188. https://doi.org/10.1007/s10551-016-3163-1.

Delmas, M. A., & Pekovic, S. (2013). Environmental standards and labor productivity: Understanding the mechanisms that sustain sustainability. *Journal of Organizational Behavior, 34*(2), 230–252. https://doi.org/10.1002/job.1827.

Desai, R. M., Kharas, H., & Amin, M. (2017). Combining good business and good development: Evidence from IFC operations, 103. *Global Economy & Development*. https://www.brookings.edu/about-us/annual-report/.

Douglas, E., Van Holt, T., & Whelan, T. (2017). Responsible investing: Guide to ESG data providers and relevant trends. *The Journal of Environmental Investing, 8*(1), 92–114.

Eichholtz, P., Kok, N., & Quigley, J. M. (2010). Doing well by doing good? *The American Economic Review, 100*(5), 2492–2509. https://doi.org/10.1257/aer.

Endrikat, J., Guenther, E., & Hoppe, H. (2014). Making sense of conflicting empirical findings: A Meta-analytic review of the relationship between corporate environmental and financial performance. *European Management Journal, 32*(5), 735–751. https://doi.org/10.1016/J.EMJ.2013.12.004.

Freeman, R. E. (1984). *Strategic management: A stakeholder approach*. Boston: Pitman.

Friede, G., Busch, T., & Bassen, A. (2015). ESG and financial performance: Aggregated evidence from more than 2000 empirical studies. *Journal of Sustainable Finance & Investment, 5*(4), 210–233. https://doi.org/10.1080/20430795.2015.1118917.

Fulton, M., Kahn, B., & Sharples, C. (2012). *Sustainable investing: Establishing long-term value and performance*. https://papers.ssrn.com/sol3/papers.cfm?abstract_id=2222740.

Gao, H., & Zhang, W. (2017). Employment nondiscrimination acts and corporate innovation. *Management Science, 63*(9), 2982–2999. https://doi.org/10.1287/mnsc.2016.2457.

Garavan, T. N., Heraty, N., Rock, A., & Dalton, E. (2010). Conceptualizing the behavioral barriers to CSR and CS in organizations: A typology of HRD interventions. *Advances in Developing Human Resources, 12*(5), 587–613. https://doi.org/10.1177/1523422310394779.

Godfrey, P. C. (2005). Philanthropy and shareholder wealth: The relationship between corporate a risk management perspective. *Academy of Management Review, 30*(4), 777–798.

Golicic, S. L., & Smith, C. D. (2013). A meta-analysis of environmentally sustainable supply chain management practices and firm performance. *Journal of Supply Chain Management, 49*(2), 78–95. https://doi.org/10.1111/jscm.12006.

Gray, R. (2010). Is accounting for sustainability actually accounting for sustainability…and how would we know? An exploration of narratives of organisations and the planet. *Accounting, Organizations and Society, 35*(1), 47–62. https://doi.org/10.1016/J.AOS.2009.04.006.

Griffin, J. J., & Mahon, J. F. (1997). The corporate social performance and corporate financial performance debate. *Business and Society, 36*(1), 5–31. https://doi.org/10.1177/000765039703600102.

Haffar, Merriam, & Searcy, C. (2018). The use of context-based environmental indicators in corporate reporting. *Journal of Cleaner Production, 192*, 496–513. https://doi.org/10.1016/J.JCLEPRO.2018.04.202.

Haskel, J., & Westlake, S. (2017). *Capitalism without capital: The Rise of the intangible economy*. Princeton: Princeton University Press.

Herring, C. (2009). Does diversity pay? Race, gender, and the business case for diversity. *American Sociological Review, 74*(2), 208–224. https://doi.org/10.1177/000312240907400203.

Hubbard, D. W. (2014). *How to measure anything: Finding the value of intangibles in business* (3rd ed). New York: Wiley. https://doi.org/10.1016/j.jclepro.2017.07.048.

Hunt, V., Prince S., Dixon-Fyle, S., & Yee, L. (2018). *Delivering through diversity*. McKinsey & Company. https://www.mckinsey.com/~/media/McKinsey/Business%20Functions/Organization/Our%20Insights/Delivering%20through%20diversity/Delivering-through-diversity_full-report.ashx.

IFC & Deloitte. (2014). *Financial valuation tool for sustainability investments*. https://www.fvtool.com/downloads/user-guide-april2014.pdf.

Ioannou, I., & Serafeim, G. (2019). Corporate sustainability: A strategy? (19-065). *SSRN Electronic Journal*. https://doi.org/10.2139/ssrn.3312191.

Joseph, G. (2012). Ambiguous but tethered: An accounting basis for sustainability reporting. *Critical Perspectives on Accounting, 23*(2), 93–106. https://doi.org/10.1016/j.cpa.2011.11.011.

Khan, M., Serafeim, G., & Yoon, A. (2016). Corporate sustainability: First evidence on materiality. *The Accounting Review, 91*(6), 1697–1724. https://doi.org/10.2308/accr-51383.

Kiron, D., Unruh, G., Kruschwitz, N., Reeves, M., Rubel, H., Meyer, A., & Felde, Z. (2017). Progress toward our common future in uncertain times. *MIT Sloan Management Review, 58*(4). http://sloanreview.mit.edu/sustainability2017.

Lev, B. (2001). *Intangibles: Management, measurement, and reporting*. Brookings Institution Press. https://www.jstor.org/stable/10.7864/j.ctvcj2rf2.

Lev, B., & Gu, F. (2016). *The end of accounting and the path forward for investors and managers*. Hoboken, NJ: Wiley.

Lubin, D. A., & Krosinsky, C. (2013, December). *The value driver model: A tool for communicating the business value of sustainability* (pp. 1–26). UN Global Compact Leaders Summit 2013: Architects of a Better World.

Miras-Rodríguez, M. d. M., Carrasco-Gallego, A., & Escobar-Pérez, B. (2015). Are socially responsible behaviors paid off equally? A cross-cultural analysis. *Corporate Social Responsibility and Environmental Management, 22*(4), 237–256. https://doi.org/10.1002/csr.1344.

Marcuzzo, S. F. (2015). *Novo campo program: A strategy for sustainable cattle ranching in the Amazon*. Instituto Centro de Vida, Alta Floresta-MT. https://www.icv.org.br/wp-content/uploads/2015/09/Cartilha-Novo-Campo-ING.pdf.

Margolis, J. D., Elfenbein, H. A., &. Walsh, J. P. (2009, March). Does it pay to be good...and does it matter? A meta-analysis of the relationship between corporate social and financial performance. *SSRN Electronic Journal*. https://doi.org/10.2139/ssrn.1866371.

McElroy, M. W., & van Engelen, J. (2012). *Corporate sustainability management: The art and science of managing non-financial performance*. Earthscan. https://books.google.com/books/about/Corporate_Sustainability_Management.html?id=OFMju0mjWj0C.

McWilliams, A., & Siegel, D. (2000). Corporate social responsibility and financial performance: Correlation or misspecification? *Strategic Management Journal, 21*(5), 603–609. https://doi.org/10.1002/(SICI)1097-0266(200005)21:5%3c603:AID-SMJ101%3e3.0.CO;2-3.

Milne, M. J., & Gray, R. (2013). W(h)Ither ecology? The triple bottom line, the global reporting initiative, and corporate sustainability reporting. *Journal of Business Ethics, 118*(1), 13–29. https://doi.org/10.1007/s10551-012-1543-8.

Orlitzky, M., Schmidt, F. L., & Rynes, S. L. (2003). Corporate social and financial performance: A meta-analysis. *Organization Studies, 24*(3), 403–441. https://doi.org/10.1177/0170840603024003910.

Peloza, J., & Yachnin, R. (2008). *Valuing business sustainability: A systematic review*. Research Network for Business Sustainability. https://api.van2.auro.io:8080/v1/AUTH_6bda5a38d0d7490e81ba33fbb4be21dd/sophia/blox/assets/data/000/000/018/original/NBS-Systematic-Review-Valuing.pdf?1492523365.

Porter, M. E., & Kramer, M. R. (2006, December). Strategy and society: The link between competitive advantage and corporate social responsibility. *The Harvard Business Review, 84*(12), 78–92.

Porter, M. E., & Kramer, M. R. (2011, January–February). The big idea: Creating shared value. *The Harvard Business Review, 89*(1–2), 62–77.

Rappaport, A. (1986). *Creating shareholder value: The new standard for business performance*. New York and London: Free Press.

Reed, D. (2001). *Stalking the elusive business case for corporate sustainability*. Washington, DC: World Resources Institute. https://www.worldcat.org/title/stalking-the-elusive-business-case-for-corporate-sustainability/oclc/875646874&referer=brief_results.

Salzmann, O., Ionescu-Somers, A., & Steger, U. (2005). The business case for corporate sustainability: Literature review and research options. *European Management Journal, 23*(1), 27–36. https://doi.org/10.1016/j.emj.2004.12.007.

Schaltegger, S., & Figge, F. (2000). Environmental shareholder value: Economic success with corporate environmental management. *Eco-Management and Auditing, 7*(1), 29–42. https://doi.org/10.1002/(SICI)1099-0925(200003)7:1%3c29:AID-EMA119%3e3.0.CO;2-1.

Schneider, T. E. (2011). Is environmental performance a determinant of bond pricing? Evidence from the U.S. pulp and paper and chemical industries*.

Contemporary Accounting Research, 28(5): 1537–1561. https://doi.org/10.1111/j.1911-3846.2010.01064.x.

Searcy, C. (2012). Corporate sustainability performance measurement systems: A review and research agenda. *Journal of Business Ethics, 107*(3), 239–253. https://doi.org/10.1007/s10551-011-1038-z.

Searcy, C. (2016). Measuring enterprise sustainability. *Business Strategy and the Environment, 25*(2), 120–133. https://doi.org/10.1002/bse.1861.

Steger, U. (2006). Building a business case for corporate sustainability. In *Managing the business case for sustainability: The integration of social, environmental and economic performance* (pp. 412–443). Sheffield, UK: Greenleaf.

The New York Times Magazine. (1970, September 13). The social responsibility of business is to increase its profits. https://doi.org/10.1007/978-3-540-70818-6_14.

The World Business Council for Sustainable Development. (2017). *Sustainability and enterprise risk management: The first step towards integration*. https://www.wbcsd.org/contentwbc/download/2548/31131%0A.

The World Business Council for Sustainable Development. (2019). *Materiality in corporate reporting—A white paper focusing on the food and agriculture sector*. https://www.wbcsd.org/Programs/Redefining-Value/Resources/A-White-Paper-focusing-on-the-food-and-agriculture-sector.

Turban, D. B., & Greening, D. W. (1997). Corporate social performance and organizational attractiveness to prospective employees. *Academy of Management Journal, 40*(3), 658–672. https://doi.org/10.2307/257057.

United Nations ESCAP. (2009). *Eco-effciency indicators: Measuring resource-use effciency and the impact of economic activities on the environment*. Greening the Economic Growth Series. https://sustainabledevelopment.un.org/content/documents/785eco.pdf.

Vitaliano, D. F. (2012). Corporate social responsibility, ethics, and corporate governance. *Social Responsibility Journal, 10*(5), 653. https://doi.org/10.1108/14720701011085544.

Voegtlin, C., & Pless, N. M. (2014). Global governance: CSR and the role of the UN Global Compact. *Journal of Business Ethics, 122*(2), 179–191. https://doi.org/10.1007/s10551-014-2214-8.

Waddock, S. A., & Graves, S. B. (1997). The corporate social performance-financial performance link. *Strategic Management Journal, 18*(4), 303–319. https://doi.org/10.1002/(SICI)1097-0266(199704)18:4%3c303:AID-SMJ869%3e3.0.CO;2-G.

Whelan, T., & Fink, C. (2016). The comprehensive business case for sustainability. *Harvard Business Review, 21.* http://everestenergy.nl/new/wp-content/uploads/HBR-Article-The-comprehensive-business-case-for-sustainability.pdf.

Whelan, T., Zappa, B., Zeidan, R., & Fishbein, G. (2017). How to quantify sustainability's impact on your bottom line. *Harvard Business Review, 23*. https://hbr.org/2017/09/how-to-quantify-sustainabilitys-impact-on-your-bottom-line.

Wood, D. J., & Jones, R. E. (1995). Stakeholder mismatching: A theoretical problem in empirical research on corporate social performance. *The International Journal of Organizational Analysis, 3*(3), 229–267. https://doi.org/10.1108/eb028831.

CHAPTER 15

To Control or Not Control: A Coordination Perspective to Scaling

Funda Sezgi and Johanna Mair

The question of how social initiatives can effectively scale their impact to reach individuals and communities that benefit from their innovations has received increasing attention over the past few years. A number of scholars adopt a strategic perspective and investigate the mechanisms to scale social *organizations* (Bradach, 2003; Oster, 1996), while others argue that scaling organizations is not necessarily sufficient to scale *impact* (Uvin,

Sezgi, F., & Mair, J. (2010). To control or not control: A coordination perspective to scaling. In G. Dees, P. Bloom, & E. Skloot (Eds.), *Scaling social impact -- New directions in research* (pp. 34–60). New York: Palgrave Macmillan.

F. Sezgi (✉)
Norrsken HQ, Stockholm, Sweden
e-mail: funda@norrskenfoundation.org

J. Mair
Hertie School, The University of Governance, Berlin, Germany
e-mail: mair@hertie-school.org

R. Bali Swain and S. Sweet (eds.), *Sustainable Consumption and Production, Volume II*,
https://doi.org/10.1007/978-3-030-55285-5_15

1995; Wei-Skillern & Anderson, 2003). The latter group of authors argues that scale is not a particularly good proxy for the effectiveness of the programmes (Frumkin, 2007), and that becoming large is only one of the many other possible ways of expanding impact in terms of the number of beneficiaries served (Edwards & Hulme, 1992; Uvin, Jain, & Brown, 2000). These authors emphasize that instead of focusing on growing organizations, we need to turn attention to more effective and inclusive ways to address social problems.

Current discussions on scaling predominately concentrate on how to enhance social *impact* and include a broad spectrum of activities:

> expanding the quantity and improving the quality of the services provided directly by [the focal] organization; enabling other organizations to provide a higher quantity and quality of direct services; changing the political, cultural, or economic environment to reduce the need or problem; attracting more or improving the productivity of resources devoted to addressing the need or problem. (CASE, 2006: 9)

In this chapter we deliberately assume a narrow view and adopt an organizational perspective on scaling. This allows us to reengage with an important stream of literature that has emphasized the role of control in organizational achievements. Although the level of control exerted differs from one organizational setting to another, control is essential in any type of organization to coordinate organizational members towards coherent goals. In this chapter we analyse an eye care system, representing a tightly controlled setting, in order to disentangle the mechanisms underpinning coordinated efforts towards scaling.

Scholars define three modes for scaling social innovations: branching, affiliation and dissemination. Accordingly, an awareness of the potential options help social entrepreneurs in specifying the core of the strategy for scaling their organizations' social impact. While we know that moving along a continuum, from dissemination to affiliation to branching, organizations require larger amounts of resources and an increasing degree of control (Dees, Anderson, & Wei-Skillern, 2004), we know little about how such control is exerted. A better understanding of how organizations scale, the mechanisms they put into use for achieving differing degrees of control under different organizational modes, can help both organizations and entrepreneurs align their strategies with appropriate design features. In order to shed light on the mechanisms at play, we investigate Aravind Eye Care System,[1] a non-profit organization based in India providing eye care services to poor people. Aravind serves as a unique setting for zooming inside organizational modes since it is a rare example of an organization that applies the three modes simultaneously. Based on our interview data as well as on longitudinal data for a number of past and ongoing scaling efforts that employ different organizational strategies and structures, we identify the mechanisms employed by Aravind under the three organizational modes. It is our hope to provide social entrepreneurs with the know-how to design the tools they need for exerting differing degrees of control once they decide on the organizational mode for scaling their social impact.

Scaling Social Impact: An Organizational Perspective

Recently, there has been an increasing interest among organizational scholars to conceptualize the strategies that social organizations pursue in their scaling attempts (Bradach, 2003; Dees, Anderson, & Wei-Skillern; 2002, Dees et al., 2004; Uvin, 1995; Uvin & Miller, 1996; Uvin et al., 2000; Wei-Skillern & Anderson, 2003). Three dominant organizational modes for scale are described in the non-profit world as branching, affiliation and dissemination. A case study survey on social enterprises reveals that 77% of the organizations investigated for the study employed branching, 41% affiliation and 36% dissemination as their scaling strategy (La France Associates, 2006).

Accordingly, *branching* is a direct activity (Uvin et al., 2000), where all units are legally part of one organization: a setting analogous to company owned stores (Dees et al., 2002). This mode is the closest one to 100% replication of the original model as it involves only a few adaptations. In *affiliation* mode, independent legal entities are tied with the founding structure through a formalized contract that specifies the procedures and practices to be shared by all sites (Dees et al., 2002). Organizations employing this mode can increase impact both directly—by delivering

[1] Hereinafter referred to as Aravind.

services to a larger number of people—and indirectly—by inducing partners to undertake new activities that are geared to enlarging the overall impact (Uvin et al., 2000).

Finally, *dissemination* typically relies on contractual agreements and the focal organization actively shares information with the recipient organization for the adoption of the model (Dees et al., 2002: 5). Frequently referred to as diffusion, spread or political scaling out, the dissemination mode is an indirect means for greater impact, where "non-profits that are capable of learning the lessons from their operational programmes diffuse the resulting knowledge through training, information sharing, consultancy and advice whether to other non-profits, governments, or international donors" (Uvin et al., 2000: 1414). While the process of spreading ideas or knowledge is not amenable to a great deal of control (Frumkin, 2007), dissemination mode is advantageous in that it not only allows non-profits to increase their impact without expanding in size (Uvin et al., 2000), but is also a prerequisite for learning which elements of the programme are relevant to be routinized for expansion through large-scale operations (Korten, 1980).

Dees et al. (2004) suggest that all these organizational modes—branching, affiliation and dissemination—should be considered as a continuum in terms of increasing degree of central coordination and resource requirements towards branching. The authors argue that dissemination is the simplest and usually the least resource-intensive mode since "the originating organization has at most a short-term agreement to provide technical assistance to those who would use this information to bring the innovation to a new locale" (Dees et al., 2002: 5). However, according to the authors, the disseminating organization has little control over implementation in new locations (Dees et al., 2004). Dees and his colleagues (2004) argue that branching, at the other end of the spectrum, offers the greatest potential for coordination and commonly requires the greatest investment of resources by the focal organization.

In this chapter, we seek to go beyond static descriptions of organizational modes adopted by social enterprises in their attempts to scale social impact. We seek to contribute to the organizational perspective on scaling impact through a systematic analysis of the mechanisms employed by a non-profit organization to activate varying degrees of control in three organizational modes. By unpacking the "nuts and bolts" of a successful initiative, we hope to provide tools for social enterprises in determining the design features of their organizations to achieve fit with their intended strategies.

Organizational Control

Control is one of the main pillars of organizational design. Tannenbaum (1968) defines control as "any process in which a person (or group of persons or organizations of persons) determines or intentionally affects what another person, group, or organizational will do" (p. 238). Control can be conceptualized as how much power an organization has over its other resources and subunits (Floyd & Lane, 2000; Jaeger & Baliga, 1985; Kirsch, 1996; Tannenbaum, 1968), or as the processes by which the firm coordinates the activities (Lebas & Weigenstein, 1986; Ouchi, 1979, 1980; Tushman & Nadler, 1978). To date, scaling scholars have focused on the former perspective and analysed the degree to which organizations can control the implementation of its practices in new locations. In this chapter, we adopt the latter perspective and investigate the mechanisms that enable coordination within and between subunits once the organization chooses the organizational mode(s) through which it scales its impact.

Control is crucial in ensuring that organizational members direct their efforts towards the attainment of organizational objectives (Olsen, 1978). In designing the control system, it is important to keep coherence with the strategy, and to implement features that ensure progress towards desired organizational and social outcomes (Chenhall, 2003). A study on social enterprises replication efforts supports these arguments suggesting that one of the key questions to be addressed in a replication strategy is "what level of control does the social enterprise want to have over replicated entities?" (UnLtd Ventures, 2008). Accordingly, the degree of control the organization seeks to exercise is important in ensuring that the appropriate structure is chosen for replication of the social innovation in new locations. However, understanding how much control the focal organization can employ is not sufficient. We need a better understanding of the design features that enable the activation and maintaining of the level of control the organization seeks to exercise under various organizational modes.

This study is based on an instrumental case study research design. Our research setting, Aravind, uniquely combines three modes of scaling discussed in the popular literature on scaling, namely branches, affiliation, and dissemination. The mission of the organization is to eliminate needless blindness by (1) providing compassionate and high quality eye care for all in its branch hospitals, (2) working with socially committed partners in underserved areas of India and other developing countries in its affiliated hospitals, and (3) providing teaching, training, capacity building, advocacy, research and publications in its dissemination mode.[2] As suggested by the literature, all those modes/strategies require different levels of resource commitments and control properties. In the rest of the chapter, we provide an analysis of how the focal organization in this study coordinates its activities around the sub-purposes mentioned earlier. We build on longitudinal archival data as well as interviews and observations from multiple field trips to conduct a comparative analysis on the specific coordination mechanisms characterizing each mode.

Aravind Eye Care System

Aravind was founded in 1976 with the objective of overcoming preventable blindness in resource-poor settings, India being the initial target. According to World Health statistics,[3] as of 2009, there are about 314 million visually impaired people worldwide, of which 45 million are blind. Geographic distribution of people with visual problems is not even: approximately 87% live in developing countries. In India, in particular, over 12 million people—of which 63% are cataracts—are visually handicapped (IndiaStat, 2004). It is estimated that more than 6 million operations are needed per year to tackle the rising incidence rate (Bhandari, Dratler, Raube, & Thulasiraj, 2008). Infrastructure deficiencies in India to meet this need energized Dr. Govindappa Venkataswamy—known to many as "Dr. V."—to start Aravind Eye Care System.

The initial goal of the organization was to provide quality eye care surgeries at reasonable cost. Over time, however, Aravind built a self-sustaining business model, where the quality of eye treatment combined with compassionate care and the efficiency of operations are its main strengths. Aravind charges below-market prices for patients who can afford the surgery and cross-subsidizes the income generated therein for the patients who cannot afford to pay. Today, approximately 60% of the all operations at Aravind are provided for free or at a low cost (Bhandari et al., 2008).

[2] Source: Aravind Eye Care System Activity Report (2008–2009).

[3] http://www.who.int/mediacentre/factsheets/fs282/en/index.html (last accessed 22 October 2009).

The ability to provide free and/or low cost surgeries to poor people while being financially self-sustaining is due to the efficiency achieved at Aravind. Two key components of the innovative Aravind model are among the many things that help explain the level of efficiency achieved: cost cutting through establishment of Aurolab, the lens manufacturing division of Aravind, and the large volume of surgeries thanks to the flow of operations. From its establishment until 1992, intraocular lenses needed for cataract surgeries were donated by American manufacturers for Aravind to fulfil its social mission. However, the fast growth in the number of surgeries proved the model based on donations infeasible. To overcome the dependence on other parties in its operations, Aravind established Aurolab in 1992 and started producing its own lenses for ten dollars each while the market price for the same variety was two hundred dollars in the United States.

The other key component of the Aravind efficiency model is the "serial production model" inspired by the McDonald's food chain model (Bhandari et al., 2008). Young girls hired from villages are trained for two years to become mid-level ophthalmologists (MLOPs) who can fully prepare patients for operation. The doctor, having two operating tables one next to another, takes solely six minutes to perform a cataract surgery and has the next patient ready by the time he finishes one operation. These two examples illustrate many of the innovative dots of the Aravind business model through which it sought to increase productivity at the lowest cost possible, and hence to serve as many people as possible.

Efficiency is the key to success in this type of setting, and Aravind puts utmost effort into maintaining quality while providing large volume of eye care service. The organization emphasizes "treating rich and poor people alike" as the core principle of the organizational culture, and is driven by values such as modesty, sincerity, dedication, teamwork, conservatism, growth, spirituality, discipline, and energy to help the poor sector. According to the founders, commitment to the value system established at Aravind is vital to the sustainability of the model over years and across contexts.

Since its inception, therefore, Aravind is faced with two major conflicting challenges that are common to many social enterprises: (1) How to scale up their innovative health service business model to build capacity for achieving their strategic objective of delivering one million eye surgeries per year by 2015? (2) How to cultivate and maintain value consistency across the system throughout expansion?

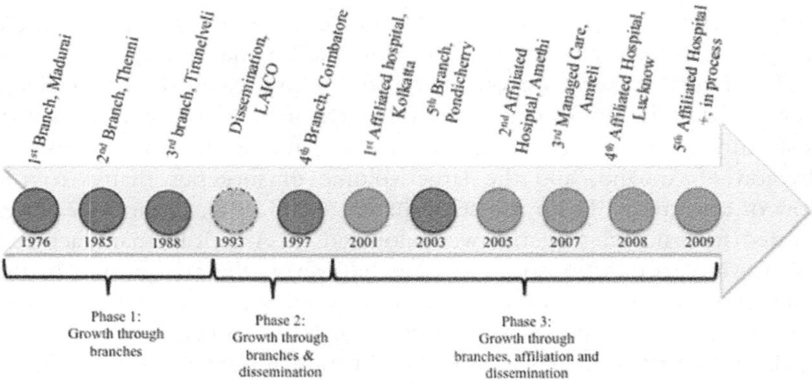

Fig. 15.1 Timeline and phases of the Aravind Eye Care system evolution

Organizational Evolution

Having started with an 11-bed capacity, Aravind increased its number of cataract surgeries from a total of 29,928 in 1988 (Natchiar, Thulsiraj, & Sundaram, 2008) to 269,577 in 2008, performed at five branches. Today, Aravind Eye Care System is the largest provider of eye care in the world: the organization performs approximately 270,000 surgeries per year and serves over two million patients in its branch and affiliated hospitals; it has provided consulting and capacity building services to 216 hospitals across India, South East Asia and Africa.[4] Figure 15.1 provides an overview of the evolution of the organizational modes adopted by Aravind over time.

As Fig. 15.1 suggests, Aravind expanded only through branches in *Phase 1*. After expanding its capacity to 250 beds in Madurai, the organization built its Thenni branch in 1985 and Tirunelveli in 1988. By the beginning of 1990s, Aravind had obtained "proof of concept" through its hospital in Madurai and the successful replications of the main hospital in two other Indian cities. The success of the Aravind model attracted the attention of other organizations that sought to collaborate with it in different ways. *Phase 2* started with Lions Clubs International Foundation approaching Aravind to join forces for overcoming blindness. Lions had raised money to fight cataract blindness and the organization

[4] See www.aravind.org.

decided to use the fund for improving poorly performing hospitals around India instead of building new ones. Leveraging the knowledge base it accumulated over years, in 1993 Aravind standardized its practices and created templates for strategies to generate demand, provide low cost high quality services, and achieve financial viability. In 1996, Lions Institute of Community Opthalmology (LAICO) was officially established through which Aravind started disseminating knowledge by training healthcare and managerial personnel in the development and implementation of efficient eye care services. *Phase 3* started in 2001 when Aravind, for the first time, was approached by a third party organization to establish affiliated hospitals. From then onwards Aravind has been expanding its impact through a combination of all three organizational modes mentioned in scaling literature: branching, affiliation (a.k.a. managed care in Aravind terminology), and dissemination (a.k.a. consulting and capacity building projects through LAICO).

Today, Aravind has five branch hospitals with nearly 4000 bed capacity, four affiliated units and plans of reaching a target of 25 affiliated hospitals and 1 million surgeries by 2015, and has provided capacity building services to 216 hospitals and indirectly helped them increase their performance significantly. Figure 15.2 provides an illustration of the performance data on Aravind branch hospitals. Social impact achieved through these direct (branching and affiliation) and indirect ways of scaling (dissemination) is evident: the evolution described has played a major role in increasing the cataract surgery rate in Tamil Nadu (from 2039 in 1988 to 7633 in 2005) and in India as a whole (Natchiar et al., 2008).

However, as mentioned earlier, since its inception, Aravind has endeavoured to fulfil dual objectives simultaneously: scaling social impact to overcome blindness and keeping value consistency within the system throughout expansion. In the rest of the chapter, we illuminate the key mechanisms at play under the three organizational modes employed by Aravind to demonstrate its efforts to serve those dual purposes. As suggested by previous research on scaling, we also observe that Aravind has greatest control over its resources in branches and decreasingly so towards the dissemination mode. However, our analysis pushes the thinking on control issues in social enterprises by providing a coordination perspective where we systematically investigate the mechanisms enabling the functioning of a complex system encompassing three organizational modes simultaneously.

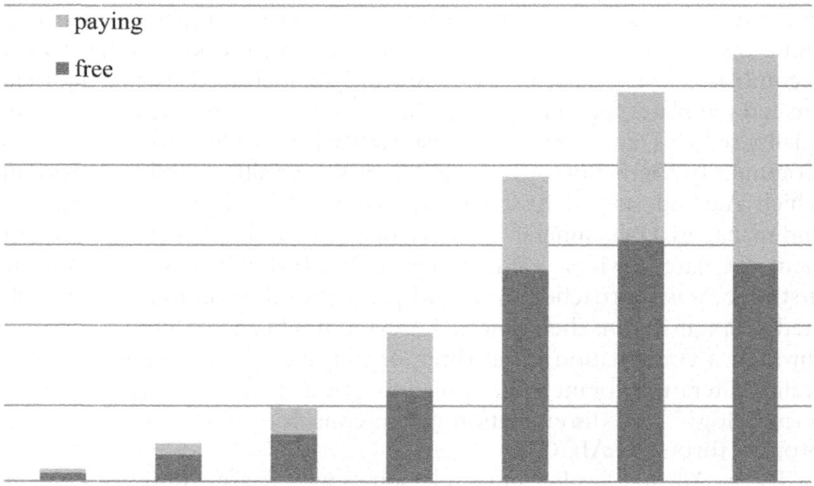

Fig. 15.2 Number of surgeries performed in branches over years

Mechanisms at Play

Our data reveal that in trying to maintain consistency across the system in terms of practices, procedures and values, Aravind uses patterns of coordination activities that are organized under four mechanisms: *training*, *mobility*, *communication* and *sharing of knowledge through templates*. That is to say, the organization attempts to: (1) train organizational members in order to teach them skill and cultivate values, (2) rotate organizational members to cultivate values in newly established hospitals and maintain values in existing ones, (3) ensure communication between the hospitals mainly to monitor performance measures and also to reinforce the other two mechanisms, and (4) provide up-to-date templates reflecting its best practices to be shared with third party hospitals. However, as the following analysis demonstrates, differences between organizational modes in terms of their subgoals determine whether a mechanism is employed by an organizational unit and, if yes, to what extent.

Training

Training is necessary in establishing control because while providing organizational members with the necessary abilities to be functional in the organization, it allows the organization to communicate and cultivate its expectations (Jaeger & Baliga, 1985). At Aravind, there is a strong emphasis on training. Especially in branches and affiliated hospitals where Aravind seeks to establish tight relationships with its partners, training serves as a mechanism to establish and maintain consistency not only in terms of operations but also in terms of values and culture. Differences remain, however, between branches and affiliated units since affiliation mode limits the organization's span of control. At the other end of the spectrum, Aravind provides training services mainly to share its best practices with other hospitals. Therefore, training is less intensive in terms of duration and levels of organizational members involved from the third party hospitals.

More specifically, in the *dissemination* mode, clinical and management staff from clients, and managers from funding agencies receive training mainly at LAICO that is located at the base hospital. Depending on the need, however, other branches also get involved in training of the consulted hospitals under dissemination mode. While the standard version of the training provided in this mode is a one-week vision-building workshop, depending on the demand from the client, duration of the training ranges from several days up to a year.

Training in affiliated units and branches, however, goes beyond short- to long-term workshops. In the case of *affiliated hospitals*, clinical and management staff get trained in the responsible branch, although for slightly shorter periods than the staff that are employees of branches. Doctors of affiliated units are sent to Madurai for three months: two months for organizational orientation and one for surgical training; and the duration of the MLOP training varies between six months to one year, while locally recruited doctors and other medical staff receive bundled training in various branches for one to several months. Aravind puts great effort into going beyond teaching operating skills through their training programmes in affiliated hospitals. According to one of our interviewees, operating skills are easy to learn; what makes the difference is the "attitude toward patients" that organizational members acquire throughout training.

In *branches*, same as affiliation units, all clinical and management staff gets trained; however, training in this mode takes place only at base branch. This centralized approach ensures the highest level of homogeneity possible. In branching mode, training of the branch staff is considered to be an ongoing activity, as the organization considers branches as the originating points for disseminating the original business model and the staff there is considered to be learning-by-doing on a continuous basis. Moreover, training takes more time in this mode. For instance, MLOP training is two years instead of one in branches. Our informant responsible for the training of the staff explains that the first year of branch MLOP training includes teaching skills and values, and the second year is for "moulding" them for Aravind culture.

Table 15.1 compares branches, affiliated hospitals, and dissemination mode in terms of their use of mechanisms. As shown, training gets more intensive towards branches. Drawing from the literature on control mechanisms and our observations, we expect that organizational subunits that are subject to more intensive and centralized training are likely to be more coordinated with the original model.

Table 15.1 Coordination mechanisms at use under different organizational modes

	Branches	*Affiliated Hospitals*	*Dissemination*
Training	• Centralized • Longer	• Decentralized • Shorter	• Decentralized—centralized • Shortest
Communication	• Larger scope in terms of levels of staff involved • Higher frequency	• Smaller scope in terms of levels of staff involved • Lower frequency	• Smallest scope in terms of levels of staff involved • Lowest frequency
Mobility	• Larger scope during establishment • Larger scope and higher frequency at established hospitals	• Smaller scope during establishment • Smaller scope and lower frequency at established hospitals	• Smallest scope • No repetition, merely visits
Templates	No templates	In process	Extensive use of templates

Communication

Communication is also crucial in establishing and maintaining control, because as Stacey (1993) puts it: "control operates through self organization: through the spontaneous formation of interest groups and coalitions around specific issues, communication about those issues, cooperation and the formation of consensus and commitment to a response to those issues" (p. 242). In other words, communication is a means to control and helps build commitment. Although at varying degrees among branching, affiliation, and dissemination modes, communication is extensively used by Aravind as a mechanism to monitor various performance outcomes in its lightest form, and to be aware of changes taking place in different parts of the system, to be informed about emerging problems, to harmonize problem solving efforts, and to acknowledge accomplishments.

Under the *dissemination* mode, communication is limited. While the heads of client hospitals and involved funding agencies receive reports from Aravind regarding the general outcomes of consulting projects, in return, they provide Aravind with monthly standardized reporting on financial and outcome measures.

In *affiliated units*, standardized performance reports are produced and shared with the branches. Moreover, subjective reporting on outcomes and quality are exchanged on an individual basis between hospital heads and AMECS staff at the headquarters. There is also ongoing emailing and telephone calls on a nonstandardized basis between management, clinical staff (doctors and nurses) with senior staff from branch in charge. One of our interviewees explains that he meets with doctors at the end of the month to discuss the reasons for the complications, how they handle them and how they could be overcome. Moreover, every six months all supervisors gather to have an interaction with one of the founding members and discuss what they have been doing. In these meetings, information is presented to the vice chairman and is then spread throughout the system.

Within the *branches*, there is continuous exchange of information and experience between staff at all staff meetings. Moreover, communication is more frequent and the tools used more elaborate in comparison to affiliation units. Other than the standardized and comprehensive reporting agendas on finance, performance, and quality measures, there is ongoing teleconferencing, internal mailing lists, internal newsletters and journal clubs to share experiences, frequent meetings of hospital, clinical, and nursing heads at the base hospital and semiannual auditing team visits that are still to be standardized. One of the hospital administrators interviewed explained that every change made in the branch hospitals is communicated to the main branch, and that the change is integrated into the system if it is considered valuable to the system.

As Table 15.1 suggests, in branch hospitals, communication is more frequent and covers a larger scope of staff levels. As we move along the continuum, however, smaller numbers of staff levels get involved in coordinating the activities and communication channels are less frequently utilized. Therefore, while in the case of branching communication serves as a strong mechanism to ensure coordination and consistency across units, in the dissemination mode, it barely has positive effects on the performance of the consulted hospitals.

Mobility

One distinctive practice employed by Aravind to ensure consistency throughout the system is the continuous movement of organizational members. This mechanism is predominantly evident in managed care and branch hospitals. The rationale behind this mechanism is to establish commitment to organizational values in newly established hospitals, and to maintain Aravind value system across the already existing hospitals. Mobility is effective in maintaining consistency across the system because it goes beyond formal training methods by teaching values through role models. Value training or socialization is an interpersonal process of informally or implicitly teaching organizational values and behavioural expectations to organizational members to bring them in line with what is required for successful participation within the organization (Etzioni, 1961; Jaeger & Baliga, 1985). The use of this mechanism varies significantly across organizational modes at Aravind.

In the *dissemination mode*, clinical and management staff from hospitals involved in capacity building projects visit Aravind hospitals to observe the functioning of the system, only for short durations though.

In *affiliated units*, both clinical staff (doctors and nurses) and management staff (hospital and department administrators) rotate on a temporary basis. Especially during the establishment of the affiliated units, senior clinical staff and one hospital administrator move temporarily to the unit until the system is in place. This generally takes about two years. Moreover, for their training purposes, MLOPs visit the branch associated with the affiliated hospital they will eventually settle down in. MLOP training used to take four months in the making of the affiliation mode; however, it is now increased to one year to enhance learning. Nurses interviewed confirm that spending time in branch hospitals is key to understanding the Aravind-way-of-doing-things. However, this process is not repeated after the training period is over. Once the best practices are settled and core values cultivated, an unsteady circulation of the senior level staff or high potential candidates starts from branches to affiliation hospitals. This is the main distinction between mobility of staff in affiliated hospitals and branch staff, although senior management is currently considering standardizing the ongoing rotation of the former to reenergize them periodically.

In the case of *branches* there is a *steady* circulation of clinical staff and management staff. All clinical and administrative members take on duties in various branches before they settle down to one. The chief training officer for MLOPs explains that rotation during and after training ensures that branch members experience at least three hospitals before they settle in. Moreover, any organizational member can be called on duty when a new branch is to be established. So, establishment of branches involves not only senior executives, but also all levels of hospital staff, including housekeepers, MLOPs, operation theatre nurses and so on. During the establishment of one of the branch hospitals, for instance, out of 150 people needed for the new hospital, 130 were transferred from other branch hospitals to ensure that the value system was in place. One of the informants highlights that they started employing local people only after the system was settled in that new branch hospital, and when the established system could absorb those newly hired within a short period of time.

As Table 15.1 demonstrates, dissemination lies at the far end of the continuum: only hospital heads are involved in the process and they visit Aravind hospitals for only short periods of time to observe the functioning of the system. In branch hospitals, during start-up of new hospitals and ongoing operations, mobility covers the largest scope of employee levels and is most frequent. Although differences remain between branches and affiliated hospitals, people in branches and affiliated units are mobilized for ensuring that they learn the Aravind-way-of-doing-things through first-hand experience; and they are expected to serve as role models committed to Aravind values when they settle in a hospital. Therefore, while employed at varying degrees, mobility at Aravind serves a strong mechanism for establishing and maintaining consistency across the system.

Templates

Organizational literature suggests that templates are useful for sharing codifiable practices with other organizations (Jensen & Szulanski, 2007; Jensen, Szulanski, & Casaburi, 2003). Although having access to a template does not ensure that the template is used by the recipient unit, it helps the focal organization to communicate its practices and serve as a means to reproduce the complex set of interrelated organizational routines necessary when setting up a site for independent production or for improving the practices of an existing organization. At Aravind, generating templates is related both to the size of the operations of organizational modes and to the depth of content Aravind coordinates with other hospitals. Accordingly, template use becomes more salient when the focal organization seeks to coordinate the activities with a larger number of hospitals and when it seeks only to coordinate practices rather than to transfer tacit knowledge that is embedded in individuals (Nonaka, 1994; Polanyi, 1966).

Hence, template is the mechanism that is mainly used by *dissemination* mode. To share its knowledge base on human resource management, infrastructure, systems and procedures built over time at the branches, Aravind has prepared extensive templates related to demand generation, quality and financial viability. Having standardized the mainstream activities that are considered to have a positive effect on performance in terms of number and quality of surgeries and hospital performance, and having prepared simplified checklists out of them, Aravind has shared knowledge with 216 eye hospitals across India, South East Asia, and Africa to date.

There are no templates available for the *affiliated units*, although the senior management at Aravind considers having templates for this mode as an emergent necessity. One of the interviewees highlights that mistakes that were made during the making of affiliation mode might not be affordable with intended scaling efforts through this mode (i.e. reaching the target of one million surgeries per year via twenty-five affiliated hospitals to be established by 2015). Another informant also confirms that standardizing the process and generating templates simplify the scaling efforts as it prevents the organization from reinventing the wheel and helps in focusing on novel tasks.

"In the branches there is almost zero documentation: mind wise, it's more like that", says one of the senior managers regarding the use of templates in *branches*. Another informant explains that branches do not need templates due to the accumulated knowledge in humans. In other words, in trying to maintain full consistency across its branches, Aravind relies more on the other three coordinating mechanisms mentioned earlier rather than on template use.

As Table 15.1 suggests, templates are mainly used in the dissemination mode for sharing practices. Since Aravind seeks to coordinate values as well as practices in branches and affiliated hospitals, to date, templates have not been utilized under these two modes. However, the need for standardizing activities becomes more salient as the affiliation mode evolves to become a larger subsystem. Therefore, templates are in process to ensure that the basics of the complex Aravind model are shared with newly established units via templates, and higher order coordination is to be maintained through the support from the other three mechanisms.

Organizational Modes, Coordination and Scaling

The analysis presented in this chapter allows us to go beyond a brief description of the level of control implemented through different organizational modes and demonstrates the mechanisms the organization has available to activate the level of control it seeks to exert on third parties. Table 15.2 provides a comparison of the three organizational modes in terms of their use of the discussed mechanisms. The difference between modes in terms of use of mechanisms arises from the level of coordination Aravind seeks to achieve under different modes.

In the dissemination mode, Aravind merely shares strategies and best practices with consulted hospitals and does not seek to impose its value system on the recipient units. Hence, mechanisms used under this mode

Table 15.2 Intensity of coordination mechanisms used under organizational modes

	Branches	*Affiliation*	*Dissemination*
Training	+++	++	+
Communication	+++	++	+
Mobility	+++	++	0
Templates	0	In process	+++

are mainly to transfer operational knowledge and coordinate the activities of the consulted hospitals with that of Aravind. In branching and affiliation, however, Aravind seeks to go beyond replicating best practices, although differences remain between these two modes. Full ownership of its branch hospitals allows the organization to fully concert the efforts of its organizational members towards the achievement of the organizational mission, which is scaling social impact while maintaining value consistency throughout the system for Aravind. Although the same level of consistency is intended for the affiliation mode, full coordination in the mode is contingent upon the extent to which Aravind has control over its partner organizations.

These observations suggest that when the organization seeks also to ensure value consistency together with operational consistency across branches and affiliated units, there is higher reliance on informal coordination mechanisms such as training, communication, and mobility. When the objective is to coordinate only practices and procedures, as is the case in the dissemination mode, there is higher reliance on formal coordination mechanisms such as templates (although this mechanism is also enforced through communication and training). Informal mechanisms help establish a base of attitudes, habits, and values that foster cooperation and minimize the divergence of preferences among group members by exerting culture control through socialization instead of formal performance evaluations as control mechanisms (Govindarajan & Fisher, 1990; Pascale, 1985). Formalizing through templates, on the other hand, helps to share knowledge on good practices at larger scale since they are codified, standardized forms of knowledge (March & Simon, 1958) that coordinate activities without stretching human resources and at lower cost.

These observations are helpful for understanding the design features that are relevant for differing degrees of control exercised under different organizational modes. Depending on (1) the level of control a social entrepreneur seeks to exercise and (2) what it seeks to coordinate an organization needs to employ various combinations of coordination mechanisms at varying degrees. However, it should be noted that choice of mechanisms to exert differing levels of control across organizational modes is not a static decision. As the organizations evolve to scale further, they might need to revise their structural components since increasing number of employees intensifies the need for coordination in the organization (Blau, 1970). For instance, at Aravind, at its initial stage, affiliated

Table 15.3 Type of coordination mechanisms appropriate for varying degrees of coordination and scale

		Coordination of...	
		Practices only	*Practices & values*
Scale	High	Formal mechanisms	Informal & formal mechanisms
	Low	Formal & informal mechanisms	Informal mechanisms

hospitals were intended to be fully aligned with branches (to the extent that the partners' values are consistent with Aravind's). However, as the organization moved towards higher number of affiliated units, the need to generate templates for establishing and maintaining new hospitals arose.

Therefore, when the objective is to coordinate practices only, formal mechanisms are useful. Higher reliance on informal mechanisms is advisable when the organization seeks to achieve value consistency together with coordinated practices. However, as the scale of operations increases, there is a tendency to include formal mechanisms in the formula. Table 15.3 summarizes our conclusions related to coordinating mechanisms in terms of scaling and coordination considerations.

Conclusion

The difficulties around scaling and replicating good practices have been discussed widely and these difficulties are evident in the many failures to replicate new business models in different contexts. Therefore, by studying the main features of the innovative Aravind business model we seek to provide insights into the main challenge of scaling social impact while maintaining core values. Zooming in on the organizational modes employed by Aravind, we provided a systematic analysis of the mechanisms underlying the organizational structure. We identify the practices to establish and maintain differing degrees of control depending on the organizational subunit purposes. Linking our observations to "what the organization seeks to coordinate" and the scale of operations under each organizational mode, we then offered suggestions as to the types of mechanisms appropriate for organizational strategy, objectives and structure. By systematically unpacking the "building blocks" of a successful initiative, therefore, we hope to have provided know-how and possible tools for social enterprises in determining the design features of their organizations to achieve fit with their intended strategies.

References

Bhandari, A., Dratler, S., Raube, K., & Thulasiraj, R. D. (2008). Specialty care systems: A pioneering vision for global health. *Health Affairs, 27*(4), 964–976.

Blau, P. M. (1970). A formal theory of differentiation in organizations. *American Sociological Review, 35*(2), 201–218.

Bradach, J. (2003, Spring). Going to scale: The challenge of replicating social programs. *Stanford Social Innovation Review*, 19–25.

CASE. (2006). *Scaling social impact research project: Practitioner survey executive summary*. Center for the Advancement of Social Entrepreneurship, Duke University.

Chenhall, R. H. (2003). Management control systems design within its organizational context: Findings from contingency-based research and directions for the future. *Accounting, Organizations and Society, 28*(2), 127–168.

Dees, J. G., Anderson, B. B., & Wei-Skillern, J. (2002). *Pathways to social impact: Strategies for scaling out successful social innovations* (CASE Working Paper Series No. 3).

Dees, J. G., Anderson, B. B., & Wei-Skillern, J. (2004, Spring). Scaling social impact: Strategies for spreading social innovations. *Stanford Social Innovation Review, 1*(4), 24–32.

Edwards, M., & Hulme, D. (1992). *Making a difference: NGOs and development in a changing world*. London: Earthscan.

Etzioni, A. (1961). *A comparative analysis of complex organizations*. New York: Free Press.

Floyd, S. W., & Lane, P. J. (2000). Strategizing throughout the organization: Managing role conflict in strategic renewal. *Academy of Management Review, 25*(1), 154–177.

Frumkin, P. (2007). *The five meanings of scale*. Social Edge Online Discussion Forum: A Program of the Skoll Foundation.

Govindarajan, V., & Fisher, J. (1990). Strategy, control systems, and resource sharing: Effects on business-unit performance. *Academy of Management Journal, 33*(2), 259–285.

IndiaStat. 2004. *Report on prevalence of blindness and estimated number of blind persons in India*.

Jaeger, A. M., & Baliga, B. R. (1985). Control systems and strategic adaptation: Lessons from the Japanese experience. *Strategic Management Journal, 6*(2), 115–134.

Jensen, R. J., & Szulanski, G. (2007). Template use and the effectiveness of knowledge transfer. *Management Science, 53*(11), 1716–1730.

Jensen, R. J., Szulanski, G., & Casaburi, M. V. (2003). *Templates and the effectiveness of knowledge transfer*. Academy of Management.

Kirsch, L. J. (1996). The management of complex tasks in organizations: Controlling the systems development process. *Organization Science, 7*(1), 1–21.
Korten, D. C. (1980). Community organization and rural development: A learning process approach. *Public Administration Review, 40*(5), 480.
La France Associates. (2006, July). *Scaling capacities: Supports for growing impact*. LLC.
Lebas, M., & Weigenstein, J. (1986). Management control: The roles of rules, markets and culture. *Journal of Management Studies, 23*(3), 259–272.
March, J. G., & Simon, H. A. (1958). Cognitive limits on rationality. In *Organzations*. New York: McGraw-Hill.
Natchiar, G., Thulsiraj, R. D., & Sundaram, R. M. (2008). Cataract surgery at Aravind eye hospitals: 1988–2008. *Community Eye Health Journal, 21*(67), 40–42.
Nonaka, I. (1994). A dynamic theory of organizational knowledge creation. *Organization Science, 5*(1), 14–37.
Olsen, M. E. (1978). *The process of social organization*. New York: Holt Rinehart & Winston.
Oster, S. M. (1996). Nonprofit organizations and their local affiliates: A study in organizational forms. *Journal of Economic Behavior & Organization, 30*(1), 83.
Ouchi, W. G. (1979). A conceptual framework for the design of organizational control mechanisms. *Management Science, 25*(9), 833–848.
Ouchi, W. G. (1980). Markets, bureaucracies, and clans. *Administrative Science Quarterly, 25*(1), 129–141.
Pascale, R. (1985). The paradox of "corporate culture": Reconciling ourselves to socialization. *California Management Review, 27*(2), 26–41.
Polanyi, M. (1966). *The tacit dimension*. London: Routledge & Kegan Paul.
Stacey, R. D. (1993). *Strategic management and organizational dynamics*. London: Pitman.
Tannenbaum, A. (1968). *Control in organizations*. New York: McGraw-Hill.
Tushman, M. L., & Nadler, D. A. (1978). Information processing as an integrating concept in organizational design. *Academy of Management Review, 3*(3), 613–624.
UnLtd Ventures Social Enterprise Replication Series. (2008). *Social entreprise replication overview: Planning and key considerations for social enterprises planning growth through replication*.
Uvin, P. (1995). Fighting hunger at the grassroots: Paths to scaling up. *World Development, 23*(6), 927.
Uvin, P., Jain, P. S., & Brown, L. D. (2000). Think large and act small: Towards a new paradigm for NGO scaling up. *World Development, 28*(8), 1409–1419.

Uvin, P., & Miller, D. (1996). Paths to scaling-up: Alternative strategies for local nongovernmental organizations. *Human Organization, 55*(3), 344.
Wei-Skillern, J., & Anderson, B. B. (2003). *Nonprofit geographic expansion: Branches, affiliates, or both?* (CASE Working Paper Series, 4).

Correction to: Tourism as (Un)sustainable Production and Consumption

Lin Lerpold and Örjan Sjöberg

Correction to:
Chapter 8 in: R. Bali Swain and S. Sweet (eds.),
***Sustainable Consumption and Production, Volume II*,**
https://doi.org/10.1007/978-3-030-55285-5_8

Chapter "Tourism as (Un)sustainable Production and Consumption" was previously published non-open access. It has now been changed to open access under a CC BY 4.0 license and the copyright holder updated to 'The Author(s)'. The book has also been updated with this change.

The updated version of this chapter can be found at
https://doi.org/10.1007/978-3-030-55285-5_8

R. Bali Swain and S. Sweet (eds.), *Sustainable Consumption and Production, Volume II*,
https://doi.org/10.1007/978-3-030-55285-5_16

Index

R. Bali Swain and S. Sweet (eds.), *Sustainable Consumption and Production, Volume II*,
https://doi.org/10.1007/978-3-030-55285-5

T

The manufacturer's authorised representative in the EU is Springer Nature Customer Service Centre GmbH, Europaplatz 3, 69115 Heidelberg, Germany. If you have any concerns regarding our products, please contact ProductSafety@springernature.com

Printed and bound by CPI Group (UK) Ltd, Croydon, CR0 4YY
30/09/2026
02225450-0009